Latino Politics in America

Community, Culture, and Interests

John A. García

ROWMAN & LITTLEFIELD PUBLISHERS, INC.
Lanham • Boulder • New York • Oxford

ROWMAN & LITTLEFIELD PUBLISHERS, INC.

Published in the United States of America
by Rowman & Littlefield Publishers, Inc.
A Member of the Rowman & Littlefield Publishing Group
4501 Forbes Boulevard, Suite 200, Lanham, Maryland 20706
www.rowmanlittlefield.com

P.O. Box 317, Oxford OX2 9RU, United Kingdom

British Library Cataloguing in Publication Information Available

Library of Congress Cataloging-in-Publication Data
García, John A.
    Latino politics in America : community, culture, and interests / John A. García.
        p.   cm.— (The spectrum series)
    Includes bibliographical references and index.
    ISBN 0-8476-9164-0 (alk. paper) — ISBN 0-8476-9165-9 (pbk. : alk. paper)
    1. Hispanic Americans—Politics and government.   2. Political participation—United States.   3. Hispanic Americans—Social conditions.   4. Hispanic Americans—Ethnic identity.   5. Community life—United States.   I. Title.   II. Spectrum series, race and ethnicity in national and global politics.

    E184.S75G367 2003
    305.868'073—dc21   2002152244

Printed in the United States of America

♾™ The paper used in this publication meets the minimum requirements of American National Standard for Information Sciences—Permanence of Paper for Printed Library Materials, ANSI/NISO Z39.48-1992.

Latino Politics in America

THE SPECTRUM SERIES

Race and Ethnicity
in National and Global Politics

Series Editors
Paula D. McClain **Joseph Stewart Jr.**
Duke University *University of New Mexico*

The sociopolitical dynamics of race and ethnicity are apparent everywhere. In the United States, racial politics underlie everything from representation to affirmative action to welfare policymaking. Early in the twenty-first century, Anglos in America will become only a plurality, as Latino and Asian American populations continue to grow. Issues of racial/ethnic conflict and cooperation are prominent across the globe. Diversity, identity, and cultural plurality are watchwords of empowerment as well as of injustice.

This new series offers textbook supplements, readers, and core texts addressing various aspects of race and ethnicity in politics, broadly defined. Meant to be useful in a wide range of courses in all kinds of academic programs, these books will be multidisciplinary as well as multiracial/ethnic in their appeal.

TITLES IN THE SERIES

Latino Politics in America: Community, Culture, and Interests by John A. García

The Navajo Political Experience, Revised Edition by David E. Wilkins

Asian American Politics: Law, Participation, and Policy edited by Don T. Nakanishi and James S. Lai

American Indian Politics and the American Political System by David E. Wilkins

FORTHCOMING TITLES

Media & Minorities by Stephanie Greco Larson

Contents

Tables

Boxes

~~~~~~

Profiles

Acronyms

ATEDPA   Antiterrorism and Effective Death Penalty Act
CANC   Cuban American National Council
CANF   Cuban American National Foundation
CBDG   Community Block Development Grant program
CCD   Committee for Cuban Democracy
CHCI   Congressional Hispanic Caucus Institute
COPS   Community Organized for Public Services
CSO   Community Services Organization
DANR   Dominican American National Roundtable
HACR   Hispanic Association for Corporate Responsibility
HNBA   Hispanic National Bar Association
IAF   Industrial Areas Foundation
IIRIRA   Illegal Immigration Reform and Immigrant Responsibility Act
INA   McCarran–Walter Act
INS   Immigration and Naturalization Service
IRCA   Immigration Reform and Control Act
LADO   Latin American Defense Organization
LCLAA   Labor Council for Latin American Advancement
LNPS   Latino National Political Survey
LULAC   League of United Latin American Citizens
LUPA   Latinos United for Political Rights
MALDEF   Mexican American Legal Defense and Education Fund
MWVREP   Midwest Voter Registration and Education Project
NABE   National Association of Bilingual Educators
NAHD   National Association of Hispanic Dentists
NAHJ   National Association of Hispanic Journalists
NALEO   National Association of Latino Elected and Appointed Officials
NCLR   National Council of La Raza
NHCC   National Hispanic Corporate Council

OLAW	Organization of Los Angeles Workers
OMB	Office of Management and Budget
PRA	permanent resident alien
PRLDEF	Puerto Rican Legal Defense and Education Fund
PRWORA	Personal Responsibility and Work Opportunity Reconciliation Act
SHPE	Society of Hispanic Professional Engineers
SIG	special interest groups
SSI	Supplementary Security Income
SVREP	Southwest Voter Registration and Education Project
UFW	United Farm Workers
USHCC	U.S. Hispanic Chamber of Commerce
VRA	Voting Rights Act

Acknowledgments

〰〰〰〰〰〰〰〰〰〰〰〰〰〰〰〰〰〰〰〰〰〰

A not an unfamiliar statement by most authors is the long period of time that preparation of his or her manuscript consumed before its completion. In many ways, I share the feeling that this particular effort represents an indeterminable passage of time, effort, bringing to bear a multitude of experiences, research literatures, and contributors who are both known and unknown to me. It is in this vein that I try to acknowledge those individuals and related experiences that played a key role in the evolution of this book.

In 1972, with very limited training in the field of Chicano/Latino politics, but well-grounded in American politics and behavior, I begin teaching courses on minority politics and Chicano/Latino politics. To a large extent, my construction, reformulation, and modification of those courses inspired a vision to undertake a Latino politics text. In order to do this, it was necessary to examine and try to understand the critical elements of the politicization of Mexican-origin persons, originally, and then other Latino subgroups became a significant part of my academic and "active-citizen" career. In a very real sense, all of the undergraduate students who have taken my Chicano/Latino course over the years have been both participating reactants to my materials and thoughts as well as providers of input on the pertinent topics and dynamics of Latinos and the American political system. Similarly, graduate students over the years have engaged me and expanded my perspectives on Latinos and their politics. A special note should be made of two summer programs, involving young and more established Latinos, that sharpened my notions and questioned the underlying reasons of what to explore about the Chicano/Latino experience. The first was the National Chicano Research Network, initiated by Carlos H. Arce. During a summer in the late 1970s, fifteen to twenty scholars met over a two-week period to discuss issues, ideas, and perspectives about the Chicano experience. Some of the participants included Mario Barrera, Tomas Almaguer, Rumaldo Juarez, Gilberto Cardenas, David Hayes-Bautista, and later Guadalupe San Miguel, Marta Tienda, Aida Hurtado. The exchanges and challenges to my ways of seeing and understanding the Latino communities and its structural linkages immensely added to my thoughts. The second was during in the late 1980s and early 1990s, when I was the instructor in the Latino Research Seminar, also held at the University of Michigan. Over four summers, I interacted with over eighty Latina/o graduate students and faculty from seven or so academic disciplines. The richness of intellectual vitality and curiosity, the interdisciplinary mix essential to understanding the Latino experience, and an array of research interests and inquiries invigorated my interest and motivation to explore and pursue systematic work on Latinos. Many of these Latina/os have made—and continue to make—invaluable contributions to the study of Latinos in America as well as improve the status of their respective Latino communities.

Again over the years, my contact and interactions with a wide range of scholars and practitioners entailed collaborative ventures and discussions that helped clarify my approach and examination of Chicano/Latinos, and sustain the effort. These persons include Angelo Falcón, Phillip García, F. Chris García, Rodolfo de la Garza, Vilma Ortiz, Rosemary Santana-Cooney, Rodney Hero, Benjamin Márquez, David Torres, Lisandro Perez, Christine Sierra, Denise Segura, Gilberto Cardenas, Leo Estrada, Rumaldo Juarez, Maxine Baca-Zinn, Obed Lopez, David Hayes-Bautista, Lionel Maldonado, and Amado Padilla. In the past decade, a newer generation of Latino scholars has emerged as active inquisitors and committed individuals to the craft of systematic inquiry into the Latino reality, as well advocates for institutional responsiveness of professional organizations and other institutions. Persons such as Manuel Avalos, Luis Fraga, Louis Desipio, Linda Lopez, Edwina Barvosa-Carter, Gary Segura, Valerie Martinez-Ebers, David Leal, Edward Tellez, Susan Gonzalez-Baker, Matthew Snipp, Fernando Guerra, Anne Santiago, Linda Facio, Jorge Chapa, and Emilio Zamora represent a small portion of this next generation. The future of Latino scholarship and activism remains in good hands with the current generation and beyond.

It is both irreverent and unthinkable not to acknowledge family and close friends who are more outside the academic world, which has taken a good part of my time and attention, but whose assistance and support are priceless. My grandmother Amparo L. Torres and father, Ramon García, left me legacies that live on in my sense of rootedness, integrity, purpose, connections to family, community, and a vision for better than we have. Joyce Y. García has remained a close fiend, supporter, and helper in my professional and personal life. Her expertise as an interpreter and translator enabled me to build on my Spanish-language epigrams with much improved clarity, grammar, and focused statements than I could have done alone. To my daughter and son, Clarissa Olivia and Joel Armando, I welcomed the challenge and responsibility of being a parent and friend and the lessons learned in extending beyond myself, especially in a nonprofessional way. Foundations for the future are continually built on what and how we pass forward. That is everyone's responsibility. My mother, Dora

G. Garcia, remains as vital today as throughout my youth and younger adulthood. Her strength and commitment to being involved and extending the broad "boundaries" of family are facets that I affirm. While my brothers, Raymond, Frank, and Carlos, have distinguished themselves in their respective careers, family roots evidenced themselves in their service, sense of cultural and local roots, and pursuit of excellence. A deserving tribute to that family line is the action of Raymond who established an endowed chair in the name of Ramon and Dora García at the Honors College at the University of Houston.

The language and communicability of this manuscript was vastly improved through the careful and committed eyes of Rebecca Suzanne Elvin, who went through the entire manuscript editing, clarifying, and making the communication more effective. Her vigilance, character, and questioning—from a non–social scientist perspective—helped to make the book's content more accessible, hopefully, to a larger readership.

Acknowledgments should not be long litanies of my personal history and endless listings of key persons, who played major roles in my development as a social scientist and individual. As I began, contributors are both individuals, both known and less so. Clearly, the numerous activists, neighbors, organizational members, public servants, and civically aware individuals, who I have known and worked with, have made my development as a political scientist broader and deeper. My department provided me with assistance in the form of library searches, photocopying, and clerical and telephone support, which moved the book project along in important ways. In addition, I want to acknowledge specifically Rowman & Littlefield's Spectrum Series' editors, Paula McClain and Joseph Stewart, who took the initiative to challenge me to put together a Latino politics text, and exhibited much confidence in my undertaking. The whole series and its contributors represent another step in examining and informing more persons about America's diverse communities, their intricacies, and their important and positive impact on our political system and society. Similarly, Jennifer Knerr worked with me on this project and provided me with enthusiasm, support, and critical ideas for improvements and additions.

There will be my sins of omissions in this acknowledgment. This project was long in coming and a major investment of time, energy, thought, and commitment. The last element is one of which I seem to have some reservoir, and it is derived from many sources, some of which I have acknowledged in the preceding paragraphs. I refer to the study of Latino politics and the well being of these communities as a dynamic one in which changes will occur. Some are these can be predictable while others are less so. I am reminded of a phrase—"La vida te da sorpresas; sorpresas te da la vida" [Life will give you surprises and surprises will give you life]; the Latino communities will give life to themselves and to this nation and in doing so surprise themselves and others.

1

An Introduction to Latino Politics

Emprendimos una peregrinación y nos pregun-tamos ¿Donde estan nuestras raices, los hilos de la historia y las experiencias en estas tierras las conocidas tanto como las nuevas? Al hacer el reconocimiento, percibimos perspectivas de todas las direcciones y siempre miramos hacia el futuro con esperanza y dignidad.

Undertaking a pilgrimage to find our commu-nity, we ask ourselves, "Where are our roots, those strands of history and experiences in lands both known and new?" As we search, our reconnaissance takes in views from many sources, and we are always looking to the future with hope and dignity.

BE COUNTED! LET THE GOVERNMENT AND ITS AGENCIES KNOW WHO AND WHAT you are. These "simple" requests were part of the Census Bureau's efforts to carry out the 2000 decennial census with a full count of all persons living in the United States. The information collected will produce population tabula-tions with counts and detailed descriptions of all persons, including Hispan-ics. How are people classified, and what are the consequences and implica-tions of the classification? What is reported, when data is released, how accurate the information is, and how it will be used are important for Latino communities and their organizations.

The Spanish-origin question included in the decennial census first appeared in the 1970 census as an ethnic self-identifier. The information elicited by the Spanish-origin question serves as the basis for voting and civil rights legislation and implementation, as well as a variety of service delivery programs. Recently the Office of Management and Budget (OMB) decided to review the basis on which racial and ethnic data is collected.[1] After lengthy public input and feedback from federal statistical agencies, the OMB had a revised race question format for Census 2000. A person had the option of marking more than one racial category (white, black, Asian, Pacific Islander, Native American/Alaskan native and other). In addition, the OMB separated

Asians from native Hawaiians and Pacific Islanders to create five racial categories. The ability to mark more than one option enables persons of multiracial background, if they choose to self-identify, to indicate the various racial categories that are appropriate.

For persons who mark more than one race, a resulting issue lies with the method in which the population tabulation method(s) will be conducted and reported. Previous censuses reported the racial tabulations as discrete counts, and each person fell into only one racial category. For Census 2000, the tabulation was more complicated as persons could indicate multiple responses. For example, indigenous populations from Mexico and Central and South America might not be included in the American Indian category. What happens to the individual who marks herself as African American and white and checks off Spanish origin on the ethnic-origin question? How is this person counted, and in how many different ways? The classification method selected has a direct bearing on civil rights, voting rights, and program participation monitoring, as well as what the government means by Hispanics/Latinos. To further complicate the classification issue, plans are under consideration, for the future, to tabulate multiple responses on the Spanish-origin question. For example, an individual marks that he is of Spanish origin and non-Hispanic origin (i.e., of mixed Hispanic origin). How is that person counted?

With this brief and not so simple description of current governmental policy decisions and classification schemes based on the concepts of race and ethnic origin, I have begun to illustrate one key dimension of exploring Latinos and their political worlds. While significant media attention has highlighted the continual growth of the Spanish-origin population, it is not clear who we are talking about or why persons whose ancestry is tied to Chile are associated with persons whose ancestry is connected to Honduras. Public law 85-983 established the designation of Spanish origin for purposes of federal data collection, thus combining persons from twenty-two countries of origin under a single category.

Under the broad scope of Latino politics, this book addresses the dialectics of diversity and similarity among persons and communities of Spanish origin. In many ways, Latinos and their politics reflect a community that is being influenced by Latino elites and organizations, "mass" level inter-group interactions,[2] the mass media, as well as by governmental policies and agencies. Regardless of the derivation of the Latino/Hispanic concept, the idea of a group of peoples tied together by language, cultural values, and practices, similar histories in the United States, and public policies is now visible on the American landscape, and its political ramifications are very dynamic.

Critical to this discussion of Latinos and the American political system is an examination of the basis and construction of identity and the salience of group identification. This central dimension affecting Latinos residing in the United States informs the nature and basis for community among this collection of persons from twenty-plus national-origin groups. Most Latinos think of themselves in terms of their own national-origin group (Honduran, Cuban, Argentine, etc.), and this subgroup identification is an important component of the core definition of community (García et al. 1994). At the same time, a sense of **pan-ethnicity,**[3] or seeing themselves not only in national-origin terms but also as part of a broader community is a more recent development. The Hispanic or Latino label can serve as an important dimension in the formation of a Latino community. Yet it is the meaning beyond the use of the label that establishes a sense of working community and identifies common concerns, interests, and situations.

The concept of ethnicity (and, to a lesser degree, race) represents social boundaries in which group identity exists, is created, and is redefined. The **social construct of race** usually refers to a group of persons that defines itself as distinct due to perceived common physical characteristics (Cornell and Hartman 1998). This group is socially defined based on physical characteristics and is fated by biological factors. Historical precedents and policies construct a racial category such as the one-drop rule that operated in the South. A common practice in the South was to categorize any person who had any African lineage (as little as one drop) as Negro or African American. As a result, Jim Crow laws in the South defined participation in social life based on one's race. In this case, black racial identity was defined by the state as anyone with one thirty-second Negro ancestry or one drop of "Negro" blood (Payne 1998).

The work by Omni and Winant (1994) further extends the development of race as a social product of human actions and decisions. The concept can change over time in members of the racial group or through "external" social actions. Identity can be comprehensive in forming the basis for a nearly complete social organization and lifestyle or, minimally, it is symbolic and periodically emotive. In most cases, there are direct consequences for membership in a racial group. In the case of Latinos, its members can be categorized into racial groups as well as an ethnic group.

Ethnic groups deal with group attachments that are connected to descent. In reality, direct "blood" ties to ancestry are less important, with belief in a descent being more critical. This reinforces the socially constructed basis of ethnicity. The "strands" that cultivate this belief in common descent can include physical attributes, cultural practices, and a shared historical experience (Cornell and Hartman 1998, 16–17). What makes ethnicity distinctive is that this shared affinity serves as the basis for community formation.

The work by R. A. Schermerhorn (1970) reinforces this view of ethnicity by defining it as a "collectivity within the larger society having a real or putative common ancestry, memories of a shared historical past, and a cultural focus on one or more symbolic elements defined as the epitome of their peoplehood." Consistent with these definitions is the presence of self-consciousness among members of an ethnic group. Ethnicity lies within the core of one's identity. At the same time, the self-identification that a person "takes on" may be influenced by external factors such as public policies that provide punitive costs or possible benefits for ethnic group membership. Thus ethnicity operates among persons who identify with others of their descent and also influences individuals outside their group's boundaries.

Race and ethnicity differ in the greater pervasive burden and consequences for those carrying the racial designation. Movement across racial boundaries is more restricted by social traditions and customs than ethnic categories. For ethnic individuals, the demarcation by the larger society may also be externally imposed; yet affiliation with the group is usually asserted by members of the ethnic group. Race becomes a way in which defining and assigning differential status is associated with power, control, inferiority, and majority-minority group status.

Ethnicity also shares external group designation. But it includes an element of self-concept and identification that is also associated when members of an ethnic group start to define their ethnic category. They fill in their own content and meaning, casting their own histories and experiences and what it means to be an ethnic. This process can be described as the social construction of ethnicity from within. In many ways, this book is an examination of the social construction of Latinos in the United States as a viable community and how that manifests itself politically. Clearly, race and ethnicity overlap concerning a sense of group identity and the nature of **power relations** that position its members in the larger society.

While we may think of **ethnic identity** as primarily a matter of individual choice or circumstances, the development of such identities can be credited or influenced by sources or influences external from the ethnic community such as political institutions (the courts, political parties, etc.) and agencies (Equal Employment Opportunity Commission, Civil Rights Commission, Department of Justice, etc.) that designate policies (voting rights, civil rights protection, entitlements, etc.) in terms of specific group categories (minorities, African Americans, Hispanics, etc.). For example, the **Voting Rights Act** of 1965 focused initially on institutional exclusionary voting practices directed toward African Americans in the South. The prohibitions against literacy tests, grandfather clauses,[4] **limited voting** registration location(s), and so on, were policy interventions intended to open up the electoral process. Voting Rights Act amendments later incorporated the concept of linguistic minorities and implemented bi- or multi-lingual voting materials and assistance.

Legislation, official governmental data gathering, and mass media characterizations of Hispanics/Latinos have served as a way to deal with a collection of persons and groups that have become reconfigured into a simpler grouping. One of the issues confronting many Latino sub-communities is the extent to which Latino subgroups (Guatemalans, Mexican-origin, Argentines, etc.) are connected to one another and issue an inclusive appeal to work on common causes. The use of the labels Hispanic and/or Latino gives to the broader society a much simpler picture of who persons of "Spanish origin" are and what they are about. Rather than examine and assess each national-origin group in terms of "its own political needs and status," it converts them from a diverse and complex mix of groups to a simplified and a more manageable package of a new "ethnic group." This helps policy makers deal with their political world and the new demands made on it.

One result of a new formulation of group status, often referred to as pan-ethnicity, is the creation of concrete benefits to which organizations and members of this new group category can now respond. For example, bilingual educational programs are based on the existence of students who have limited English proficiency, as well as the perception that bilingualism is primarily a Latino issue. Consequently, a pan-ethnic grouping, with a much larger population base, can emphasize its need and use its sizable constituency to maintain and expand bilingual education programs. An in-depth understanding of Latinos and community building would integrate the role of public policies and social institutions (mass media, governmental agencies, decision-making bodies, etc.) into the process of sub-Latino groups' activities and developments, as well as the links that tie several Latino subgroups in collaborative efforts.

Another critical factor for community building is the general climate, mood, and awareness about Latinos held by the broader public. Public concerns about cultural and linguistic balkanization, immigration swells, multilingualism, and so on, see Latinos as problematic. These issues carry an underlying theme in which segments of the non-Latino communities see many Latinos as unwilling to Americanize and become undifferentiated Americans. Such concerns highlight their presence and increase the possible costs of being Latino.

For example, the 1997 welfare reform legislation barred "permanent resident aliens" from participating in Social Security's Supplementary Security Income (SSI) and other federal entitlement programs. Congress did not choose to differentiate between undocumented immigrants and permanent resident aliens. Similarly, initiatives in California regarding immigrant access to social services and discontinuing bilingual education programs have targeted Latinos. This has stimulated many persons of Spanish origin to assume a defensive and/or survival mode. Latino civic engagement has increased in the form of protest activities, higher voter registration and turnout levels, and greater political interest (Sierra et al. 2000). Throughout this book, I emphasize the need to understand identity, its constructions and its dynamic character, as well as the sources of identity, in order to interpret and analyze Latino politics.

Latino politics take place in many social contexts (F. C. García 1997;

Bonilla and Morales 1998), including societal institutions such as schools, federal and local decision-making arenas, referenda and initiatives, public policies, public opinion, and political representation at all levels. Yet scholars focusing on the Latino community have not thoroughly researched many of these dimensions of politics. For example, researchers have only recently begun to examine Latino community organizations and their political involvement with urban redevelopment, local school issues, and environmental "racism" (Pardo 1998; Pulído 1996). More research findings exist for the Mexican-origin population as opposed to Central and South Americans and other Caribbean groups. Only in the past five to ten years have researchers begun to examine the political domains and actions of Latinos in their own communities. At the same time, a limited number of national databases and subsequent analysis has become more readily available for discussion of Latinos and their politics.

An examination of Latinos and the political sphere needs to start with an assessment of power relations among Latinos, Latino subgroups, and the established power holders and institutions. This examination includes both historical and contemporary power relations and how Latinos have survived, adapted, and succeeded in power exchange terms. That is, have Latinos or Latino subgroups (Mexican Americans, Cubans, Puerto Ricans, Panamanians, etc.) successfully accessed political and economic institutions or placed key issues or concerns on the policy-making agenda?

William Blain Richardson (1947–)

In 1982, Bill Richardson was first elected to Congress to represent a newly created district in New Mexico. As congressman, he was a member of the House leadership and served as chief deputy majority whip. He sat on the Democratic Steering Committee, the House Energy and Commerce Committee, and the House Interior and Insular Affairs Committee. In 1996 President Bill Clinton appointed Richardson to the cabinet-level post of United States ambassador. Richardson had earlier established himself in international circles through his diplomatic trips to Central America. In 1998 Richardson was appointed secretary of transportation. He did not stay in that position long because he was appointed secretary of energy in 1999. In the 2002 elections, Richardson was elected governor of New Mexico. He promises to continue to be an important figure in Latino politics.

Bibliography

Brooke, James. "Traveling Troubleshooter Is Ready to Settle Down." *New York Times,* December 14, 1996, 11.
Crow, Patrick. "The Nominee Speaks." *Oil and Gas Journal,* July 27, 1998, 44.

Power relations focus on political resources, agenda setting, organizational development, leadership and **mobilization,** authority, influence, and legitimacy. Inquiring into governmental policies (at the federal, state, and local levels) that have influenced the Latino communities can lead to a greater understanding of the extent and use of power by Latino communities. In some respects, governmental initiatives and actions that classify persons by group terms or identities (i.e., race, **ethnicity,** and social class) can serve as an indicator of political presence. Part of the political empowerment process is recognition of the group, even in symbolic ways.

Whether or not the political system is organized to be responsive to Latino communities, political institutions through their practices and/or benign neglect clearly indicate the power basis that Latinos must develop effective strategies to contend with. The 1980s were designated as the "decade of the Hispanic." Projections of extraordinary population growth, with Latinos becoming the nation's largest minority group before 2010, have heightened an expectation of Latinos basking in the "political sun." At the same time, through the 1980s, Latinos' socioeconomic status (household income, families living below poverty, single-parent headed households, percentage of adults with a high school diploma, etc.) continued to lag even farther behind whites. Recognition and responsiveness from governmental institutions was much slower than the expansive Latino growth rate. To a significant degree, the U.S. political system was evolving from Latinos being a relatively obscure or invisible group to having some degree of political awareness and familiarity by political institutions, especially at the national level.

In addition to the contextual elements that contribute to the basis and content of Latino politics, other important factors include sociodemographic status, such as occupational locations in the labor market and economic status and residential concentration, as well as regional concentrations, access to social institutions (their own or societal), and legal prohibitions (limiting immigrant rights and participation, having impact on redistricting, etc.). The sociodemographic map identifies the resource bases for Latinos as well as possible policy issues and concerns. Given the youthfulness of the overall Latino population and the significant proportion of Latinos who are foreign-born, issues such as educational quality, persistence to stay and complete their education, immigration reform, and increased militarization of the border are all likely policy extensions of the sociodemographic profile of Latinos. In addition, the relatively lower percentage of high school graduates and college graduates for Latinos, as well as their concentration in service sector industries, has implications for political mobilization and resources. Lower levels of educational attainment, lower job status, and lesser income levels reduce the conventional type of personal resources that individuals can convert for political purposes.

Political participation and mobilization (Verba et al. 1995; Rosenstone and Hansen 1993) are closely connected to an individual's socioeconomic status, positive political predispositions (or attitudes), and available time to engage in political activities. In chapter 3, we will develop a sociodemographic "map" of Latinos to assist in the construction of the extent of their political resources and the range of issues that will compose our discussion.

The discussion in this book focuses on the creation, maintenance, and redefinition of community and the role that external stereotypes and perceptions about Latinos and/or Latino subgroups play in framing Latino politics. Culture and its expression within the Latino communities through the mass and Spanish-language media, cultural traditions and practices, and Spanish-language maintenance define and maintain a sense of community. In addition, individual membership in and attachment to the Latino community is reinforced through social networks, living in Latino residential areas, experiences with discrimination, and shared experience in the workplace. These "arenas" are at the core of creating bridges for a Latino community at the grassroots level.

Ethnicity and identity reflect self-choice in how an individual places himself within a group affiliation. Latinos who continue to use Spanish, maintain ethnically "dense" social contacts with fellow Latinos, and participate in cultural events and practices are living their Latino-ness. The whole spectrum of being Latino or Cubano or Dominicano lies in the daily routine. How one communicates, the composition and content of one's interactions, lifestyle preferences and behaviors, and extent of affinity toward persons of similar ancestry contribute to the definition of who one is and its relevance to one's life.

Immersion as a Latino, or, more likely, a Cuban, Puerto Rican, or other Latino subgroup, is related to social contexts, and the involvement of activists and organizations that link the daily experiences of Latinos with directed social and political actions. Numerical growth helps Latino communities assert their identity and command necessary resources. The key distinctions within this dynamic community between citizen status (native-born and naturalized), permanent resident aliens, undocumented persons, and political refugees are critical toward understanding the range of similarities and diversities within this community. Similarly, class differentiation within the Latino community serves to create close-knit communities or, perhaps, accentuate class bifurcation.

There is literature that deals with class bifurcation in the African American community and its impact on mobilization, organizational growth and development, and maintaining consensus on public policies (West 1994; Dawson 1994). The connectedness or lack of it between the African American underclass and upwardly mobile and successful middle class can create different policy agendas and alliances that may not include each other. The existence or extent of class bifurcation, defined for Latinos as potentially between the foreign-born and native-born cleavages, has not been researched adequately. Cultural maintenance and practices are critical for group identity and community building.

At the same time, our theme of similarity and diversity suggest that community among Latinos does not require unanimity or complete consensus in order to engage as a political community. Like many political coalitions, this discussion of Latino politics identifies common bonds, experiences, conditions, and interests that can bridge across Latino subgroups for collective actions on various occasions. These introductory comments and ideas serve as an overview for an examination of Latino politics. The rest of my commentary in this introduction delineates specific dimensions of community building and politics for the 35 million-plus Latinos in the United States.

The basis for a Latino community will be shared interests, with culture serving as the vital connection. It is important to establish definitions of ethnicity, identity, and community, as well as analyze how political institutions, processes, policies, and political actors help shape the nature and substance of Latino politics. An "inside and outside" set of processes and actions are at play. Latino activists, organizations (local and national), political parties, and national "events" such as English Only, Proposition 209, fatalities along the border, and other political events that have occurred weave a set of contributing factors that can bring people together for common purposes. One of the real challenges for this author lies with achieving sufficient breadth and depth in covering the many different Latino subgroups. In many cases, only a sparse literature is available.

Chapter 3 establishes a demographic profile of Latinos in the United States incorporating characteristics that establish shared interests, social status, cultural "indicators," geographic concentrations, and institutions within the Latino sub-communities. The demographic profiles are then linked to community building and agenda setting. The themes of diversity and similarity are interwoven throughout this book. We will explore two particular bases for community—a **community of interests** and a **community of common/similar cultures** (García and Pedraza-Bailey 1990). A community of culture exists when individuals are linked closely by their participation in a common system of meaning with concomitant patterns of customary interactions of culture. Shared cultural practices, celebrations, and traditions serve to bridge Latino subgroup boundaries and potentially provide common bases and resources for effective mobilization.

Other writers (Espiritu 1992; Hayes-Bautista 1980) refer to these dynamics as elements of a pan-ethnicity in which several national-origin groups coalesce under a broader identity and community reference. A **community of interests** represents the conditions, statuses, and experiences that Latinos share with members of other Latino subgroups. Except for Puerto Ricans, a significant proportion of each Latino subgroup consists of foreign-born persons and immigrants. The current national climate is filled with serious con-

Box 1.1   Census 2000: Identifying Latinos

The final Census 2000 tally reported a Latino population that exceeded 35 million persons. Their continued high growth marked a 53 percent increase over the decade, while the nation's overall population growth was only 13.2 percent. Another noteworthy result was 96.9 percent growth among Latinos who indicated the "other Hispanic" category, from 5.1 million in 1990 to 10 million in 2000. The Census Bureau noted that this change could have resulted from a change in census coverage, as well as a change in the question format (the question on Hispanic origin in 2000 did not include examples for the "other Hispanic" category, while the 1990 question did have examples). Also, the Census Bureau reported a possible change in identification among Hispanics and non-Hispanics (Guzman 2001).

As already noted, an important issue is identification with being Latino. Those who identify themselves as Latino or Hispanic generally do so as members of a specific Latino subgroup. The increase in the number of "other Hispanics" has created serious concerns among Latino organizations (such as the Puerto Rican Legal Defense and Education Fund, Mexican American Legal Defense and Education Fund, National Council of la Raza, U.S. Hispanic Chamber of Commerce, and National Puerto Rican Coalition). Their concern lies with the misspecification of several Latino subgroups, most notably Dominicans and Colombians in the Northeast. The absence of examples of possible Latino sub-groups not already mentioned to accompany the "other Hispanic" category is seen as the culprit for the lower number of Central and South American subgroups and Dominicans. Communication on behalf of these organizations indicates 9

cerns about immigration policies and perceived negative consequences of continued immigration. Latinos are seen as the dominant source of immigrants. Therefore immigration exerts an impact on many Latino communities and can serve as a contributing factor in developing a broader community of interests.

Chapter 4 attempts a substantive understanding of the many Latino sub-communities and includes focused discussions of the subgroups and their historical and power relations in the United States. In addition, I present an overview of how communities may exist in relative isolation from other Latino communities or linked in various ways to other Latino subgroups. An interesting aspect of inter-group dynamics is discernible in the Census 2000 findings. Not only have Latinos increased in numbers during this past decade, but their percent fewer Colombians than a decade ago, while Dominicans and Salvadorans reported a smaller population gain than had been projected. These organizations cite similar underreporting for New York City and New Jersey.

This underreporting of specific Latino subgroups resulted in diminished public awareness of the actual size of the various communities and the corresponding resources and needs of each. In addition, the possible underreporting of Latino subgroups can limit the research, based on Census 2000 data, of new and growing Latino communities. These organizations expressed reluctance, in the future, to assist the Census Bureau in outreach and promotional assistance for subsequent data collection. Discussions are under way in regard to obtaining greater Latino subgroup specification through the use of the ancestral information from the long form. (In addition to the Census 2000 general form, one in six households received the long form, which included over fifty questions asking for more detail in regard to economic information, migration, language use, and other data used for federal programs. Among the specific questions on the long form, the persons in the household are asked to indicate their ancestral origins.)

While the actual response from the Census Bureau is still in progress, undergoing analysis and evaluation, this post-Census development further illustrates the complexities of defining the Latino community and how those definitions influence the public policy and community empowerment process. It becomes mutually beneficial to identify all persons who self-identify as Latino as well as their Latino subgroup status. This issue illustrates the evolving nature of defining the Latino community and the dynamics of Latino politics in America.

migration patterns have become more regionally diverse, extending into less traditionally identified Latino areas. For example, increases among the Mexican-origin exceeding 80 percent in southern states such as Arkansas, Georgia, North Carolina, and Tennessee represent major gains in rural and urban communities. This migration of Mexican-origin persons moving to the northeast and south is substantial in terms of population and political activities.

Similarly, Central Americans (especially "refugees") since the mid-1980s have migrated in significant numbers to traditional areas of Latino concentrations with established Mexican, Cuban, or Puerto Rican enclaves. One result has been a reconfiguration of Latino issues, a more diverse organizational milieu, and inter-group competition. An analysis of Latino politics must address the dynamic nature of the composition of the Latino community and its evolving political networks. Analyzing power relations and particular public policies is one way to explore the nature and character of Latino sub-community politics and its connections to "broader collective Latino politics."

Ethnicity, group identity, and pan-ethnicity involve the social construction of identity, which occurs within the respective groups and is influenced externally. The contributing factors of culture, daily experiences, social contexts, and public policies are introduced to assess the extent and "permanence" of Latino sub-communities and the broader Latino national community. Pan-ethnicity is explored in terms of both its political utility for Latinos and the interplay of mass and elite "forces" involved in this social construction. Authors like Peter Skerry (1993) have suggested that many Latino leaders perpetuate a sense of ethnicity or "Latino-ness" to maintain their power bases. In this vein, the social construction of ethnicity and resulting community is an artificial one, or at best a contrived one for the benefits of a limited number of activists. On the other hand, our basis for community indicates that identity and affiliation of Latinos must include dimensions of self-choice and conscious acceptance of belonging to a community defined as Latino or a specific Latino subgroup. Again the basis for community will be related to the viability of pan-ethnicity.

The political participation of Latinos is discussed in a number of chapters that break down the contributing factors of participation into individual, organizational, socialization, attitudinal, and **structural factors** for Latino subgroup members. An attempt will be made to differentiate the crucial factors of foreign-born and native-born, gender, class, and regional location in our analysis of political participation. The dimensions of time, money, and skills (Verba et al. 1995) will be incorporated into the factors associated with participation. The participation chapters will then move to the many modes of participation—voting, electoral activities, organizational involvement, protest, individualized contact, and office holding. The extant research literature on specific Latino subgroups will be used to portray the variations and similarities that exist across the Latino community.

The next aspect of Latino politics is the area of political mobilization. When Latinos are asked to get politically involved, whether by organizational leaders, neighbors, or the like, who gets involved and who does not? Political involvement is not solely a function of an individual's decision. Persons can be asked, approached, and enticed to get involved. This is a simple way to define political mobilization as the "outside" forces that influence individual political involvement. Characterizing mobilization in this manner also serves as a mechanism for introducing organizations and leadership into the Latino politics equation. Using specific Latino-focused organizations, I illustrate the range of organizational goals and scope, arenas of involvement, membership and resource bases, and political impact in a variety of policy areas. We examine the extent of Latinos' involvement in organizations and how Latino organizations are involved with the Latino community and its needs.

Latinos' leadership styles, their communication skills, and linkages with the "masses" are then addressed. Leadership is studied in terms of the goal articulation conveyed to Latinos and its coherency, which can influence specific political activities. Some have suggested that Latino political empowerment would be greatly enhanced if there were one or even two national Latino leaders who had followings in all of the Latino sub-communities. Others have argued that the core of Latino interests and needs resides in local communities, where leadership activities and development are more critical. A singular leader or two or three would be a difficult challenge for any community of this size and diversity to achieve.

The role of Latino leadership serves to crystallize issues, strategies, and "targets." The issue of gender bias, which is inherent in the discussion of leadership, is examined. Viable national leaders are more likely to be males, whereas leaders at the grass roots are often women. Characterizing leadership in this manner serves to introduce the concept of vertical and horizontal leadership. Again, specific examples are adduced to illustrate the issues and impact associated with leaders.

Although great attention has been focused on the national and state levels, Latino politics at the local level is an active arena. It has been suggested that the intensity and soul of Latino politics deal with local struggles (location decisions regarding toxic waste sites, delivery of services, educational equity and quality, residential gentrification, etc.). A number of locally focused community organizations have arisen over the past two decades in several Latino sub-communities. Organizing principles, efforts, strategies, and outcomes are important dimensions of Latino politics. They are often overlooked and underanalyzed. I attempt to characterize and analyze Latino local politics in the context of Latino empowerment and political development.

An understanding of Latino politics involves a focus on the political dynamics occurring within the Latino communities, as well as external forces and actions in the larger society. In this context, legislative initiatives and policies like the Civil and Voting Rights Acts have played an important role in electoral representation, equal opportunities, and fuller civic participation. In the latter chapters of this book I examine the origin of voting and civil rights legislation and policies that have impacted Latinos. Other legislative changes (Title VI, VII, IX of the Higher Educational Act, Equal Employment Opportunity Act, etc.), lobbying efforts, and major court decisions will be analyzed as part of the political assessment of Latinos and the political system. Organizations like the Mexican American Legal Defense and Education Fund and Puerto Rican Legal Defense and Education Fund are key groups considered in this section.

This discussion of Latinos focuses on specific public policy areas to maintain consistency with our theme of community, which includes shared interests, culture, and conditions that help shape the critical issue areas for Latinos. The politics of culture is connected with language, cultural distinctiveness, **English only** initiatives, and other xenophobic movements directed toward Latinos. First-generation immigrants and international migration bring immigration policies, border enforcement, immigrant and non-citizen rights and political integration, and avenues for participation into our discussion of Latino politics. To some extent, the immigration question is a test of political loyalty, with Latinos being placed on the defensive.

Equality of opportunity issues deal with educational quality and resources, labor market participation (i.e., advancement and access to jobs, preparation for employment with job mobility, protection from discrimination, and equal and competitive pay), economic participation and income mobility, access to higher education, and social service participation. Within this context, the debate and impact of affirmative action is pertinent. To some extent, foreign policy concerns (Cuba and the Castro regime, the economic embargo of Cuba, Puerto Rican statehood/independence, the North American Free Trade Act, U.S. economic investments in Latin America, drug interdiction, etc.) are aspects of the public policy discussions, which have particular relevance to Latinos. Integral to this section is attention to an understanding of the American policy-making process. Understanding agenda setting, monitoring policy implementation, and reviewing policy consequences are an integral part of analyzing specific policy areas.

Finally, this analysis points to the future of Latino politics and revisits the concepts of community, shared interests, culture and organizations, and identity construction, as well as external factors and actions in the political system. The last two chapters look at coalition formation, within the Latino communities and other minority communities. A discussion of trends for the next millennium closes out our discourse. Where will the Latino community be in the next twenty years, and will their identity be thinner and more externally assigned rather than thicker and more assertive? Given the changing demography of the Latino community (growing numbers of Latinos from Central America and the Caribbean, greater geographic dispersion and intermixing of Latino sub-communities, etc.), will the agenda and its leadership structure also undergo some changes? I develop four possible scenarios based on different directions of community building and their political manifestations.

CONCLUSION

In this introduction I have tried to lay out important concepts from which to describe and analyze Latino politics. The challenge is to discuss the politics of Latino sub-communities without necessarily assuming that Latino politics (in its pan-ethnic sense) is the pervasive mode. That is, I define politics at the national-origin community level (Cuban, Salvadoran, Mexican-origin, etc.) for both national and local arenas. At the same time, there is a Latino political force, which, at times, is more like one group than any multiple collections of independent Latino subgroups. An important question in regard to identifying Latinos in American society is the extent to which Latinos impact political arenas and agendas as a pan-ethnic community rather than a loose consortium of semi-independent interests. The task has begun and the chapters that follow will try to analyze Latino politics with the vitality and personalities that constitute the Latino peoples.

NOTES

1. The concepts of race and ethnicity warrant additional clarification. The census recognizes five racial categories: white, black, American Indian/Alaskan native, Asian/Pacific Islander, and other. The last category, "other," represents persons who identify themselves racially in ways that are different from the other four categories. In the case of ethnicity, ancestry and/or country forms the basis on which origin is categorized. Persons who identify themselves as of Spanish origin are asked a follow-up question seeking their particular ancestral group (i.e., Mexican, Cuban, Puerto Rican, Central/South American or other [to be specified]). In essence, ethnicity in the census is limited to "Spanish origin."

2. By mass interactions, I mean inter-Latino interactions at the grassroots level. What is the extent of contact between persons of specific Latino subgroup origin with other Latinos? These interactions could be social, familial, employment based, or any one of a variety of social interactions within the local community.

3. Pan-ethnicity refers to a sense of group affinity and identification that transcends one's own national-origin group. A pan-ethnic identity does not necessarily replace national-origin affinity, but it includes a broader configuration in defining the group. Latinos or Hispanics include several national origins.

4. The grandfather clause requires a potential registrant to show that his grandfather was a registered voter before he can register to vote. For African Americans, the grandfather clause hearkened back to the period of slavery when blacks had no rights, much less voting rights.

2

Community Building
in Latino America

*Píntame un cuadro donde se representan ima-
genes de nuestra comunidad. El/la artista pinta
de acuerdo su propio punto de vista. Todas las
perspectivas, la abundancia de rostros y fig-
uras forman el carácter de lo que significa ser
parte de una comunidad que es evolucíon.*

Paint me a picture in which images of our
community are represented. The artist paints
according to his or her own point of view.
With so many perspectives, a multitude of
faces and personalities make up the character
of our changing community.

An examination of Latino politics in the United States can be viewed as a
reformulation of community within the mutual forces of diversity and similarities. With politics centered on the substance of power, influence,
resources, and interest articulation, Latino politics represents an aggregation
of persons whose origins and/or ancestry is connected to over twenty countries in Latin America and the Iberian Peninsula. The idea of a group of people
tied together by Spanish language, similar cultural values, practices, histories, and targeted public policies has been stated by numerous authors
(Gómez-Quiñones 1990; Stavans 1996; Fox 1997). Underlying this perspective is the assumption that persons occupying a common ancestry and culture will come together for common objectives and concerns.

In this chapter, I will develop some political bases for Latino politics, as
well as the resultant directions this political community would go. Prior to
the 1980s Latinos were characterized as specific national-origin groups in certain regions of the United States. The Chicanos/Mexican Americans in the
Southwest can trace their ancestors to the sixteenth century, as well as newly
arrived Mexicanos from Mexico's central plateau. Puerto Ricans live in the
Northeast, especially in the New York metropolitan area. There was a significant post-World War II out-migration from "la isla" to the industrial centers

of the "rust belt" as well as the agricultural sector in the Northeast and the South. After Fidel Castro came to power in 1959, several waves of political refugees and exiles flooded into the southern United States. Even though Cuban refugees participated in refugee placement programs that included resettlement throughout the United States, most preferred to reside in Florida. Subsequent waves of Cuban refugees in the 1980s and 1990s augmented an entrepreneurial and better-educated community in Miami-Dade County.

Mexicans, Puerto Ricans, and Cubans make up the three largest Latino communities and are more established and visible to the larger American public. At the same time, the post-1970s saw a major influx of Latinos from Central America and, to a lesser extent, South America. The liberation struggles in El Salvador, Nicaragua, Guatemala, as well as high birth rates, political instability, and inadequate economic growth and opportunities, have fueled out-migration of Central Americans into almost every region of the United States. For the most part, Central Americans have been designated as economic migrants rather than political refugees. Public policy distinctions between economic and political migrants reflect national foreign policy commitments rather than an individual's condition or situation.

Locating distinct groups under the umbrella label of Latino or Hispanic[1] implicitly assumes some degree of group membership and affinity. Consequently, we will consider the nature of community within and across the Latino sub-communities, including an assessment of the strength and character of building and maintaining community. By "community," I am referring to the connections between persons to formulate a sense of place, being, and membership into a larger whole. The origins of Hispanics or Latinos can be traced to various strands of U.S. history and events. For example, federal legislation in the mid-1970s initiated by Congressman Edward Roybal had all federal agencies maintain records and designations of persons of Spanish origin. Persons of Spanish origin were generally defined as individuals from Spanish-speaking countries, including the Iberian Peninsula. An early difficulty with the implementation of the legislation was determining a uniform "standard" to identify persons of Spanish origin. The range of standards included Spanish surname, ancestry, birthplace, and respondents with parents of foreign-born parentage, self-identification, and language when growing up.

The 1970 census also reflected the different methods to identify persons of Spanish origin. Within the short and long census forms,[2] ancestry and self-identification determined Hispanic-ness. That is, an individual who identified herself as a person of Spanish origin would do so. There were no prescribed criteria such as Spanish-language use or foreign-born status that marked Spanish origin. The self-identifier introduced in the 1970 census has become the consistent Hispanic "marker" ever since. Technically, it is referred as the

ethnicity item or Spanish-origin identifier. It might be helpful, then, to distinguish between race and ethnicity.

Many scholarly and popular literatures have discussed race in terms of phenotypes, skin color, biological traits, ancestry, and social structures. Public policies like the "one-drop rule" have reinforced the concept of race as most directly connected to skin color and some notion of racial categorization. On the other hand, ethnicity is commonly associated with ancestry or national origin. To be an ethnic is to be, for example, Irish American, Italian American, or Cuban American with ties to cultural practices and traditions. Although I do not discuss the conceptual and theoretical underpinnings of race and ethnicity, the social and historical context of these terms is an important dimension for understanding politics, power, and influence in American society. For our purposes, we will operate on the notion that ethnicity and race are interrelated concepts that establish group boundaries, behaviors, and inter- and intra-group relations.

Following the census distinction of race and "ethnicity," a Spanish-origin person can be of any race.[3] The American understanding of race and ethnicity is strongly related to skin color and serves as an external influence on group identification. Thus the first factor contributing to the configuration of "Hispanic" or "Latino" as an umbrella term was the formulation of public policy establishing the presence and characteristics of Spanish-origin persons.

The mass media was the second factor contributing to the use of an umbrella term. The mass media responded to the changing demography of the United States. Toward the end of the 1970s, the media began reporting and discussing both established and recently arrived Latinos; many major newsmagazines and newspapers starting referring to the 1980s as the decade of the Hispanics. Characterizations such as "Hispanics' day in the sun," "fastest-growing minority," and "soon to be the largest minority group" were typical references to this aggregation of persons from twenty-two Spanish-speaking countries.

Ironically, descriptors such as "an awakening sleeping giant," "the invisible minority," and "bronze/brown power" were used in the early 1960s to depict Mexican Americans in the Southwest. One parallel theme for both time periods was potentiality and promise. The focus on significant population growth and continuation in the future propelled Latinos as a new political and economic force in American society. Mass media centers in the eastern part of the United States conducted exploration and fact-finding on these relatively unknown Hispanics. In regard to clustering many national-origin groups into an almost ethnic group status,[4] both from a public policy and news reporting perspective, there is some utility in assigning one group label and identity to varied national-origin group members. I am not suggesting that subgroup differentiation does not take place, but there are advantages to parsimony.

Thus persons of Spanish origin came to be seen as composing a group with similar cultural traditions and a common language. The discovery of Latino people by the mass media served to heighten public awareness of them and to ascribe some general characteristics, for example, Spanish speaking, largely immigrant, religious, committed to family, and having traditional values. The accuracy and relevance of these images actually depend on how Latinos see themselves. Nevertheless, the configuration of persons of Spanish origin was greatly impacted by the discovery and portrayal of Hispanics by the media, especially during the "decade of Hispanics."

A third factor in the development of an umbrella term is based in the so-called Latino community itself: both the demography of the swelling growth rates among Latino subgroups and the creation of "situational ethnicity" by Latino activists. There was a significant influx of Latinos into the United States beginning in the mid-1970s. And the fastest growing elements within the Latino community were persons from Central and South America and the Spanish-speaking Caribbean. Movement initially followed their migration to the Northeast and Midwest and later to states like California and Texas, and to the South. The next chapter will provide more specific demographic profiles of these developments. One result of greater Latino migration throughout the United States was a more diverse mix of Latino subgroups. This pattern held strongly for the established Mexican American, Puerto Rican, and Cuban communities in contact with individuals from Central and South America. Such a confluence of persons with linkages to the Spanish language, colonial histories with Spain, and U.S. hegemony were possible cultural and political connections.

While each group was growing faster than the national average, its respective size and regional concentration was limited on a national scale. Mexican Americans were seen as a regional minority that was primarily concentrated in the Southwest and oriented toward regional issues. Puerto Ricans were a New York metropolitan "phenomenon." Coping with a declining manufacturing economy and living the mean streets of "El Barrio" filled their world. Cubans, on the other hand, were seen as focused on ethnic enclaves and entrepreneurship and anticommunist policies in southern Florida. These oversimplifications summarize dominant perceptions of the situational and policy domains of the three larger subgroups. The development of pan-ethnic grouping and identity becomes a means to expand the group, its scope and national visibility. Thus the outgrowth of "Hispanicity" or Latino-ness represents a strategic decision among activists to enlarge the community and, potentially, its political capital and resource base.

Changing internal Latino demography and the strategic development of an expanding Latino population base are not mutually exclusive evolutions. Some writers on Latino politics have characterized the political actions of Latino activists as perpetuating **ethnicity** or **pan-ethnicity** in order to ensure

Gloria Molina (1948–)

Best known for her articulation of community concerns and her many "firsts," Gloria Molina is California's most prominent elected Chicana official. Her firsts include being the first Chicana/Latina assemblywoman, the first Chicana/Latina Los Angeles city councilwoman, and the first Chicana/Latina on the Los Angeles County Board of Supervisors. Raised in Los Angeles, Molina completed college and became involved in community politics. From 1972 to 1982, she founded Comisión Femenil de Los Angeles (a chapter of Comisión Femeníl Mexicana Naciónal); worked in the office of Assemblyman Art Torres; became commission national chair; and served in the Department of Intergovernmental and Congressional Affairs, Department of Health and Human Services in Washington, D.C., before returning to California to work in the assembly as a Democrat despite opposition from local Chicano leaders. Molina's ability to run for city council and county board of supervisors depended on the success of lawsuits by the Mexican American Legal Defense and Educational Fund (MALDEF) challenging the gerrymandering of electoral districts. She was forced to challenge local Chicano leaders including Esteban Torres, her former mentor. Her victories established her as the leading Chicana officeholder in California and a strong force in the Democratic Party.

Bibliography

Mills, Kay. "Gloria Molina." *Ms.,* January 1985, 80–91.
Tobar, Hector. "Gloria Molina and the Politics of Anger." *Los Angeles Times Magazine,* January 3, 1993, 10–13, 24–32.

a political base and a following. Thus these leaders do not reflect the assimilation and upward mobility that many Latinos are achieving. This perspective goes to the very heart of community and community building. The realities of daily living among Latino subgroup members include contact and awareness of not only fellow "national-origin" members but also other Latinos in their community or elsewhere.

The three factors that I have identified in Latino development in the United States are intended to provide consistent themes and concepts that will carry the discussion throughout this book. The themes include (1) diversity within and between Latino subgroups, (2) common linkages across the subgroups historically, culturally, linguistically, and politically, (3) the internal dynamics among Latinos defining, refining, and strategically developing their community, and (4) the role of external forces such as public policies (Voting and Civil Rights Acts, affirmative action initiatives, etc.) and public opinion and movements (**English only,** anti-bilingual and anti–affirmative action referenda, restrictive and punitive immigration measures, etc.) that activate the Latino communities. Thus Latino politics result from the interaction of initiatives undertaken by members and organizations within the various Latino sub-communities, as well as the social and political structures, practices, and public opinion of the larger U.S. political community. I began this chapter by introducing the concept of community and how that has been and is currently being operationalized within the broader Latino communities. In the next section I provide greater clarity and direction.

IS THERE A LATINO COMMUNITY AND WHAT DOES THAT MEAN?

The delineation of Latinos or Hispanics has centered on the notions of a group of people linked by a common language, interrelated cultural traditions and values, and similar experiences in the United States. More recently social scientists have posited a central common experience such as discrimination and relegation to minority status in most facets of American life. Measures of socioeconomic and political inequality are often used to join ethnic status with unequal opportunities and rights.

Each Latino subgroup has a unique history in the United States, contact and migration to the United States, social class distribution, and legal status: political refugee status versus legal permanent resident alien or undocumented migrant. Two bases of community I will present are associated with the concepts of commonalty of culture and commonalty of interests (García and Pedraza-Bailey 1990; Cornell and Hartman 1998). Cultural communities endure when persons are tied together naturally by their involvement in a common system of purpose with accompanying patterns of traditional interactions and behaviors that are rooted in a common heritage (Cornell 1985). This common heritage or tradition includes national ancestry, language, religion, and religious customs, observance of holidays and festivals, and familial networks. For the Mexican-origin population, Keefe and Padilla (1989) explore Chicano ethnicity and identify several dimensions of culture. When familial interactions are primary and serve as conduits of cultural transmission, then the "products" are customs, folklore, linguistic loyalties, ethnic loyalty, and group identity. Thus a person can be enveloped with a sense of ethnicity, usually within a national-origin context (Mexican American, Salvadoran, Dominican, etc.). However, this sense of ethnicity does not automatically lead to community actions.

The idea of a **community of interests** revolves around persons who are united by a common set of economic and political interests. This connection may be due in part to group members' concentration in certain industries and occupational sectors, residential enclaves (Denton and Massey 1988; Croucher 1997), political disenfranchisement (Smith 1990; J. A. García 1986a), and differential treatment based on ancestry, phenotype, language, and various other cultural traits and practices. Clearly there is an intersection of cultural status and interests. The result of perceived and accepted common interests may lead to the development of a new or reinforced identity. For example, the "official usage" of pan-ethnic terms such as Hispanic may reorient a person to incorporate that label and strategically use that identity to maximize political effect. A Mexican American activist in Arizona might oppose a referendum effort to remove bilingual education programs because such programs do not ensure educational excellence and equity for all Hispanic children. The Latino sub-community is the reality experienced by Mexican-origin children; yet the broader identifier Hispanic is used to place the issue in a national, as well as local, context.

The development of a **community of common interests** works to examine and construct new "boundaries" of group affiliation, as well as an analysis of comparable conditions and the nature of structural relations between the group with social and political institutions. A central element within these analytical insights is the role played by discriminatory practices and prejudicial attitudes in the larger society and public policies.

For example, the Immigration and Naturalization Service (INS) may conduct "sweeps" of residential areas only or primarily in Latino neighborhoods. If only persons who appear "Latino" are detained to show proof of legal status, then that policy action has a disparate impact on Latino communities. This dimension, discrimination, is certainly attached to being recognized as a minority. For our purposes, minority status is a relational concept in which minority group members have limited access, opportunities, power, and influence. Thus issues of empowerment, representation, equity, power, access, and participation become a major part of defining community and their interests.

The dimension of commonalty—community linkages, bonds, affinity, interactions, and individual affiliation—is important in our discussion of Latino community. This collectivity is a nexus of various associations, but this does not suggest uniformity or complete consensus among all of the Latino sub-communities. The theme of diversity and similarity emphasizes that conformity and unanimity are not real expectations for community membership and operations. While not totally analogous, variations in character, lifestyle, personality, and so on, that can be found within most families do challenge the maintenance of a family entity.

If the Latino sub-communities can share commonalties of culture and interest, each can play an interactive role with the other. That is, cultural cues and symbols can encourage persons of Spanish origin to adhere to specific goals and objectives. At the same time, cultural maintenance and practices can serve as the political content of a Latino political agenda. For example, the persistence of Spanish language, or at least exposure to Spanish, while growing up serves as a common cultural experience. It also serves as a point of political conflict in respect to English as the official language of the United States, structuring and maintaining bilingual educational programs, and loyalty and assimilation to American society. The politics of culture is fueled by the persistence of Latino culture. In our broadest sense, commonalty of culture and interests can be seen as perceptions and experiences among Latinos, which reflect positive affinity and substantial interactions and awareness of Latinos in the various sub-communities.

In the past decade a growing body of literature has developed the concept of pan-ethnicity (Espiritu 1992; Hayes-Bautista and Chapa 1995; Cornell and Hartman 1998). The work by Padilla (1986) explores this concept in the context of the Latino population in Chicago. Padilla espouses the idea of Latino consciousness, which includes both an ideological and a pragmatic sense of group identity. The ideological aspect conceives the interrelatedness among persons of Spanish origin in terms of their communal cultural values and routines in addition to political, economic, and social conditions and consequences. The latter connection ties in structural biases and policies that disadvantage persons who are Mexican, Guatemalan, Colombian, and so on. Thus there is a cost to being Latino, in terms of opportunities, equity, access, and rights, that transcends any specific Latino subgroup.

The pragmatic dimension of Padilla's Latino consciousness contemplates the potential benefits of expanding community beyond national-origin boundaries. In this way, a group is significantly enlarged. I have already referred to the demographic explosion within the Latino sub-communities. Rather than 1 million Cubans in the United States, we can talk about 30 million Latinos. The larger population base and greater national geographic dispersion serve to enhance greater political effectiveness. At the same time, larger numbers do not necessarily translate into guaranteed political power. In some ways, the pragmatic nature of creating a Latino community is a strategic move to expand the potential political resource base by accenting both commonalties of culture and interests.

I am using the concepts of commonalty of interests and culture as two foundational bases for the creation and maintenance of the Latino community. I explicitly view these clusters as both perceptions and experiences that can produce positive affinity toward and meaningful interactions between activists in the various Latino sub-communities. I present two significant challenges: converting the conceptual discussion into explicit operational indicators of these links of community and the availability of data and other measures to explore community building. I have chosen to use some demographic information to move beyond the conceptualization of community.

Referring to the results of the Latino National Political Survey (LNPS) (de la Garza et al. 1993), I will examine cultural factors and socioeconomic status among persons of Cuban, Puerto Rican, and Mexican-origin. My later challenge, available data for the full spectrum of Latino sub-communities, is reflected in my initial analysis of community for the three largest Latino subgroups.

Spanish Language Use among Latinos

Spanish language has consistently been identified as one of the cultural glues for Latinos. And the LNPS supports this identification. While there were several items that tapped Spanish language, we chose to use the language of the interview that the Latinos employed in the survey. This is a more direct measure of language use than self-reported language (Padilla 1974). While Spanish is still prevalent among the Latino communities, there are some variations by each of the three subgroups. More than 70 percent of the Cubans answered the survey in Spanish, while 55.2 percent and 47.4 percent of Puerto Rican and Mexican origin respectively conducted their interviews in Spanish. Two salient factors that influence the extent of Spanish-language persistence are age and place of birth. For example, more than 86 percent of the Cuban respondents were born in Cuba, and they are older, on average, than the other two Latino subgroups.

Age Structure and Latinos

Another way to illustrate differentiation due to age is examining Latinos who are under twenty-five. For this age-group, only 35.8 percent of all of the Latino respondents completed the survey in Spanish, as opposed to 75.1 percent of Latinos over the age of fifty-five. Similarly, 80 percent of Latinos born outside the United States answered in Spanish, compared to 15 percent for U.S.-born Latinos. Thus the issue of connectedness among Latinos is only partially demonstrated in the language that these respondents used in the LNPS. Other aspects related to language—its use, awareness, loyalty, and exposure—also contribute to the language domain of Latinos. For example, the growth of Spanish-language media—especially television (Telemundo, Galávision, and SIN)—serves to confirm the Spanish-language markets and mass media transmission of culture and Spanish language. The number one radio station in the Los Angeles metropolitan area is KMEX.

Educational Attainment Levels

Another demographic dimension common to Latino group members is educational attainment. The extent of education achieved provides valuable political resources as well as potential areas of common interest. In the LNPS, we find that Puerto Ricans and Mexican-origin persons differ noticeably from Cubans. Almost 30 percent of the Cubans had completed thirteen years of schooling or more, compared to 19.4 percent and 16 percent for Puerto Ricans and Mexican-origin respectively. Again, the factors of age, language use, and nativity proved to be key determinants of educational attainment for all Latinos. The latter point is pertinent for Puerto Ricans and persons of Mexican origin, as non-U.S. born persons had significantly lower educational levels. The nature of Cuban migration and selective class out-migration reinforced exodus of the professional and educated classes from Cuba (Portes and Rumbaut 1990; Pedraza-Bailey 1985). The Mexican-origin respondents have the greater concentration of persons at the lower end of the educational range (i.e., 31.4 percent with six years of schooling or less), as well an overrepresentation of foreign-born persons in the lower educational categories.

Household Income among Latinos

Another dimension of similarity is economic resources and household income. Relative to the other two groups, Puerto Ricans have lower household income. More than one-fourth (27.5 percent) of the Puerto Rican households earn less than $9,000 per year, compared to 12.9 percent and 15.8 percent respectively for the Mexican-origin and Cubans. At the other end of the income spectrum (households with $75,000), twice as many Cubans (4.3 percent versus 2.1 percent and 2.0 percent Mexican-origin and Puerto Ricans respectively) fall into this upper-income level. The majority of all of Latino households fall into the middle-income category ($20,000–$40,000).

Religious Affiliation and Religiosity

Commonalties of culture and interests include the religious dimension. The popular view of the religious affiliation of most Latinos is that Catholicism dominates across all of the subgroups. If we look at the religious affiliation of the LNPS respondents, we find general support for this characterization. Fully 77.4 percent of all Latinos are Catholics with some subgroup variations. Puerto Rican Catholics are closer to 70 percent, while 80.6 percent of Cubans are Catholics. On the other hand, 14 percent of Latinos are affiliated with Protestant denominations and the balance (8.8 percent) some other religion or no affiliation. The centrality of Catholicism is a major aspect of Latino communities.

Another view of religion, its significance and commonalty, is a follow-up question of LNPS respondents regarding frequency of religious attendance. The Latinos were asked to indicate how often they attended church (from every week, once/twice a month to almost never).[5] Slightly more than a third of the Latinos responded to almost every week, yet there were noticeable differences between Catholics and non-Catholics. Of the Latino Protestants, 58.8 percent attended church weekly compared to 34.8 percent for Catholics. In addition, the LNPS included an item that asked Latinos how much religion served as a significant guide for their daily lives. Again there were some differences between Latino Catholics and Protestants. For Mexican-origin and Puerto Rican Protestants over 50 percent responded that their religion provides a great deal of guidance compared to their Catholic counterparts' 27.9 percent and 22.6 percent respectively. While I am not examining religious affiliation and religiosity, this information can help establish that one commonalty—religion—has a foundation within the Latino community. But Latinos are not monolithic and religiosity is stronger among Latino Protestants. The critical point is that culturally there is warrant to consider religion as a connector for Latinos.

The Pan-ethnic Dimension and the Latino-Hispanic Label

Pan-ethnicity, as discussed so far, refers to the process of group formation due to common conditions and bases for community. The other critical component lies with the situational nature of pan-ethnicity. Individuals consciously choose a group identity that serves a specific utility—political, for our purposes. Since Latinos can be viewed as an aggregation of over twenty national-origin groups, I would posit that there need not be a "natural" clustering based on that connection. Works by Padilla (1986), Espiritu (1996, 1997), Nagel (1996), and Cornell and Hartman (1998) have helped develop the concept of pan-ethnicity.

Group consciousness and social identity constitute a significant building block for this concept. "Group consciousness" refers to the cognitive elements of group attachment; a person incorporates group identity(ies) as part of his social identity, along with evaluative assessments about the group's relative position in society. This identity represents an attachment and affinity to social groupings. For our purposes, persons of Mexican, Dominican, Colombian origin, for example, can include a sense of group attachment and affiliation in addition to national origin/ancestry and any other social identity (parental roles, work groups, etc.). While the literature on social identity and group consciousness focuses on the individual dynamics of identity, clearly the social context serves to establish or reinforce the basis for group affiliation and affinity. For students of American politics, a long-standing phenomenon is the transformation of ancestral groups into minority groups. Minority status is associated with differential treatment and power and, identifiably, group awareness. For Latinos, language, customs, phenotype (to some extent), and social networks help promote that identifiability. At the same time, stereotypes and prejudicial attitudes toward Latinos, as well as unfair treatment, serve to perpetuate identifiability.

The "Latinization" of the United States (Cuello 1996) over the last three decades has been accompanied by the transformation of immigrant and indigenous groups into minority groups (Wilson 1977). Miami is now recognized as a Latino city in which Cubans have both important political and economic influence. Los Angeles with its sizable Mexican-origin and growing Central American communities rivals cities in Latin America in terms of population concentrations. One out of every five persons in Chicago is Latino with a mix of Mexican, Puerto Rican, and Central American origin. New York has not only a large Puerto Rican population but also fast-growing Dominican, Colombian, and Peruvian communities. Three national Spanish-language television networks broadcast daily throughout the United States and Latin America. In sections of many U.S. cities most residents do not speak any English and streets are lined with Latino-based and oriented businesses. As pointed out by Cuello (1996), this nation has undergone dramatic and cultural changes in a very Latino sort of way.

For our purposes, the Latinization of the United States can bear a direct impact on the U.S. political system and processes. I have already defined this connection in terms of building community among these diverse and similarly based sub-communities. In this section, the focus on pan-ethnicity reflects the cognitive and psychological dimensions of group identity and consciousness. Group identity refers to an individual's affinity to and sense of attachment to a social category that is largely defined in ethnic, racial, gender, and age-related terms. Obviously, other social groupings can serve as the basis for group identity. Among Latinos, evidence of group identity is concentrated within national group boundaries (García et al. 1994); each person is attached to a Mexicano, Cubano, or other Latino subgroup country.

The concept of group consciousness (Verba and Nie 1972; Miller et al. 1981; J. A. García 1982) builds on the presence of group affinity by adding two other dimensions: an evaluation of one's group status politically in American society and a collective orientation toward social and political action. For Latinos, individuals with a group consciousness have a positive affinity for being Latino; they assess their group's sociopolitical status as experiencing lower levels of socioeconomic and political status and are inclined to participate in some collective activity to change the situation. My reference to pan-ethnicity falls within the general discussion of group identification. That is, instead of a Guatemalan thinking of himself in exclusively national-origin terms,[6] this person could include Latino (a broader group aggregation) as well. I introduced this concept earlier in this chapter. Works by Padilla (1986), Espiritu (1992), Nagel (1996), Hayes-Bautista and Chapa (1987), and Nelson and Tienda (1985) have used, in varying degrees, the concepts of group identity and group consciousness to construct pan-ethnicity.

We are exploring the extent of "Latino-ness" or "Hispanicity" in terms of community building or bridging across the twenty-plus Latino national-origin groups. In addition, we are examining the relevance and impact of such community formation on the political system. The latter point encompasses the identification of issues and public policy preferences, organizational and leadership development, political **mobilization,** electoral politics and representation, and policy implementation. While much attention has been directed toward the phenomenal population growth of Latinos over the past two decades, our perspective does not revolve around growth per se. Population size and geographic location/concentration can serve as a resource base, but converting numbers of persons into an effective political base requires additional elements.

Consistent with the internal and external dynamics affecting Latino community building, the process of constructing or developing a Latino identity and affinity can be the result of situations and conditions within the Latino sub-communities and general societal developments. For example, work by Felix Padilla (1986) in Chicago highlights the conscious efforts by leadership in the various Latino communities (Mexican, Puerto Rican, Cubans, etc.) to promote a pan-ethnic identity. The use and social meaning of Latino to reflect a community of Spanish-speaking and culturally and politically similar groups was evident in the early 1970s.

One of the focus groups conducted as part of the Latino National Political Survey in 1989 was held in Chicago. A central area of exploration was identity and labeling. A group of fifteen to twenty Latinos (of varied national origins and ages) participated in a discussion of how each saw himself or herself. For the most part, each person included being Latino as part of his or her social identity. In addition, their characterization of what that meant reflected a sense of community among all persons of Latino background. For our purposes, the inclusion of being Latino or Hispanic indicates the integral role of that identity without being the only identity a person internalizes.

Another example from one of the two Chicago focus groups is the set of responses from young adult Latino siblings. Their parents were of "mixed" Latino background—one parent Puerto Rican and the other Mexican. The sister had married an Italian and lived in a South Side Polish Catholic neighborhood. Their parents were divorced. Then the sister described a series of situations in which her four-year-old daughter was already attuned to her sense of identity. When visiting her grandmother, the granddaughter refers to her Mexican-ness, and when visiting her grandfather, the young girl accented her Puerto Rican identity. At the same time, while living in her South Side neighborhood, the young girl places greater emphasis on her father's Italian ancestry. In school, the young girl is more likely to refer to her European or white ethnic background. When traveling on the CTA bus from the far South Side to the Loop (downtown commercial area), she is quick to identify herself as a minority or person of color. Finally, with her mother and her uncle, she refers to herself as a Latina.

CONCLUSION

This real-life illustration is intended to present a clearer picture of the identity process and how situations help influence it. Persons can assume a multiplicity of identities without feelings of divided loyalties or confusion. It also illustrates how within-group socialization and external cues influence the identification process. For our purposes, the development of a sense of being Latino can be a "product" of shared cultural values and practices (language, origins, traditions, etc.), inter-group interactions, and societal constructs (positive, but usually negative) of persons of Spanish origin. As we examine the development and existence of community among persons of Latino origin in the United States, our primary purpose is to explore the linkages of community to the political realms of agenda setting, political mobilization, political resource development, and public policy outcomes and implementation.

NOTES

1. The terms "Hispanic" and "Latino" are used interchangeably to indicate persons from Mexico, Central America, South America, the Spanish Caribbean, and the Iberian Peninsula living in the United States. I prefer to use "Latino" as a pan-ethnic term, while recognizing the extensive use of "Hispanic" by the mass media, public officials, and the public.

2. The U.S. decennial census is an attempt to enumerate all persons living in the United States on April 1 of each decade. The short form includes basic information such as number of persons in the household, ages, race, gender, and relationships of household members. The short form is distributed to all households. The long form is sent to one in six households, randomly, with much more detailed items (labor market, migration, ancestry, language use, etc.).

3. Racial categories in the census include the following categories: white, black, Asian/Pacific Islander, American Indian/Alaskan native, and other. For the 2000 census, race included the same categories but separated Asian populations from the

Pacific islanders, making five racial categories. Also, individuals were instructed to mark all racial categories that apply.

4. The creation of cross-national groups into a more singular ethnic group happened for not only Latinos but also Asian Americans, Arab Americans, and American Indians. The basis for group aggregation is perceived cultural similarities, which are usually couched in cultural, linguistic, and religious terms.

5. Only Latinos who indicated having a religious affiliation answered this question.

6. This example does not suggest that our hypothetical Guatemalan would see himself in only national-origin terms. An individual could incorporate gender roles, work roles, or familial identities as well.

3

Culture and Demographics

¿Somos parte de la amplia comunidad de latinos o principalmente parte de una comunidad específica y bien definida? Los valores, el idioma, las tradiciones y estilos de vivir son aspectos del carácter de cada uno de nosotros. ¿Las dimensiones de las culturas comunes y las circunstancias diarias son nuestra realidad o dudamos eso?

Are we part of an extended Latino community or primarily a part of a specific, well-defined community? Values, language, traditions and lifestyles are aspects of the character of each one of us. Are these dimensions of our common cultures and our daily circumstances part of our reality or do we doubt that?

In this chapter, I introduce another way to amplify these bases for community among Latinos in the United States. Clearly, there is a greater awareness among the larger public about the presence of Latinos. Recent releases by the U.S. Bureau of the Census 2000 of the racial and Spanish population counts have sparked dozens of articles about Latinos. Two major themes have been continuing high population growth and the presence of Latinos throughout the United States. The visible "impressions" about Latinos' significant population growth (in which immigration is a major contributor) and their cultural persistence (manifested mostly through Spanish-language use) have reinvigorated public interest in these communities. Who are Latinos? How many are there? Where do they live and what are they like? Our basic theme of community building is grounded in the understanding that Latinos come from a number of countries and/or are connected ancestrally to these Spanish-origin countries. The terms "Latino" and/or "Hispanic" are used to identify persons of Spanish origin. In most cases, these are persons who come from or are ancestrally from Mexico, Central and South America, the Spanish-speaking Caribbean, and the Iberian Peninsula. At the same time, some Latino communities can point to long-established communities in the United States dating to the seventeenth century. Latinos are among the oldest groups in America and yet are some of the more recent newcomers.

Group affinity is neither automatic nor positive. Individuals are more likely to have stronger affinities to their country of origin than to a larger, "primordial" grouping or cluster called Latino. By primordial I mean the fundamental characteristics that attach individuals to a group, such as language, ancestry or bloodline, phenotypical traits, and other aspects of culture and tradition. It should be quite clear that an essential part of Latino politics is bridging national-origin boundaries and developing an additional sense of being connected to other persons and communities of Spanish origin ancestry and background. Thus we are exploring the expanded boundaries of social identity that incorporate a sense of group consciousness and connectedness that goes beyond national boundaries. A brief demographic profile of the Spanish-origin communities will help identify some important features of these populations and essential background information that contributes to a sense of being Latino in America.

By 2000, the Hispanic or Latino population numbered over 35 million persons. This represented approximately 12.5 percent of the total U.S. population (see table 3.1). Our theme of significant population growth can be seen over a longer period than the past few years. In the 1970 census, the Spanish-origin population (Hernández et al. 1973) was slightly greater than 9 million (9,072,602) and constituted some 4.4 percent of the U.S. population. The following growth was most evident between the 1970 and 1980 decennial censuses. The Latino population increased by over 61 percent to reach 14.6 million persons (the total U.S. population increased by 11.5 percent). Subsequently, the 1990 census revealed the same pattern as Latinos increased by 53 percent (compared to 9.8 percent for the overall population) to number 22.4 million. At the beginning of a new millennium, Latino growth continues to outpace the general non-Hispanic populations (32.9 percent versus 4.7 percent). The growth trajectory predicted that Hispanics would assume the "title" of the largest minority group by 2005; yet Census 2000 indicated that mark was reached by 2001.

This substantial growth rate is attributed to the three primary factors associated with most population increases: (1) significant portions of the female population in the fertility age range, (2) higher birth rates than the general population, and (3) international migration. In table 3.2, the magnitude of the Latino population growth is well illustrated. In addition, we can see the major subgroup composition of Latinos. The Mexican-origin community is historically the largest subgroup, composing almost 60 percent of all Latinos. Mexican-origin, Mexican Americans, or Chicanos have had even higher growth rates than the overall Latino rate (92.9 percent from 1970 to 1980 and 54.4 percent from 1980 to 1990). This pattern continued into the 1990s with both higher birth rates and immigration contributing to these gains. The second largest com-

Rodolfo "Corky" Gonzáles (1928–)

Of all the leaders who emerged during the Chicano power movement, no one was more closely identified with urban youth than Rodolfo "Corky" Gonzáles. As a popular boxer in Denver, Colorado, Gonzáles became an active member of the city's local Democratic political machinery during the 1950s. Known for being brash and fiery, Gonzáles's ability as a community organizer garnered him positions as codirector of Colorado's Viva Kennedy campaign in 1960 and as director of Denver's Neighborhood Youth Corps (1964) and the city's War on Poverty program (1965). By 1966 Gonzáles founded the Crusade for Justice after becoming disillusioned with party politics. In works such as *Yo Soy Joaquín,* Gonzáles called for a cultural and political revolution among Chicano youth to establish bilingual education, independent Chicano schools, and economic and political separation from Anglo society.

While Gonzáles earned the adoration of thousands of students, he alienated a significant portion of the Mexican American community with his controversial separatist rhetoric. Many criticized Gonzáles as self-promoting for not only the absolute control he maintained over the Crusade for Justice, but for his negative critiques of popular leaders such as Jose Angel Gutiérrez and César Chávez. Moreover, many Mexican American women and men rejected the machismo boxing chauvinism that Gonzáles's militant rhetoric embodied. Despite these criticisms, Gonzáles helped inspire a new generation of Chicano youth to articulate forcefully the demands of an increasingly urban Mexican American community.

Bibliography

Gonzáles, Rodolfo "Corky." "Chicano Nationalism: The Key to Unity for La Raza." In Wayne Moquin, ed., *A Documentary History of the Mexican American.* New York: Bantam, 1972.

Marín, Christine. *A Spokesman of the Mexican American Movement: Rodolfo "Corky" Gonzáles and the Fight for Chicano Liberation, 1966–1972.* San Francisco: R & E Research Associates, 1977.

ponent of the Latino communities is the Puerto Rican or Boricua population, which now numbers 3.4 million persons. The next largest group is the Cubans or Cubanos who are 4 percent of all Latinos (1.2 million). Beyond these three largest Latino subgroups, greater specificity is more difficult to achieve.

Demographically, the "rest of the Latino community" is consolidated into two general categories: Central Americans and South Americans, includ-

Table 3.1 Latino-Origin Population in the United States, 1970–2000

	1970	1980	1990	2000	Growth (%) 1970–1990	Growth (%) 1990–2000
Total population	203,211,926	226,545,805	248,709,873	281,421,906	22.4	13.2
Hispanic population	9,072,602	14,608,673	22,354,059	35,305,818	146.4	57.9
Non-Hispanic population	194,139,324	211,937,132	226,355,814	246,116,088	17.0	8.7
Mexican descent	4,532,435	8,740,439	13,495,938	20,640,711	197.8	52.9
Puerto Rican descent	1,429,390	2,013,945	2,727,754	3,406,178	90.8	24.9
Cuban descent	544,600	803,226	1,043,932	1,241,685	91.7	18.9
Other Hispanic descent	2,566,177	3,051,063	5,086,435	10,017,244	98.2	96.9
Dominican Republic descent	NA	NA	520,151	764,945	NA	47.1
Central American descent	NA	NA	1,323,830	1,685,937	NA	27.4
South American descent	NA	NA	1,035,602	1,353,562	NA	30.7

Sources: Thomas D. Boswell, *A Demographic Profile of Cuban Americans* (Miami: Cuban American National Council and Current Population Survey, 1998); *Hispanics in the United States* (Washington, D.C.: U.S. Bureau of the Census, 1997); *Census 2000 Paints Statistical Portrait of National Hispanic Population,* CB 01-81 (Washington, D.C.: U.S. Bureau of the Census, 2001).

Table 3.2 Growth of the Latino Population in the United States, 1970–2000

	Growth (1000s) 1970	1980	1990	2000	Growth (%) 1970–1980	1980–1990	1990–2000
Total	203,212	226,546	248,710	281,422	11.5	9.8	13.2
Total non-Latino	194,139	211,937	226,356	246,117	9.2	6.8	8.7
Hispanic	9,073	14,609	22,354	35,306	61.0	53.0	57.1
Mexican	4,532	8,740	13,496	20,641	92.9	54.4	52.9
Puerto Rican	1,429	2,014	2,728	3,406	40.9	35.5	24.9
Cuban	545	803	1,044	1,242	47.3	30.0	19.0
Other	2,566	3,051	5,086	10,017	18.9	66.7	96.9

Sources: Jorge del Pinal and Audrey Singer, "Generations of Diversity: Latinos in the United States," *Population Bulletin* 52, no. 3 (1997): 13; Betsy Guzman, *The Hispanic Population: Census 2000 Brief.* C2KBR/01-3. (Washington, D.C.: U.S. Bureau of the Census, 2001).

Table 3.3   **Composition of the Latino Population in the United States, 1970–1997 (percentage)**

	1970	1980	1990	1997	Growth[a] 1970–1990	Growth[a] 1990–1997
Mexican descent	49.9	59.8	61.2	58.5	26.7	−5.5
Puerto Rican descent	15.8	13.8	12.1	9.6	−22.8	−13.1
Cuban descent	6.0	5.5	4.8	3.5	−21.7	−10.6
Other Hispanic descent	28.3	20.9	3.9[b]	28.4	NA	NA
Dominican Republic descent	NA	NA	2.4	2.2	NA	NA
Central American descent	NA	NA	6.0	4.8	NA	NA
South American descent	NA	NA	4.7	3.8	NA	NA

Sources: Thomas D. Boswell, *A Demographic Profile of Cuban Americans* (Miami: Cuban American National Council, 1994); National Association of Hispanic Publications, *Hispanic-Latinos: Diverse People in a Multi-Cultural Society,* Special Report (Washington, D.C., 1995); Current Population Reports, *Hispanic Population in the U.S.,* 1997 (Washington, D.C.: U.S. Government Printing Office, 1998).
[a]These columns represent the group-specific gains or losses for each Latino subgroup relative to the overall Latino population for these periods.
[b]The drop in percentage of "other Hispanic" in the 1990 census is the result of a new delineation between Central and South Americans and persons who mark the "other Hispanic" category.

ing persons from El Salvador, Guatemala, Panama, and Nicaragua; Spanish-speaking South American countries such as Colombia, Peru, Venezuela, and Argentina; and the other Spanish-speaking areas of the Caribbean, particularly the Dominican Republic. In many respects, these segments of the Latino communities represent the faster growing elements for the decade of the 1990s. These Latino subgroups include more immigrants and refugees[1] (less so native-born persons) and are settling in longer established Latino communities throughout the United States. The more recently arrived Latinos are settling in already established Latino communities (e.g., Miami, New York, Chicago, and Los Angeles), in the South, and in certain eastern suburban communities. The influx of Latinos into areas of previously low concentration became quite significant during the decade of the 1990s. For example, Central Americans have become the largest Latino element in Washington, D.C.; Dominican and Colombian populations are rivaling the Puerto Ricans in New York City.

There are also variations within the broad Latino sub-communities. In table 3.3, we can see the intra-Latino group percentages relative to each other. As already noted, the Mexican-origin population has been the largest subgroup. Over the past three decades Chicanos continued their population "dominance" and high growth rates. While Puerto Ricans continue to be the second largest Latino group, their proportion of the Latino population has been declining noticeably. What is not directly apparent from this table is that the growth within the Latino communities comes from the Central and South American segments more than any other segment.

Box 3.1   Defining Hispanic/Latino via the Census

With the population growth of Central and South Americans and Domini-cans, there has been some debate over the accuracy of their count. The Spanish-origin question in the census form asked persons to indicate if they were Hispanic/Latino or not. If the answer is affirmative, specific options that a person could mark include Mexican, Puerto Rican, Cuban, or other Hispanic, the last option is followed by a underline which can be used to indicate a specific group—Salvadoran, Panamanian, Colombian, and so on. From these responses the Census Bureau counted the numbers of per-sons in the "other" Hispanic category. Debate erupted between cities like New York and Dominican and Colombian organizations over the structure of the census question, which led to a major undercount.

For example, New York City planners estimate an undercount of more than 150,000 Dominicans and more than 35,000 Colombians. A sociolo-gist, John R. Logan (SUNY-Albany), has issued recalculated figures for these groups and has the support of New York City officials for the adjustments. (The contents of this vignette are taken partially from a *New York Times* story, "Expert Offers New Estimates of City Hispanic Population," by Janny Scott [July 6, 2001].) While part of the controversy centers around the choice of the "other Hispanic" option and a line for the person to indicate a specific group, there are additional considerations. While many persons selected the "other Hispanic" category, they left the line blank as to which specific Latino subgroup they belonged to. As a result, it is difficult to say how many Dominicans, Colombians, and Panamanians are identified.

The Census Bureau offered one explanation for the number of "other Hispanics": This term has become such a broad-based expression that indi-viduals do not choose to make specific references. This situation demon-strates how specific counts of the various Latino subgroups are important to local governments and Latino organizations for political purposes, funding, and service programming. Rising numbers of persons falling into the "other Hispanic" category may indicate a broader sense of identifying oneself or perhaps confusion as to how some Latinos identify themselves more specif-ically. Clearly the discussion of community is dynamic and evolving.

While Latino population growth has been substantial, Latino residential communities have been concentrated in certain regions and states of the United States rather than "randomly" distributed throughout. Table 3.4 presents the distribution of Latinos by state. Almost 86 percent of the Latino population can be found in ten states. California and Texas are home to almost one-half of all Latinos, nearly 17.5 million. Other states with significant Latino populations include New York, Florida, Illinois, New Mexico, and Arizona. Latinos reside in large, populous states, with substantial electoral votes and industrial and expanding service economies. The numbers of Latinos for these primary state residences have exceeded a critical mass status.[2] This point illustrates that a Latino political presence has been established and **mobilization** is the critical element for further political development.

In 1998 Governor George W. Bush of Texas incorporated a targeted effort to seek Hispanic support through public policies such as bilingual education reform and funding, as well as opposing **English only** and anti-immigrant legislative initiatives. On the other hand, former Governor Pete Wilson of California in 1994–1998 supported several statewide propositions (e.g., opposing immigration, affirmative action, and bilingual education) that resulted in increased Latino **political participation** and declining support for the Republican Party.

The information in table 3.5 further reflects the population growth within the various states for this decade. For example, while Latinos represent one-third of the state population of California, their 29.1 percent increase has occurred since 1990. Similarly, in states like Texas and Florida, the Latino population increases since 1990 are both over 30 percent. Gains in

Table 3.4   U.S. Hispanic Population by State

	Census 2000 Population	Percentage of Hispanics in the State	Cumulative Percentage of Hispanics in the United States	Within-State Percentage Change, 1990–2000
California	10,966,556	31.1	31.1	42.6
Texas	6,669,666	18.9	50.0	53.7
New York	2,867,583	8.1	58.1	29.5
Florida	2,652,715	7.6	65.7	70.4
Illinois	1,530,262	4.3	70.0	69.2
Arizona	1,295,617	3.7	73.7	45.1
New Jersey	1,117,191	3.2	76.9	28.2
New Mexico	765,386	2.2	79.1	19.6
Colorado	735,601	2.1	81.2	31.1
Massachusetts	428,729	1.2	82.4	24.7
Rest of the states	6,276,512	17.8	100.0	47.3[a]

Source: Betsy Guzman, *The Hispanic Population: Census 2000 Brief.* C2KBR/01-3. (Washington, D.C.: U.S. Bureau of the Census, 2001).

[a]This percentage represents an average percentage change across the forty-two states, plus the District of Columbia.

Table 3.5 The Latino Population in the United States and Selected States, 1990 and 2000

	1990			Census 2000			Percentage Increase in Latino Population 1990–2000
	Total	Latino	Percentage Latino	Total	Latino	Percentage Latino	
United States	249,439,545	22,574,761	9.1	281,421,906	35,305,818	12.5	20.8
Arizona	3,679,225	688,736	18.7	5,130,632	1,295,617	25.3	88.1
California	29,929,011	7,688,110	25.7	33,871,648	10,966,556	32.4	42.6
Colorado	3,303,919	425,378	12.9	4,301,261	735,601	17.1	72.9
Florida	13,018,036	1,591,040	12.2	15,982,378	2,682,712	16.8	68.6
Illinois	11,446,412	918,002	8.0	12,419,293	1,530,262	12.3	66.9
Massachusetts	6,018,123	293,121	4.9	6,349,729	428,729	6.8	46.3
New Jersey	7,757,228	742,215	9.6	8,414,350	1,117,191	13.3	50.5
New Mexico	1,519,984	576,977	38.0	1,819,046	765,386	42.1	32.7
New York	18,001,855	2,213,304	12.3	18,976,457	2,867,583	15.1	29.6
Pennsylvania	11,895,176	244,427	2.1	12,281,054	394,088	3.2	61.2
Texas	17,045,892	4,346,397	24.8	19,439,337	5,722,535	29.4	31.7

Source: Betsy Guzman, *The Hispanic Population: Census 2000 Brief.* C2KBR/01-3. (Washington, D.C.: U.S. Bureau of the Census, 2001).

political representation are becoming more evident in these top ten states since the 1990s. The decennial census for 2000 resulted in congressional seats being reapportioned in most of the top ten states for Hispanics. Even in states that may lose some congressional seats (New York, Pennsylvania, Massachusetts, etc.), Latino gains will position them to compete actively for the redrawn congressional districts and/or serve as a critical voting bloc. We will examine the electoral activities and outcomes in a later chapter.

As we approached the 2002 national elections, Latino concentration in states such as California, Texas, Florida, New York, Illinois, and other large Electoral College states would see them playing a more pivotal role in congressional and statewide campaigns. Clearly the results of the first five tables in this chapter reinforce and amplify the theme of substantial population growth for Latinos over the past three decades. At the same time, a more recent publication by the U.S. Bureau of the Census (1999) presented population projections for the United States until the year 2050. Latino growth continues at a higher rate than the general population, and Latinos should soon constitute over one-fifth of the U.S. population.

CULTURE, LATINOS, AND DEMOGRAPHICS

So far, this demographic profile has centered on the size and national-origin makeup of the Latino communities in the United States. We have also suggested that an important element of the community of culture would include language and foreign-born origin. The common perception is that the Spanish language unifies Latinos. In 1990, about 14 percent of the U.S. population spoke a language other than English at home. Spanish was the most common non-English language, spoken by over 54 percent of all non-English speakers. This represents over 17 million persons (age five years and older). For all Latinos, nearly 78 percent reported speaking Spanish at home while growing up. In contrast to the percentage of Spanish-speaking Latinos, the second largest non-English language group was French (6.1 percent). About one-half of Latinos indicate that they speak English well.[3]

The data in table 3.6 provide another way to look at Spanish-language use among Latinos. Again, data from the 1990 census asked follow-up questions of respondents indicating they spoke a language other than English. These individuals were questioned about their self-reported English-speaking proficiency. As already mentioned, among all Latinos slightly more than one-half speak English very well. Yet variations surface when the language dimension is examined by Latino subgroups. The Mexican-origin population mirrors the overall percentage of Latino Spanish use. On the other hand, higher percentages of Central Americans and Dominicans do not speak English very well (65.5 percent and 63.7 percent respectively). Almost 55 percent of Cubans do

Table 3.6   Language Spoken at Home by Ability to Speak English for Selected Latino Groups, 1990

	Percentage Who Speak Spanish and Do Not Speak English "Very Well"	Percentage Who Speak Spanish and Speak English "Very Well"
All Latinos	50.8	49.2
Mexicans	50.9	49.1
Puerto Ricans	41.4	58.6
Cubans	54.5	45.5
Dominicans	63.7	37.3
Central Americans	65.5	35.5
South Americans	54.6	45.4
Spaniards	31.9	68.1

Source: United States Bureau of the Census, *We the Americans . . . Hispanics* (Washington, D.C.: Department of Commerce, 1993.)

not speak English well, while Puerto Ricans have the lowest percentage of persons not speaking English very well.

Speaking Spanish is still a fairly universal experience for most Latinos. Exposure to Spanish language in the home setting is not uncommon in Latino households. At the same time, the ability to speak Spanish (to whatever degree) and understand/speak English well connotes a bilingual language environment more than a predominantly non-English speaking, isolated population. Thus issues of English-only and political loyalty continue to occupy the political landscape, while Latinos look more like a bilingual group than one that is steadfastly holding on to their mother tongue exclusively. The role of Spanish-language use, the extent of language loyalty, and how the public arena reinforces or discourages bilingualism are some aspects of Spanish-language persistence and the public arena for Latinos. In addition, the growth of Spanish-speaking media, particularly networks like Univision and Telemundo, and Spanish-language radio help meet the service needs of Latinos. Spanish-language media also provides a vehicle for Spanish-language maintenance and acquisition among primarily younger and native-born Latinos. The role and impact of Spanish-language media will be discussed in latter chapters, especially in relation to campaigns and elections.

A significant element of Latino communities is composed of persons born in Spanish-origin countries. Thus nativity, or the significant presence of foreign-born persons, perpetuates language, customs, and traditions. Since the 1970s, more Latinos have immigrated into the United States than any other group. The composition of U.S. immigration has changed dramatically in the latter half of this century as Latin American and Asian immigrants predominate the migration stream. Almost two-fifths of all Latinos residing in the United States are foreign-born. Table 3.7 displays the nativity status of Latinos. While the percentage of American permanent resident aliens overall is slightly greater than 10 percent,[4] the overall percentage for Latinos is 38.4 percent (6.1 percent for non-Hispanics). At the same time the proportion of immigrants for Cubans is the highest of any group.

The number of Latino foreign-born varies across the different Latino subgroups. Over 70 percent (71.8 percent) of Cubans are foreign-born, as well as 67 percent of Central and South Americans. The Cuban community's foreign-born status is that of refugees with access to specific governmental assistance programs. While the percentage of Mexican-origin persons is lower (36.9 percent), the sheer number of Mexican foreign born exceeds the total for all of other Latino immigrants. Finally, the distinction of Puerto Ricans born in the United States or on the island of Puerto Rico is not associated with citizenship status: Puerto Rico is a commonwealth, and Puerto Ricans are U.S. citizens. At the same time, perspectives and experiences among Puerto Ricans may be affected by their place of birth.

Language and nativity (foreign-born) are critical cultural dimensions that help define the Latino community of culture. The coexistence of native-born and "immigrant" living in the same or proximate neighborhoods, familial social networks, and common work environments and business interactions provide a regular basis for cultural exchanges and experiences. These interactions can reinforce cultural expressions and values or, perhaps, create cultural tensions over assimilation, acculturation, or even cultural authenticity. Cultural dynamics would be less likely to exist without the persistence of Spanish language and a steady influx of immigrants. In addition, the sizable percentage of foreign-born in Latino communities helps bring forth the extended and complex set of issues and policies related to immigration, rights and legal standing, and access to services. Thus population figures show the extensiveness of the foreign-born segment within the Latino community.

A clear political link for Latinos with a significant foreign-born segment is the extent of naturalization or lack of it. Citizenship status has a direct link with electoral participation that tends to offset the rapid growth rate that Latinos have experienced. Table 3.8 reports the size and naturalization status of foreign-born persons in the United States. A person who is a legal permanent resident alien can pursue U.S. citizenship after five years' residence. This includes demonstrating good moral character, knowledge of U.S. government and history, respect for the law, competence in the English language, completing a personal interview process, and paying the naturalization filing fees.

There are almost 28 million foreign-born persons, of whom 41 percent are Hispanics. Of this population, 35.1 percent of all foreign-born persons are naturalized citizens, in comparison to 21.6 percent for Hispanics (the rate is 45.8 percent for non-Hispanics). Examining those rates by specific Latino subgroups reveals some variation. For the Mexican-origin immigrants, only 14.6 percent are naturalized citizens in comparison to 51.2 percent for Cubans. To

Table 3.7 Nativity Status for Latinos by National-Origin Background, 1997 (in 1000s)

	Origin			Latino Subgroups				
	Total	Hispanic	Non-Hispanic	Mexican	Puerto Rican	Cuban	Central and South Americans	Other Hispanic
Total	266,792	29,703	237,089	18,795	3,152	1,258	4,292	2,206
United States	237,207	16,578	220,089	11,584	1,824	343	1,327	1,500
Puerto Rico	1,364	1,299	65	9	1,241	4	25	20
Outlying areas	115	15	99	1	14			
U.S.-born parents	2,314	417	1,898	263	43	7	65	40
Foreign-born	25,792	11,394	14,398	6,939	31	904	2,875	646

Source: U.S. Bureau of the Census, *Current Population Survey Reports, March 1997, Race and Ethnicity* Table 10.1 (Washington, D.C., 1998).

Table 3.8 Foreign-Born and Citizenship among Hispanics and Non-Hispanics, March 1997 (in 1000s)

	Origin			Latino Subgroups				
	Total	Hispanic	Non-Hispanic	Mexican	Puerto Rican	Cuban	Central and South Americans	Other Hispanic
Total	27,779	11,393	14,386	6,937	31	904	2,875	646
Naturalized	9,043	2,456	6,586	1,104	22	463	734	223
	(35.1%)	(21.6%)	(45.8%)	(14.6%)	(72.9%)	(51.2%)	(25.5%)	(34.5%)
Not a citizen	16,736	8,936	7,800	5,923	8	441	2,141	423
	(64.9%)	(78.4%)	(54.2%)	(85.4%)	(27.1%)	(48.8%)	(74.2%)	(65.5%)

Source: U.S. Bureau of the Census, *Current Population Survey Reports, March 1997, Race and Ethnicity* Table 10.7 (Washington, D.C., 1998).

some degree, designation as a political refugee facilitates the naturalization process for Cubanos. The naturalization percentage for Central and South Americans is also low, as 25.5 percent are citizens. The consequences of lower numbers of Latino citizens among the foreign-born are connected to elections, job opportunities, immigration petitions,[5] and scholarship opportunities. Again, several research studies examine the factors that influence naturalization. This demographic sketch serves to establish the size and extent of the group of foreign-born Latinos. Its implications will be analyzed in latter chapters.

COMMUNITIES OF INTEREST

Language and immigrant status are two purveyors of culture and linkage to one's country of origin. In sociological terms, the social networks of Latinos can be very ethnically dense with interactions that incorporate Spanish language, cultural practices, and familial contacts with recent arrivals. At the same time, common conditions and situations contribute to a sense of community. Matters such as differential treatment, societal stereotypes, and similar socioeconomic status are examples of common situations that can serve to connect elements of the Latino community. One such area lies with educational attainment and Latinos. Table 3.9 provides some recent information on the levels of schooling for Latinos and non-Latinos. For the adult population over twenty-five years of age, almost 25 percent graduated from college, and over 80 percent graduated from high school. In comparison, only 9 percent of Latinos are college graduates and 57 percent are high school graduates. There are indications that younger cohorts of Latinos are completing more schooling than older ones, yet the gap between non-Latinos and Latinos is widening.

In terms of subgroup educational attainment, some differences are present. The Mexican-origin segment fares less successfully, as 47 percent are high school graduates, whereas 64 percent of Cubans graduated from high school.

Another important consideration is the differential in the educational attainment between U.S.-born Latinos and foreign-born (70 percent versus 42 percent high school graduates respectively). Again we see how immigrant status influences socioeconomic status and highlights certain institutions and policy areas. In addition to Latino subgroup status, the age structure for each group is relevant. For example, the Mexican-origin and Puerto Ricans are a young population while the Cubans are older than the median age for non-Latinos. Therefore, the presence of Latino children in our school systems comes primarily from these particular Latino subgroups. The gamut of relevant educational issues includes bilingual education, quality of educational facilities and programs, access for immigrant children, school retention rates and discipline policies (Meier and Stewart 1991; San Miguel 1987), and par-

Table 3.9   Educational Attainment of U.S. Residents by Race and Ethnicity, 1996 and 2000

	Number (1,000s)	Less Than Fifth Grade	Less Than Ninth Grade	High School Graduate or Higher	BA/BS or Higher
		Highest Level of Education (%)[a]			
Total population, age 25+[b]	175,230	1.6	5.4	84.1	25.6
Non-Latino	160,689	1.0	6.0	85.0	25.0
White	130,784	.5	3.7	88.4	28.1
Black	19,445	1.6	5.1	78.9	16.6
Asian and Pacific Islanders	6,667	3.6	4.9	85.6	43.9
Hispanic	19,979	8.7	18.6	57.0	10.6
Age-group					
25–34	8,489	3.7	15.0	61.5	9.7
35+	11,490	10.9	20.3	55.0	11.1
Origin					
Mexican	8,691	13	36	47	7
Puerto Rican	1,592	5	19	60	11
Cuban	821	6	23	64	19
Central and South American	2,272	7	25	61	14
Other Hispanic	1,165	5	18	66	13
Place of birth					
United States	5,672	4	13	70	12
Outside United States	8,869	15	41	42	8

Sources: Jorge del Pinal and Audrey Singer, "Generations of Diversity: Latinos in the United States," *Population Bulletin* 52, no. 3 (1997): 32; U.S. Bureau of the Census, *Educational Attainment of U.S. Population Fifteen Years and Older by Race and Spanish Origin.*
[a]Estimated attainment data from Current Population Survey, 1997.
[b]The figures for the educational attainment for both Latino and non-Latinos were derived from special reports on Hispanic origin for census 2000.

ticipation in school decision making. A later discussion of public policy will relate these issues to the Latino community.

Another aspect of socioeconomic life for Latinos lies in the labor market. Labor force participation rates, especially for Latino males, have been higher than those of the general population. In addition, Latinos are more concentrated in blue-collar jobs and in service and manufacturing/construction industries. Thus, if more Latinos tend to be occupationally "stratified" and located in particular industry sectors, then issues, problems, and union or organizational connections serve as a common bases for mobilization and actions. Table 3.10 presents occupational information for Latinos and non-Latinos. One significant feature lies in the differential unemployment rate between Latinos and non-Latinos. Latino unemployment for males and females is 50–100 percent greater than for their non-Latino counterparts.

Two general occupational clusters (professional, administrative and sales,

Table 3.10   Selected Labor Force Characteristics in the United States by Race and Ethnicity, 1996 (percentage)

| | Unemployed | | Occupation of Employed Workers | | | |
| | | | Men | | Women | |
	Men	Women	Professional, Administrative, Sales	Service, Skilled/ Unskilled Labor	Professional, Administrative, Sales	Service Skilled/ Unskilled Labor
Total	7	5	48	52	72	28
Non-Latino	6	5	50	50	74	26
White	5	4	51	49	76	24
Black	14	9	34	66	61	39
Other non-Latino	7	5	58	42	67	33
Origin						
Hispanic	10	10	27	73	56	44
Mexican	10	10	23	77	55	45
Puerto Rican	10	11	37	63	64	36
Cuban	6	6	44	56	72	28
Central and South American	8	10	29	71	48	52
Other Latino	16	7	45	55	60	40
Place of birth						
United States	10	9	41	59	72	28
Outside United States	9	11	18	82	40	60

Source: Jorge del Pinal and Audrey Singer, "Generations of Diversity: Latinos in the United States," *Population Bulletin* 52, no. 3 (1997): 38.

and service skilled and unskilled) illustrate a common foundation among Latinos. Whereas non-Latino males are evenly divided between the professional/administrative and skilled/semiskilled occupations, the distribution among Latinos is more skewed toward the service and skilled/unskilled jobs (27 percent and 73 percent). In a similar pattern for Latinas, the disparity exists but is not as extreme (74 percent/26 percent for non-Latinos versus 56 percent/46 percent for Latinas).

Latino subgroups show measurable differences between most of the subgroups and the Cubans. While Cubans are still below the non-Latino males in percentage employed in professional/administrative (50 percent versus 44 percent), the other Latino subgroups range from a low of 23 percent to 37 percent. A similar pattern exists for Cubanas in comparison to other Latinas. Finally, the occupational location of Latinos is also influenced by nativity, as U.S.-born Latinos fare better occupationally. As labor force participation rates continue to increase, especially for Latinas, all Latinos in the labor market will play a greater role in the composition of the workforce, contribute more to the social security system, and have more human resource labor force mobility[6] (Morales and Bonilla 1993). Thus issues like job mobility, job training and educational preparation, discrimination in the labor market, and entrepreneurship become salient issues for Latino communities. This dimension of an element of a **community of interests** will appear in the discussion of public policy and Latinos.

This introductory discussion of the foundations of the Latino community next examines the Latino family, presenting information on family income status, Latino families living below poverty, and family type. A substantial literature, both social scientific and literary, portrays the central value of family life for Latinos as a source of social and financial support, as well as cultural reinforcement. Values such as respecting elders, maintaining extended families, supporting familial social and cultural rituals, as well as the centrality of family for identity and well-being, have been identified as core for Latinos. In a way, this demographic information has dimensions of both culture and common situations (i.e., interest).

Table 3.11 provides data on the number of Latino families relative to all families in the United States for 1995. Whereas Latinos represent over 11 percent of the total U.S. population, they constitute 9 percent of all families. As the following table shows, an important factor is the larger size of Latino families. Another relevant aspect of Latino families is the percentage of households born outside the United States (60.8 percent). This is a substantial difference, given the percentage of foreign-born Latinos in the total Latino population.

If we check the family income status of Latinos in comparison to non-Latinos, then economic disparities are quite evident. Percentage-wise, more than twice as many Latino families have incomes less than $10,000 (16 percent versus 7 percent) than non-Latinos. In the case of Puerto Rican families, the rate is three and a half times greater for family income under $10,000. At the other income end ($25,000 or more), the lag between Latinos and non-Latinos is that two-thirds as many Latino families fall into this category as non-Latinos. Again, Cuban families display similar percentages of families as non-Latinos with slightly lower percentages at the upper end (62 percent versus 72 percent). For the most part, family income for Latinos is significantly lower than for non-Latinos.

Another indication of the economic disparities between non-Latinos and Latinos is the percentage of families living below poverty level. Among all family types (two parents, female headed, etc.), three times as many Latino families live below poverty level than non-Latinos. In the case of female-headed families, almost one-half of all Latina-headed families live below poverty level. The rate is considerably higher for Puerto Rican female-headed households (64 percent). The interrelated factors of a youthful age structure

Table 3.11 Family Income and Poverty Rates in the United States by Race and Ethnicity, 1995

	Number of Families (1,000s)	Percentage of Family Income			Percentage Below Poverty		
		Under $10,000	$10,000– $24,999	$25,000+	All Families	Female- headed	Elderly
Total	69,597	7	21	72	11	32	6
Non-Latino	63,311	7	20	74	9	30	5
White	52,861	5	18	77	6	22	4
Black	7,871	19	29	51	26	45	17
Other non-Latinos	2,579	10	20	70	15	33	10
Origin							
Hispanic	6,287	16	35	49	27	49	18
Mexican	3,815	15	37	47	28	50	18
Puerto Rican	742	26	29	45	36	64	19
Cuban	312	10	28	62	16	29	12
Central/South American	929	11	35	54	22	35	19
Other Latino	489	20	26	54	25	50	20
Place of birth							
United States	2,466	15	29	56	22	47	16
Outside United States	3,821	17	38	45	30	51	20

Source: Jorge del Pinal and Audrey Singer, "Generations of Diversity: Latinos in the United States," Population Bulletin 52, no. 3 (1997): 40.

Table 3.12 Family Type and Poverty Status among Hispanic and Non-Hispanics, March 1997 (in 1000s)

	Origin			Latino Subgroups				
	Total	Hispanic	Non-Hispanic	Mexican	Puerto Rican	Cuban	Central and South America	Other Hispanic
Total	70,241	6,631	63,609	4,007	780	367	962	515
Type of family								
Couple	53,604	4,520	49,083	2,892	424	282	627	295
	(76.3%)	(68.2%)	(77.2%)	(72.2%)	(54.3%)	(76.9%)	(65.2%)	(57.3%)
Male householder	3,847	494	3,353	307	49	23	77	37
	(5.5%)	(7.4%)	(5.3%)	(7.7%)	(6.3%)	(6.2%)	(8.0%)	(7.1%)
Female householder	12,790	1,617	11,173	807	307	62	258	183
	(18.2%)	(24.4%)	(20.2%)	(39.4%)	(39.4%)	(16.9%)	(26.8%)	(35.3%)
Family size								
2	29,780	1,731	28,049	943	227	153	255	153
	(42.4%)	(26.1%)	(44.1%)	(23.5%)	(29.1%)	(41.8%)	(26.5%)	(29.6%)
3	16,239	1,571	14,668	862	212	100	240	157
	(23.1%)	(23.7%)	(23.1%)	(21.5%)	(27.2%)	(27.4%)	(24.9%)	(30.5%)
4	14,602	1,555	13,046	926	201	71	241	116
	(20.8%)	(23.5%)	(20.5%)	(23.1%)	(25.7%)	(19.5%)	(25.1%)	(22.5%)
5+	9,620	1,774	7,846	1,275	141	42	226	920
	(13.7%)	(26.8%)	(12.3%)	(31.8%)	(18.0%)	(11.3%)	(23.5%)	(17.3%)

Source: Jorge del Pinal and Audrey Singer, "Generations of Diversity: Latinos in the United States," *Population Bulletin* 52, no. 3 (1997), tab. 9, p. 40.

(especially for Mexican-origin and Puerto Ricans), residential locations in central cities, and declining urban economies are contributing elements for many Latino families. With the centrality of family as a positive value for many Latinos, the economic condition for a substantial segment of Latino families warrants concern and attention. Thus the linkage of family economic status as a common interest is quite likely.

A complementary demographic presentation is a profile of Latino families. Table 3.12 presents data information on family type as well as family size. Our previous profile of Latinos confirms a greater number of household members than non-Latino households. In 1997 both Mexican-origin and Cubans families as couples have a similar percentage as non-Latino "couple" families (72.2 percent, 76.9 percent, and 77.2 percent respectively). On the other hand, female-headed households are much more prevalent among Mexican-origin, Puerto Ricans, and "other Hispanic." The more telling information lies with the size of families. Latinos are three-fifths less likely to fall into the category of families with only two persons.

On the other hand, Latino families are 2.2 times more likely to include five or more persons in the household. Mexican-origin households are 2.6 times more likely to have five or more members in the family. Central and South American families exhibit a similar larger family situation among the other Latino subgroups. Larger family, lower levels of family income, and corresponding higher rates of family poverty place Latino families at risk in terms of quality of life (e.g., housing conditions, educational isolation,[7] limited employment opportunities, economic segregation, and vulnerability to violent crime), which suggests both common ground and limited political resources to mobilize for effective change.

CONCLUSION: COMMUNITY OF INTERESTS AND CULTURE

In this chapter, I have developed some demographic indicators supporting the concepts of community of culture and community of interests. If Latinos of various national origins share some commonalties that are central to life's experiences and situations, then these commonalties can serve as bases for common and collective actions. The following chapters will examine and discuss developments within the Latino community in a variety of political arenas and activities. In the community of culture segment, the dimensions of Spanish language and nativity (or extent of foreign born) constitute a significant constellation of cultural connections. Spanish-language persistence, reinforced to a large degree by continuous Latino migration, establishes and expands Latino enclaves, maintains "ethnically and culturally" dense social networks, contributes to a sustained Latino presence and visibility in the United States, and creates demands for business and media services.[8] The net effect is that culture is dynamic and extends beyond the traditional boundaries of Latino national-origin communities.

The community of interests dimension consists of similar socioeconomic conditions and status. I have presented information on occupational status, educational attainment, and family type among different Latino groups. There are more similarities or clustering among Latinos subgroups than substantially differential statuses. The one group that is less similar is the Cuban population. Nevertheless, the basis is evident and open to greater community-building efforts. I am not suggesting that either or both set of similarities will automatically result in political empowerment or influence. Rather, if some forms of community are present, then the accompanying factors of active and effective organizations and effective leadership can serve as a conversion component for political potential. In addition, situational conditions such as negative activities and legislation targeting Latinos, or even positive appeals to the Latino communities by businesses, political parties, and the like, assist in the dynamic formation of communities of interest and culture. The basis and direction of community building across Latino communities does serves as the crux of the analysis and discussion of Latino politics in this volume. In the next chapter, we will focus on the psychological dimension of identity and the dynamics of political mobilization relevant to Latinos.

NOTES

1. In terms of U.S. policy, refugee refers to political status and official designation—a person who is fleeing a totalitarian regime, experiencing political persecution and a threat to life. Seeking political asylum in the United States is a formal process. The State Department is primarily responsible for determining which regimes are totalitarian. This has been a particular point of contention, especially for Central Americans, whose countries have experienced significant political turmoil and violence.

2. In this context, the idea of critical mass would suggest that Latinos now compose a major community of presence and possibly political and economic influence to influence their state's decision-making process.

3. The items from the census that are used to determine English-language proficiency are a self-reported three-item sequence. The first question asks the person if he or she speaks a language other than English. The person who answers affirmatively is then asked what that other language is. Finally, the respondent is asked how well (or not) she speaks English.

4. In 1997, the percentage of foreign-born persons in the U.S. population reached a record high since record levels in the early 1900s.

5. One of the requisites in petitioning to be admitted into the United States is having a sponsor. The two primary bases for admission are family reunification or needed job skills. In the case of family reunification, there are preferential categories

among the different types of family members, and U.S. citizens have higher priority as sponsors than permanent resident aliens do.

6. It has been documented that the traditional American workforce is aging, and the newest and most expansive segments of the workforce are women and minorities. Given the youthfulness of Latinos, they should continue to increase their proportion of the workforce, as well as contribute significantly to the social security system.

7. The idea of educational isolation refers to students who attend racially and/or ethnically segregated schools, with lower-quality school facilities and less-qualified instructional staff, and poorer educational outcomes (dropout rates, high school completion, disciplinary actions, standardized test scores, etc.).

8. This point illustrates the demand structure that can result with a critical mass of culturally similar persons, such as businesses that cater to Latino customers and serve as desirable employees for ethnic enterprises. In addition, the mass media (print, radio, television), especially Spanish-speaking, serves to highlight and inform the public about Latinos, as well as help to establish the economic impact of Latinos as consumers.

4

Latino Subgroups
in the United States

Los latinos somos de muchas nacionalidades distintas. Pero, dime que nombre prefiere, y yo puedo calibrar nuestra afinidad como una familia más grande. Pues, quizás no pueda. El proceso de extenderse más alla de familia, de patria, depende en las experiencias que compartimos y como nos entendermos y nuestras interacciónes. Pero, primero necesito definir a cual grupo pertenezco.

Latinos are of many distinct nationalities. But tell me which name you prefer and I can gauge our relationship in the larger family. Well, perhaps I cannot. The process of extending ones' identity beyond family and country depends on the experiences that we share, how we understand one another, and our interactions. But, first, I need to decide to which group I belong.

Understanding Latinos and their political involvement is better accomplished by examining community formation and inter-group linkages. Even though Latinos have been grouped together by the mass media and governmental policies, the extensiveness of community across the Latino subgroups tends to be hidden. National (Latino National Political Survey, CBS news, CNN-All Politics Polls, etc.) and regional social surveys by Florida International University, Texas A & M University, UCLA, and others, still portray many Latinos as being more familiar and interactive within their own national-origin group than with other Latinos. This pattern partly results from the regional concentration of each Latino subgroup (80 percent of Mexican-origin are in the Southwest; 60 percent of Cubans in Dade County, Florida; 80 percent of Puerto Ricans in the Northeast; etc.). But the lack of opportunities to interact across "inter-Latino" groups is not limited by geography alone but is also related to family, common experiences, and historical and homeland connections. Finally, the results of Census 2000 indicate that the Latino mix throughout the United States is becoming more diverse.

In this chapter I provide direct characterization of Latin subgroups in addition to the demographic profiles in the following chapter. I present a short syn-

Box 4.1   The Changing Faces of Latino America

The historically Mexican face of the Texas Latino community has changed in the past decade. Lori Rodriquez of the *Houston Chronicle* ("Latino Mix Becomes More Diverse," *Houston Chronicle*, May 23, 2001) provides some real faces and stories about the diverse mix over the past decade. She describes the Chanax family (from Guatemala), which over the past twenty years has migrated to Texas. The seven nephews of Don Esteban worked, started families, and settled in the city. He speaks minimal English, but one daughter speaks with a "Latin lilt" and his son Giovanni, a college-bound marine veteran, speaks English with a Texas accent. They represent a non-Mexican influx into Houston that has more than doubled (from 10.3 percent to 24 percent) as a proportion of the state's Latinos. The proportion of Mexican-origin shrank from 80 percent to 73 percent in Harris County. Similarly in Brazoria County (part of the Houston metro area), the proportion of non-Mexican population grew from less than 10 percent to 23 percent, with similar jumps in the other counties in the metro area. Whereas Mexican Americans have been in the 90 percent range of all Latinos in Texas, the abrupt shift to other Latinos now residing in the state is quite striking. The same patterns are evident in Austin (12.7 percent to 23.3 percent), El Paso (4.7 percent to 16.7 percent), Dallas (12 percent to 17 percent), and San Antonio (8 percent to 30 percent).

In Houston, Guatemalan immigrants have secured employment in one of the city's largest Supermarkets: Randall's. It has been estimated that Randall's employs over a thousand Guatemalans. Other indicators of an ethnic mix are found in the Randall's bakery, which offers coronas, roscas, and other traditional Guatemalan breads next to bolillos, pan de huevo, and other Mexican pastries. Nestor Rodriquez (University of Houston), who has examined migration to the Houston area, notes the significant migration from Central and South America with a "sprinkling" of Puerto Ricans and Cubans. While this is documented in Houston and in Texas, similar additions of other Latinos into traditional concentrations of either Mexican, Puerto Rican, or Cuban areas are evident in Florida, New York, California, and other regions with established Latino communities.

opsis of several Latino subgroups in terms of their settlement and historical development in the United States. There is a wealth of historical and interpretative accounts of Latino subgroup experiences over an extended period of their history in the United States. I include some of those references in the bibliography. Some of the gains in Latino immigrants have occurred in the past decade, and accounts and analyses of these communities are in the process of being written. These brief sketches hopefully will give a fuller picture of the many sub-communities that make up what we call Latino or Hispanic.

MEXICAN-ORIGIN COMMUNITIES: GROWING THROUGHOUT THE UNITED STATES

Historically, the Mexican-origin population has been the largest and oldest of the Latino subgroups. They consistently represent more than three-fifths of the total Latino population, and they predate the English settlements in the eastern section of the United States. Spanish expeditions to what is now the American Southwest began in the early sixteenth century. The pattern of establishing mission settlements lined much of the region, particularly in the states of California, New Mexico, Arizona, and Texas. The presence of Spanish Mexicans and mestizos (i.e., descendants of Spanish and Indian or indigenous cultures) is also reflected in the names of many southwestern states (Nevada, Montana, Colorado, Nuevo Mexico, etc.), as well as numerous cities and towns. At the same time, Mexican-origin people include recent migrants (both legal resident aliens and undocumented persons). These migratory patterns to the agricultural regions and industrial sections of the United States were established in the latter part of the 1800s and early 1900s. Now it is the service sectors of the American economy that serve as destinations for many newly arrived Mexicanos.

For much of the period since the Treaty of Guadalupe to the present, Mexicanos have been concentrated in the five southwestern states. Largely heavy manufacturing in steel, auto, and railroads influenced the noticeable migratory stream to the Midwest. As the new millennium begins, the presence of Mexican people is also evident throughout the other regions of the country (Northwest, Northeast, and South). For example, meat processing plants, textiles, and service industries in states like Arkansas, Florida, and North Carolina have become destinations for Mexican immigrants. Similar patterns are still developing in the other regions mentioned. Obviously the physical proximity to Mexico and its economic dependence on the American economy serve as major contributors to the flow of goods and people across the border. Similarly, U.S. immigration policy has provided impetus for freer and, at times, more restricted movement across the border. Finally, Mexico's proximity and continuous migration have also served to maintain cultural contact and economic exchanges with family, relatives, and other social networks.[1]

In this brief accounting of the Mexican-origin population, the themes of long-standing residence and continuous international migration coexist as the context for Mexican American/Chicano political life and issues. The demographics of this group, as well as its cultural maintenance (largely in terms of social affinity and identification, bilingualism, and familialism), contribute to the people's experiences in the United States and their political integration. Regions of the Southwest (southern Texas, northern New Mexico, and southern California) provide examples of power and economic relations for Mexican Americans. The preponderance of Mexicanos in South Texas (el Valle de Rio Grande) serves as evidence that population alone does not translate to political and economic power and influence.

The Mexicanos served as a labor force and flexible labor pool for the agricultural economy but did not control property or the means of production. It was as if two separate societies existed—the owners and the others—with workers and **ethnicity** being the dividing line (Montejano 1987). The 1960s saw the advent of Chicano power and major efforts by Mexican Americans to achieve political control. The rise of a third party movement (La Raza Unida) in primarily rural south Texas saw a number of city councils, school boards, and county offices secured by Chicano candidates. While the "electoral takeover" was short-lived, it set the foundation for subsequent political efforts and organizational development. Middle-class organizational efforts among workers and targeted educational reforms assisted ensuing political advances and **mobilization** (Shockley 1974; Foley 1988). The following chapters will focus on the political resource development (socioeconomic and psychological predispositions or political attitudes), organizational expansion in resources, strategies, and skills, and leadership development, which are primary components of Latino political involvement.

The Hispano experience in New Mexico differs from that of rural South Texas, where economic and political subjugation has been a long-standing reality (Montejano 1987). The Hispanos included a propertied and business class before the Mexican-American War of 1848. Even though the advent of territorial government and resulting statehood saw Hispanos' economic and political power diminish, they maintained political leverage. Ironically, contemporary New Mexico has experienced significant interregional migration of non-Latinos into the state, particularly in the north. Hispanos, with two-fifths of the state's population, continue to serve as "players" yet engage in continuous political struggles to maintain their political position. The 2000 elections in New Mexico saw the statewide election of Hispanos as attorney general, secretary of state, state treasurer, and state auditor. In 2002, Bill Richardson, a Latino, was elected governor.

Southern California represents the legacy of the Californios (Pitt 1966), but even more the rise of extensive Mexican migration to this state. After World War II, noticeable numbers of Mexican Americans migrated from Texas to California in search of better opportunities and less discrimination. After the 1960s California became the major destination state for international migration, especially from Mexico. The combination of push-pull factors (lack of job opportunities in Mexico, peso devaluations, proximity to the

U.S border, economic pull of jobs, and an established Mexican-origin community) contributed significantly to the growing Mexican-origin population. The expansive California economy (in the service sectors, traditional agricultural sections, high-tech manufacturing operations, etc.) made it the major port of entry for immigrants. The translation to appreciable political and economic influence did not become evident until the 1990s.

During the previous decade, redistricting, activism by Mexican American organizations (Mexican Legal Defense and Education Fund, Southwest Voter and Education Project, etc.), and anti-immigrant and nativism movements set the stage for increased Mexican American political group awareness and activities. In the mid-1990s, state initiatives such as Propositions 187, 209, and 237 served as a stimulus for Mexican Americans and their organizations to mobilize and register to vote. One of the results of this increased activism has been rising numbers of elected officials at the state and federal levels (Lt. Governor Bustamante, Speaker of the Assembly Montearroyos, Congresspersons Sanchez and Roybal, etc.). For over four decades the Mexican-origin community has been portrayed as "the sleeping giant," "an awakening minority," and "a group whose time for a place in the sun has arrived." As we begin the next millennium, these projections will become concrete.

The Mexican-origin population has grown from a territorial minority (de la Garza et al. 1973) to a national presence and expanding political involvement. Mexican American organizations have been able to diversify their goals and objectives as well as their constituency base, incorporating other Latino subgroups into their membership as well as focusing on a broader range of issues and policy. For example, the National Council of La Raza (NCLR) was originally the Southwest Council of La Raza in the late 1960s. Its primary goals were economic development, social services, and advocacy on behalf of Mexican Americans. Since its inception, the organization has taken a national orientation with its headquarters in Washington, D.C. Its constituency base includes all Latinos, with membership and board members representing most segments of the diverse Latino community. It has developed a film production company, supplies venture capital for small businesses, provides resource development for community-based organizations, and engages in applied research, policy analysis, and advocacy. NCLR illustrates the evolution of Mexican American organizations in the latter half of the twentieth century.

The wider dispersion of Mexican Americans throughout the United States has broadened their contact with other Latino subgroups and expanded their identity beyond purely national origin. For example, the concept and label use of "Latino" in Chicago is widespread among Latinos of Mexican, Puerto Rican, Cuban, Salvadoran, and Central and South American ancestry. While conducting field research with several Latino community-based organizations in the early 1970s, I encountered a consciously constructed Latino identity. The activist elements instilled a sense of identifying as Latinos to help broaden the "population base" of the emerging Latino community. Almost twenty years later, when the Latino National Political Study was conducting focus groups in Chicago, the presence of a Latino identity was evident. Focus participants had integrated a sense of national-origin awareness and identity, as well as broader group identification as Latinos. As Mexican Americans are the largest Latino subgroup, broadening inter-group contacts and incorporating a pan-ethnic[2] identity serve as building blocks for a Latino community.

The long-standing Mexican American community has established social networks, traditions, and cultural practices that contribute to the definition and maintenance of community. In addition, the evolution of Mexican American organizations (e.g., mutual aid societies, labor movements, cultural organizations, civil rights, professional groups, and advocacy/litigation organizations) represents a substantial history of organizational activities and definable agendas. In general the core of that agenda has focused on civil rights, access and participation in the economic and political arenas, educational quality, and greater political empowerment.

Its leadership has expanded from grassroots and labor leaders to include others with "corporate skills" and a national scope. The continuous migration of Mexicanos adds to the population growth and the geographic dispersion of the Mexican-origin people. At the same time, it draws national attention to immigration, its varied consequences, generally restrictive public policies, and the need to integrate more recent immigrants into the body politic. While the larger proportion of the Latino community is of Mexican origin, its role in coalescing all of the Latino subgroups has not always been dominant.

PUERTO RICANS: MANHATTAN OR LA ISLA BORINQUEN (PUERTO RICO)?

The popular notion about Puerto Ricans is one of island transplants, largely migrating after World War II to the New York metropolitan region. But the current population of slightly over 2 million has a longer history in the United States. In the late nineteenth century, some Puerto Ricans migrated to the Northeast, attracted to agricultural labor and cigar making. With the Spanish-American war, Puerto Rico became a U.S. possession. The Jones Act of 1917 established Puerto Ricans as U.S. citizens and allowed them a congressional "observer" without a vote. In 1947 the act was amended to enable Puerto Ricans to elect their governor and other officials except for the Supreme Court.

The status of Puerto Rico has been a long-standing concern. As a commonwealth, it enjoys a degree of autonomy while participating in entitlement programs and citizenship benefits. The independence movement in Puerto Rico reached an apex on July 25, 1952, with a push for a free associated state for Puerto Rico. Alternatives to commonwealth status include free associated state status, statehood, and independence. There have been a number of plebiscites (1967, 1993, and 1998: HR 856 United States–Puerto Rico Political Status Act). In each case, the status quo, commonwealth, has received the greater number of votes. The statehood option has been the second most preferred option, with independence a distant third. The status of Puerto Rico is a major issue on the island and among many Puerto Ricans on the U.S. mainland. Enmeshed in the discussion of political status lie issues of culture, identity, and political expression.

For Puerto Ricans living on the mainland, there are a number of dimensions related to the political status question. The first is an interest in being directly involved in the discussion and vote. With the framing of House Bill 866, one of the points of contention was whether Puerto Ricans living on the mainland would be allowed to vote in the plebiscite. The close cultural and familial contact and affinity between Puerto Ricans and Puerto Rico stirred both interest and support from Puerto Rican organizations to ensure mainland participation in the plebiscite. Second, cultural and group identity among Boricuas in the United States interprets the political status issues as embedding issues of cultural identity, maintenance, and pride, which are important on the island and the mainland. The terms "Boricua" and "Newyorican" refer to Puerto Rican populations in the United States. Third, the question of political status can serve as focal point for the political status of Puerto Ricans in the United States. Empowerment, active political involvement, cultural maintenance, and policy advocacy from their own perspective (Jennings and Rivera 1984; Jennings 1994; Cruz 1998) motivate the Puerto Rican community.

Puerto Ricans remain concentrated in the Northeast. Whereas over 80 percent once lived in the New York metropolitan area, however, in 1995 that percentage dropped below 70 percent. Other Puerto Rican communities are located in Massachusetts, Connecticut, Chicago, Miami, and Los Angeles. The status and conditions of Puerto Rican communities can be compared with many of the other Latino subgroups. A generally young population, Puerto Ricans face problems with housing, education, employment, single-headed households, poverty, and residential segregation. Their primary location in the New York metropolitan area has highlighted these problems. The elimination of low-skill central city manufacturing jobs, economic globalization, and relocation have contributed to higher rates of joblessness, social welfare participation, inferior schools, and limited and substandard housing (Kasarda 1989, 1985).

Herman Badillo (1929–)

In 1972 Herman Badillo became the first Puerto Rican U.S. congressman; he represented New York City. In 1974 he sponsored the Bilingual Education Act of 1974. He is a practicing attorney and sits on the board of the City University of New York.

Bibliography

"Courting Badillo: A Last Hurrah as Comptroller." *New York Times,* May 20, 1993, B1(L).
"Mr. Badillo's First Salvo." *New York Times,* October 6, 1994, A28

Denton and Massey's work on residential segregation (1988) highlights the formation and perpetuation of sub-cultural practices and social networks that have impeded the incorporation of Puerto Ricans into mainstream economic and social life. Torres-Saillant and Hernández (1998) and Moore and Pinderhughes (1993) suggest that the distinctive Puerto Rican island culture and language, along with targeted labor recruitment by certain industries (e.g., agricultural and manufacturing) and racial discrimination, contributed to economic disparities and barriers in the housing market.

Clara Rodríquez (1998, 2000) discusses the American basis of race and how it constitutes a different racial order from the one found in Puerto Rico. Whereas Rodríquez characterizes race in America as white and other (primarily black), in Puerto Rico there are a multiplicity of "racial categories" or distinctions—blacks, indigos, triguenos, negros, morenos, and white or Spanish. Thus the U.S. schema, which categorizes persons as white, black, possibly white, not white, and not black, leaves Puerto Ricans outside the racial order. Rodríquez contends that race, ethnicity, and culture are interconnected in the Puerto Rican experience and inconsistent with the American view of race and who fits what category. For Puerto Ricans, the phenotypical variations are an integrated system. Yet America and its institutions may differentiate between Puerto Ricans by different racial categories when they identify themselves in cultural terms with race as a subset. The introduction of race and ethnicity also brings forth discriminatory theories that preclude Latinos from equal opportunities and access to many realms of life in the United States.

The issues confronting the Puerto Rican communities center around housing costs and access, urban relocation due to gentrification and urban renewal, educational quality and curriculum (including the dropout problem, language and bilingual education and participation in higher education), unemployment, female-headed households, poverty and children living in poverty, and crime and public safety. Especially since the 1960s, Puerto Rican organizations have targeted community improvement, adaptation, and empowerment goals. For example, from the origins of the Puerto Rican Forum came ASPIRA and the Puerto Rican Community Development Program (Fitzgerald 1971). The leadership of Antonia Pantoja was instrumental in the development of all three organizations.

Organizations like the Puerto Rican Merchants Association and the Puerto Rican Civil Service Employees Association address the economic dimensions of life in the United States. Our theme of connectedness with the Commonwealth of Puerto Rico is further reinforced by the presence of its office in New York City to assist Puerto Ricans with referrals. In the 1980s the commonwealth office also participated in a voter registration campaign in the city. Finally, organizations like the Puerto Rican Legal Defense and Education Fund and the Institute for Puerto Rican Policy deal directly with issues of political empowerment and policy advocacy. Limited studies on Puerto Rican political behavior indicate lower rates of **political participation,** especially in the electoral process (Nelson 1979; Falcón 1993). Ironically, levels of electoral participation among Puerto Ricans on the island exceed those in the United States.

Nelson's (1979) analysis of Puerto Rican political involvement saw assimilation as aiding greater degrees of political activities. Only in the case of voting did the "more assimilated" Puerto Ricans participate at higher levels. Nelson found a negative association between participatory attitudes and assimilation. Although Puerto Ricans have a lower voting rate, they are oriented toward signing petitions, protesting, and joining community organizations.

The Puerto Rican communities, while still concentrated in the Northeast, have broadened their geographical presence and are actively engaged in local politics and policies. The social and economic issues mentioned in the demographic profile constitute much of the political agenda for Puerto Ricans. Continued close ties with Puerto Rico and well-established neighborhoods on the mainland have served to maintain a strong sense of cultural identity, Spanish-language use, and pride (Cruz 1998; Rodríquez 1998; Jennings 1994; Jennings and Rivera 1984). Again, culture, ancestral ties, limited socioeconomic mobility, and discrimination compose a significant portion of Puerto Rican experience and are the foundation for community empowerment.

CUBANOS: STILL AN EXILE COMMUNITY?

Likely descriptors for Cubans in the United States would include living primarily in southern Florida, Fidel Castro, anticommunists, *el son y boleros* (forms of Cuban music and rhythms), and political involvement. While the broader public knowledge about Cubans usually begins with the political demise of Fugenia Batísta in 1957, Cubans in the United States have an earlier presence. Historically, Cubans have lived in Florida since the 1850s along the American Gulf Coast. Major numbers populated the Key West area, largely involved in the cigar industry. Trade, labor, and commerce connected Cuban labor and entrepreneurs during the expansion of cigar production for much of the latter part of the century. The Spanish-American War and subsequent U.S. control of Cuba established both political and economic ties. American investments, export partnerships, and extended foreign relations almost made Cuba a U.S. satellite.

In a more contemporary context, the rise of Fidel Castro and his communist regime helped create an exile community for many Cubans. Accounts of Cuban migration, since the late 1950s, have been referred to as the "golden exile," the exodus of Cuban elites and professionals from the Castro regime. These exiles were primarily white, well-educated professionals and entrepreneurs, urban residents. Between 1963 and 1972, 296,000 Cubans were resettled into twenty-four hundred communities. Because they immigrated as political refugees, American refugee policy provided assistance in the following areas: job training, English instruction, college loans, free certification for health professionals, housing subsidies, food stamps and food surpluses, and citizen exemption for certain jobs. Between 1961 and 1971, federal allocations for Cuban refugee assistance equaled $739 million. In addition, federal funds went to Dade County schools ($120 million) to assist with refugee children and youth. When federal immigration law changed in 1965, the Cuban Adjustment Act of 1966 exempted Cubans from the newly imposed 120,000-immigrant ceiling for persons from Western Hemisphere countries. Cubans share a similar immigrant segment that is characteristic of other Latino subgroups.

The status of political refugee and the corresponding federal legislation differentiate Cubanos from other Latinos. The contrast lies in the program and financial assistance they received to facilitate adjustment to life in the United States, and their political motivation to leave Cuba, which carries a strong sense of political issues and concerns. For many Cubans, anti-Castroism and anticommunism are central elements of their politics and activities. Organizations like the Cuban American National Foundation (CANF) (previously led by Jorge Mas Canosa) and movements such as Brigade 2506, Alpha 66, and Omega 7 focus their activities on efforts to wrestle control of Cuba from Fidel Castro and his regime. Military efforts, economic sanctions and embargoes, Radio and TV Martí show why Cubans have been referred as an exile community.

Cuban migration underwent significant socioeconomic, racial, and political changes with the Mariel boatlifts. This wave of refugees was more likely to include single adults, service and semiskilled workers, social misfits , rural people, and to be less educated than their pre-1980 counterparts. Racially, this wave of Cubans included more Afro-Cubans than the predominantly white, elite refugees of earlier years. Politically, Cuban refugees had enjoyed a receptive climate as exiles leaving a communist regime and producing economic and social successes in America (e.g., major entrepreneurial ventures, educational advances, stable and supportive family structures, economic revitalization of urban centers). Yet the nature and timing of the Mariel flotilla was seen as Fidel Castro's "dumping" of social misfits and criminals, and a growing anti-immigrant hostility was developing in the United States. The unsuccessful efforts of Haitian émigrés to gain a favorable entry status, with their boatlifts being turned back, angered African Americans and heightened the sense of inter-group competitive conflict in South Florida. For example, the Dade County Commission passed an English-only ordinance despite the positive contributions that the Cuban community had made to the revitalization of the South Florida economy.

The politics of the exile community focused on containing Castro's Cuba in the short term and policies that would achieve the "demise" of Fidel Castro and his communist regime, continued family reunification in the United States, and long-term resettlement assistance. For example, the Cuban American National Foundation lobbied the Clinton administration to support the Cuban Democracy Act, which tightened trade embargoes with tougher sanctions for firms involved with Cuba, and the establishment of Radio-TV Martí. Radio Martí, situated in South Florida, conducts news and informational broadcasts targeted at Cuba, similar to the Radio Free Europe model for eastern European communist countries. Yet by the early 1990s, Cuba and its leadership was only one of a broader range of domestic agenda issues. Some persons have described this development as a transition from exile to American ethnic politics. Nevertheless, changes occurred in the Cuban community. In 1995, Florida International University's Cuban Research Institute conducted a survey on attitudes toward Cuba and found that 84 percent favored continued sanctions, 57 percent supported military invasion, 68 percent viewed dialogue as a tactic to advance democratization, and 46 percent favored reestablishing dialogue. There are indications of some impatience with the old policies.

Interestingly, second-generation Cubans display some political attitudes that differ from their parents'. This generation includes persons who experienced more of their childhood in the United States (Hill and Moreno 1996). They expressed lower levels of trust toward the U.S. government, diversity in partisan preference, less closeness to the Cuban community, and favored decreased governmental spending (Moreno and Warren 1992, 1996). In addition, second-generation Cubans are more likely than their parents to use a pan-ethnic identity (i.e., Latino or Hispanic) by a percentage of 27.7 percent to 5.8 percent. This generation speaks Spanish less frequently, and whereas 58.9

percent of their parents see no discrimination, the second generation responded at 23.5 percent. There are other indications of a more moderate orientation toward Castro's Cuba. Organizations like Cambio Cubano and the Committee for Cuban Democracy (CCD) describe themselves as moderate and support a willingness to negotiate with Fidel Castro. Gutierrez-Menoyo's return to Cuba (Elliston 1995) was marked by the government's show of tolerance and respect. Marcelino Miyares of CCD advocates dialogue, reconciliation, and respect for Cuban sovereignty. At the same time, a desire for democratization is a central element among the moderate segments of Cuban Americans. The election of Alex Perales as Dade County executive mayor marks the rise of second-generation Cubans to elective office.

Another central feature of Cubanos is their entrepreneurship. The numbers of Cuban entrepreneurs and the growth of firm receipts and new firms far surpass any other Latino subgroup and other minority entrepreneurs. It has been suggested that this changing exile community's elite background and geographic concentration in southern Florida contributed significantly to the development of ethnic enclaves and enterprises (Portes and Mozo 1985; Portes and Stepnick 1993). Personal resources and attitudinal dimensions such as motivations tied to family ambitions, entrepreneurial role models, and family norms for independent business formation, influenced the rise of the Cuban business class (Petersen 1995). In addition, a large Spanish-speaking social network provided consumer demands and access to a Cuban labor force. Loans were available, if necessary, and when resources were lacking, a rise in partnerships occurred. The opportunity structure, market conditions, resource mobilization, and access to ownership propelled the Cuban community to experience a faster rate of upward economic mobility than any other Latino group. At the same time, their entrepreneurial successes helped revitalize the southern Florida economy and serve as a major U.S. gateway for Latin American trade.

The Cuban community maintains its share of exile fervor as the new millennium begins while expanding its focus to include domestic issues (economic development, civil rights, immigration policy, etc.). Cuban leadership was instrumental in the passage of the Cuban Liberty and Solidarity Act,[3] and it includes expropriations after 1959. At the same time, the exit polls in the 1996 presidential elections indicated more support for William Clinton than in his previous presidential race. The Cuban community exhibits the character of a resource-affluent group, with active leadership and a focused agenda emphasizing U.S. relations with Cuba. It is generally well organized, geographically concentrated, culturally immersed, and politically active. Within our theme of examining the various Latino subgroups as dynamic communities, the Cuban community exhibits common ground with other Latinos (e.g., social welfare policies, civil rights, language and immigration, economic mobility), as well as distinct policy perspectives and priorities regarding economic sanctions and isolation policies for Castro's Cuba, lower levels of support for affirmative action, lower perceptions of discrimination toward Latinos, political refugee status, and arguments for "pro-democratization" initiatives.

CENTRAL AND SOUTH AMERICANS: AMERICA'S OTHER HISPANICS

Public awareness of Latinos/Hispanics is usually limited to some knowledge of Mexican Americans, Cubans, or Puerto Ricans, particularly the rapid growth rate for all Latinos. Yet, as I have shown in breaking down the various Latino subgroups, the "other Hispanic" category is increasing at the highest rate. Under the rubric of Central and South Americans, we are identifying the Latinos from Central and South American countries. The Central American countries include Guatemala, Honduras, Nicaragua, Panama, El Salvador, and Costa Rica. The South American countries include all of the Spanish-speaking countries of that continent. Brazil is sometimes excluded from this cluster and sometimes included. Among all Latinos, this cluster has the highest proportion of foreign-born persons and constitutes those more recently entering the United States. We should note that labor migration among Central and South Americans occurred in the late 1800s and early 1900s. Industries such as cigar factories, munitions factories, sugar cane and other agricultural product processing, and shipyards are examples of earlier labor market relations between Central and South Americans and the United States (Figueroa 1996). More significant migration has occurred since the mid-1970s and continues at a high rate. Whereas the three largest Latino subgroups tend to concentrate in certain regions of the United States, Central and South Americans are more widely distributed.

Salvadorans are the largest Latino group in Washington, D.C., and the greater metropolitan area (one of every four Latinos are from El Salvador). At the same time, almost two-fifths of Salvadorans live in the Los Angeles metropolitan area. Similarly, 49 percent of Guatemalans live in the Los Angeles region.[4] Ecuadorians (60 percent), Colombians, and Peruvians are more concentrated in the New York metro area. Hondurans and Nicaraguans are settling in the Gulf Coast region, particularly in southern Florida and New Orleans. While the residential patterns of the Central and South Americans are distributed in many parts of the United States, there is a close proximity of their geographic location with the communities in which established concentrations of Mexican Americans, Puerto Ricans, and Cubans are found.

The relatively broad geographic distribution of Central and South Americans throughout the United States and their close proximity to the three larger Latino subgroups serves to maintain their own community identity and extend the range of interactions with other Latino groups. The Latiniza-

Box 4.2   Latinos in the District of Columbia

The *Washington Post* did a feature story on Bolivians in the Washington, D.C., metro area (Emily Wax, "For Area Bolivians, Cherishing the Past, Looking to the Future," *Washington Post,* June 7, 2001). The description includes Sunday morning soccer games on a field behind the Pentagon City mall. Besides soccer balls, Bolivians brought résumés, homemade pastries, and pages of job and house listings. Similar scenes are repeated on Sundays in south Arlington and Crystal City. This network celebrates cultural gatherings even as it shares advice about parenting, jobs, and immigration law. In a way, these soccer games serve as cultural glue that connects Arlington's rapidly growing Bolivian community. The concentration of Bolivians in this area is referred to as "little Cochabamba" (one of Bolivia's major cities). The Washington region is home to the largest Bolivian population in the United States, with the largest concentration in Arlington. With evidence of upward mobility and growing affinity to living in America, Bolivians also work to retain their culture. For example, Escuela Bolivia is a Saturday school aimed at keeping Bolivian children connected to their mother country and fluent in Spanish. In addition, two Bolivian newspapers, *Bolivia Today* and *El Bolivariano,* cover cultural events, politics, and other issues in the local community as well as Bolivia. While a detailed population count of Bolivians is not available, it is estimated that between 60,000 and 100,000 live in the D.C. area. Some Bolivians left Bolivia in the late 1960s and 1970s to escape political and economic upheaval. In the 1980s, a second wave came when high inflation hit the Bolivian economy. There is now evidence of political activity, particularly in trying to get more Bolivians on local school boards and local government. The characterization of the Bolivian community in Arlington displays patterns of maintaining a community of culture and transforming common interests into directed political involvement.

tion of a national community can be assisted by the presence of diverse Latino subgroups living in the same urban areas. The nature and extent of inter-group contact will establish a positive, supportive relationship or a competitive, conflictual one. As a fast-growing segment of Latinos, Central and South Americans are establishing their presence and impact in the United States, as well as altering the mix and "chemistry" of Latinos and their primary interests.

While relatively little research literature has been generated about Central and South Americans, one important dimension is the extent of foreign-born and immigrant standing that characterizes these communities. Overall, Latinos constituted almost half of the foreign-born population in the United States in 1996 (Hansen and Faber 1997). The percentage of foreign-born among Central and South Americans exceeds three-fifths of their residential population. Political instability and revolutions in El Salvador, Guatemala, Honduras, and Nicaragua forced many Central Americans out of their homes into neighboring Mexico and the United States. Gaining entry to the United States as political refugees and the U.S. role in military and covert operations and foreign policy in that region are major concerns for Central Americans.

Since obtaining political refugee status was difficult for Central Americans, undocumented migration became more prevalent in the 1980s and beyond. One of the accompanying results of many Central Americans' plight was the advent of the "sanctuary movement" in which religious organizations and other groups established an underground network to help Central Americans enter the United States. In addition, these organizational efforts focused on obtaining official political refugee status for Central Americans. Providing proof of clear persecution and personal endangerment upon returning home due to political beliefs and activities was very difficult. Individuals who were caught in the cross-fire between government and rebel forces were considered victims of a civil war or political instability rather than political dissidents. While we will not analyze the merits of U.S. refugee policy for Western Hemisphere countries versus other parts of the world, the immigrant segment of Central Americans clearly represents a major policy domain.

Immigration policy and rights are central issues for Central Americans. Besides the question of political refugee status, specific areas of concern include equal protection, actions of the Immigration and Naturalization Service, access to entitlement programs, and discriminatory practices in the labor market and housing. Organizations like the Task Force for New Americans, the Latino Coalition for Racial Justice, and Sanctuary for Salvadorans (Jordan 1995) represent actions to protect and advocate on behalf of Central American immigrants and their families. The organizational development within the Central American communities is still in the early stages, straining to develop resources, stable organizational structures, and maturing leadership. In 1996, over 2.9 million Central Americans resided predominantly in nine states.

While issues of immigration, a deteriorated and inadequate home country economy, and economic opportunities in U.S. labor markets for Central Americans have been characterized as primarily political in nature, there are complementary factors. Largely economic forces of

Box 4.3   The Colombian Community

An example of the growth and involvement of the Colombian community was highlighted in *Semana* ("Colombians Are Fastest Growing Latino Group in the U.S.," *Semana*, May 14, 2001). In early May 2001, Colombian Americans held their first Convention of Colombian organizations in the United States in Atlanta, Georgia. It was emphasized that a half million "legal" Colombians reside in the United States (primarily in Miami and New York), representing a 60 percent increase since 1990. The story also mentioned that an estimated 1.5 million undocumented Colombians could be living in the United States. In addition, it is estimated that remittances of $2.5 billion annually are sent to Colombia. Concerns about political clout and representation constituted much of the convention discussions. Part of the difficulty lies with the group's geographic dispersion and need for better political cohesiveness. The belief held by many Colombians that they will eventually return to their homeland could deter political organizing for American politics and issues. In the next Colombian election, Colombians living abroad will be able to elect a senator to represent their interests in Bogotá, solidifying their link with the homeland. This brief example serves to demonstrate the growth of the "other Latino" communities, as well as the effort and challenges of engaging in the American political system.

devaluation, high inflation rates, significant market fluctuations for goods and materials, and political instability drive the immigration factors for South Americans. Significant contributing countries are Colombia, Venezuela, Peru, and Ecuador. Again, their settlement patterns are primarily in the Northeast, California, and Florida. Like many immigrant communities, their organizational scope entails adjustment issues (labor market information and opportunities, the educational system, housing availability and affordability, treatment and immigrant rights) and cultural practices and traditions.

The growth of these communities has created some competitive pressures with other Latino subgroups. For example, growing numbers of Colombians and Ecuadorians in New York City have generated demands for greater involvement and participation in Latino politics and leadership. These demands include more attention to immigration and rights, political recognition, and greater allocation of governmental resources for South Americans. There have been greater levels of political involvement by these Latino subgroups around local issues and an expanding national network centering on immigration legislation and proposals. For example, the 1997 Immigration

Reform Act, which significantly curtailed access by permanent resident aliens to federal entitlement programs, was a major focal point for Central and South American communities. In addition, a noticeable proportion of these Latinos are U.S. born and/or educated, which will alter the resource base and possibly the policy agenda in the future.

Any discussion of Central and South Americans as part of the Latino aggregation tends to be speculative rather than informed through systematic research and study. It is both the "youngest"[5] and the fastest-growing element of the Latino community. Their American "character and demeanor" is still in the process of taking a more definitive form. U.S. born and/or educated Central and South Americans are exerting an effect on their organizational development and goals and defining their public policy concerns. Their residential location in areas proximate to the existing major Latino subgroups can both broaden the scope of what is Latino and heighten intergroup competitiveness. Their increasing demands entail greater focus on immigration and immigrant rights, access to social programs, and inclusion in the Latino leadership. At the same time, there are some indicators of cooperative ventures among Puerto Ricans, Dominicans, and Colombians. Overall, the expanding presence of Central and South Americans in the Latino landscape defines the changing parameters of evolving Latino politics.

LOS DOMINICANOS

The Dominican population in the United States has been experiencing continuous growth, particularly since the mid-1960s. This predominantly immigrant community is slightly over 70 percent foreign-born. In 1997, their population almost numbered 1 million, with primary residences in the New York metropolitan area. Other areas of concentration include New Jersey (11 percent), Florida (less than 3 percent), and Massachusetts (less than 1.5 percent) (Waldinger 1989; Torres-Saillant and Hernández 1998). The Washington Heights area on the Upper West Side of Manhattan represents the largest concentration of Dominicans (41.1 percent). It has been the site of many organizations (Centro Cívico Cultural Dominicano, Alianza Dominicana, Asociación Communal de Domincanos Progresistas, etc.) and police-community conflicts.

The more notable migration of Dominicans was most evident since 1966. During the twelve-year regime (1966–1978) of President Balaguer,[6] family planning policies and economic forces stimulated the migration of Dominicanos to the United States and Puerto Rico. Economics policy, high unemployment, external debt crisis, high international interest rates, and the deterioration of commodity prices motivated them to go the urban areas of the East Coast. Even though the Dominican Republic altered its economic policy to establish free trade zones, expand tourism, and export nontraditional products, the economic push factors continued to be strong. Dominican migrants are primarily persons from rural areas who are less educated, unskilled, and of lower socioeconomic status. Disproportionate numbers of women are in the migration stream, as well as persons between the ages of twenty-five and forty-four.

The initial waves of Dominican migration to the New York metropolitan area occurred during the economic restructuring from a manufacturing to a service economy. Many Dominican workers were employed as operatives in manufacturing or in wholesale segments of the service/manufacturing sectors. The demographic profile of Dominicans in New York reflects slightly lower rates of labor participation (60.7 percent versus 67.9 for Latinos versus 68.3 for all workers) (Torres-Saillant and Hernández 1998). Their **human capital** resources (or their lack of resources) contribute to their depreciated socioeconomic status. For example, the Dominican poverty rate is 45.7 percent, compared to 37.2 percent for all Latinos or 23.8 percent citywide. In addition, the percentage of Dominican female-headed households exceeds that of other Latinos (49.7 percent versus 44.1 percent) and also the citywide rate (25.6 percent).

The rise of organizations has accompanied the growth of the Dominican community, especially in the Northeast. Initially, many organizations reflected the cultural and immigrant-related adjustments of newcomers to the United States. Their focus centered on immigration, the educational system, and employment and social counseling (Sassen-Koob 1985; Guarnizo 1994). Groups like the Centro Cívico Cultural Dominicano, Asociación Dominicanas, and the Club de San Juan Pablo Duarte represent efforts of voluntary organizations to facilitate the transition to life in a new country. Some of these organizations date back to the early 1960s, with a movement toward advocacy and political empowerment taking shape in the late 1980s. For example, the Asociación Communal de Dominicanos Progresistas incorporated activities dealing with employment, empowerment, financial support, and advocacy for more responsive social institutions. In addition, gender-specific organizations have emerged (Collectivo de Mujeres Provincianas) that advocate for services and opportunities for women. Similarly, there are increasing numbers of professional or work-related organizations such as travel agents, accountants, and so on.

Until recently, Dominicans have been portrayed as almost invisible politically. Given the high percentage of foreign-born, they rank ninth in naturalization rates. Currently they represent 11 percent of Latino voters and 2 percent of all New York City voters (Falcón and Santiago 1993). To some extent, anti-immigrant sentiment and policies have activated greater political interest and activity among Dominicans. For example, immigration reform legislation potentially eliminated participation in some entitlement programs by permanent resident aliens. Issues like immigrant rights, policy backlash that targets the foreign-born, crime and drugs, and representation are part of the political agenda for Dominicans.

Dominicans, like many other Latino subgroups, are confronting issues of cultural and political identity and political orientation focused on the United States. Recent gains in electoral representation to city and state levels serve as indicators of political development in the Dominican community. Yet there is support for a state of mind that remains engaged with one's own native country, while becoming acclimated to the norms and activities in U.S. society. Some researchers have referred to this as "political duality." A person has double loyalties and interests in both the home country and the "host" country. Political duality became an option for Dominicans in 1996 as the Dominican Republic provided for dual citizenship. The impact of this policy will not be evident for a few years.

The advent of Dominican studies at City University of New York and continued organizational growth and activity should advance Dominicans' political development as a community in the United States. Greater activity and involvement will open more interactions within the New York metropolitan region with other Latino subgroups. The growth of the Dominican and Colombian communities in the Northeast is already reconfiguring the larger Latino community in this region. For example, there is some indication of competitiveness between Dominicans and Puerto Ricans for political visibility, advantage, and systemic attention from the major institutions. The future of Latino political activity lies with not only community formation across national-origin boundaries but also with the bases for independent and interdependent agendas and strategies[7] across all Latino subgroups.

CONCLUSION: LATINO AMERICA— RICH IN DIVERSITY AND COMMONALTIES

This brief portrayal of the histories and experiences of the different Latino subgroups in the United States is intended to provide insights about the nature and content related to each of these subgroups. The demographic profiles that follow furnish a picture of the size, socioeconomic status, and residential location for each group. These portrayals take into consideration our dimensions of **community of interests** and cultural themes. The factors of language, Spanish influences on cultural practices, institutions, religion, and the like, cut across all of the Latino subgroups. At the same time, unique experiences and variations occurred in the Dominican Republic versus Cuba versus Peru, and so on. The immigrant strand that is prevalent among the Latino subgroups helps define much of the Latino experience in relation to continued ties with one's home country, adjustment to most phases of life in the United States, and focus on cultural maintenance.

The socioeconomic status of many Latino subgroups (educational levels, labor market participation, income levels, family structures and household size, etc.) is quite similar and present opportunities for joint cooperative ventures. The overlap of residential location in areas with significant concentration of Puerto Ricans, Cubans, and/or Mexican-origin affords some opportunities for different kinds of interactions, particularly for the Central and South Americans. These interactions can be beneficial, conflictual, or very infrequent. Yet common cultural orientations and customs and situational conditions that warrant action can stimulate the bases for contact and interactions. Next we will focus on the sociodemographic underpinnings of community for Latinos. The nature and existence of common cultural and socioeconomic situations have a fundamental linkage to political resources and involvement.

NOTES

1. This latter point has been an area of some discussion and debate regarding the lower levels of Mexican American political participation. Close attachment to Mexico and the supportive system of political involvement in Mexico seems to suppress political involvement and interest in the American political system.

2. The term "pan-ethnic" refers to a socially constructed group identity that extends beyond the traditional national origin groupings like Irish, Mexican, Panamanian, and so on. The pan-ethnic movements represent an "umbrella" cluster of similar but distinctive group members. The labels American Indian, Asian American, and Latino serve as good examples of **pan-ethnicity.**

3. This legislation, also strongly pursued by Senator Jesse Helms, would allow lawsuits in U.S. Courts against traffickers who seize property belonging to Cubans living in the United States.

4. Eighteen percent of Latinos live in the Los Angeles standard consolidated area alone.

5. I use the youngest descriptor to indicate the relatively recent Central and South American migration and residency in the United States. The majority of these Latinos arrived during the 1970s and later.

6. Joaquín Balaguer was president of the Dominican Republic on three different occasions: 1960–1962, 1966–1978, and 1986–1996. He held posts under dictator Rafaél Trujillo, as vice president just prior to Trujillo's demise. He was ousted by the military in 1962 and returned in 1965 at the time of the U.S. military intervention. He won the presidency in 1966, and again in 1970 and 1974. His election in 1994 was

so marred by fraud that opposition protests and international pressures forced Bala-guer to agree to resign after an abbreviated two-year term.

7. A basic element in this book is that examination and discussion of Latinos consists of their own group interests and infrastructure with the bases for connections with other Latino subgroups. With this dynamic, it becomes quite possible to advance one's own specific group interest and/or the interests of the broader Latino communities.

5

The Politics of
Interest and Culture

Nuestro pueblo, la comunidad, nuestra gente, todos son expresiónes de haber entendido que somos una familia con una voz fuerte y unida. Sin embargo, igual que muchas comunidades, nuestras vidas son diferentes con relación a la comunidad, la cultura, la política y la familia. El gran desafío para la comunidad latina es de utilizar esos elementos de nuestra cultura y experiencias para tener verdadero poder político.

Our town, our community, our people—all are expressions of having understood that we are a family with a strong, united voice. Nevertheless, like many communities, our lives vary in relationship to the community, the culture, politics, and the family. The great challenge for the Latino community is to use these common elements of our culture and experiences in order to obtain real political power.

So far in this book, discussions of Latinos have explored community and all of its contributing factors that can develop a sense of commonalty and group affiliation. Referring to the concepts of "community of cultures" and "community of interests," I have tried to identify and describe aspects of the various Latino subgroups that serve to build community. Implicit in this discussion is the idea that the construction of a Latino community is the result of external forces (**structural factors,** social movements, and public attitudes) and activities within the Latino community and organizational efforts to connect across subgroup boundaries. In this chapter I add another dimension to the community-building process: the sense of belonging to a group or community has some psychological and emotive connections.

Latinos may share common cultural traditions and practices, as well as similar situations in the workplace, in education, and the like. Yet identification with and emotive attachment to a community builds and maintains community and works on behalf of its interests. Since Latinos come from a number of national-origin ancestries, this discussion includes the concept of **pan-ethnicity:** a sociopolitical collectivity made up of people of several different national origins (Espiritu 1992). In doing so, individuals undergo a shift in their level of identification from smaller boundaries to broader affiliations. These individuals augment their national-origin identity by including a broader identity of Latino/Hispanic.

Various works by Espiritu (1992), Nagel (1996), and Cornell and Hartman (1998) have explored the world of pan-ethnicity, which transcends the long-standing group status of **ethnicity** and race. In the United States, Latino/Hispanic identity has been developing for over two and one-half decades. The introduction of a self-identified Spanish-origin item in the 1980 census (Fernández 1985) was an early attempt to cluster persons from Spanish-speaking countries of the Western Hemisphere and the Iberian Peninsula as a major ethnic group. Almost at the same time, legislation initiated by Mexican American congresspersons sought to have federal agencies collect and report statistical information on Spanish origin.

The national media "discovered" the rapidly growing Latino population, and major news and feature stories were produced during the late 1970s and the 1980s. The 1980s were designated the "decade of the Hispanics" by many of the national news magazines. In the U.S. context, ethnicity took on a different character, since groups were not limited to persons of particular national origins or ancestries. Pan-ethnicity for Latino persons also affected American Indians and Asians. The American mosaic was dramatically changing, and minority standing incorporated the notion of "pan-ethnics."

For the most part, ethnicity was thought of in terms of national origin and ancestral origin: Italians, Poles, Irish, and Mexican Americans were American ethnic groups. Before the 1970s, the Latino world was made up of many groups, primarily of Mexican-origin, Puerto Ricans, Cubans, and other Latino subgroups. Each had a history of its own, organizations, leadership, and internal ethnic networks. Ethnicity was thought of as an emotional force in which persons maintained affinity to and affiliation with others from their country or ancestry. Cornell (1988) describes ethnicity as a web of sentiments, beliefs, worldviews, and practices that individuals hold in common. A sense of ethnicity was a guarantee that group solidarity was a natural companion. Culture, traditions, and language served as the "glue" for this attachment.

Internal group definitions and experiences did not solely define the nature and origin of ethnicity, as structural conditions and treatment have also created ethnic groups. Legislative policies that categorize individuals by groups and define them by national origin, ancestry, race, and so on, control benefits and/or enforcement in the areas of civil rights and increasing access to educational opportunities, labor markets (job training, language classes, etc.), and health services. Yet there are other costs of this type of policy categorization, including stigmatization and victimization, in addition to creating benefits for being a group member. How political and economic institutions treat and interact with persons from different "ethnic" groups can help impose and define ethnicity. In this sense, ethnicity has dimensions of voluntary status as well as imposed group affiliation.

An example of this in the case of Latinos is Mexican Americans' experience since the 1960s and the development of the pan-ethnic term "Hispanic." As already indicated, the term became widely used after the 1970s. Critics like Gómez (1992) suggest that the term was a product of Madison Avenue public relations firms, Capitol Hill press corps, major media outlets, and governmental bureaucrats. This analysis sees the rise in marketing efforts (Mattel's Hispanic Barbie, Coors's Decade of the Hispanic, etc.) as reinforcing the evolution toward identifying Mexican Americans and other Latinos as Hispanics. This helped to blur distinctions across the various Latino subgroups. Consequently, both print and visual media and governmental reporting promoted usage of the term, which has now exploded throughout the country. Hispanic has become the primary descriptor for both specific Latino national-origin groups like Mexican Americans or Chicanos and all clusters of groups of Spanish origin.

Thus the term "Hispanic" was the product of external forces trying to simplify and homogenized a diverse aggregation of Latino subgroups. A data-gathering agency, the Census Bureau, is credited with institutionalization of "Hispanic" by including it in the 1980 census. Yet Edward Fernandez of the Census Bureau's Ethnic and Spanish Division (Del Olmo 1998) indicates that the impetus for the Spanish-origin category came from Mexican American policy groups who were trying to respond to undercounts of Mexican Americans and other Latinos. The adoption of this broader term was one way to ensure a fuller portrayal of Latinos, as well as nationalization or pan-ethnic labeling of all the various Latino subgroups.

For the Mexican American community, there had been a long evolution of labels to differentiate this population, from Mexicanos to Spanish Americans to Latino Americans to Mexican Americans and Chicanos (Acuña 1988; Gómez-Quiñones 1990). Distinguishing in-group and out-group contexts was an important factor with the derivation and use of specific labels. There were in-group preferences for specific labels, which varied by class, region, and generational distance from Mexico (J. A. García 1982). Labels like "pocho," "Mexicano," "Raza," "Chicano," "Manito," "Mestizo," and others were used by different segments of the Mexican-origin community. The various ethnic labels usually reflected class, national origin, nativity, racial identification, cultural traditions, and language use (J. A. García et al. 1994; Patterson 1975). In addition, during the 1960s, labels also indicated political orientations and ideologies. For example, the Chicano label (Hirsch and Gutierrez 1973, 1974; Gómez-Quiñones 1990) incorporated a more radical political ideology and approaches for social change and justice. In a contemporary sense, the "endorsement" of Hispanic by some Mexican American political elites recognizes a modern form of **ethnic identity.**

For our purposes, ethnic identity is dynamic and multidimensional and has symbolic and instrumental functions. While Mexican-origin political activists used Mexican American and Chicano during the 1960s and 1970s, the use of labels has been broadened and altered. Mexican Americans, like other individuals, have changing multiple ethnic and social identities. Broader inclusiveness and multiple layers of affinity and loyalty reflect the contemporary nature of identity. Thus a Mexican American can have multiple identities that connect her with local situational factors and the larger social context that can trigger a variety of specific identities. For example, a Mexican-origin person may identify herself as a minority, a Hispanic, a Mexican American, of Mexican ancestry, a Spanish speaker, and bicultural. Each identity can serve to extend a person in a variety of networks and frames of reference. Modern ethnicity, including Latinos, results from a dynamic, fluid, and contextual process.

"Hispanic" defines who is not Hispanic more than who is Hispanic. Padilla (1986) outlines the Latinization of groups in Chicago in which as a pan-ethnic label (Latino, in this case) expanded the size of the local community and forged an added identity for greater political mobilization. The dynamics related to ethnicity, national origin, and race are constantly changing. The advent of pan-ethnicity and the broadening of its scope beyond national origin has redefined group parameters but remains a "loose coupling" that does not precisely explain what determines who is a Hispanic at all times and in all situations. The Latino pan-ethnic community has developed into a perceived and actual interest group that shares cultural traditions, situations, and practices. At the same time, the involvement of Latino elites and activists affects the evolution and development of an identifiable Latino community.

LATINO POLITICAL ELITES AND ACTIVISTS

Political elites and activists translate and interpret political and social necessities and realities. They frame critical meanings and context for the Latino community to advance political agendas and enhance their empowerment. Thus Latino leaders inform, educate, and motivate members of the Latino community to relate their own circumstances and opportunities/obstacles toward governmental institutions, policies, and actions. The Latino community is further defined and identified, increasing its involvement with American political life. The use of the terms "Hispanic" and "Latino" broadens the size of these sub-communities and creates greater visibility in national arenas like Congress, the national media, and federal agencies. Many leaders of national Mexican American organizations participated in discussions focusing on clarifying some common denominators for this loose aggregation of Latino national-origin subgroups.

Box 5.1   Defining Community and Descriptors

One of the debates about Latinos and their political potential is the reality of community. Although there may be a web of networks, cultural links, and common circumstances, the Latino subgroups can choose to pursue their own course of action. The Latino growth rate revealed in Census 2000 led to characterizations of them as the nation's largest minority group. Journalists and scholars are now challenging the accuracy of this depiction. Orlando Patterson (Harvard University), a well-known scholar of African American and minority politics, analyzes not only Latinos' response to the "Hispanic question" but also their responses to race. Patterson notes that a majority of Latinos mark themselves racially as "white." At the same time, the second largest racial option selected is "other race." Thus depicting America as less "white" is not accurate if the Latinos who "check off" the racial option white are recognized. Patterson also notes the range of diversity among persons who fall under the Hispanic/Latino "umbrella." He questions the extent of cohesiveness and agreement among the different Latino subgroups on public policies, issues, leadership support, and other elements deemed critical for effective minority group politics. Linda Robinson of *U.S. News* has also presented this theme ("Hispanics Don't Exist," *U.S. News* Special Report, May 11, 1998). She emphasizes the diversity among the many Latino subgroups and the absence of a common Latino subculture. She brings out the variations among Latinos but acknowledges the "existence of pan-ethnic pockets in which occasional alliances are struck on specific issues." Her discussion ends with a categorization of seventeen distinct Latino subcultures that are largely regionally based.

The 1980 census incorporated the ethnic term "Spanish origin," which applies to persons in over twenty Spanish-origin countries. This ethnic category has expanded the size and geographic base of the "Latino community" vis-à-vis non-Hispanic political elites and has won support at the grassroots level. This new "ethnic group" has national force as a significantly larger and more geographically dispersed group than a single Latino subgroup like Mexican Americans. A Latino/Hispanic community created and shaped by Latino political elites can project both potential and actual power and influence. It can create more opportunities for political mobilization, broaden the scope of awareness for group affinity and membership, and expand a larger resource base for Latino interests. All of these factors represent central elements of Latino community building.

Bob Martínez (Robert Martínez) (1934–)

Bob Martínez was the first Hispanic mayor of the city of Tampa and later the first Hispanic governor of Florida. Noted for his energetic antidrug policies as well as for his strong actions in favor of the environment, he served in the U.S. capital as director of the Office of National Drug Control Policy, or "drug czar."

Voters found Bob Martínez to be an efficient mayor who turned the city's fortunes around at a time when Tampa was in poor administrative condition. He did this by unhesitatingly ditching his earlier pro-union position and cracking down on city unions. The money he saved was put into infrastructure projects. In this way, in the course of his tenure Tampa began to be held up as an example of what could be done to improve smaller cities around the country.

During this time, Martínez switched to the Republican Party and found favor among national leaders of the party, including then-president Ronald Reagan. In 1984 and 1988, Martínez spoke at the party's national conventions.

In 1986 he was elected governor of the state of Florida, to a great extent on the basis of promises not to raise taxes. But one of his first projects as governor was to establish a service tax. The move backfired badly and had to be abandoned, and his administration was off to a bad start. But his concern as governor for a traditionally liberal cause, the environment, led him to set up a land protection plan, Preservation 2000, that earned him a Conservationist of the Year award.

Key components in the Latino community include some degree of group identification, affinity, and attachment among persons of Spanish origin with other persons of "Spanish origin." Consensus, solidarity, and cohesion are objectives of community building but are not absolutely essential for its operation. Elements of community (group identity and affinity, common interests and circumstances) provide pragmatic opportunities to engage in collective efforts. Thus the presence and perception of a national community serves as political capital for Latino leaders. It becomes the primary responsibility of leadership to capitalize on the various "strands" of Latino community life to direct its members toward specific actions and connections with regard to the policies in the public and private sectors.

Communities of culture and interests and the resulting networks that are established across the Latino sub-communities serve as connections from which communication, interactions, and collaborative opportunities are cre-

In other respects he acted as a staunch conservative, beginning to stand out in the fight against narcotics, with an approach that put greater emphasis on prosecution and on building more jails than on educating people away from drug consumption. He called out National Guard in the fight against smuggling, opposed abortion and sex education, and cracked down on obscenity and brutality in pop song lyrics.

Martínez lost his gubernatorial reelection bid in 1990 to a Democratic senator, Lawton Chiles, despite campaign support from the family of President George H. W. Bush, but his anti-drug credentials quickly came in handy when President Bush appointed him "drug czar." In this capacity Martínez stressed education, and he had the satisfaction of seeing drug-use levels descend among young people. His period in office was controversial, however, with regard to administrative practices. Martínez was charged with being imperious and disorganized.

Martínez held that post from 1991 until the end of Bush's term in 1993, when he returned to private business with his own marketing firm in Tampa.

Bibliography

Division of Historical Resources. "(Robert) Bob Martínez, Portrait and Biography." Available online: dhr.dos.state.fl.us/governors/martinez.html. Downloaded October 10, 2000.

Tardiff, Joseph C., and Mpho Mabunda, eds. *Dictionary of Hispanic Biography.* Detroit: Gale Research, 1996.

U.S. Senate Committee on the Judiciary. *Mr. Robert Martínez to be Director of National Drug Control Policy.* Washington D.C.: U.S. Government Printing Office, 1991.

ated. The extent of consensus, coherency of interests and actions, and unity are all components of community in which variation will exist at any given point in time. The Latino community is evolving and developing on the foundation of common culture and situations. Latino organizations and leadership have made direct efforts that recognize the connections and build on them. Dialogue about the development of pan-ethnicity is an example of the community-building process among Latinos.

The Latino community's political capital is enhanced with the appearance of coherency and unity. This is an important resource because on many occasions political leaders, officials, and institutions (Congress, state legislatures, etc.) place the onus on Latino leaders to present their issues, positions, demands, and so on, as one voice. Otherwise an absence of consensus is assumed, which undermines any legitimacy of the organization(s) and its leadership. The development of Latino pan-ethnicity (and community) pro-

vides a broad set of group parameters in which ambiguity and loose boundaries (regarding the inclusiveness and total cohesiveness of Latinos) do not
necessarily undermine the effort. This highlights the strategic nature of pan-
ethnicity and its flexibility and fluidity.

An umbrella descriptor for a wide range of Latino subgroups takes on a
more pragmatic and broader issue orientation. It also promotes the formation
of inter-group political coalitions among Latino subgroups not limited to
purely national-origin and regionally driven groups and issues. Consequently,
the use of Latino and Hispanic shifts the emphasis of community-based activities from primarily local to electoral and policy advocacy at the national and
state level.

A larger Latino configuration, which has been influenced internally by
the Latino sub-communities and externally by political institutions and officials and the national media, is a realistic characterization of Latino development at the beginning of the twenty-first century. Regardless of the origin of
"Hispanic" or "Latino," the role of Latino leaders is to define its meaning and
relevance. The movement to redefine the boundaries of communities com-
plements strategies of Latino political elites to promote and add specific
meaning to pan-ethnic terms. Three specific developments have contributed
to the movement toward a broader definition of ethnicity for Latino subgroups: (1) the transition to modern ethnicity that further interconnects race,
ethnicity, culture, class, and gender[1] into broader categorizations; (2) the contextual nature of ethnic labels and identity; and (3) the coexistence of multiple identities (Barvosa-Carter 1999) with salient ones influenced by utility
and context.

Our theme of community building includes pan-ethnic group awareness
and identification. I am not suggesting that pan-ethnic identity takes the
form of "primordial" affinity and attachment. It becomes an acquired identity whose meaning and relevance is contextually defined and interpreted. It
delineates loosely defined parameters of group membership and interests.
Such broad characterizations may be more effective in identifying non-Hispanics than providing clear, concise identifications of Hispanics.

Puerto Rican, Cuban, Central and South American political elites have
followed a similar evolution and development. The broader distinction of the
Latino "umbrella" has enabled different Latino subgroups to advance their
issues and concerns in both local and national arenas. For example, the El Salvadoran and Guatemalan communities have focused significant efforts on
obtaining political refugee status in order to facilitate the legal status of many
Salvadoran and Guatemalan immigrants. In addition to pursuing policy
changes within their own organizations, the broader inclusion of Central
Americans with other Latinos, especially immigrants, helps expand the constituency base, political visibility, and potential clout to affect immigration
reform and policy adjustments. The Central American segment represents

the most recent influx of Latino subgroups and the fastest growing Latino segment. The utility of adding the Latino identity and labeling themselves as such fuels the well-established image of a fast-growing population.

Community building among Latino subgroups does not preclude the persistence of Latino subgroup organizations or targeted efforts for their respective community needs and interests. The recognition that an individual has multiple identities has a parallel politically. Thus political involvement on behalf of Latinos may be salient at times, while on other occasions Latino subgroup interests (Dominican, Cuban, etc.) may be more prominent. This exploration of community among individuals and Latino subgroups reveals a network of connectors in which some degree of affinity and attachment occurs. It manifests itself politically with enough frequency to sustain a sense of community and, perhaps more importantly, to establish a stronger sense of community.

LATINO IDENTITY: TWO VIGNETTES

The utility of Latino identity and its promotion by Latino activists and leaders is illustrated through two incidents that took place in Chicago some sixteen years apart. The first involved cross-communication between two local Latino community organizations and the latter was a focus group discussion of identity.

In 1971–1972, I engaged in fieldwork with several progressive neighborhood-based community organizations (Brown Berets, LADO, Young Patriots, Black Panthers, Young Lords, etc.) that were involved in free health clinics (J. A. García 1977). All of these organizations were very politicized and had community control and radical reform as central parts of their mission. During this time, the city of Chicago was determined to close the clinics by requiring physician ownership. Each clinic was independent, and there was very little contact and communication between the different organizations. Ironically, they faced similar problems and there was a potential for cooperative and coalitional efforts. The Brown Beret clinic—Benito Juarez—and the Latin American Defense Organization (LADO) clinic—Pedro Albizu Campos—had arranged a joint meeting to discuss possible cooperative activities to deal with pressure coming from the Richard J. Daley political machine.

The meeting was held in the Brown Beret neighborhood (Pilsen) with many members of each organization attending. The Brown Beret membership was youthful and had a militaristic style of dress and demeanor. At the meeting, they marched in formation into the room with their leaders at the head of the line. LADO was based in Westown in an area with a mix of Latino subgroups—primarily Puerto Rican and Mexican-origin. Its organizational membership was a combination of families, young persons, and seniors. They entered the meeting in a less structured way and its members were diverse in terms of age and family status.

The Brown Beret perceived the LADO organization as primarily a Puerto Rican group and less tied to the U.S. mainland. They saw themselves as cultural nationalists concerned about liberation politics. As a result, the meeting highlighted national origin, cultural nationalism, and cultural differences rather than similarities of ideology, organizational goals, and culture. The meeting became tense and little progress was made in finding common ground and joint initiatives. Some of the LADO members, lacking child care, had to bring their young children. The divisiveness of the two organizations centered on their national-origin and perceived cultural differences.

At one point, a Brown Beret leader pointed to a couple in LADO—the male Puerto Rican and the female Mexican American. Their three-year-old daughter was also present. He reminded the parents that their daughter would one day have to decide whether she was Puerto Rican or Mexican American/Chicana. The LADO parents, without consulting each other or hesitating, simultaneously responded, "She does not have to decide that, she is a *Latina*!"

Some sixteen years later, I was a co-principal investigator for the Latino National Political Survey (the first probability sampling of Cuban, Mexican-origin, and Puerto Rican adults living in the contiguous United States). As part of the preparation of the survey instrument, a series of ten focus groups in five cities were conducted in 1988. Chicago was the site of two focus groups. One of the primary topics of discussion was how individuals see themselves and the area of social identity. A group of fifteen to twenty Latinos (bilingual or primarily English speakers) agreed to talk for a couple of hours. As the conversation on identity progressed, many of the participants comfortably identified themselves as Latino(a). Over the previous fifteen to twenty years, Latino activists had made concerted efforts to promote Latino identification. At the same time, each participant assumed several other identities such as Puerto Rican, Salvadoran, Mexican(o), immigrant, and so on.

The group included a brother and sister with one Puerto Rican parent and one of Mexican origin. The sister was married to a man of Italian ancestry living on the South Side of Chicago in a primarily white ethnic neighborhood. The Latina had a daughter who attended a parochial school in the neighborhood. A discussion followed in which the Latina described a series of identities and situations for her daughter. When visiting her grandmother, the daughter emphasized and identified herself as a Mexican American. While visiting her grandfather (the grandparents were divorced), she was a Puerto Rican. At home, the daughter's identity was Latina. She attended a parochial school in the neighborhood. At school, the daughter took the ethnicity of her father. Finally, the mother described trips they took together on the Chicago Transit Authority bus. On their bus route toward the Loop (central retail and business section of the city), the daughter was aware of her minority status and identity. Many of the other bus passengers were African Americans and the daughter recognized the broader concept of "people of color." It was clear from the focus group setting that these siblings were cognizant of their multiple identities and how different situations "trigger" a different identity and label. The multiplicity of identities that are a part of an individual can be transferred and learned by children. The socialization process has been researched in terms of the development of identities (gender, racial, ethnic, etc.) and how early that process begins (Bernal and Martinelli 1993). Chicago continues to be a primary area in which pan-ethnic identity is developed and maintained on a daily and individual basis.

LATINO COMMUNITY BUILDING AND MOBILIZATION: THE CRITICAL POLITICAL LINK

Community building among Latino subgroups is directly connected to political domains of American society. A community includes common interests, circumstances, experiences, cultural traditions and values (in this case for Latinos), personal networks, and affinity. Consequently, a Latino community and its subgroups participate in various political arenas to pursue their interests and goals. The examination of Latinos and their politics does not assume that political dynamics occur only because some basis for community exists. The other essential element is the mobilization of individuals and group members to act collectively. Mobilization is the process by which political candidates, political parties, activists, and groups try to induce other people to participate. Effective mobilization occurs when efforts by these individuals or groups increase the likelihood of involvement by others (Tilly 1978; Rosenstone and Hansen 1993).

Political participation in the United States declined through much of the latter half of the twentieth century. In the electoral arena, fewer persons voted in national, state, and local elections. One of the ironies is that registration systems and access to the registration process have been made easier (motor voter legislation, deputy registrars, mail-in registration, same-day registration, etc.). Yet election 2000 showed that problems still exist, especially for minority populations. Outdated voting machines, inaccurate voting lists, challenges to voting status, and intimidation were among the problems identified by the U.S. Civil Rights Commission study in Florida (U.S. Civil Rights Commission 2001). Political scientists have examined the decline of political involvement since the beginning of the discipline. More recently, such factors as declining social and political trust, heightened cynicism, decline of community and social networks as some of the primary contributors have been identified (Putnam 2000; Nie et al. 1996).

Clearly political participation is viewed as individually driven. It is up to each person to determine how, when, and why to get politically involved. Participation is mostly episodic, and only a small proportion of the citizenry maintains a continual practice of involvement. For our purposes, participation involves the process of influencing the distribution of social goods and values (Rosenstone and Hansen 1993). These may be public or private actors in the political arena using direct or indirect means to influence. We know that on an individual basis, the critical factors for involvement are resources, time, opportunities, beliefs, values, ideology, and participatory political attitudes. Participation is affected by contact with organizations, leaders, and political parties who strategically choose to activate specific individuals and/or groups. Thus a person's participation is due to choices she makes and the incentives to participate that are available. Overall, the "pull factors" than can motivate a Latino to participate are the nature of political life (interest, impact, excitement, etc.), important social networks for which politics is a key element, contact with political actors and activists, available time, issues, and group identification.

A Latino who becomes involved in the political process faces both opportunity costs and resource requirements, including time, skills (communicative, organizational, etc.), money, knowledge, self-confidence, and efficacy (Rosenstone and Hansen 1993; Verba et al. 1995). The acquisition of education (usually in terms of schooling) translates into greater accumulation of pertinent knowledge and familiarity with the political processes and institutions. In addition, more schooling is associated with the development of political skills—letter writing, oral presentations, research and informational access, and so on. Individuals with a strong sense of personal and political efficacy are more likely to be self-confident and competent in political arenas. Time, resources, and positive predispositions constitute the key ingredients for an active citizenry.

While costs and resources tend to differentiate individuals who choose to and do participate in politics, there are benefits and rewards for political involvement. Researchers (Verba et al. 1995; Wolfinger and Rosenstone 1980; Rosenstone and Hansen 1993) have categorized the political benefits as material, solidary, and purposive. Material benefits are tangible rewards that are converted to a monetary benefit like a job, a tax break, and so on. The solidary rewards are intangibles such as status, deference, and friendship (Rosenstone and Hansen 1993). Finally, purposive benefits are inherent rewards that a person derives from participation in and of itself. Even within this schema, the reward system can extend beyond personal rewards. Political involvement can result in the attainment of collective rewards that have diffuse group benefits.

For example, the extension of the **Voting Rights Act** with bilingual provisions for election information and assistance could have both individual and collective benefits for Latinos. Clearly, the community has a direct stake in the well-being and advancement of Latinos with political involvement and outcomes. As more Latinos vote and make use of bilingual materials and assistance, then the community has a potentially louder voice. Latinos who do not need bilingual election services can be supportive of such policies for both overall community benefits and the symbolic value of addressing the Latino community. As community is defined in terms of its essential elements and interests, preferences are articulated with specific political outcomes in mind. Latinos who identify with Latino organizations (locally and nationally) and with Latino leaders and advocates, develop a strong psychological attachment and become more likely to engage in a variety of political arenas.

A significant amount of research on Latinos and/or Latino subgroups portrays a relatively politically inactive population. The general political participation research literature (Verba et al. 1995) suggests why some persons do not participate. One segment does not participate because they are unable to do so. The largest segment of such persons is not old enough or may be non-citizens. Age and citizenship are requirements for the major kinds of participation. Nevertheless, many young people and non-citizens engage in political activities such as electoral campaigns, community-based organizations, or discussions of community issues with coworkers and neighbors.

Another segment consists of persons who are not interested in participation, because of either non-participatory attitudes or inadequate resources. For example, Latinos who are cynical or alienated from politics, its institutions and processes, are less inclined to get involved, especially in the more conventional modes of political involvement (voting, partisan activities, campaigning). Viewing politics as highly complicated or incomprehensible (J. A. García 1989) can distance an individual from things political. Orientations such as political trust (or distrust), inefficacy, and political interest (or its lack), can serve as disincentives for political involvement. The final category for nonparticipation is the absence of communication and contact with others who might ask an individual to get involved in a particular situation or activity, or around a given issue. A *Los Angeles Times* California survey (*Los Angeles Times*, 1994b) reported that during the 1994 California election period, any political party or organization soliciting their support or involvement had not contacted over four-fifths of the sampled Latino electorate. Thus, beyond individual motivation, interest, resources, and beliefs, individuals need to be approached, encouraged, and "directed" toward participation. This latter segment highlights the role of political mobilization with individuals and identifiable communities.

So far this discussion has focused on the distinction between individually motivated involvement and the role of mobilization, which is stimulated by persons or groups. Mobilization involves conscious efforts by organizations, political candidates, and activists to induce persons to get involved and participate politically. In very concrete ways, mobilization deals with the social temperament of political life. The identification and use of social networks, key influencers in those networks, and the knowledge of persons' concerns make political involvement more personal and translatable to one's personal situation and everyday world. A person who is connected to a political matter generally is more likely to respond favorably and get drawn into political affairs.

Over the past twenty years there have been many national debates, actions, policies, and public perceptions about immigration, especially undocumented migration. This policy area holds the attention of both the public and policy makers. Obviously the immigrant community is well aware of the policies and circumstances related to immigration, labor and housing markets, law enforcement, educational access, and adjustment to life in the United States. The California State initiative, **Proposition 187,** directly targeted access to education and health services among undocumented and permanent resident aliens. The mobilization that took place within the Latino community regarding Prop. 187 involved local neighborhood organizations as well as national civil rights groups. The result was raised awareness and increased voter registration for the upcoming elections, as well as public rallies and protests around Prop. 187. More Latinos ran for elective office in California and their numbers increased in state and local government, accentuating the rising level of political expression and involvement among Latinos.

In chapters 9 and 10, we will focus on the policy areas of immigration, education, and voting rights, as well as examine the political involvement of the immigrant segments of the Latino community. Immigrants (both legal and undocumented) found ways to involve themselves politically on the Proposition 187 initiative, even though they were unable to vote. Political expression and involvement extends the ballot box. Mobilization efforts by leaders, activists, and Latino-based organizations induced Latinos to get involved through a number of different venues and forms of political interest.

Political mobilization includes both direct and indirect forms of inducement and persuasion. The direct form lies in opportunities to participate such as signing petitions, posting campaign signs, registering to vote, or attending rallies. By creating participatory venues, the mobilizers subsidize political information and personal costs of involvement. Mobilization usually does not take the form of a blanket call for involvement but is more strategic in nature. **Targeted mobilization** involves identifying persons who, when contacted, are more likely to respond to the calls for involvement. The targeting has to be done efficiently, as resources are always limited. So the "kinds" of people who are likely to be contacted are those who are knowledgeable about politics and issues, those positioned in established networks, those whose actions are effective, and those likely to respond (Rosenstone and Hansen

1993). For the general population these persons are more likely to be employed, belong to organizations, be more affluent, have higher levels of educational attainment, and be more partisan. For the Latino community, it is likely to be persons who are opinion leaders in their neighborhood or at work, who possess political knowledge and are positively disposed to involvement.

We know that individuals with higher socioeconomic status (education, income, and occupation) are more likely to participate politically than those at the lower end. Higher socioeconomic status affords the person greater skills, resources, and opportunities for participation. In the case of Latinos, the current socioeconomic distribution of community members (education, occupational status, and income levels) is generally lower than the non-Latino population. Consequently, enhanced issue awareness and greater salience coupled with a sense of group identity become an additional cueing element for targeted mobilization. Considerable research (J. A. García, 1998; de la Garza et al. 1994) has documented relatively lower levels of political involvement among Latinos, while at the same time income and occupational status are not as strong as "determinants" for political participation as with other groups (J. A. García 1995).

More recent research (Hardy-Fanta 1993; Pardo 1998; Saito 1998) has found that political activism and interest among Latinos is quite evident at the local and neighborhood levels. For example, state and local government initiatives to locate a prison facility and waste management site in the East Los Angeles section of the county activated strong concerns among Latino residents, especially mothers and other women in the area. As a result, the Mothers of East Los Angeles was formed to oppose these two projects (Pardo 1998). Eventually they were successful, but in the process of organizing and strategizing around these issues, the Mothers and other involved Latinos developed a better understanding of the political processes and empowered themselves. Community struggles against unfavorable governmental proposals and actions enabled leadership development and heightened interest in a wide range of community issues. Success in achieving objectives provided greater incentive to pursue other issues of importance and interest with similar energy and commitment. Similar events occurred in other communities with Latino populations such as Miami (Portes and Stepnick 1993), New York City (Falcón 1993), and other major metropolitan cities (Jennings 1992, 1994; Cruz 1998).

The timing dimension of mobilization is critical for efficient and effective campaigns. Persons who are contacted need to be ready to follow leaders and have an interest in the issue. The directed activity needs to have a consequential effect (eventually) on the problem or issue. Also, the action is timed to occur when decision-making is impending and the outcome is "hanging in the balance." The timing is not allowed to compete with other concerns that may diminish a response and commitment to act. For example, in its earlier organizational development, the Southwest Voter Registration and Education Project (SVREP) began extensive voter registration campaigns. Cities and neighborhoods were selected and an organizing local committee conducted the campaign. There were registration campaigns during years in which elections were several months away or when no elections were held.

As a result, newly registered persons did not vote or they let their registration lapse. Subsequently SVREP timed its registration campaigns to election years and closer to primary and general elections. In addition, volunteers would talk to prospective registrants about local problems and concerns. These exchanges served to increase awareness about linkages between community problems and the political system. If not having a voice in government or non-responsiveness were concerns, then registering to vote became a real tie to political participation and change. Finally, Latino political mobilization is directed toward legislative arenas, which are overtly political and visible, rather than bureaucratic ones.

CONCLUSION

This discussion in this chapter centered on the bases for community among Latinos with an important ingredient of group identity and the resulting linkages with political involvement. There is a clear link between individual motivation and resources to participate and mobilization efforts by organizations and activists to assist that process. The individual component provides insight about the motivations and capacities that a person develops and his cumulative experiences in different political arenas. Participation in America is voluntary, which contributes to overall participatory rates, as politics must contend with work, family, social interests, and other daily activities and concerns. For Latinos, limited resources, language barriers, a historic lack of political engagement in the United States, and lack of contact with recruitment networks have all contributed to lower levels of political involvement.

The following chapters will focus on the individual and mobilizations aspects of Latino participation. We will examine participation in a variety of different venues (voting, campaigning, organizational involvement, partisan activities, school-related activities, letter writing, etc.). For the most part, our knowledge about specific participation levels is limited to a few Latino subgroups (primarily Mexican Americans, Cubans, and Puerto Ricans) and the more common data is pertinent to only particular participatory modes (primarily voting and election returns). It is only in the last five or so years that information, studies, and accounts of the political participation of the "other Latinos" are becoming available. The extant research information will be used to characterize a participation "map" for these politically emerging communities. In addition to characterizing Latino participation, we will present the essential factors that influence those who become involved and in which arenas. As indicated earlier, politically inactive Latinos cite a lack of time or interest or a perceived lack of relevance and no understanding of politics (Verba et al. 1995) as their major reasons.

Finally, this discussion would not be complete without considering the mobilization dynamics intersecting individual political behavior and attitudes with the targeted actions of organizations and activists. With the development of a stronger Latino community, how do Latino-based organizations and Latino leaders/activists motivate and influence fellow Latinos to get more involved in the American political process? Does organizational affiliation and engagement, whether the group is specifically political or not, provide interest, knowledge and networks from which to mobilize? Does greater attention and visibility of Latinos on the American landscape become an extra incentive to be more political? How does issue salience serve to activate Latinos and/or provide mobilizers the substance to encourage and reduce the costs for Latino participation?

NOTE

1. Even though I have not developed gender consciousness and its ideological aspects related to pan-ethnicity, there are discussions and analyses of its impact in the chapter on political community for Latinos.

6

Latino Political Participation

~~~~~~

Y ¿que tal tu vida cívica? ¿Aprendiste de tus padres? ¿Qué talentos desarrollaste para trabajar en la comunidad? Si se te pide que trabajes en la comunidad ¿cómo vas a responder?

And how is your civic life? Did you learn from your parents? What talents have you developed to serve better our community? If someone asks to join in the effort with other members of our community, how will you respond?

~~~~~~~~~~~~~~~~~~

The "Y2K problem" seemingly applied to Latino **political participation** in the highly active political year 2000: we faced a presidential election that did not include an incumbent, and we had to work to maintain control of Congress and political advantages in many state legislatures and gubernatorial mansions. As the next millennium begins, will the rising trajectory of Latino political involvement be reconfigured or does it backtrack to earlier low levels of collective involvement? Or will it surge to even greater impact and visibility on the American political landscape? For Latinos, solving their Y2K bug means converting a growing adult population into a more politically oriented and politically immersed population. In this chapter we will examine current patterns of Latino political participation, critical contributing factors, and areas for which there is little systematic information.

The American political culture envisions political participation as a fundamental right and obligation of each person to have a role in political processes and institutions. Having access, pursuing political interests, knowing the rules of the game,[1] developing effective political resources, having responsive representatives, and influencing the policy-making process are central dimensions of political participation.

Political participation can be described as the involvement of an individual or group of individuals with the central objective of influencing the policy-making process and substance. This entails accumulating and utilizing resources, developing positive participatory orientations, and recruiting others to get involved. Political resources include time, money, and communication and organizational skills. Resources equip a person to engage in the political arena with knowledge, available time, and the pertinent skills to articulate and effect change. Participatory orientations develop political attitudes that are conducive for participation: political and personal efficacy, political trust and interest, and a sense of group consciousness. The third side of the participation triangle is recruitment. A person may initiate his or her own actions, *as a result* of being encouraged by persons or organizations to get involved in a particular way. A person may become active because he or she was asked to do so.

The literature on political participation (Verba and Nie 1972; Verba, Scholzman, and Brady 1995; Milbrath 1977; Rosenstone and Hansen 1993) identifies who, when, where, and how individuals participate. As already noted, who participates is largely a function of available and amassed resources. One of the most critical resources is educational attainment. Persons who have attained more years of schooling and educational credentials (degrees, professional certification, etc.) are more likely to participate. Greater "amounts" of education increase levels of political knowledge and efficacy. Education can provide the communication skills that people need to enter the political realm. Education can provide access to higher-status and better-paying jobs, knowledge about political matters, contact with others engaged in political activities, and civic skills such as writing and public speaking.

Early socialization experiences also play a critical role in the development of an individual's participatory future. Family discussion of things political and exposure to political events such as rallies and campaigns can make a lasting imprint on a young person. Similarly, early pre-adult experiences such as involvement in extracurricular activities, activities in religious organizations, and having politically active parents make a strong impression on children and help teach them. Such background characteristics as gender, race, and **ethnicity** also have an important role in early socialization. If the family expects girls to be less involved or even not involved, a woman's political participation can be affected. Being subjected to discriminatory treatment can cause a person to become politically involved to combat such treatment in the future (de la Garza and Vaughn 1984). The cycle of life experiences and early socialization establishes the foundation from which an individual chooses to get involved or not. However, early socialization does not completely predetermine any individual's participatory life.

According to Verba, Scholzman, and Brady (1995), participation involves (1) resources, (2) psychological orientation, and (3) recruitment. Resources include the accumulation of time, money, and skills. Time means having opportunities to participate and the availability of time to do so. Money pro-

vides a valuable resource for engaging in political activities and being identified in networks. Skills include the ability and confidence to engage in political activities. Education plays a major role in skill acquisition. Educational
attainment provides greater political knowledge and information, as well as
communication skills (writing, public speaking, organizing thoughts and
ideas, etc.). Higher levels of educational attainment generally position a person in higher-level jobs and income. In addition, positive participatory orientations like personal and political efficacy, political trust, and sense of civic
duty are associated with greater educational attainment. Finally, higher levels of education are generally associated with organizational affiliation and
involvement.

All of these ingredients for political participation center on an individual's abilities and acquired skills, position in a job setting, and resource base
from which to engage in political matters. As already noted in the demographic profiles, Latinos as a group do not possess the necessary time, money,
and skills in great quantities—yet. A discussion of participation must include
recruitment and mobilization: persons get politically involved when they are
asked to be active. Political mobilization entails efforts by political parties,
organizations, candidates, and leaders to persuade individuals to participate.
Mobilization efforts can be direct, contacting and encouraging persons for
specific actions and responses, or indirect, using social networks to commu-
nicate the message. The primary networks are based in the workplace or the
neighborhood.

So far, I have identified political participation as originating in the individual or in targeted efforts by third parties to persuade persons to get
involved in a specific activity or issue. The results of **targeted mobilization**
include creating opportunities to participate, subsidizing the costs of gathering political information, and subsidizing the costs of political activism. The
latter point refers to providing materials, rides to the polls, individuals to
assist, and the like so that the "targeted" individual does not have to expend
as much time and energy as he would if he were participating alone. Thus the
act of mobilizing entails identifying people to contact and persuade and the
most efficient manner to reach them. In the identification process mobilizers
have a good sense that the persons contacted will likely respond to the call for
action. Research by Rosenstone and Hansen (1993) indicates that persons
more likely to be targeted are persons who are employed, belong to organizations, are leaders in the organization, are more educated, have higher income
levels, and have some partisan (political party) history.

Mobilization efforts tend to be more successful if the contact is made
between persons who know each other. Personal connections establish a
more receptive setting for the message and request. Another important "characteristic" for targeted mobilization is that once contacted, the person will be
effective and well positioned to solicit the help of others in their networks.

Timing is the other essential ingredient. When you ask someone to participate, the issue (e.g., city council hearing on an ordinance) or event (e.g., election date) is usually very near. Thus the outcome is hanging in the balance and there are identifiable consequences that will affect the individual.

Political participation centers on obtaining volunteers when other circumstances, situations, opportunities, and "distractions" compete for people's involvement. Most Americans' political participation is very limited and sporadic. Participation involves time, resources, opportunities, knowledge and interest, and the motivation to engage in a wide range of possible political activities. Non-participants are individuals who cannot participate or do not want to or have not been asked to get involved. Persons who cannot participate are excluded by restrictions like age requirements, citizenship status, language barriers, felon status, and the like. Persons who do not want to participate are usually not interested; find other "things" more important to do, do not have enough time, and find politics too complicated and/or boring or feel distrustful and cynical about politics. The last category of non-participants is never asked by anyone or any organization to get politically involved. This occurs because the mobilizers do not perceive such individuals as likely participants or being positioned in useful networks. The size of the non-participant group varies by the type of political activities available.

How and where do Americans participate politically? The most common form of political participation centers on elections. The United States holds the greater number of elections each year. As a result, political participation is seen as election dominated, and voter registration and turnout become the primary indicators. In addition to voting, political campaigns involve making campaign contributions, doing volunteer work, posting campaign signs or wearing campaign buttons, and attending rallies.

The penultimate form of participation is seeking political office, but a very small fraction of persons actually obtain it. At the same time, political participation extends beyond the electoral arena in both individual and collective ways. Persons can make direct contact with public and/or bureaucratic officials regarding an individual problem or on behalf of their neighborhood or group. The other dimensions of political participation include belonging to organized groups. The organization can be explicitly political or nonpolitical. As already mentioned, involvement with an organization as a member, financial contributor, or leader enables the person to gain access to information and knowledge, policy preferences, organizational skills, and experience with collective efforts. Other forms of political participation include protest activities, talking about politics or trying to persuade another individual to support a given candidate or proposition, and partisan activities. The opportunities for political participation are substantial, and many persons choose to become politically engaged.

While active political participation is an integral part of a viable democ-

César Chávez (1927–1993)

César Chávez organized the first successful major labor action against the employers of California's exploited migrant farmworkers—most of them Mexican Americans. He then expanded his work to meet the needs and aspirations of the Hispanic-American community in general and to liberal and civil rights causes for all minorities. Through his work, he became one of the best-known Hispanic leaders in the United States and was hailed far and wide almost as a lay saint of the oppressed.

Chávez was born on March 31, 1927, in Yuma, Arizona. His family owned and worked a plot of poor-quality land, but they lost even this land during the Great Depression of the 1930s. The Chávez's then had to join the armies of rootless farmhands who followed the crops on the West Coast.

Chávez served in the navy during World War II and then returned to work in the Californian fruit and vegetable fields. In 1950, he lived in a neighborhood of San Jose that was so bad that it was called *Sal Si Puedes* ("Get Out If You Can"). At that time he was contacted by a worker for the CSO (Community Service Organization), a group created by Saul Alinsky, a pioneer in community organization in the United States.

Working for the CSO, Chávez quickly demonstrated his talent for convincing people. He signed up more than 4,000 new voters within two months, while continuing to work in the fields during the day.

At the same time, he began to suggest to his fellow farmhands that they form a union to fight against the miserable working conditions. When his employer found out about this, he immediately fired Chávez. Chávez then went to work for the CSO as a staff member. By 1958, he was CSO general director for California and Arizona.

In 1962 Chávez decided it was the time to act. He asked the CSO to back him in trying to organize a union. Both he and the other CSO activists knew that, since 1903, Mexican American and Asian farmworkers in California had made many attempts to organize. They had also tried to strike for better pay and working conditions. The landowners had defeated every attempt, even resorting to physical violence against the workers.

This knowledge did not stop Chávez from wanting to try again, but it did stop the CSO, so Chávez quit.

With his savings of $1,200, he founded the National Farm Workers

Association (NFWA)—which later became the United Farm Workers of America (UFW)—and began to recruit members. To do so, he had to resist brutal pressure not only from the employers but from other sources as well.

His opposition included the Teamsters Union. The Teamsters tried to take over the operation, but Chávez mistrusted the huge union's motives. He wanted to keep the union a grassroots organization whose members would feel closely involved.

In 1965 the union staged its first strike. Chávez was unsure the union was really prepared for it (the NFWA strike fund amounted to less than $100). Still, the strike was necessary in order to support Filipino grape pickers who had begun a work stoppage near Chávez's headquarters in Delano, California.

In 1968 Chávez launched a nationwide grape boycott, asking consumers everywhere to simply stop eating grapes until the workers who picked the fruit were paid decent wages and were given acceptable working and living conditions. He succeeded in making millions of people aware of the plight of the migrant workers and willing to support the boycott enthusiastically. The refusal to buy California grapes spread even to Europe.

Chávez viewed the struggle—which he and his followers called *La Causa*, "the cause"—as more than a labor dispute. It was a statement of the equal worth of Hispanics as human beings. Chávez would, in time, extend his movement to deal with other abuses and inequities in U.S. society. He was a forceful supporter of the civil rights movement and became a hero to the dispossessed everywhere.

Bibliography

Day, Mark. *Forty Acres: César Chávez and the Farm Workers.* New York: Praeger, 1971.

Faivre, Lynn. *Chávez: One New Answer.* New York: Praeger, 1970.

Griswold del Castillo, Richard, and Richard García. *César Chávez: A Triumph of Spirit.* Norman: University of Oklahoma Press, 1995.

Levy, Jacques E. *César Chávez: Autobiography of La Causa.* New York: Norton, 1974.

Matthiessen, Peter. *Sal Si Puedes: César Chávez and the New American Revolution.* New York: Random House, 1969.

Pitrone, Jean. *Chávez: Man of the Migrants.* New York: Pyramid Communications, 1972.

Taylor, Ronald B. *Chávez and the Farmworker.* Boston: Beacon, 1975.

racy, and laws, practices, and traditions try to reinforce an individual's regular political engagement, the actual practice of participation is very uneven. I will try to construct a systematic picture of Latino political participation and examine why the current picture exists. This portrait will have some "open spaces" because social scientists, marketers, and journalists have only recently chronicled Latinos in the political system.

LATINO POLITICAL PARTICIPATION

Early works (Tirado 1970; García and Arce 1988) on Latino political participation focus almost exclusively on Mexican-origin people. Over the past thirty years, systematic examination of Mexican American and other Latino political behavior has been restricted to specific communities or limited forms of political participation (e.g., voting or organizational activities) (Briegal 1970; Márquez 1985; Allsup 1982; J. A. García 1986a, 1998; Chapa 1995). General conclusions regarding Latino political participation may be summarized as follows: (1) overall rates of participation are lower than those of the general population; (2) there is evidence of accepting participatory orientations, but participation does not necessarily follow; (3) rates of organizational involvement and activities are lower; (4) rates of voter registration and turnout are lower; (5) a significant proportion of the Latino sub-communities are foreign-born and are not citizens; and (6) there is a feeling of distance from and disinterest in the political world (J. A. García 1997; Falcón 1992; Moreno and Warren 1992).

The three primary sources for my portrayal of Latino political participation include the Participation in America II study by Sidney Verba, Kay Scholzman, and Henry Brady (1995); the Latino National Political Survey (de la Garza et al. 1995); and the Current Population Surveys by the Bureau of the Census. I begin by examining participation levels among Latinos compared with those of Anglos and African Americans for a broad range of political activities.

The following tables are based on the Verba et al. study in which the Latino respondents are reported as all Latinos and only Latino citizens. Table 6.1 includes nine political activities. For voting, there are very noticeable differences between Latinos and the other groups. There is a greater than 30 percent gap between Latino voter participation and that of Anglos. The situation improves if the voter base is only Latino citizens and the gap is now 21 percent. Interestingly, in the area of campaign involvement, there is no difference between Anglos and Latinos (citizens or not), and both are lower than African American rates. On the other hand, the percentages of Latinos contributing to political campaigns are significantly lower (almost 50 percent) than that of the other two groups. I will discuss in a later section the political

Table 6.1 Participation in a Range of Political Activities for Anglos, African Americans, and Latinos (percentage)

Specific Political Activity	Anglos	African Americans	Latinos	Latino Citizens
Voting	73	65	41	52
Campaign work	8	12	7	8
Campaign contribution	2	22	11	12
Contact with officials	37	24	14	17
Protest activity	5	9	4	11
Informal community activity	17	19	12	14
Board membership	4	5	1	5
Affiliation with organization	52	38	24	27
Mean number of activities involved	2.2	1.9	1.2	1.4

Source: S. Verba, K. Scholzman, and H. Brady, *Voice and Equality: Civic Volunteerism in America* (Cambridge: Harvard University Press, 1995), tab. 8.1, p. 233.

implications of a significant non-citizen segment within the Latino community, both electorally and in other realms of political participation.

In domains outside the electoral arena, Latino political participation is lower as well. Individual, direct contact with public officials is a preferred way of expressing political viewpoints and concerns. Latinos are much less likely to contact officials, and not much difference exists between all Latinos and Latino citizens (14 percent and 17 percent respectively). On the other hand, twice as many Latinos indicated that they have participated in protest activities—demonstrations, marches, and the like. This is much truer for Latino citizens, although it needs to be noted that this survey was taken in 1989. Developments, particularly in California, and the rise of activism around immigration policies have seen greater involvement of non-citizens (*Los Angeles Times* 1994b).

The other noteworthy area of political activity lies with organizational involvement and informal community activity. Historically, research on organizational involvement among Latinos, especially Mexican Americans (Tirado 1970; Márquez 1993; J. A. García and de la Garza 1985; J. A. García 1989) reflects a limited degree of organizational involvement. The consistent characterization is low rates of organizational affiliation and leadership positions. The data in the Verba et al. survey do not alter significantly that pattern. Whereas 52 percent of Anglos belong to some organization (political or nonpolitical), 24 percent of all Latinos and 27 percent of Latino citizens are group members. At the same time, membership on an organizational board is low for all respondents, but there is no difference for Latinos.

The category of informal community activity usually involves being immersed in neighborhood issues, school-related matters, or other locally

Table 6.2   Organizational Involvement in Nonpolitical Groups among Anglos, African Americans, and Latinos (percentage)

Nonpolitical Organization	Anglos	African Americans	Latinos	Latino Citizens
Nonpolitical organizational affiliation	71	58	40	42
Active in nonpolitical organization	39	34	19	20
Time for charitable activities	38	34	27	29
Make charitable contributions	71	56	47	52

Source: S. Verba, K. Scholzman, and H. Brady, *Voice and Equality: Civic Volunteerism in America* (Cambridge: Harvard University Press, 1995), tab. 8.3, p. 242.

Table 6.3   Range of Political Activities among Anglos, African Americans, and Latinos and by Gender (percentage)

Type of Political Activity	Total Respondents	Anglo Males	Anglo Females	African American Males	African American Females	Latino Males	Latinas
Voting	71	75	71	63	66	58	40
Campaign work	9	9	8	9	12	10	5
Campaign contribution	24	28	22	19	22	18	5
Informal community activity	17	18	15	17	18	16	14
Contact with official	54	40	33	33	19	23	9
Protest activity	6	5	6	10	8	5	3

Source: S. Verba, K. Scholzman, and H. Brady, *Voice and Equality: Civic Volunteerism in America* (Cambridge: Harvard University Press, 1995), fig. 8.5, p. 258.

based activities. Overall, the level of Latino informal activity is comparable to the other two groups, especially for Latino citizens. The overall mean number of activities involved still reveals the lower levels of involvement for Latinos (i.e., 1.4 mean number of activities versus 2.2 for Anglos). Clearly an understanding of Latino political participation needs to go beyond an overall summary of activities and explore specific political arenas. The electoral arena has been well examined, and Latinos have made slow progress. The other area of concern lies with the organizational realm and relatively limited participation in organizations, whether political or not.

In table 6.2, we can see the level of organizational involvement in specifically nonpolitical groups (Verba et al. 1995). Whereas more than seven in ten Anglos have membership in an organization, the numbers are appreciably lower for both all Latinos and Latino citizens (40 percent and 42 percent respectively). Africans Americans tend to fall midway between Anglos and Latinos. Affiliation is one aspect of organizational involvement as active participation extends beyond dues paying. Again, Latino active participation is almost one-half that of Anglos (20 percent versus 39 percent). Similar disparities exist in time for charitable activities as well as giving charitable contributions.

So far, we have examined Latino participation by differentiating all Latinos from Latino citizens. Table 6.3 introduces the gender dimension, another critical component of Latino political behavior. While differing rates of political participation exist among Latinos, Anglos, and African Americans, there are some noteworthy gender differences. In the electoral area, there is a real gender-voting gap among Latinos(as), with an 18 percent differential. Percentage-wise, twice as many Latinos have been involved in campaign work than Latinas, and Latinos contributed three times more to campaigns. Whereas the gender gap has closed for non-minority groups, it seems to persist within the Latino community.

Gender differences persist in matters of contacting public officials, yet their respective participation in protest activities is comparable. An area in which Latino gender differences are much less evident is that of informal community activities. Their respective percentages are virtually identical (16 percent versus 14 percent). Recent works (Pardo 1998; Hardy-Fanta 1993; Montoya et al. 2000; Hardy-Fanta and Cardoza 1997) focusing on activism at the local level demonstrate the critical and pervasive leadership roles that Latinas have played. Matters regarding schools, education, public safety, and undesirable facilities like prisons, waste dumps, basic city services, and gangs have served as key organizing issues. Latinas have advanced these causes and directed many of these efforts.

As already noted, personal political resources enhance political engagement. Persons need to have skills, time, and economic resources to participate effectively. Table 6.4 displays a number of political resources by race, ethnicity, and gender. The job skills dimension deals with the degree of autonomy a person has on the job (decision making, use of discretion) and communication opportunities such as directing meetings, making presentations, and preparing interoffice communications.[2] Out of four possible job skills, the overall average for all respondents was 1.4 in comparison to 1.5 for Latino males and 1.0 for Latinas. Males had higher than average job skills regardless of race or ethnicity. In addition to developing nonpolitical skills that are transferable to political activities, being recruited for political action is another element of participation. From the work of Rosenstone and Hansen (1993) persons targeted for political recruitment are usually employed, participate actively in social networks, and have social status and economic resources. A vast majority of Americans are seldom asked to participate in political action. Table 6.4 shows that one in seven respondents were asked, and Latino males reflected this level of recruitment. For Latinas, the ratio was more like one in twenty-five. One observation we can make is that the par-

Table 6.4   Distribution of Politically Relevant Resources, Organizational Involvement, and Recruitment Contact for Anglos, African Americans, and Latinos and by Gender

Political Resources, Organizations and Recruitment	All Respondents	Anglo Males	Anglo Females	African American Males	African American Females	Latino Males	Latinas
Mean number of job skills	1.4	1.8	1.2	1.4	1.0	1.5	1.0
Percent recruited for political action	14	16	13	13	12	13	6
Percent affiliated with nonpolitical organization	68	71	72	63	54	47	35
Mean number of meetings attended	.83	.82	.86	.77	.86	.59	.55
Mean number of organizational skills	.53	.59	.56	.44	.39	.24	.14
Percent recruited for political action by own organization	23	27	21	25	16	17	6

Source: S. Verba, K. Scholzman, and H. Brady, *Voice and Equality: Civic Volunteerism in America* (Cambridge: Harvard University Press, 1995), tab. 8.2–3, pp. 236–43.

ticipation lag that we saw earlier in this chapter for Latinos is not as present for politically relevant resources.

Our examination of organizational skills is a variation of the job skills battery of items.[3] The mean number of organizational skills is low for all respondents (mean of .53) versus even lower ones for Latinos (.24) and Latinas (.14). This pattern of low organizational involvement is also reflected with the scores on the mean number of meetings attended. Both Latinos and Latinas are the lower scores with .59 and .55 (which is almost one-fourth less than the other groups). Finally, recruitment on the job is already demonstrated to be low, yet being associated with an organization slightly improves the chances of outside contact. One in four respondents reported being recruited by their own organization for political action. The percentage drops considerably for Latinos, 17 percent and 6 percent for males and females respectively.

Our earlier discussion of political participation introduced the concepts of political engagement, interest, efficacy, and relevant information. Persons more likely to be politically involved are individuals who are psychologically oriented toward participation and its relevance to their lives. Knowledge, interest, and personal and political efficacy all contribute to active involvement. Table 6.5 summarizes participatory scores for all respondents, males

Table 6.5   Summary of Participatory Scores for the Respondents in the Participation in America Study

Indicator of Participatory Measures	Political Engagement Scores	Political Interest Scores	Political Efficacy Scores	Political Information Scores
All respondents	19.1	5.8	9.2	4.6
Anglo males	20.4	6.0	9.6	5.3
Anglo females	18.8	5.8	9.1	4.5
African American males	18.5	6.0	8.8	4.0
African American females	16.9	5.5	8.6	3.2
Latino males	17.8	5.3	9.1	3.8
Latinas	14.8	4.6	8.0	2.5

Source: S. Verba, K. Scholzman, and H. Brady, *Voice and Equality: Civic Volunteerism in America* (Cambridge: Harvard University Press, 1995), fig. 12.4, p. 349.

and females.[4] Interestingly enough, the disparities by racial/ethnic groups and/or gender vary by the different indicators. For example, in the political engagement dimension, the range of scores is 20.4 for Anglo males to 14.8 for Latinas. Latinos fall on the lower end of this dimension. Similarly, summary scores of political interest reflect a drop among African American females and Latino(as). On the other hand, political efficacy is viewed as an important set of political attitudes to encourage involvement. The score range is relatively narrower with Latinas at 8.0 (at the lower end) and Anglo males at 9.6 (at the higher end). Finally, noticeable differences are evident with political information scores. Again Latinos and African American females have the lower scores. Our brief view of participatory measures indicates the negative impact of participatory levels affected by both gender and ethnicity (i.e., being Latino and female).

In order to complete a full picture of the participatory profile of Latinos, we will draw on the only national probability survey[5] of Latinos, the Latino National Political Survey. As in the Verba et al. survey, Latinos were asked about their political involvement in a variety of political activities and types of organizational involvement. Nonpolitical organizations were identified that ranged from work, charitable, sports, and other types of groups. As already noted, individuals who are involved in groups tend to derive political information, develop useful political skills, and have interest in political activities and issues. Specific political activities included signing petitions, writing letters to the newspaper, attending public meetings, wearing campaign buttons, going to rallies, making political contributions, and volunteering for a political party. The LNPS also included a sample of non-Latinos in the same areas for which Latinos were interviewed. Table 6.6 presents the results of Latino organizational involvement.

Table 6.6   Organizational Involvement of Latinos and Anglos by Membership in Different Types of Groups (percentages)

Organization Type	Mexican	Puerto Rican	Cuban	Anglo
Work	16.7	10.4	16.0	26.2
Charitable	30.8	18.1	31.7	38.8
Social	3.5	3.4	10.6	18.2
Sports	15.7	8.2	17.6	25.8
None	42.9	62.7	42.1	24.7
Number of respondents	878	587	312	416

Source: De la Garza et al., *Latino Voices: Mexican, Puerto Rican, and Cuban Perspectives on American Politics* (Boulder: Westview, 1993), tab. 8.2, p. 115.

There are disparities in organizational involvement between Latinos and Anglos, as well as between the three Latino subgroups. Similar to findings in the Participation in America II study, Latinos, as a group, belong to fewer organizations than their Anglo counterparts. As a matter of fact, more than two out of five Latinos (42.9 percent) do not belong to any organization. The numbers of Latinos interviewed in the LNPS was more than five times greater than the Verba study. The greater numbers of Latinos interviewed allows us to examine the between-group variations. Puerto Ricans appear to have the lower level of organizational involvement, as almost three-fifths of the respondents indicate no organizational membership. Similarly, Puerto Ricans are less likely to belong to work and charitable organizations than their Mexican and Cuban counterparts. In many respects, Mexican and Cubans mirror each other on the extent and type of organizations in which they are members. Relatively, lower levels of political involvement in many political activities should reflect Latinos' lower level of organizational involvement.

In table 6.7, we can see the extent of Latino political involvement for a variety of political activities. In contrast with the Verba et al. Participation in America II study, the disparities between the three major Latino subgroups are not as marked in some categories. For example, while 21.2 percent of the Anglo respondents have attended a public meeting, the range for the Latino subgroups is from 12.4 percent for Cubans to 17.7 percent for the Mexican-origin respondents. The act of wearing a campaign button drew similar percentages of Latinos and Anglos as did attending political rallies. The larger disparities appear in persons signing petitions and, to a lesser extent, making political contributions. Partisan volunteering is almost identical for all the comparison groups, with the Mexican-origin having the highest percentage (7.0 percent).

While the results from the LNPS suggest that participatory disparities are not as great when examined across the three larger Latino subgroups and Ang-

Table 6.7   Participation in a Range of Political Activities among Latinos and Anglos (percentages)

Political Activities	Mexican	Puerto Rican	Cuban	Anglo
Sign petition	29.9	20.7	23.8	49.4
Wrote to newspaper	12.1	9.1	14.4	20.2
Attended public meeting	17.7	16.6	12.4	21.1
Wore campaign button	17.9	17.8	18.1	21.7
Went to rallies	9.1	7.9	8.9	9.2
Volunteered for political party	7.0	4.4	4.5	4.6
Made political contribution	9.0	6.4	7.0	12.6

Source: De la Garza et al., *Latino Voices: Mexican, Puerto Rican, and Cuban Perspectives on American Politics* (Boulder: Westview, 1993), tab. 8.11, p. 120.

Jose Angel Gutiérrez (1944–)

Jose Angel Gutiérrez was one of the civil rights leaders who helped stage the Chicano student walkout in Crystal City, Texas, in 1968. As a result of that protest, he was elected to the city council and also served on the city's school board, where he was a strong advocate for bilingual education. In 1970 he founded the Mexican American political party, La Raza Unida, to work for political participation and empowerment of Mexican Americans. In 1986 he became the executive director of the Greater Texas Legal Foundation and was appointed an administrative law judge in Dallas in 1990. In 1993 he ran an unsuccessful U.S. Senate campaign for the seat of Lloyd Bentsen.

Bibliography

Garcia, Ignacio. *United We Win.* Washington, D.C.: University Press of America, 1989.

los, some features of the LNPS are worth noting. The LNPS was a face-to-face interview with bilingual and bicultural interviewers. Both response rates and personal rapport may have contributed to the response patterns. In addition, the Anglos interviewed in the LNPS came from the same areas as the Latinos. In this manner, the political milieu and/or culture are similar for all respondents. Finally, separating out the three groups enables the reader to note any real variations.

For example, 50 percent more Mexican-origin respondents indicated that they volunteered for a political party than the other two Latino subgroups. In addition, Cubans were less likely to attend public meetings (approximately

Table 6.8   Involvement in School-Related Matters by Latinos and Anglos (percentage)

School-Related Activity	Mexican	Puerto Rican	Cuban	Anglo
Meet with teacher	62.5	55.6	39.3	—[a]
Attend PTA	41.8	40.4	30.1	47.1
Meet with principal	47.6	43.0	31.4	54.0
Attend school board meeting	18.1	20.2	13.6	19.8
Vote in school board elections	28.1	21.2	15.3	43.1

Source: De la Garza et al., *Latino Voices: Mexican, Puerto Rican, and Cuban Perspectives on American Politics* (Boulder: Westview, 1993), tab. 8.12, p. 120.
[a]This question was not asked of the non-Latino respondents.

25 percent less) than Puerto Ricans or Mexican-origin. Within the political participation research literature, the types of political activities focused on are seldom in specific political arenas (local, state, school districts, etc.). The LNPS included a battery of items that focused on Latino participation in school-related matters and in local arenas.

One of the ongoing debates regarding Latino involvement and interests is in the educational policy arena. Some studies (Meier and Stewart 1991) cite low socioeconomic status, immigrant background, and cultural barriers for Latinos to explain low involvement. Other studies (Carter and Segura 1979; San Miguel 1987) find levels of aspirations and commitment to children's educational attainment, significant percentages of Latinos in the school age ranges, and an immigrant base that seeks to improve their children's future as indicators of Latino support and interest in education.

Table 6.8 presents a unique set of items that focus on Latino involvement in school-related matters. Latino participation is higher in this arena than in the conventional categories of political activities. More than three-fifths of the Mexican-origin respondents indicated that they had met with a teacher. Their attendance at PTA meetings is comparable to that of their Anglo counterparts, with Cubans having the lowest percentage. The Cuban respondents are, on average, fifteen years older than their Mexican-origin and Puerto Rican counterparts. The Cubans, on average, are fourteen years older than Latinos in the other subgroups, reducing the number of parents with school-age children.

Attendance at school board meetings represents almost one-fifth of the respondents with little variation between the four groups. The major difference between Latinos and Anglos lies with participation rates for voting in school board elections. Many Latinos' non-citizen status is a contributing factor here. One of the summarizing observations from table 6.8 is that Latinos, education, and their participation in the area are quite notable. The concomitant arena that has not been pursued systematically is Latino participation in local affairs. Most of the polling and opinion data has focused on their partic-ipation at the national level, especially federal elections.

Our discussion of Latino political participation portrays a population that is less active than their non-Latino counterparts. At the same time, the LNPS provides us with a more detailed view of variation between Latino subgroups. The earlier discussion of community emphasized the coexistence of com-monalty and diversity. That is, commonalties of culture and interests con-nect the various Latino subgroups, while at the same time each has unique experiences and situations.

CONTRIBUTORS TO LATINO POLITICAL PARTICIPATION

The preceding discussion of political participation outlined essential factors that affect a person's propensity and level of political activity: individuals or groups of persons trying to influence the policy-making proccss. In the polit-ical arena, political resources are critical for active involvement. The primary contributing factors are time, money, communication and organizational skills, and participatory orientations. For the most part, Latinos have been characterized as less politically involved than other segments of the Ameri-can body politic.

Research results reinforce that overall assessment, yet it is not univer-sally the case. Clearly the demographic profile of Latinos provides a mixture of liabilities and potential. Liabilities include a youthful population, a signif-icant proportion of the community that is foreign-born, relatively lower lev-els of education attainment, greater proportion of non-English or limited Eng-lish speakers, lower rates of organizational affiliation and involvement, lower income attainment levels and higher rates of poverty, and low rates of natu-ralization. The assets could include a rapidly growing population that will also increase its proportion of the adult population, population concentra-tions in large, populous states and metropolitan areas, and slowly improving socioeconomic status.

The liabilities are generated by limitations on political resources that come with youthful, lower socioeconomic status, and significantly immi-grant-based groups. The youthfulness of Latinos tends to be negatively asso-ciated with high rates of political participation. Younger persons are less ori-ented to organizational and community involvement as well as less interested in politics. The relatively lower levels of education and income afford Latinos fewer opportunities and resources of time, knowledge, infor-mation, and money to get involved. The significant proportion of foreign-born Latinos presents a number of potential liabilities. For one, the legal status of "resident alien"[6] places limitations on the electoral arena because permanent resident aliens cannot register or vote. Naturalization requirements, as well as continued connections to their mother country, keep naturalization rates lower than the overall average for all immigrants. In addition, some research (J. A. García 1981; Desipio and de la Garza 1998) indicates that levels of political integration and political involvement and knowledge are lower for immigrant populations. Similarly, they have lower rates of organization affiliation and participation.

The assets related to this Latino profile are manifold. The continued high growth of this community creates a substantial political base from which to mobilize and exercise political influence. In addition, the concentration of Latinos in nine states (over 90 percent of all Latinos are found there)[7] puts them in highly urban and more populous states. Recently Latinos began to transform this population potential to political activity in California. Several ballot propositions (Prop. 187, 211, 209)[8] heightened Latino interest and involvement in elections. As the "targets" (if not exclusively) of the propositions, Latinos were responded by mobilizing in Latino areas and seeking involvement by Latino organizations.

The past two elections in California saw a rise in the number of Latino elected officials in the state legislature and a Latino lieutenant governor. I cite this example as an illustration of the conversion of the Latino political base through external catalysts. The other asset area is the slowly expanding Latino middle class. Although there are disparities between Latino and non-Latino households and individuals, the percentages of Latinos earning over $40,000 per year has increased by 71.9 percent between 1979 and 1999, as well as the numbers of high school graduates and college students. Latinos must accumulate socioeconomic resources as we move to the next millennium to ensure increased political participation and effective mobilization.

CONCLUSION

In this chapter, I laid out the basis for political participation in America and how the Latino community conforms or does not conform to those patterns. For the past twenty-five years, that characterization has been one of limited and/or marginal participation. At the same time, the social science knowledge base has existed for only thirty years, and the primary focus has been the Mexican-origin community. It is only since the 1990s that information about Latino political participation has been published and researched. We know a little about the patterns of involvement for the other Latino subgroups, primarily Puerto Ricans and Cubans. Social science knowledge about Central and South Americans is virtually nonexistent.

Part of the nature of trying to understand Latinos and their politics is the dynamic and changing situations and developments that are ongoing.

In the next chapter, we will examine the electoral area to explore further Latino political participation. We will look at past and present voting registration and turnout patterns, partisan and candidate choices, partisan affiliation and ideology, and the development and role of Latino organizations.

NOTES

1. The principle of "the rules of the game" entails the requisites for political involvement (citizen or permanent resident alien), knowledge about the political system, registered status, knowing access points to the political system, information about procedures and decision making, and so on.

2. The specific nonpolitical job skills asked in the Verba et al. study are as follows: writing a letter, attending a meeting and participating in making a decision, planning or chairing a meeting, and giving a presentation or speech.

3. The organizational skills items used in the Verba et al. survey included the following: serving as an officer of a club or organization, serving on a committee for a local organization, making a speech, and attending a public meeting on local or school affairs.

4. The components of the additive participation scale are as follows: voting in the 1988 national election; working as a volunteer for a candidate running for office; making a contribution to an individual candidate, party, or political action group; contacting governmental officials; taking part in a protest, march, or demonstration; working informally with others in the community to deal with some community issue and problem; serving in a voluntary capacity on any local governmental board or council; and being a member of or giving money to a political organization.

5. The Latino National Political Survey was designed as a national probability survey; persons of Mexican, Puerto Rican, and Cuban origin residing in the U.S. had a chance to be selected for this survey. These three groups represent the three largest Latino subgroups (approximately four-fifths of all Latinos). The sample design ensures a higher selection ratio for Cubans and Puerto Ricans to acquire greater numbers of respondents for inter-group comparisons and analysis. The LNPS was conducted in 1989–1990, and a total of 2,814 Latinos were interviewed in a face-to-face interview.

6. Foreign-born living in the United States can be permanent resident aliens, can hold a temporary visa as a student or businessperson, or can be undocumented persons. The latter category includes individuals who come into this country illegally without formally petitioning the Immigration and Naturalization Service. Other terms are used to describe this segment of the population. Some wish to label the "undocumented" in more pejorative terms. For this reason, I place the term "illegal alien" in quotation marks.

7. The nine states with the most Latinos are California, Texas, New York, Florida, New Jersey, Arizona, New Mexico, Illinois, and Massachusetts (in descending order of population size).

8. The following propositions were state initiatives to enact policy in areas that directly impacted Latinos and made them the subject of targeted blame and/or perpetrators of the problem area. Proposition 187 would limit access to social services (medical, welfare) and public education to undocumented populations in California. Proposition 207 would remove state affirmative action provisions for employment and higher education in California. Finally, Proposition 209 would end bilingual programs as currently constituted in California and create transitional immersion programs for a one-year period.

7

Latinos in the Electoral Arena

Su voto es su voz. Ya conozco este llamado desde mucho antes del comienzo de este siglo. Las decisiones, los candidatos, los temas, los derechos, las campañas y hasta adquirir más atencíon. ¿Y qué hago? ¿Con quién consulto, y sobre que? Ya basta. Me tengo que mover tengo que actuar.

Your vote is your voice. I know that call from long before the beginning of this century. Decisions, candidates, issues, rights, and campaigns—they all require attention. And what do I do? With whom do I consult and about what? Enough! I have to get going and act.

Our preceding examination of **political participation** among Latinos noted two major themes: (1) a pattern of generally lower rates of political participation (although in the past five to eight years, it has improved significantly) among Latinos in most arenas[1] of political involvement; (2) the first evidence was driven largely by research on the Mexican-origin populations of the Southwest. It was only through the Latino National Political Survey that a more detailed participation picture became available regarding the broader Latino political communities. At the same time, the richness of the LNPS (both its sample size and significant numbers of Mexican-origin, Puerto Ricans, and Cubans) does not provide information on the full array of all Latino subgroups, especially the "other Latinos" who now represent over 20 percent of Latinos. As a matter of fact, this segment of the Latino community has the highest rates of population grown. Thus discussion of political participation at this time is limited primarily to the three major Latino subgroups.

Social science research results, governmental reports, polls, and journalistic accounts give us a contemporary portrayal of Latinos in the electoral arena. The electoral arena—candidates, campaigns, fund-raising, issues, partisanship, and elections—usually receives the main focus of attention when individuals think or talk about politics. Popular notions of political involvement tend to

Dennis Chávez (1888–1962)

Dennis Chávez was the first Hispanic American Democrat ever elected to the U.S. Senate from New Mexico; he served from 1935 to 1962. Prior to his election, he was a member of the U.S. House of Representatives, where he had spent four years. Chávez began his political career with the help of Senator Andrieus A. Jones from New Mexico. Chavez served as a clerk in the office of the secretary of the Senate. Concurrently, he pursued a law degree at Georgetown University. After receiving the degree and passing the bar, he went back to New Mexico and began practicing law. His first stop on the way to becoming a U.S. senator was the New Mexico House of Representatives, where he served for one term.

Bibliography

Keleher, William A. *Memoirs: 1892–1969, A New Mexico Item.* Santa Fe, N.M.: Rydal, 1969.
Perrigo, Lynn I. *Hispanos: Historic Leaders in New Mexico.* Santa Fe, N.M.: Sunstone, 1985.

describe Latinos as less active in the electoral arena than other groups in the United States. Lower voter registration and lower voter turnout rates characterize their less-than-active role. A major contributing factor to this historic pattern lies with the significant segment of the Latino population that is foreign-born and non-citizens. In addition, data cited in the previous chapter indicates that Latinos participate less in campaigns and tend to donate less money to campaigns. Overall, the discussion of Latinos in the electoral arena has concentrated on their potential to play a significant role in electoral outcomes rather than determine who gets elected. In this chapter, we will examine the electoral participation of Latinos focusing on emerging patterns that deviate from general notions of limited Latino electoral participation.

SETTING THE ELECTORAL SCENARIO

A major interest regarding Latinos and elections lies in their electoral impact on national elections, especially when there are competitive presidential races. The 2000 presidential election was the closest in history. The impact of that election will be highlighted later in this chapter. For the most part, close presidential races since 1960 have been fairly infrequent, with the Kennedy-Nixon race (1960) being the closest one prior to 2000. Thus I will focus this discussion of Latino electoral participation on the national level. How have Latinos been important in overall electoral situations? Are there certain conditions or circumstances in which their role is pivotal in national outcomes? Another important aspect of Latinos and elections is the extent of bloc voting among Latinos for candidates and political parties. Effective Latino bloc voting has been seen as motivating Latinos to vote in "unison" for the same candidates and political party to provide the candidate/political party with a winning margin. The third aspect of an effective Latino voting strategy is converting its large population base into a sizable registered and voting electorate. Continued population growth among Latinos and its potential significance politically, economically, and culturally hinges on conversion into a stronger voting force. This remains a high priority for Latino organizations and leadership. Finally, the salience and coherence of identifiable policies and issues motivate Latinos to vote as well as become important constituencies for political parties and candidates. We will focus on this constellation of critical factors as we examine in greater detail the patterns and dynamics of Latino electoral participation. Yet the universe of Latino political participation does not revolve exclusively around national elections and voting. An old axiom about politics is that all politics are local. In many respects, the proximity of local concerns and issues has initiated significant **mobilization** of Latino communities with carry over effects for other local and/or state and national issues and movement. To some degree, the governmental level that has jurisdiction over the issues will receive the Latino response.

LATINOS AS A CRITICAL DETERMINANT OF ELECTION OUTCOMES

While much attention was directed to the 2000 presidential election, the closeness of the outcome as well as the circumstances of the final decision caused much speculation as to what factors and/or voters influenced the outcomes. To some degree, with such close voting totals in many states, different voting blocs (the "religious right," labor, Latinos, African Americans, etc.) would indicate that their votes made the difference. Yet some forty years previously the Kennedy-Nixon presidential race was also a tightly contested election. Perhaps in a prophetic manner, the League of United Latin American Citizens generated a white paper regarding the 1960 presidential election. The policy paper outlines a scenario in which the concentration of Latinos in Illinois, Texas, California, and New York could affect the outcome of the 1960 election. The basic premise revolved around Latino bloc voting, moderate turnout levels, and Democratic candidates as the primary benefactor of the Latino vote. If the election was close, then the states with significant numbers of Electoral College votes would determine the final outcome. States with a large number of electoral votes and Latino concentrations were key ingredients in the LULAC white paper. The Kennedy-Nixon race produced one of the closest votes in American presidential history. Analysis of the Texas returns indicated that the Latino vote (primarily Mexican American) was a critical factor in John Kennedy's victory. Since that white paper, the "critical swing vote" thesis has been a major theme in discussions of Latino electoral participation at the national level.

The LULAC white paper of the 1960s identifies some basic assumptions about Latinos (in 1960, the primary reference was to Mexican Americans, while now the scope includes a broader range of Latino subgroups). Yet the arguments mirror the base arguments used to examine the contemporary status of Latino electoral politics. The decades of the 1980s and even the 1990s were portrayed as an era of great expectations (J. A. García 1986) in which Latinos would have a significant impact on American politics and the national economy. The notion of potentiality and near conversion has persisted since the early 1960s. Captions such as "Sleeping Giant," "Invisible Minority" and "Their Time in the Sun" were illustrative of this theme. There has been some debate among researchers (de la Garza and DeSipio 1993; de la Garza and Desipio 1996; Falcón 1992; Rodríquez 1998) about the potency of Latino politics. The debate centers on whether the Latino electorate has finally become a more active electorate or is still a potential force. Those who argue the potentiality point to the still large gap between Latino voter registration and turnout and that of non-Hispanics. In addition, the youthfulness of Latinos (over two-fifths are under eighteen years old) as well as the large proportion of foreign-born non-citizens explains the unrealized potential.

Proponents of a truly active Latino electorate will point to the rise of Latino elected officials at both the federal and state/local level. In California alone, Latinos now hold 762 elective offices, 20 percent of assembly and senate positions, and six members of the state's congressional delegation (Verdin 2000). The year of the Latino voter was declared in 2000 as they became 8 percent of the national electorate (a 60 percent increase from 1996) and were openly courted by the major political parties and presidential candidates (Milbank 2000). Newspapers such as the *Dallas Morning News* and news services such as the Associated Press and CNN identified the Latino community as a critical voting bloc, a deciding factor, and the "soccer moms of 2000." In addition, changes in voter registration and turnout, as well as increased naturalization among foreign-born Latinos, indicate a more active Latino electorate.

The themes of Latinos as a potential electoral force or as active electoral participants appear to have coexisted into the 1990s and into the current millennium. There is evidence that Latino electoral activism is on the rise, especially in California. For example, the Tomas Rivera Center reported that there are now 7.7 million registered Latino voters. In addition, the number of Latinos voting increased from 2.5 million in 1980 to 5.7 million in 2000. Concrete indicators include (1) the growing Latino percentage of the state electorate;

(2) increases in registration levels and voter turnout (both absolute and relative);[2] (3) increases in the number of Latino candidates as well as greater numbers elected to office; and (4) greater Latino awareness about elections and campaigns, as well as greater Latino organizational involvement in the elections.

In states like Arizona and New York, gains in the above-mentioned areas have not been as evident. For example, an examination of the voting-age population in the United States and Arizona from 1994 to 1998 shows substantial population gains but virtually no gains in the number of voters. The national voting-age population increased from 177.2 million to 183.5 million over the four-year period. At the same time, the number of voters declined from 85.7 million to 83.8 million. In the case of Latinos in Arizona, their voting-age population grew from 382,000 to 496,000, yet the number of Latino voters decreased from 122,000 to 120,000. In some respect by Latinos holding steady and the non-Latino electorate declining, their electoral strength can have an unexpected boost. The challenge remains for Latinos to convert even further their growing populations into a larger and more effective electoral base.

Box 7.1   Latinos and the 2000 Elections

The 2000 presidential and other federal and state elections were filled with many firsts and an unusual series of events. Closely contested elections and uncertain results filled the news reporting on election night coverage. Obviously the determination of the presidential outcome (*Gore v. Bush* 2000) marked a first as the Supreme Court ruling on Florida's vote count made the determination in which George W. Bush was elected president. Subsequently, a plethora of factors have been identified as contributing to the eventual outcome. One dimension of election 2000 was the role of the Latino community. Extensive campaigning, money spent on targeted Latino campaign advertising, candidates making direct appeals and integrating Spanish phrases in campaign presentations, active voter registration and education campaigns, and media speculation of the pivotal role that Latino voters had on the election outcome were indicators of their impact on election 2000. To some degree, the 1960 LULAC white paper scenario portrayed some visible elements that were present in the 2000 elections.

The Latino impact on election 2000 includes the following elements: (1) the Latino electorate increased in size as a proportion of the electorate; (2) candidates Bush and Gore campaigned in key states with significant Latino populations and appeared before Latino organizations and Latino-based causes (Gore shows support for the janitor strike in Los Angeles); (3) the media characterizes Latino voters as the "soccer moms" of 2000 and as a crucial voting bloc in a predicted close election (Milbank 2000); (4) Bush strategists calculated a 30–50 percent Latino vote would boost his overall national edge by 1.6 percent; and (5) the key Electoral College states with Latino presence extended beyond the Southwest region, Florida, Illinois, and New York to include New Jersey, Michigan, Wisconsin, and Ohio.

Both major political parties and the presidential candidates actively sought the Latino vote. The Democratic Party reinforces the Democratic "tradition" among most Latinos and emphasizes its policy record on education, immigration, and economic reforms; the Republican Party outreach emphasized Republican principles of hard work, self-reliance, patriotism, and a "caring conservatism" as the basis for their support. Selectively, both candidates made appearances or opted to "skip" gatherings of Latino organization conventions (National Council of La Raza, LULAC, National Hispanic Women's conference, etc.). Both Gore and Bush attempted to either expand or cultivate their Spanish-speaking capabilities by taking Spanish lessons and incorporating Spanish into their speeches.

Exit poll results (CNN Election 2000) indicated that Latinos supported Albert Gore overall—65 percent—to 35 percent for George W. Bush. Latinos represented 7 percent of the electorate. Other than African Americans, Latinos were the largest ethnic voting bloc for Gore and Lieberman. There were some variations among the Latino vote by state. In California, Latino voters supported Gore by a 68 percent to 29 percent margin (14 percent of the electorate); in Texas, a majority of Latinos (54 percent) voted for Gore, but Bush received 43 percent of the Latino vote. In Florida, Bush and Gore divided the Latino vote with 49 percent each. Partisan competitiveness among Latinos in Florida has been evident since 1996. While Cubans are the dominant Latino subgroup in the state, they are now less than 50 percent and the influx of other Latinos could be altering voter patterns. In New York, 80 percent of Latino voters supported Al Gore compared to 18 percent for Bush. Finally in the states of New Jersey, Colorado, and New Jersey the percentage of Latino voters for Gore were 58 percent, 68 percent and 66 percent respectively. While George W. Bush received the second highest percentage of Latino voters (Ronald Reagan in 1984 received approximately 40 percent), the nature of presidential elections, partisan support, and shifts do not, at this time, indicate a major Latino partisan shift from the Democratic Party. Voters' choices for president and their partisan affiliation do not always coincide, and voters cross party lines for the presidential candidates while voting along partisan lines for other offices at the state, local, and congressional levels. Finally, exit polls in Texas and California indicated that Albert Gore received 54 percent and 67 percent of the Latino vote overall; but in heavily Latino precincts, it was 73.8 percent and 81 percent respectively.

The results of the 2000 national elections did indicate continued Latino support for Democratic candidates and an increase in the number of Latinos seeking and being elected to political office. A noticeable gain was most evident among Latinas as candidates and as elected officials. Another aspect of election 2000 was the issues that were highlighted by the major candidates. While the campaigns directed attention to obtain the voting support of Latinos, the "pressing" concerns were more generic in nature. Social security solvency, access to prescription drugs for the elderly, overall educational reform, and a stronger defense occupied the major campaign themes. Absent were directed campaign themes and discussions dealing with immigration, bilingual education, **English only,** militarization of the border, and social welfare access for permanent resident aliens. There was a national issue strategy that portrayed the key issues in the most generic terms to ensure broad appeals, while in Latino group settings the major candidates used their presence to indirectly signify concern for support of the group's interests.

With the election of George W. Bush, there were expectations that significant Latino appointments would follow at the highest levels. When the newly elected President Bush was assembling his cabinet, only one Latino (Mel Martínez as HUD secretary) was appointed after Linda Chávez withdrew as the Department of Labor nominee. In comparison, two or more members of other minority communities were selected as members of the president's cabinet. The other high-level Latino appointee was Antonio González (former Texas Supreme Court justice) as chief counsel to the president.

A wide range of situations and electoral forces affected the outcome of a very close and controversial election in 2000. Did Latinos play a role in affecting the outcome of election 2000? Yes they did, along with many other voting constituencies, organizations, PACs, and various elements of the American electorate. Latinos' continued preference for the Democratic Party and geographic areas in which Republican candidates made some inroads raises the political capital for Latinos. The Democratic Party will continue to direct its attention to maintaining and expanding Latino voter support, and the Republican Party will work further to define and to operationalize its commonalities with Latino interests. Meanwhile, it is in the best interests of Latino organizations and leadership to activate further and mobilize the Latino electorate, especially building on recent gains through naturalization and higher voter registration rates. While trying to reinforce the pivotal role that Latinos can play in close elections, Latino leadership has the larger objective of demonstrating the critical role played by Latinos in most elections. Latinos constitute a real and growing voting bloc at local, state, and national levels throughout the United States.

LATINO VOTING PATTERNS AND SUBGROUP VARIATIONS

The effect of collapsing the various Latino subgroups into one general group can overstate and/or misdirect researchers, policy makers, and journalists' discussion of Latinos as primarily a singular, "unified" group. Their voting patterns are not uniformly identical, and we know little about the electoral patterns of many of the Latino subgroups. Our knowledge base of Latino electoral participation is rooted primarily in studies of the Mexican-origin community. A consequence of dealing with the Latino communities as primarily one large group is that the distinctiveness and specific history of each subgroup is muted. Nevertheless, one of the themes of this book is the extent of community and connectiveness across the various Latino subgroups. Consequently, my reporting of Latino voting patterns will reflect their aggregate totals, with the exception of data derived from the Latino National Political Survey.

LATINO VOTER REGISTRATION AND TURNOUT:
PATTERNS AND EXPLANATIONS

Voting registration and turnout patterns among Latinos are informed by critical factors. In this section we examine Latino electoral patterns as well as what changes and actions by organizations and leaders may produce different results.

Generally there are two major requisites for persons to register and vote in American elections: the age requirement and citizenship. With the passage of the Twenty-fifth Amendment, all eighteen-year-olds could vote in all elections in the United States.[3] The second major requirement is U.S. citizenship, either native-born or naturalized. On both counts, as previous demographic presentations of the Latino population demonstrate, Latinos are negatively impacted. First, the youthfulness of the Latino population (the median age of Latinos is approximately ten years younger than the general population) significantly erodes the overall Latino population base. Second, with about 40 percent of the Latinos being foreign-born and having lower naturalization rates (J. A. García 1982; Pachón and Desipio 1994), the translation of a Latino voting base is made even more difficult. The first problem will "take care of itself, partially." Over time, a greater proportion of the Latino community will attain voting age. The subsequent challenge will be mobilizing younger Latinos to get involved in the electoral arena, with voter registration being the first step (Wolfinger and Rosenstone 1980; Milbrath and Hoel 1977).

Naturalization rates among Latino immigrants need to be increased. (Immigration and Latinos will be addressed in more detail in the chapter on the political world of Latino immigrants and immigration policy.) The 1990s saw rising Latino naturalization rates, especially for Mexican immigrants. For the most part, incentives to convince Latinos to become citizens have not been sufficient (acquiring voting status, attaining access to government employment, American patriotism, etc.) to alter the naturalization rate. As we will see in the public policy chapter, external factors such as anti-immigrant attitudes and referenda directed toward limited access and participation of Latinos and immigrants have played a major role in motivating Latinos to become electorally involved. The proximity of one's homeland is also a factor in choosing to become a citizen or not. Next we will consider in greater detail the factors that influence permanent resident aliens (i.e., individuals who have sought and have been approved for legal residence by the Immigration and Naturalization Service) to pursue or not pursue citizenship.

The **Voting Rights Act** of 1965 included a provision that mandated the reporting of registration and voting data for presidential and congressional elections by race, Hispanic origin, and gender; thus we have access to this information. These figures represent *national* registration and voting rates, and they do not differentiate among the different Latino subgroups.

Table 7.1 provides us with a longitudinal record of registration of Americans for the presidential elections since 1968. Overall, there has been a decline of voter registrants. The gender gap for male/female registration has disappeared over the past thirty years, and now women have higher electoral rates. The differential between Hispanics and non-Hispanics is substantial. If you compare Hispanic registration with that of Anglo registrants, there is a consistent thirty-point difference. The gap does not change over this roughly thirty-year period.

Recalling that there is a smaller electoral base for Latinos due to their youthfulness and higher percentage of foreign-born, the percentages of registered voters are based on the voting-age population for each group. This population base does not exclude non-citizens (over eighteen years of age), which partially explains the substantial gap. Yet the persistent lower levels of registered status present the challenge of converting potential electoral "muscle" into a stronger force. If we remove the non-eligible Latinos (i.e., non-citizens), the gap is closed by half. Similarly, if we compare the percentage vote based on the registered voters only, then the gap is 10–12 percent between Latinos and non-Latino whites. We will now examine the Latino turnout (or voting) rates over the same period of presidential elections derived from the Census Bureau.

Again the figures for American voter turnout exhibit a continuing voter decline since the 1960s (see table 7.2). The 1996 election marked the lowest presidential turnout in the latter part of this century. That decline in voter turnout cuts across all racial and Hispanic-origin groups and all age groupings. The figures for Latino voters are significantly lower than for any other grouping. They are lower than the 18–24 year group, which usually includes those least likely to vote.

Again, the low percentage of Latinos voting is partially attributed to the inclusion of all Latino adults, including non-citizens, except for the 2000

Table 7.1 Reported Registration by Race, Gender, and Age: U.S. Presidential Elections, 1968–2000 (percentage)

	2000	1996	1992	1988	1984	1980	1976	1972	1968
Total voting age (in 1000s)[a]	202,609	193,651	185,684	178,098	169,963	157,085	146,548	136,203	116,535
Overall registered	69.5	65.9	68.2	66.6	68.3	66.9	66.7	72.3	74.3
Race									
White	71.6	67.7	70.1	67.9	69.6	68.4	68.3	73.4	75.4
Black	67.5	63.5	63.9	64.5	66.3	60.0	58.5	65.5	66.2
Hispanic origin[b]	57.3	35.7	35.0	35.5	40.1	36.3	37.8	44.4	NA
Gender									
Male	68.0	64.4	66.9	65.2	67.3	66.6	67.1	73.1	76.0
Female	70.9	67.3	69.3	67.8	69.3	67.1	66.4	71.6	72.4
Age-group									
18–24	50.7	48.8	52.5	48.2	51.3	49.2	51.3	58.9	56.0[c]
25–44	63.3	61.9	64.8	63.0	66.6	65.6	65.5	71.3	72.4
45–64	75.4	73.5	75.3	75.5	76.6	75.8	75.5	79.7	81.1
65+	78.4	77.0	78.0	78.4	76.9	74.6	71.4	75.6	75.6

Source: Current Population Report Series P20, nos. 192, 253, 322, 370, 405, 440, 466, 542; November 1996 Current Population Survey.
[a]Civilian, noninstitutional population.
[b]Hispanics may be of any race.
[c]Prior to 1972 data for people 21–24 years of age with the exception of those 18–24 in Georgia and Kentucky, 19–24 in Alaska, and 20–24 in Hawaii.

Table 7.2 Reported Voting by Race, Gender, and Age: U.S. Presidential Elections, 1968–2000 (percentage)

	2000	1996	1992	1988	1984	1980	1976	1972	1968
Total voting age (in 1000s)[a]	202,609	193,651	185,684	178,098	169,963	157,085	146,548	136,203	116,535
Voted	59.5	54.2	61.3	57.4	59.9	59.2	59.2	63.0	67.8
Race									
White	61.8	56.0	63.6	59.1	61.4	60.9	60.9	64.5	69.1
Black	56.8	50.6	54.0	51.5	55.8	50.5	48.7	52.1	57.6
Hispanic origin[b]	45.1	26.7	28.9	28.8	32.6	29.9	31.8	37.5	NA
Gender									
Male	58.1	52.8	60.2	56.4	59.0	59.1	59.6	64.1	69.8
Female	60.7	55.5	62.3	58.3	60.8	59.4	58.8	62.0	66.0
Age									
18–24	36.1	32.4	42.8	36.2	40.8	39.9	42.2	49.6	50.4[c]
25–44	56.1	49.2	58.3	54.0	58.4	58.7	58.7	62.7	66.6
45–64	67.8	64.4	70.0	67.9	69.8	69.3	68.7	70.8	74.9
65+	69.6	67.0	70.1	68.8	67.7	65.1	62.2	63.5	65.8

Source: Current Population Report Series P20, nos. 192, 253, 322, 370, 405, 440, 466, 542; November 1996 Current Population Survey.
[a]Civilian, noninstitutional population.
[b]Hispanics may be of any race.
[c]Prior to 1972 data for people 21–24 years of age with the exception of those 18–24 in Georgia and Kentucky, 19–24 in Alaska, and 20–24 in Hawaii.

Current Population Report. Nevertheless, the percentages of Latinos who are both registered and voting remains much lower than the other groups and significant gains do not seem visible over this period. If we take into account the high population growth rate among Latinos, even unchanged registration and turnout rates can have an impact. For example, Latinos in California have increased in population by 42.6 percent since 1990. Their growth rate is five times that of the non-Hispanic population. Even though their registration and voter turnout rate have not changed appreciably, their proportion of the electorate has increased by "natural growth." In 1990 Latinos were 7 percent of the state's electorate and 2 percent in 1996.

These kinds of gains can enhance the Latino electoral base but represent slow process toward greater electoral empowerment. Dramatic gains can be accomplished by adding more native-born Latinos who are not currently registered. These additions can enhance Latinos' gains with a relatively "constant" or declining registration and turnout levels for all voters. As a result, the percentage of Latinos both registered and voting should increase, since all other groups are voting and registering at lower levels.

CRITICAL FACTORS AFFECTING LATINOS' ELECTORAL PARTICIPATION

What other factors affect the level of Latino electoral involvement? The possibilities can be discussed based on two different data sources: (1) the Current Population Series for the Voting Rights provisions and (2) the extant social science research literature on voting and elections. After the November 1998 elections, the Current Population Survey included a battery of items among voting-age respondents and asked their reasons for not voting in the election. Overall, of the 21.3 million people who reported they were registered but did not vote in 1998, more than one in five reported they could not take the time off from work or school or because they were too busy (see table 7.3). Another 17 percent did not vote because they were not interested or did not care about elections and politics. This predisposition is often associated with political cynicism, apathy, and inefficacy (García 1998; Desipio 1996). If you compare these responses with those of nonvoters in 1980, almost three times as many (7.6 percent in 1980 versus 21.5 percent in 1998) indicated no time or too busy to vote. Finally, the other noteworthy reasons given by nonvoters in 1998 were: being ill or disabled (15 percent); not preferring any of the candidates (13 percent); being out of town (11 percent); forgetting to vote or having no way to get to the polls (4 percent each); and the lines were too long (1 percent).

Therefore, the decline in voter turnout seems to be centered on voter apathy, disinterest, and some degree of cynicism. If we look at Hispanic nonvoters, their responses do not differ substantially from the responses of other nonvoters. One-fifth were too busy or had no time off, while another one-

Table 7.3 Reported Reasons for Not Voting among Those Who Reported Registering but Not Voting by Race, Gender, and Age, November 1998 (percentage)

	Number (1000s)	Total	No Transportation	No Time Off/ Too Busy	Out of Town	Ill/Disabled/ Emergency	Didn't Like Candidates	Not Interested	Other Reasons[a]
United States, total	40,006	100.0	1.8	34.9	8.3	11.1	5.5	12.7	10.2
Race									
White, non-Hispanic	31,442	100.0	1.5	34.6	8.3	11.2	6.0	13.3	17.9
Black, non-Hispanic	4,729	100.0	7.5	32.1	4.9	12.8	3.5	10.2	20.5
Hispanic	1,090	100.0	2.3	39.3	5.8	8.2	4.1	10.8	22.3
Asian and Pacific Islander	728	100.0	0.6	48.8	6.8	7.5	2.4	10.2	15.9
Gender									
Male	18,267	100.0	1.0	37.4	10.3	7.3	5.5	13.3	16.5
Female	21,739	100.0	2.6	32.7	6.7	14.3	5.5	12.2	20.2
Age									
18–24	5,763	100.0	1.2	38.6	9.8	2.6	3.0	9.8	21.3
25–44	19,014	100.0	1.3	43.3	6.5	5.7	5.1	13.0	18.8
45–64	10,103	100.0	1.5	30.9	10.1	11.3	7.5	14.0	19.3
65+	5,126	100.0	5.3	7.4	10.1	40.2	5.8	12.2	15.2

Source: Jennifer Day and Avalaura Gaither, *Voting and Registration in the Election of November 1998*, 2000 Current Population Reports, P20-523RV (Washington, D.C.: U.S. Bureau of the Census).

[a]The other reason category includes forgetting, long lines, registration problems, other reasons. The "don't know" or refused responses are not reported in this table, so the row total is less than 100 percent.

seventh (14.4 percent) were not interested in the elections. Hispanics were about 50 percent (13.0 percent versus 9.4 percent) less likely to not vote because they disliked the candidates. Overall, Hispanic nonvoters seem to parallel the same reasons that all other non-voters cite.

The 2000 CPS voting and registration report (Jamieson, Shin, and Day 2002) also provided reasons for not voting (for all nonvoters), and too busy (20.9 percent) was the most prevalent response. It was followed by illness or emergency (14.8 percent), not interested (12.2 percent), out of town (10.2 percent), and not liking the candidates (7.7 percent). Men, younger adults (18–44 years), Latinos, and the more educated were likely to report they were too busy (Jamieson et al. 2002).

SOCIOECONOMIC STATUS, RESOURCES, AND VOTING

The existing research literature offers other insights and findings to explain voting and nonvoting. In many cases, when research examines the electoral arena, the question of who votes is answered in terms of important sociodemographic characteristics, psychological orientations, and situational and **structural factors** associated with the individual. The socioeconomic model (Verba and Nie 1972; Wolfinger and Rosenstone 1980) identifies educational attainment, income, and occupational status as the key factors that differentiate voters from nonvoters. Persons with higher levels of educational attainment, higher levels of income, and higher occupational status (professionals, entrepreneurs, etc.) are much more likely to vote than individuals with less **human capital.**[4] The concept of human capital is found in the economics and political science literature. The idea is that as individuals invest in their human resource "portfolio" with more education, greater training, more experience and are strongly motivated, they are advantaged with greater returns in the job market via earnings. The acquisition of greater human resources is advantageous economically. In a sense the idea of human capital can be thought of as political capital: individuals with greater skills, knowledge, and interest in the political process can be more effective in their actions (Putnam 2000).

Acquiring these resources will inform the person with relevant political information and a better understanding of the political process. With higher levels of educational attainment, the person not only has pertinent knowledge but communication and organizational skills and social status, which serve as beneficial assets for electoral participation. Similarly, higher levels of income afford an individual the economic resources to get involved in electoral activities and contribute to campaigns. Possessing a high-status job and money does enhance a person's available time and ability to see the direct benefits of political involvement.

The other key demographic characteristics are age and gender. In the case of the former, researchers use the idea of a life cycle. As a person becomes more "settled" in her work and household, she has a more direct stake in what happens politically. An older person is likely to be a home-owner, situated in a higher tax bracket, have children in school, and so on, which motivates him to be more aware of public policy and policy impacts. In table 7.3, the voting participation by age certainly reflects the life cycle postion.

Until the early part of this decade, much attention and discussion was directed toward the idea of a gender gap. With women historically excluded from the political process, there were noticeable differences between women's and men's political participation. The idea of politics being a man's game was reinforced by relative absence of women as political and organizational leaders, as active voters and campaign contributors, and partisan activists. The gender gap was highlighted in the electoral arena as fewer women were registered than men and voted less. As we saw in tables 7.1 and 7.2, the gender gap has closed electorally and the voting gap no longer exists. Our discussion of the role of sociodemographic factors on voting has application to other forms of political involvement. We will explore other aspects of political involvement, specifically organizational involvement and local community activities, in chapter 8.

The other contributing factors influencing who votes or not includes psychological orientations, situational factors, and structural factors. The political orientations of efficacy, trust, and interest generate greater awareness and motivation to get involved in the political process and public policies. The sense of political and personal efficacy empowers an individual to get involved and feel that he can make a difference. Researchers like Verba and Nie (1972) and Rosenstone and Hansen (1993) point to socialization experiences as major factors in the development of these participatory attitudes, with family and schools being the primary agents.

The structural factors have to do with the rules of the games and how political institutions function, especially focusing on access, an individual's or group's legal standing, rights and protections, and the formal requirements for participation. Such practices as the poll tax, the white primary, literacy tests, limited registration locations, as well as economic and physical intimidation (Grofman et al. 1992) serve as examples of structural impediments for racial, ethnic, gender, and social classes in the United States. The Civil Rights Act of 1964 and the Voting Rights Act of 1965 were intended to remove and eliminate some of these structural barriers. The situational factors revolve around salient issues, controversies, charismatic candidates, and the like, which stir interest in specific elections, office races, and propositions. Measures such as **Proposition 187** (limiting immigrants' access to social services and education) or **Proposition 227** (ending bilingual educa-

Ileana Ros-Lehtinen (1952–)

The first Hispanic woman, and also the first Cuban American, to be elected to the United States Congress, Ileana Ros-Lehtinen used this position to become one of the strongest and most visible spokespersons against Cuban leader Fidel Castro. She has been described frequently as "the darling of the Cuban community."

The daughter of an accountant, Ileana Ros was born in Havana, Cuba, on July 15, 1952. When she was seven years old, Cuba's right-wing military dictatorship was overthrown by Fidel Castro. His government became openly communist, and the next year, 1960, her family fled to Miami, where Ros went to school and college. She received an A.A. degree from Miami Dade County Community College in 1972, a B.A. from Florida International University in 1975, and an M.S. in education from the same school in 1987. Ros continued her studies of education at the doctoral level at the University of Miami.

In 1982 Ros, a Republican, was elected to the Florida legislature; she was a representative until 1986 and a state senator from that year until 1989. She married her fellow legislator and later U.S. attorney Dexter Lehtinen, in Miami, and adopted the name Ros-Lehtinen.

She ran for the U.S. House of Representatives in 1989 to fill the vacancy left by the death of the incumbent congressman. No Cuban American had ever been elected to Congress, nor had any Latina of any national ancestry. Dade County, her district, had not sent a woman to Congress in a half century. Although President George H.W. Bush helped in her campaign, the election was decided mainly along ethnic lines. Ros-Lehtinen's Democratic opponent was Jewish, and the race proved highly divisive for the area, which was at the time almost precisely 50 percent Hispanic.

tion) in California serve as situational factors to stimulate Latino voters' interest and involvement.

STATEWIDE PROPOSITIONS AS MOBILIZING FACTORS

The recent set of statewide propositions in California, beginning with Proposition 187 (limiting immigrants access to health and social welfare services), were couched in terms of the negative impacts of undocumented and legal immigrants. The issue framing this proposition targeted prima-

When she obtained 53 percent of the vote and her victory was announced, singer Celia Cruz, who had strongly backed her, expressed it this way: *"¡Los cubanos han ganado!"* ("The Cubans have won!") However, Ros-Lehtinen quickly showed a capacity to heal campaign wounds and to expand her following. She had to face reelection the following year, and this time she won with 60 percent of the vote.

In Washington, Ros-Lehtinen used membership on the House Foreign Affairs Committee to further her struggle to secure democracy in Cuba. She has ties to the main hard-line anti-Castro organization in the United States, the Cuban American National Foundation (CANF), founded by Jorge Mas Canosa. In particular, in 1995 Ros-Lehtinen was one of the country's most vocal critics of President Bill Clinton's Cuban policies, which were designed to avoid more waves of Cuban refugees reaching the United States. Their effect, she said, was to relax U.S. pressure at a time when it should have been tightened.

In 2000, during the struggle between the United States and Cuba over custody of a six-year-old boy, Elian Gonzalez, Ros-Lehtinen was one of a group of three legislators who offered to help Elian's father remain in the United States. The other members of Congress in the group were Lincoln Díaz-Balart and Bob Menendez.

Also in 2000, Ros-Lehtinen was reelected to the U.S. House of Representatives, where she continues to serve.

Bibliography

Nodal, Elizabeth. "Office of Congresswoman Ileana Ros-Lehtinen." Available online: www.house.gov/ros-lehtinen. Downloaded October 11, 2000.

Telgen, Diane, and Jim Kamp, eds. *Notable Hispanic American Women.* Detroit: Gale Research, 1993.

rily Mexicans and other Latinos as the sources of a range of economic and social problems in the state. These factors included designating all immigrants as a burden, characterizing the "culprits" as Latinos who negatively impact the economy, increasing social service budget expenditures and overcrowding health facilities. These kinds of targeting rhetoric stirred heightened political involvement by Latinos and Latino-based organizations. Voter registration campaigns, mass demonstrations, ad hoc organizations in opposition to Proposition 187, statements by the Mexican consul, and so on, were directly associated with the dynamics of Proposition 187.

Subsequently, in 1996 and 1998, other propositions in California were introduced raising issues about affirmative action, eliminating bilingual education in the public schools, and requiring unions to receive prior approval by its membership before making campaign contributions. These initiatives served as catalysts to increase Latino political involvement. It has been noted that when the political system has a direct impact on you, then your interest and motivation are significantly enhanced. The activated electoral involvement of Latinos in California not only had a direct impact on these initiatives but also carried over into a number of state legislative and local races. That is, the number of Latinos in the state assembly and senate increased as Cruz Bustamante was elected lieutenant governor in 2000. Finally, the stimulus of policy initiatives, particularly negatively directed toward Latinos, motivated Latino organizations and leaders to mobilize broader segments of their communities.

So far, I have outlined the major contributing factors that explain why individuals vote and participate electorally: the combination of sociodemographic (status attainment) characteristics, participatory attitudes and orientations, structural impediments, and situational factors. While the research literature has been long established in political participation, the findings for Latinos are both sparser and more recent. In addition, relatively speaking, we know much more about the electoral participation of the Mexican-origin population than any other Latino group. About Central and South Americans, we know virtually nothing. Nevertheless, it is possible to relate how well or not these identified contributing factors fit the Latino subgroups.

LATINO ELECTORAL PARTICIPATION: SOCIAL SCIENCE FINDINGS

The socioeconomic status model, which is at the heart of the electoral participation model, does not fit exactly the same for Latinos as other populations. Educational attainment makes a difference for Latinos (J. A. García 1996) in terms of being more likely to be registered and to vote regularly. As greater numbers of Latinos achieved high school graduate status and beyond, gains in Latino registration and turnout will continue. On the other hand, the strength of higher income attainment and occupational status does not have the same positive effect for Latinos that it does for non-Latinos. That is, there is no strong, explicit association for Latinos in higher income levels to be significantly more electorally active than those at lower economic levels. Similarly, Latinos in higher occupational status positions are not significantly more electorally active than Latinos in lower status occupations. Part of the possible explanation might lie with the relative concentration of Latinos in lower occupational positions and in lower income categories. The emerging Latino middle class is a recent phenomenon and its

Table 7.4   Voter Registration Status among Mexican-Origin, Puerto Ricans, and Cubans from the Latino National Political Survey

Registration Status	Mexican-origin	Puerto Rican	Cuban	Anglo
Respondent ever registered to vote				
Yes	676 (77.1%)	431 (73.7%)	256 (82.3%)	401 (90.0%)
No	201 (22.9%)	154 (26.3%)	55 (17.7%)	45 (10.0%)
Currently registered to vote (1989–1990)				
Yes	574 (65.4%)	375 (64.0%)	243 (78.0%)	347 (77.8%)
No	303 (34.6%)	211 (36.0%)	69 (22.0%)	99 (22.2%)
Total[a]	877	585	312	446

Source: R. de la Garza et al., Latino Voices: Mexican, Puerto Rican, and Cuban Perspectives on American Politics (Boulder: Westview, 1993), tab. 8.13, 8.14, pp. 122–23.
[a]The totals for the respondents in this table represent Latinos who are U.S.-born or naturalized citizens. As a result, the original numbers of respondents in the Latino National Political Survey is reduced from the total of 3,456 to 2,220.

impact electorally is a matter of speculation at this time. As more Latinos experience greater socioeconomic mobility, as well as a greater percentage of the community becomes over eighteen, then we may see stronger relationships between socioeconomic status and Latino voter registration and turnout.

Latinos tend to be less politically interested and less aware of political events and information (J. A. García 1995). Correspondingly, with lower levels of political awareness and interest, there is lower electoral involvement. On the other hand, Latinos exhibit levels of political trust (i.e., basic confidence in the fairness and evenness of governmental actions and actors) that are comparable to those of other voting segments of the population. This political orientation should reinforce people's belief in the political system and provide a motivation to exercise their vote. For Latinos, this association is a weak one, and some studies find an inverse relationship (J. A. García 1995; García and Arce 1988; Desipio 1996; Hero 1992).

This is somewhat ironic in that Latinos respond with a positive orientation toward the U.S. political system (indicating confidence in how it works) yet do not register or cast their vote in comparable degrees to non-Latinos. There is clearly a linkage problem or inconsistency in that evidence of political support for the American political system by Latinos does not translate into a more active role as a voting public. Some researchers (DeSipio 1996; F. C. Garcia 1988) have used the concept of **political incorporation** to assess the extent of involvement persons have with the political system. Individuals are politically incorporated via a socialization process that instills the core political values and beliefs of the American political system (de la Garza et al. 1996), as well as assuming various roles of a participatory "citizen." Moving beyond socioeconomic status can lead us to another series of explanations for the lower rates of political participation, especially electoral behavior.

CULTURE, NATIONAL ORIGIN, AND LATINOS

The concept of political incorporation, although focusing on how persons learn and involve themselves with the American political system, is generally directed toward newcomers to the political system (either as young persons assuming adult status or immigrants) and "marginalized" populations such as minority group members. For our purposes, political incorporation is the process by which group interests are represented in the policy-making process (Browning et al. 1990). Obviously, a central focus of this book has been the efforts of the Latino community to become a more active and effective "interest group" in the American political system. In this chapter, we have been examining indicators and factors affecting Latino electoral behavior. In addition to socioeconomic status effects, mobilization by Latino organizations and leaders, as well as situational circumstances (anti-Latino backlash, Latino "targeted" referenda, partisan outreach, etc.), contributes to the political incorporation of Latinos. The use of political incorporation also has centered on the systemic factors (discrimination, segregated institutions, exclusionary practices, etc.) that minimize or severely restrict the extent of incorporation by individuals and as group members.

A critical element of the Latino community, in terms of political incorporation, is the "immigrant" segment. Latino immigrants are exposed to a different culture (culturally, politically, and civic-wise) and require adjustment time to integrate into the American culture and mainstream. In his work on political adaptation of immigrants (1986b), García outlines a three-step process involving political incorporation (integration). The first is the adaptive process, in which adjustments are made in terms of social relations, language, societal roles, and familiarity with institutions, norms, and values. After some degree of socialization has occurred, the second step deals with integration; the development of organizations serves as the vehicle for contact with social and political institutions, informational networks, and communication. This organizational development establishes the presence of the migrant community and its interests with the host society and pursues societal responses. The last stage of incorporation is described as societal absorption in which their political and economic participation is "regularized" (or falls within the conventional realm of political involvement) and is recognized as an active group interest engaged in the American policy-making process. Thus one of the challenges for the Latino communities is the integration of the Latino "immigrant" segment into all of the other dimensions that connect Latinos (national-origin subgroups, class, regional location, varying histories in the United States, etc.).

In the case of the immigrant Mexican-origin community and other Latino immigrant subgroups, there is considerable debate about how to view Latinos. Are they a series of major waves of incoming immigrants from different political cultures, or are they part of a stream of indigenous populations? Historians like Acuña (1976, 1981, 1998), M. García (1989), and political scientist Mario Barrera et al. (1979) have analyzed the Mexican-origin experience in the Southwest as an indigenous population that was politically and economically subjugated. Since the 1970s the influx of Mexican migrants into the United States serves to augment the Mexican-origin community and start to undergo the adaptation period. As a result, this community can represent both an indigenous and a migrant population simultaneously. Analysis of other Latino immigrant subgroups (Dominicans, Puerto Ricans, Cubans, etc.) by Sasoon-Koob (1988) and Morales and Bonilla (1993) focuses on the global economy and how Latino migration is "manipulated" so that there is movement from less developed countries to more industrialized ones. The perspective suggests that an individual's migration decision is not solely determined by his desires and motivation, but also by structural conditions (especially economic opportunities or the lack of them in the country of origin). These factors serve as the backdrop to understand the Latino political incorporation process and the varied experiences that can either bridge or divide the Latino communities. Our discussion of political incorporation of Latinos' needs focuses on the adjustments and the congruence (or not) with the American political culture.

Thus the concept of political incorporation entails full and articulated political involvement and activities and how populations adjust to core American values and political practices (de la Garza et al. 1996). For Latinos, politics coalesces as a **community of interests** and a **community of common cultures.** We have numerous accounts about the political incorporation of European immigrants such as the Irish, Italians, and Jews (Fuchs 1990). Part of that discussion lies in the analysis of how cultural values and practices (self-help associations, residential clustering, closed social networks, etc.) played a central role in the adjustment to living in America. Cultural factors such as language, values, political culture of country of origin, familialism, extent of ties with mother country, presence or absence of organizational life, for example, can be key determinants for the extent of political incorporation among Latinos (Almond and Verba 1963; Wilson 1977; Esman 1995).

For Latinos, a partial explanation for their "limited" political incorporation (Desipio 1996) lies with persistence of Spanish language use, coming from more autocratic, less democratic, and elitist political systems that produce a legacy of limited participatory experiences, a sense of fatalism, lack of

Box 7.2   A Latino's Cultural and Political Realities

An El Salvadoran living in Washington, D.C., could be employed as a computer engineer with very good English language proficiency and a non-Latina spouse. At the same time, he belongs to a Salvadoran social club and lives in the Mount Pleasant area of the district; most of his friends are Salvadorans or Guatemalans. Thus acculturation entails degrees and/or areas of cultural values and practices while acquiring "American" customs and practices. The acculturation scenario leads to a pluralist model of American politics. That is, Latinos are an organized interest group to whom **ethnicity** and identity provide a primary basis for membership, resources, and issues. Whichever route is taken, the road to participation involves major adjustments and critical strategies from the Latino community to be effective in the American political system. This explanation focuses on how the individual adjusts to life in American society and makes a variety of choices. The role and impact of culture and language are the central elements from this perspective, as well as understanding how they operate in the American political system. Structural analysis offers another basis for examining and explaining levels of political participation for Latinos.

organizational experience, and cultural/linguistic isolation (Skerry 1993; Desipio and de la Garza 1998). Latinos come from non-participatory political cultures, and ethnic group cultural maintenance is seen as a deterrent for active participation in the American political system. For example, a strong sense of familialism would tend to keep Latinos (Tirado 1970; Márquez 1993) from being inclined to join secondary groups or formal organizations. As a result, primary social networks and knowledge gathering about the social and political system would come primarily from familial and other Latino members.

This discussion of political involvement shows that organizational affiliation and involvement are directly connected to heightened political participation (Verba et al. 1995; García and de la Garza 1985). Thus being a Latino can be a liability in terms of political incorporation due to lesser organizational affiliation and involvement. Cultural values and traditions can serve as obstacles to integration into the American political system and group effectiveness. At the same time, maintaining Latino identification can serve as a basis for group mobilization around particular concerns or issues. These perspectives are not mutually contradictory but represent realities that exist within the Latino community and make up part of the challenges for Latino political participation.

Proponents of these explanations can take two different routes. The first suggests that unless assimilation (Gordon 1965) takes place (i.e., political, cultural, social, associational, identificational, and marital), then Latinos will be located in a marginal position both in the society at large and as political participants. The assimilation process would involve departure from traditional cultural practices and values. It would involve becoming Americanized such that any distinctiveness as Latinos or as part of a specific Latino subgroup would be, at best, symbolic (Barrera 1988). The second route suggests that although assimilation is a necessary "precondition" for greater political involvement, the process of acculturation is a more "realistic" characterization of what happens in American society. That is, assimilation does take place yet it is not a one-way process that by necessity includes complete loss of group identity, affiliation, practices, and social networks. This latter perspective portrays the American political system in cultural and politically pluralistic terms.

SOCIAL STRUCTURES AND PARTICIPATORY ROLES

Given the adjustments that have been discussed, are Latinos assured of comparable levels of participation with non-Latinos and being effective on policy making? To construct a fuller picture of the variety of factors that can influence participatory roles, we need to introduce the role of social structures. This is the strand of participation explanations that involves structural conditions and institutional practices and customs (Barrera et al. 1972; 1979). Concepts such as equality, fairness, discrimination, institutional racism, ethnocentrism, and subordination are used to describe **power relations** between the dominant society and minority populations. This perspective examines factors other than merely individual characteristics, orientations, and behaviors that can lead to specific levels of participation. Laws that exclude persons from voting, registering, participating in political parties, and so on, serve as examples of social structures and institutional practices. As a result, Latinos are viewed as marginalized—economically, socially, and politically.

This line of analysis sees low rates of participation as purposive actions by the political system and its representatives to have minorities serve as subjects rather than active participants. In the electoral arena, restrictive policies such as poll taxes, literacy tests, limiting registration places and time, hostile polling locations, physical intimidation, and so on (J. A. García 1986a), are structural examples that have negatively affected Latinos and other minority voters. The net effect ranges from the outright prohibition of participation to the active discouragement of Latino political involvement. Similarly, political institutions such as legislatures, city councils, and school boards can operate under election systems and rules (**at-large** elections, off-year elections, nonpartisan elections, etc.) that can disadvantage Latino communities (Grofman and Davidson 1992) in terms of representation and productive participation.

The legacy of such structural conditions can be passivity, acquiescence, and/or withdrawal. To apply this perspective to Latinos, we will examine the provisions of the Voting Rights Act and its subsequent amendments, focusing on linguistic protections in the form of bilingual ballots, more facilitative registration systems, **preclearance** of election law changes prior to their implementation, and specified protective status for Latinos' civil and voting rights purposes.[5] These provisions identify some of the existing structural conditions and systematic responses that have been used to limit Latino electoral participation. The legal remedies listed represent policies to remove these obstacles.

Active civil rights leadership and organizations, in combination with a number of other social liberation movements, have applied both political and economic pressure for the removal of biased practices that inhibit political participation (Tarrow 1998; Piven and Cloward 1998, 2000). Continuous advocacy and monitoring is still required to ensure protection from structural barriers. As a result, organizations like the Mexican American Legal Defense and Education Fund (MALDEF), Puerto Rican Legal Defense and Education Fund (PRLDEF), and Southwest Voter Registration and Education Project (SVREP) serve as vigilant Latino interest groups to ensure a fair and equitable electoral system and process.

Another example in this area is the litigation efforts by the MALDEF and PRLDEF for voting rights protection. Since the 1970s, these organizations have engaged in class action litigation involving districting[6] plans and existing electoral systems (at-large election systems, multimember districts). The primary target in this litigation was at-large elections (Brischetto and de la Garza 1983; J. A. García 1986a), which made electing minority candidates very difficult. As the result of many successful class-action suits and favorable interpretation of the Voting Rights Act and its amendments, the use of district or ward elections became more of the "norm." Subsequently, when reapportionment and redistricting occurred after each decennial census,[7] these organizations reviewed and proposed district configurations that included the consideration of the racial and ethnic makeup of the area. During the 1980s and early 1990s, there have been appreciable gains in the number of Latino elected officials.

By the mid-1990s, court rulings like *Shaw v. Reno* and *Vera v. Bush* raised constitutional questions regarding "racial gerrymandering"[8] and its legal appropriateness. As a result, the Supreme Court has made it difficult to design "majority minority districts" in the future. The chapter on public policy issues goes into greater detail on voting rights legislation and Latino political empowerment. This example illustrates how a particular set of policy strategies (i.e., class action litigation) has impacted the electoral system by increasing opportunities to elect Latino representatives. At the same time, this strategy has become somewhat less effective due largely to recent court rulings and, to some degree, public sentiment and reactions to "majority minority districts." Thus Latino efforts to address structural conditions and barriers remain a dynamic and evolutionary process to further greater electoral participation and representation.

AFTERMATH OF THE 2000 ELECTIONS AND LATINO EMPOWERMENT

The closeness of the presidential election, growth of the Latino electorate, notable partisan attention directed to the Latino communities, and more Latinos seeking elected office all provide evidence for the political gains that Latinos take into the new millennium. Amid another round of elections (2002), at all levels there are important developments that Latinos can impact, as well as be impacted by. Both parties are vigorously contesting for control of both chambers of Congress; the latest round of redistricting opens more opportunities for Latino office competition; gains in naturalization and voter registration afford another chance to exercise political clout; and both political parties are continuing their targeted efforts to expand their respective Latino support. We can move this chapter along further by examining briefly some of the implications and developments of post-2000 elections.

The National Arena and the Bush Administration

As already noted, gains in political representation, increased participation, and impact on the public policy-making process have been continuous objectives for the Latino community. Following the 2000 elections, there were high expectations among Latinos for gains in presidential appointments at the cabinet and White House staff levels. At this time, only one Latino (HUD Secretary Mel Martínez) serves in the cabinet, and Antonio González serves as special counsel to the president, there have been other Latinos appointed to various sub-cabinet positions, commissions, and some judgeships. President George W. Bush initiated the first presidential radio broadcast in Spanish in 2002 as part of his (and the Republican Party's) efforts to establish closer links with the Latino community. In addition, the Republican Party initiated a weekly "news-oriented" broadcast on Spanish-language television. To some extent, the Democratic Party has sought to strengthen its support within the Latino community through policy proposals focusing on immigration reform, greater access by permanent legal residents to social welfare programs, minority small business support, health care coverage, and racial profiling. Thus the carryover from the 2000 elections of directed attention by the major political parties continues.

Box 7.3   Hispanics in the U.S. Congress

Hispanic Representative	Years Served	State	Partisan Affiliation	Congressional District
House of Representatives				
Romualdo Pacheco	1877–1878	California	Republican	4th
Ladislas Lazaro	1913–1927	Louisiana	Democrat	7th
Benigno C. Hernandez	1915–1917, 1919–1921	New Mexico	Republican	at-large
Dennis Chavez	1931–1935	New Mexico	Democrat	1st
Joachim O. Fernandez	1931–1941	Louisiana	Democrat	1st
Antonio M. Fernandez	1943–1956	New Mexico	Democrat	1st
Joseph Montoya	1957–1964	New Mexico	Democrat	1st
Henry B. González	1961–1998	Texas	Democrat	20th
Edward Roybal	1963–1993	California	Democrat	33rd
Eligio de la Garza	1965–1997	Texas	Democrat	15th
Manuel Lujan Jr.	1969–1989	New Mexico	Republican	1st
Herman Baldillo	1971–1977	New York	Democrat	21st
Robert García	1978–1990	New York	Democrat	21st
Anthony L. Coehlo	1979–1989	California	Democrat	15th
Matthew Martínez	1982–2001	California	Democrat	31st
William B. Richardson	1983–1997	New Mexico	Democrat	3rd
Solomon Ortiz	1983–	Texas	Democrat	27th
Esteban Torres	1983–1999	California	Democrat	34th
Albert G. Bustamante	1985–1993	Texas	Democrat	23rd
Ileana Ros-Lehtinen	1989–	Florida	Republican	18th
Jose E. Serrano	1990–	New York	Democrat	16th
Ed L. Pastor	1991–	Arizona	Democrat	2nd
Frank M. Tejada	1993–1997	Texas	Democrat	28th
Xavier Becerra	1993–	California	Democrat	30th
Henry Bonilla	1993–	Texas	Republican	23rd
Lincoln Díaz-Balart	1993–	Florida	Republican	21st
Robert Menendez	1993–	New Jersey	Democrat	13th
Lucille Allard-Roybal	1993–	California	Democrat	37th
Nydia M. Velasquez	1993–	New York	Democrat	12th
Luis Gutierrez	1993–	Illinois	Democrat	4th
Silvestre Reyes	1996–	Texas	Democrat	16th
Ruben Hinojosa	1997–	Texas	Democrat	15th
Ciro D. Ródriquez	1997–	Texas	Democrat	28th
Loretta Sanchez	1997–	California	Democrat	46th
Joe Baca	1999–	California	Democrat	42nd
Charles A. González	1999–	Texas	Democrat	20th
Grace Napolitano	1999–	California	Democrat	34th
Hilda Solís	2001–	California	Democrat	31st
United States Senate				
Octaviano Larrazolo	1928–1929	New Mexico	Republican	
Dennis Chavez	1935–1962	New Mexico	Democrat	
Joseph M. Montoya	1964–1977	New Mexico	Democrat	

Box 7.4   Hispanics Who Have Served as Cabinet Secretaries

Hispanic Cabinet Officer	Years Served	President in Office When Nominated	Cabinet Office Held
Mel Martínez	2001–	George W. Bush	Dept. of Housing and Urban Development
William Richardson	1998–2000	William Clinton	Dept. of Energy
Federico Peña	1997–2000	William Clinton	Dept. of Energy
	1993–1997	William Clinton	Dept. of Transportation
Henry Cisneros	1992–1997	William Clinton	Dept. of Housing and Urban Development
Martin Lujan	1989–1992	George H. W. Bush	Dept. of Interior
Lauro Cavazos	1988–1992	Ronald Reagan	Dept. of Education

In May 2002, poll results from eight hundred Latinos were presented at a gathering of the New Democratic Network: support for President George W. Bush would draw even against Al Gore if the two were to meet in the 2004 presidential elections. In the 2000 election, Al Gore outdistanced George W. Bush by 20 percentage points, but the current poll results indicate a near toss-up (46 percent versus 44 percent) if the election were held today. Explanations for closing this gap are attributed to a rising Latino middle class, policy responsiveness by the Bush administration (i.e., Bush reiterated continued support of U.S. economic embargo of Cuba), and a "softening of the GOP's image." Part of the White House strategy is based on the 7–8 percent of the electorate that Latinos now assume and building on the 35 percent Latino vote received in 2000. The other finding was that the same Latinos indicated support for the Democratic congressional candidate (49 percent to 23 percent) over Republican candidates.

This raises a question of the expected trickle-down effect of President Bush's popularity to other GOP candidates and possible partisan shifts. Ronald Reagan enjoyed similar levels of popularity among Hispanic voters, receiving over 40 percent of the Latino vote in his reelection in 1984. At the same time, levels of Democratic support for all other offices remained solidly high among Latinos. It is not unusual for voters to distinguish between their choices for president and for congressional and other political offices. While presidential races are clearly couched in a partisan context, appeals to the political center often transcend partisan appeals and crossover voting takes place, while more conventional partisan voting occurs for all other races.

This discussion of the post-2000 election has focused on the political parties and, to a lesser extent, the efforts and attention directed toward Latinos. The overall political "equation" would not be complete without examining the Latino community's actions and strategies. Even with specific strategies by the major political parties and their leadership, Latino organizations advance their own agenda and enhance their political empowerment. An assessment for Latinos to make is to distinguish between the rhetoric and actual results and behaviors of the political parties. In addition, identifying their primary political objectives for the short term (targeting more Latinos for state level and/or congressional offices, pursuing specific policy reforms and/or initiatives, expanding the electoral base, etc.). Such a determination will shape the future political development of Latinos. It is the seizing of opportunities and pursuing policies that will define the dynamics between Latinos and the American political system.

- According to ABC News, the 1998 vote analysis indicated that the surge of electoral participation by women, the young, African Americans, and Latinos, particularly in California, Texas, New York, and Florida had a significant effect on partisan victories.
- The Association of Hispanic Advertising has launched (September 1999) a public service campaign on television, radio, and print media to promote voter registration and participation. A total of $5 million has been donated in time and the campaign runs through November 2000.

The State and Local Levels and Latinos

The post-2000 election period has made a significant impact at the state and local levels as well. Although Latinos have in the past been absent at the gubernatorial level, governors' mansions and state legislatures have been targeted by Latinos for increasing their representational levels. In 2002, Latinos vied for the governorships of New Mexico and Texas. In the Texas case, the Democratic primary was a contest between two Latinos, Dan Morales and Tony Sanchez, with Sanchez winning out to face Republican governor Rick Perry. Despite record minority turnout and significant financial backing, Sanchez lost to Perry in a race characterized by negative campaigning, high stakes spending, the incumbency factor, and eleventh hour stumping by President Bush on behalf of his gubernatorial successor. In New Mexico, Bill Richardson faced a Republican Latino opponent who was closer to the electorate but less well established politically. Richardson was elected Governor of New Mexico in 2002 with a sizeable margin of victory.

Box 7.5   Latinos and the 2002 Midterm Elections

There were heightened expectations among Latinos and political parties and candidates about the importance and impact of the 2000 elections. A similar level of expectations existed for the 2002 midterm elections. Given divided partisan control of both chambers of Congress, both major parties sought to regain control of the House (Democrats) and the Senate (Republicans). Close races were evident in states such as New Jersey, Minnesota, Georgia, and Colorado. Similarly the major political parties were contesting many gubernatorial races. Both parties raised and spent record amounts of money on campaigns (with rising numbers of negative advertisements), and major party officials, especially President George W. Bush, "stumped" for their respective party's candidates. The outcome for Hispanics can be summarized as threefold, consistent with the themes have developed in this chapter.

Electorally, more Latinos sought elected office than in previous years. As I mentioned earlier, three Hispanics vied for the governorships of Texas and New Mexico (the Democratic and Republican candidates were both Latinos). The results showed gains among Latino elected officials at both the congressional and legislative levels. Three new Latinos were elected to the House of Representatives—Mario Díaz-Balart (R-FL), Raul Grijalva (D-AZ), and Linda Sanchez (D-CA)—which included two sets of Latino siblings serving concurrently. Loretta (47th district-CA) and Linda Sanchez (39th district-CA), became the first sisters to serve in Congress. Similarly, Lincoln and Mario Díaz-Balart (R-FL) are two Cuban-origin brothers serving southern Florida congressional districts.

Besides a gain of three more congresspersons, nine Latinos will serve in statewide offices, including Bill Richardson (D), who was elected New Mexico's first Latino governor in nearly two decades. Five of the nine Latinos are found in New Mexico, ranging from attorney general to state auditor. The other statewide elected officials are in Colorado (attorney general), California (lieutenant governor), Nevada (attorney general), and Oregon (superintendent of public instruction). At the state legislative level, Latinos had a net gain of five seats in state senates and eight in the lower houses. The state senate gains occurred primarily in California and Illinois; while in Georgia and Massachusetts, Sam Zamarripa (GA) and Jarrett Barrios (MS) became the first Latinos to serve in their state senate.

In the state lower houses, Latinos gained some additional seats in New York (3), Georgia (2), Illinois (2), Maryland (2), Texas (2), Arizona (1), and Florida (1). Again in Georgia and Maryland, these Latinos were the first elected to the lower house. The two newly elected representatives in Maryland are Salvadorans. According the NALEO Executive Director Arturo Vargas, the additional election of Latinos in 2002 represent "Latino progress in state houses . . . because state legislators have the power to address the issues that Latinos and all Americans care about the most—education, health care, good jobs, and better housing."

The other significant development of the 2002 elections and Latinos is the record amount of money spent by the major political parties on Spanish-language television ads. Candidates and parties spent $16 million trying to persuade Latino voters. Both national parties and forty or more gubernatorial, Senate, and House candidates placed Spanish-language ads for the 2002 election. In 2000, candidates and parties spent $12 million on similar ads. At the same time, Latino voters remained about the same percentage as the 1998 midterm elections (5–7%). Partisan-wise, the Greenberg poll indicated that 64 percent of Latinos voted for Democratic congressional candidates, compared to 35 percent Republican votes. This compared to 60 percent Democratic and 39 percent for Republicans in the 2000 elections. This pattern reinforces the development of more sustained attention by both major political parties for their voting support. It is not expected to wane with the upcoming 2004 national and state level elections.

Our brief discussion of some of the results of the 2002 election seems to be consistent with the activation and increasing political capital of Latinos in the electoral arena. While the electoral progress is not overly dramatic, steady gains are evident and penetration at the state legislative and statewide offices shows signs of some progress and continual challenges. In addition, the absence of any Latinos in the U.S. Senate will receive attention in the next round of elections. Another general observation is the election of Latinos in "nontraditional" areas and states. This coincides with the greater geographic influx and growth throughout the United States. Finally, the recruitment of Latino candidates, greater organizational skills, and more financial resources contribute to present and future success.

Another important development following the 2000 elections is the current round of **redistricting.** Clearly, the significant growth of Latinos carries over to the drawing of congressional, legislative, and other jurisdictional districts. Using the Voting Rights Act coverage (see chapter 10) and greater political leverage, Latino activists and organizations have submitted redistricting plans to state legislative committees and independent redistricting commissions. In general, these strategies maintain heavily Latino majority districts and create high-growth Latino districts.[9] The use of litigation to challenge redistricting plans remains an option under the Voting Rights Acts. Redistricting plays an important role in Latino empowerment as redrawing or adding new districts affords greater opportunities to seek and secure more political offices. For the past three decades there have been noticeable gains in the number of Latino elected officials after each redistricting period.

Representation and the penetration of more political institutions remains a consistent objective for Latinos at the state level. Focus on key appointed positions, especially judicial appointments, are key concerns among Latinos at the state level. In addition, the persistence of statewide referenda/initiatives will confront Latino interests and concerns. For example, there are efforts underway to have an initiative to prohibit the collection by state/local governments of information that includes reference to race and ethnicity. In concluding this discussion of Latino politics at the state and local levels, I offer the following items:

- According to the Immigration and Naturalization Service, as of April 1996, 850,000 persons had submitted naturalization petitions. For 1981–1990, 2.4 million petitions were filed and 2.2 million were approved. From 1990 to 1996, 3.9 million petitions were filed and 2.8 approved.
- In the Los Angeles INS regional office, the number of citizenship applications is up 500 percent since 1990. This office received 25,000 applications per month during 1995.
- From the 1992 census of governments (released in June 1995), although Latinos represented 9.2 percent of the population, they make up 1.2 percent of all local elected officials, up from 1.1 percent in 1987. The percentage of Latino elected officials who are women increased from 18.4 percent to 22.6 percent. Overall, the percentage of Latina locally elected officials increased by 33 percent, whereas their male counterparts increased by 3 percent.
- According to *CNN Inside Politics*, Latinos constitute the following percentages of voting age population for these states: California, 13 percent; Texas, 17 percent; Florida, 9 percent; New York, 12 percent.
- In California, Liz Figueroa was the first Salvadoran elected to the state assembly and was elected to the state senate in 1998.
- In the 1998 state and federal elections a number of Latinos were elected to statewide offices as well as increasing representation on state legislatures. According to the National Association of Latino Elected and Appointed Officials (NALEO) they included Cruz Bustamante, lieutenant governor (CA); Tony Garza, railroad commissioner (TX); Ken Salazar, attorney general (CO); and Peter Madrid, attorney general, Domingo Martinez, state auditor, Rebecca Vigíl-Giron, secretary of state, and Michael Montoya, state treasurer (NM). In addition, two new Latino congresspersons were elected: Grace Napolitano (CA) and Charlie González (TX). Finally, Latino gains in both chambers of the state legislatures were the following: Senate—Arizona (+1); California (+3); Colorado (+1); House—California (+3); New Mexico (+2); Arizona (+1); Col-

orado (+1); Michigan (+1); Wisconsin (+1); and Massachusetts (+3). These gains represented a 13 percent and 14 percent increase in the state Senates and Houses respectively.

- While Latinos constitute only 13 percent of the San Jose population, Ron Gonzales was elected as mayor in 1998. Salinas, California, elected Anna Caballero as mayor. Loretta Sanchez was successfully reelected to Congress (CA), defeating Robert Dornan again.

Local Politics and Latinos

Latinos have been very active politically at the local levels. The greater concentration of Latinos in the major cities has also resulted in more contested mayoral elections. In 2001 and 2002, Latinos sought the mayoralty in Los Angeles, New York, Houston, San Antonio, and San Jose. They were successful in the latter two cities. Despite the unsuccessful efforts of Fernando Ferrer (New York City), Orlando Sanchez (Houston), and Antonio Villaraigoiza (Los Angeles), their strong campaigns demonstrated more political experience that can carry over to subsequent elections. It also points out the competitive and cooperative relations that can occur between the African American and Latino communities. (See chapter 11 for more discussion of coalitions.) In Los Angeles, Mayor Hahn received substantial support from the African American community over Antonio Villaraigoza; while in New York, Ferrer gathered significant support from African Americans over Bloomberg. The greater likelihood of significant Latino and African American populations in our major cities will be an important ingredient in electoral politics. Finally, in the mayoral runoff between incumbent Lee Brown (African American)and Orlando Sanchez, there were voter polarization patterns with the respective racial/ethnic background of the candidates.

Increasing mayoral competition has not been limited to the largest American cities, as gains among Latino officeholders are increasing for communities of all sizes, and for other local offices. In addition, the presence of Latino candidates from subgroups other than the Mexican-origin, Puerto Rican, and Cuban communities are becoming more evident. For this decade a larger pool of candidates will come from these Latino subgroups. For example, Ana Maria Sol Gutiérrez, former school board member in Prince George County, was the first Salvadoran to run for the Maryland state legislature in 2002. She was elected to the Maryland Assembly in November, 2002. The pool of Latino candidates holding local offices becomes the next wave of Latinos vying for state and federal offices. In some cases, there will be competition between Latinos of different subgroup status. For example, the Chicago congressional district held by Luis Gutiérrez (D-Puerto Rico) is being challenged by a Mexican American candidate, and issue positions are more similar than not. Besides contesting more local offices, matters of service delivery, social service programs, education quality and funding, policy-community relations, and profiling continue to serve as the gamut of policy concerns for Latinos. I offer a few more illustrations of the types of local Latino politics that are occurring.

- In May 2001, thirty-two-year-old Edward Garza was elected mayor of San Antonio, Texas, avoiding a runoff in an eleven-candidate race. He was able to pull significant Latino as well as Anglo support. He is an urban planning graduate and was previously a member of the city council. In the same month, Samuel Rivera was elected mayor of Passaic, New Jersey. As a city council member and former policeman, he ran for the office four years previously. A high turnout and a decisive margin produced results as his closest competitor, former city administrator Imre Karaszegi, was more than a thousand votes behind (in a four-candidate race). An incumbent and a first-time elected Latino are now on the Passaic city council (Gerardo Fernandez and Jose García respectively). Turnout was 44.2 percent compared to 28.7 percent in the 1999 municipal election.
- In April 2001, Houston city council member Orlando Sanchez joined the 2001 mayoral race to challenge incumbent Lee Brown and fellow council member Chris Bell. Sanchez was Cuban American in a predominantly Mexican-origin Latino community. Although it was a nonpartisan race, Sanchez (a Republican and long-time resident of the city) was banking on support from Republican voters and contributors. At the same time, he was highlighting his Latino heritage and integrating campaign themes and Spanish language (*Podemos hacer mejor:* "We can do better") in his campaign.
- Fernando Ferrer, Bronx borough President, entered the New York City mayoral race of 2001 and was the leading vote getter in the primary. His major competitor was Mark Green, the city's public advocate. Ferrer campaigned extensively in Latino areas and received endorsements from Al Sharpton and Charles Rangel. In a close primary, Green received 51 percent (391,297) of the vote to Ferrrer's 49 percent (372,249). Owing to disputes over the count and errors, final validation did not occur until October 23, 2001. The runoff race was scheduled to take place on September 11 but was rescheduled for October.
- In June 2001 Antonio Villaraigoza faced city attorney James Hahn in a runoff election for mayor of Los Angeles. Villaraigoza sought to become the first Latino mayor in over one hundred years. James Hahn won 53 percent of the vote in the June 5 election. At the same time, Hispanic leaders were cheered not only by the fact that Villaraigosa won a large segment of the city's Hispanic vote but that the vote made up 22 percent of all ballots cast. In 1993, the last time there was a Los Angeles mayoral election without incumbents, Hispanics accounted for only 8 percent of the vote. In addition to the Hispanic vote, the African American community played a significant role in the outcome with strong support for Hahn.
- The *Economist* reported the election of Alex Penales (D) as Dade County mayor in 1996. Mayor Penales is U.S.-born Cuban American. In 1998 Ron González was elected as mayor of San Jose, California.

LATINO ELECTORAL PARTICIPATION, KEY FACTORS, AND THE FUTURE

In this chapter I have provided basic information about the level of Latino electoral participation as voters and the various explanatory factors that contribute to Latino voting patterns. Historically, Latinos have had lower rates of voter registration and turnout. Part of the difficulty lies with the significant proportion of the Latino population that is foreign-born. In addition, the youthfulness of Latinos overall (on the average ten years younger than the general population) also reduces potential voting strength. From these two starting points, we also see the effects of socioeconomic status, participatory orientations, structural factors such as discrimination, and cultural factors such as nativity, language, and the political culture of Latinos' homeland. Finally, the effects of Latino voting behavior and choices are also affected by given situations and issues that arise, such as a series of statewide propositions directly impacting Latinos.

Our focus in this chapter has been on elections, voting behavior, and Latinos. I have tried to paint a contemporary portrait of Latino registration and turnout. While there have been some periodic improvements as well as backsliding, the electoral gap is still quite evident. In terms of trends in Latino voter participation, gains made have been made, assisted by Latino organizations and leaders, in stimulating more Latinos to become involved in the American electoral system. Part of that attention has been directed toward increasing the number of Latino foreign-born who become citizens. In addition, more targeted and sophisticated voter education and registration drives have been more prominent during the latter part of the nineties. The latter part of the past decade saw greater evidence that conversion of the Latino potential voting clout is being realized more significantly. Gains have been made in the absolute number of Latinos registered and voting as well as their percentage of the total electorate. Given the greater percentage of Latinos over the age of eighteen and gains in numbers of legalized Latino immigrants, naturalized citizens should add to recent electoral Latino gains.

CONCLUSION

I conclude this chapter with recent indicators of significant changes among the Latino electorate that could carry over beyond 2000 and into the new millennium. Since the mid-1990s there have been some very specific developments and activities that could well indicate upsurges in the electoral liveliness of Latino communities. These developments appear to have long-term implications and will alter the existing definition of the electoral profile for Latinos for the future. In a real sense the future was tested in 2000 with the presidential election, as well as the plethora of federal, state, and local elections.

Loretta and Linda Sanchez

The First Sister Act in Congress

The midterm elections of 2002 yielded a milestone in Latino politics as well as in the history of the House of Representatives. On November 5, 2002, Democrats, Latinas, and sisters, Loretta and Linda Sanchez, were elected to Congress from two different districts in California, running on similar platforms and yet with distinctive styles. They are the first pair of sisters to serve in the House and are expected to serve with a stir. Interestingly, the House also has a Latino "brother act" coming out of the 2002 elections. Lincoln and Mario Diaz-Balart were elected from two different districts in Florida. Latinos in Congress are growing in number and clout, although, at present, there are no Latino Senators.

Sources: The *Orange County Register* and the *Washington Post.*

Recent electoral developments and activities can be viewed as positive indicators that Latino electoral participation is realizing more of its promised potential. Specific trends involved rising voter registration rates among Latinos. Although many of the specific examples are set in California, there is evidence of increased voter registration throughout "Latino America." This increase is even more noteworthy in light of declining voter participation among other Americans. Two key segments within the Latino community that are becoming more involved in the electoral arena are those under thirty and the foreign-born. The youthfulness of the Latino community contributes to its overall growth; yet a large proportion remains too young to vote. The 18–30 age-group will be the fastest growing segment into the next decade and, potentially, new voters. The data on increased naturalization petitions is a major shift in the 1990s and projected to continue into the next decade. To some extent, the anti-immigrant climate and restrictive policy initiatives following September 11, 2001, have served as catalysts for permanent resident "aliens" to pursue naturalization. In addition, Mexico's new policy of allowing dual citizenship has reduced the stress of maintaining Mexican citizenship at the expense of not pursuing American citizenship. Thus the conversion of the continued development of the Latino communities into a more significant electoral actor has become increasingly evident since the mid-1990s.

Increasing electoral competition among Latinos for political offices is now seeing success at the statewide level and in areas where Latinos are not the "dominant" demographic population. Part of the gain in representation is the result of an expanding and increasingly active Latino electorate; yet more energetic and effective Latino organizations and leadership are impacting the Latino political realm. Finally, external factors such as a negative climate directed toward Latinos, public policies and initiatives that directly impact Latino communities, direct partisan appeals by both major parties, and broader public networks of information and connections among the diverse Latino communities are important sources of increased Latino electoral participation. The role of Latino organizations and leadership and their concomitant mobilization is the subject of the following chapter. The intersection of Latinos with leaders and organizations soliciting, directing, and encouraging participation and involvement will convert political potential into concrete actions.

NOTES

1. I use the term "arenas of participation" to identify electoral activities, organizational, protest, and individualized involvement at various levels of government and impacting the policy-making process.

2. By "absolute gain" I am referring to positive increases among Latino voters and registrants from the previous election period. By "relative gain" I am assessing the Latino gains in voting and registration relative to non-Latino populations. For example, if the Latino voter turnout rate in 1996 was 45 percent and non-Latino was 60 percent, how much did it change in the subsequent election year? A concrete relative gain would exist if Latino turnout was 48 percent and non-Latino turnout was 59 percent. In this example, Latinos closed the gap from 15 percent to 11 percent over the two election periods.

3. States have primary responsibility for election laws and regulations within the protections of the U.S. Constitution. Some states, such as Georgia, Kentucky, Alaska, and Hawaii, allowed eighteen-, nineteen-, and twenty-year-olds the right to vote prior to the passage of the Twenty-fifth Amendment.

4. The concept of human capital is found in the economics literature. The idea is that as individuals invest in their human resource "portfolio" by obtaining more education, greater degrees of training, and more experience and are strongly motivated, they advantaged for greater returns in the job market via earnings. The acquisition of greater human resources is advantageous for economic returns. Human capital also can be thought of as political capital in that individuals with greater skills, knowledge, and interest in the political process can act more effectively.

5. The specification for which racial, national origin, or linguistic groups are covered by the Civil and Voting Rights Acts constitutes a clarification and delineation of constitutionally protected rights for members of certain groups.

6. In this case, I am referring to the manner in which elected officials are selected within a political jurisdiction. District systems tend to be geographically drawn (ward), at-large, or a combination of the two. Thus an at-large district configuration allows all voters within the jurisdiction to elect all of the representatives, whereas a ward system enables voters within the geographic district only to elect their own rep-

resentative. In a mixed-mode system, some representatives are elected in a ward configuration whereas other officials in the same body are elected at-large.

7. Following the U.S. Constitution, after each decennial census, Congress has to be reapportioned for the states according to population changes. This process has been further clarified in a cluster of court rulings regarding "one person, one vote," equal-sized districts, compactness, and contiguity. Once reapportioned, each state (usually its legislature) is responsible for drawing up districts (federal, state, and local) within constitutional guidelines. In this process racial and ethnic "representativeness" has been a factor in the design of districts.

8. The concept of racial gerrymandering involves critical consideration of the racial and ethnic makeup of a political district in delineating geographical boundaries. In this context, more concentrated inclusion of racial/ethnic groups increases their proportion of the district's makeup.

9. This concept tries to take advantage of areas in which Latinos have experienced significant growth but do not constitute a majority. Thus in a district that is 25–40 percent Latino, it becomes possible to create a "district of influence." Latinos are a sizable enough population in these kinds of districts that representatives would find it difficult to ignore them.

8

Latino Organizations and Leadership

La maquinaría de la edad moderna, estas estructuras sociales que pretenden representar nuestros sentimientos, nuestros puntos de vista pero realmente son personas de carne y hueso que dirigen estas máquinas sociales y estas son el vínculo con el pueblo.

The machinery of this modern age, these social structures that seek to represent our feelings, our points of view, are directed by real people—and they are the connections with our community.

Our examination of voting and elections centered on the number of Latinos who register and vote in U.S. elections. I outlined and discussed the major contributing factors that affect Latino electoral participation—socioeconomic status, participatory orientations, structural conditions and practices, and cultural dimensions. Progress has been made in terms of increasing Latino electoral and other modes of political involvement. In the past decade, Latinos have shown gains in educational attainment, household income, and rates of naturalization. There is a greater percentage of Latinos over eighteen years of age, and the Latino voting-age population has increased by 34.2 percent (U.S. Bureau of the Census 1999) while the general increase was 8.1 percent. At the same time, as noted in the previous chapter, organizational **mobilization** and leadership play very positive roles in increasing Latino political involvement. This mobilization can take the form of continuous efforts to activate the Latino community, as well as responding to external movements like **English only,** anti-immigrant initiatives, and proposals to eliminate bilingual education.

In this chapter, we will focus on the role of organizations and leaders in the political life of Latinos. We are seeing these elements as linkages and/or bridges between individual Latinos and the American political processes and institutions. Our earlier discussions of political involvement and participation noted how increased individual political capital can position a person to join and be active in organizations and develop communication skills, and be part of social networks that reinforce becoming and/or staying active. Therefore the political resources that a Latino can develop and obtain have payoffs for organizational involvement as well as leadership enhancement.

Beyond individual factors and experience, how do organizations serve the Latino political community? What role do leaders play in linking Latino community interests and experiences to focused activities in political arenas? Being asked to participate, especially by someone who plays an important role in whether and how a person may become politically active serve as a key ingredient in activating Latino participants. Organizations are part of the mobilizing "force" that can subsidize (reduce the costs of individual participation) political involvement for individuals by providing information, access to decision makers, forums for discussion, and potential benefits (employment, services, tax benefits, etc.). Just as the Latino population has grown dramatically over the past three decades, the rise of newer organizations, as well as the expanded scope of long-standing Latino organizations, is quite evident. Let us begin by examining, in a general manner, the purposes and basis for the existence of several Latino-based organizations.

LATINOS AND ORGANIZATIONS: HISTORICAL ORIGINS

One of the benefits of sustained and directed research about Latinos,[1] particularly since the late 1960s, is the extent of knowledge about Latino organizations, past and present. We know that organizations are an aggregation of individuals with common interests. For Latinos in the United States, the existence of Latino-based organizations served a number of purposes and/or objectives. We know much more about Mexican-origin organizations than any other Latino subgroup due to the extensive research literature. For the most part, Mexican American or Chicano organizations can be grouped by major purposes or goals (Tirado 1970): mutual aid societies/mutualistas, cultural/home community clubs (largely immigrant-based groups), adaptation/adjustment focused organizations, civil rights and advocacy organizations, social service providers or facilitators; political organizations, professional (occupationally related) organizations, and community (locally based) organizations.

It is important to understand the different bases from which Latino organizations are formed. Each basis for organizational existence impacts the organizational base (grassroots membership, immigrants, local residents, elites or professionals, etc.) and the principal strategies employed. At the same time, there are other important dimensions to identify and understand in examining organizations and their links to Latino political involvement. In addition to the membership base, organizational size and resources, goals and objectives, and modes of political action link Latino organizations with specific political arenas. Is the organization a mass-based group or is it composed of elites?

For example, the Mexican American Legal Defense and Education fund is composed primarily of attorneys and other professionals but acts on behalf of a broader Latino constituency. Is the organization primarily local or national in scope? For a Latino-based group, what is the role of culture, group identity, and national origin in attracting members and influencing the agenda or mission of the organization? Do class and/or gender come into play regarding the group's mission, membership base, and major organizational issues? Has assimilation or cultural pluralism, cultural nationalism or political integration affected the formation of the Latino organization, its strategies, and its membership base?

During the mid-1980s and beyond, the development of **pan-ethnicity** extended across all Latino subgroups, which placed different organizational pressures and expectations on existing Latino organizations as well as new ones. Latino organizations are trying to represent the wider spectrum of all Latinos in national arenas. For example, the National Council of La Raza (NCLR) was originally the Southwest Council of La Raza with its primary constituency Mexican Americans/Chicanos. While its goal of reducing poverty and discrimination, as well as improving opportunities for Mexican Americans, has not changed, its activities target all Hispanics/Latinos. Similarly, the arena is concentrated in Washington, D.C., and focuses on national issues. It has extended its chapters into the Northeast, Midwest, and South. The research and advocacy unit of NCLR focuses much of its activities on national policies such as immigration reform, social welfare reform, and affirmative action policies. We will explore these pan-ethnic efforts and developments in organizations that have adjusted their base, strategies, and political arenas later in this chapter. Clearly, obtaining a full grasp of Latino organizations involves more than identifying the organizations and their primary objectives and mission.

In this chapter, I try to weave the critical components of the origins and life cycles of Latino organizations through organizing principles that emerge from the previous set of questions that I raised, and through specific Latino organizations. A general graphic representation of the central elements found in Latino organizations, as well as most organizations in American political life, is presented in box 8.1.

The key components include the following: (1) membership base, (2) primary organizational objectives or goals; (3) geographic base and focus of operation; (4) organizational structure and leadership; (5) organizational strategies and approaches; (6) role of culture, class, and gender in organizational devel-

Box 8.1   Latino Organizations

Organizational Dimensions	Organizational Aspects
Membership base	Mass or elite base (professionals), class based, gender based
Goals/Objectives	Specific (material benefits, services, job placement, etc.) or general (assimilation, pluralism, equality, etc.), cultural maintenance, social, civil rights
Strategies	Electoral, voting, lobbying, direct actions/protest, coalitions, etc.
Organizational structure	Decentralized, local chapters, regional, centralized, permanent professional staff
Geographic base	Local or citywide, neighborhood base, national policy making, regional
Organizational resources	Membership dues, foundation grants, federal grants/funds, litigation judgments
Leadership	Autocratic, charismatic, popularly elected, bureaucratic, institutionalized, regularized

opment; and (7) organizational resource base and adaptations to pan-ethnicity developments.

The existence and activity of Latino-based organizations have been evident since Latinos inhabited the pre- and existing United States. As mentioned earlier, there is significant documentation of Mexican-origin communities and their organizations. Organizations like Orden de Los Hijos de America and La Alianza HispanoAmericano (Briegal 1970) operated in the nineteenth century largely to assist Mexicanos with surviving in the United States (providing burial insurance, rotating credit associations, cultural maintenance, etc.). The Alianza established chapters throughout the Southwest and even into Mexico. Its adaptability over the next sixty years[2] was its involvement in social service delivery programs directed to the Mexican-origin community, especially its immigrant segment. These organizations reflected the segregated and marginalized position that Mexicanos held in American society. Day-to-day survival and adaptation was the focus of early Mexican American organizations.

The turn of the nineteenth century saw a major influx of Mexicanos into the Southwest, partially due to political turmoil and the Mexican revolution.

As a result, migration continued to the Southwest and industrial, manufacturing sites in the Midwest (J. R. Garcia 1980, 1995). Industries like steel, automobiles, the railroad, tanneries, and the like served as employment magnets for many Mexican workers. In the Southwest, Mexican American organizations formed around labor groups/unions, mutual aid societies, social clubs based on communities of origin, and groups that promoted assimilation into mainstream American society.

League of United Latin American Citizens

A good example of the latter type of Latino organization is the League of United Latin American Citizens (LULAC). Formed in Texas in 1927, this group was made up of Mexican American citizens who sought to acquire the rights and privileges of American citizenship, as well as honor the duties and responsibilities of being an American. Membership was restricted to Mexican-origin citizens and loyalty to the United States was a central aspect of the organization's creed. Nevertheless, LULAC (Márquez 1988) engaged in activities that dealt with Mexican culture and pride. Initially the group focused on promoting the use of English, educational achievement and opportunities, economic opportunities (jobs and job training), and **political participation** and access. Thus the LULAC community did not include all Mexican-origin persons, although social service activities were not limited to citizens. For example, in the 1950s it founded the Little Schools of the 400, which was a preschool program to equip Mexican American children with a four-hundred-word core vocabulary prior to entering public school.

Politically, this group saw itself as a nonpartisan policy advocacy organization. In the late 1940s and early 1950s it sought to eliminate segregation of Mexican students (San Miguel 1987) in both California and Texas through litigation. Education has consistently been a central issue for LULAC. More recently, LULAC has concerned itself with access to higher education and school financing for Latinos, as well as continuing its efforts to generate greater scholarship awards. It located its central offices in Washington, D.C., and gave its executive director considerable latitude, with appropriate staffing, to engage in national lobbying on Latino issues. In the mid-1980s, LULAC joined organizational forces with NCLR, MALDEF, and the Congressional Hispanic Caucus to defeat and then significantly modify the **Immigration Reform and Control Act** of 1986 (Sierra 1991).

Over the course of its organizational development, the group has adapted its scope, broadened its membership base, and become more involved at the national level. The scope was widened to deal with issues of immigration, civil rights, affirmative action, and bilingualism (in areas not restricted to bilingual education). Its base was expanded to include non-citizens and all Latinos, not just Mexican Americans. LULAC chapters were formed in

Antonia Hernández (1948–)

Antonia Hernández is president and general counsel for the Mexican American Legal Defense and Education Fund (MALDEF), the major Latino rights advocacy organization in the United States. Born in Mexico, Hernández immigrated to the United States and obtained her law degree from UCLA. She came to MALDEF after working with advocacy groups, holding a position with the United States Senate Judiciary Committee, and acquiring some political campaign experience.

Bibliography

"Hernández Leads Huge Legal Staff." *Rocky Mountain News,* September 27, 1997, 54A.
Jackson, Robert. "A. Hernández a Pioneer Lawyer." *Rocky Mountain News,* May 10, 1994, 62A.

regions outside the Southwest and in Puerto Rico as well. While LULAC did not exclude other Latinos, as a southwestern organization its core base was the Mexican-origin population. LULAC characterized itself as a national organization, but it has been "fully entrenched" in Washington, D.C., with federal policy makers since the 1970s. A national office with sufficient staffing, sustained lobbying efforts, and national media attention are the elements of LULAC. It maintains a decentralized organizational structure with localized chapters, officers, and an annual national convention at which national officers and policy decisions are determined.

Civil Rights, Litigation, and Latino Organizations

While LULAC can be seen as a Latino organization that has evolved into a national advocacy organization, its strategies have been largely constructed around a large "mass-based" membership that provides its leadership with a loud and sizable voice to exert pressure on issues important to the Latino community. Other Latino organizations have a different membership base and pursue different strategies for Latino sociopolitical advancement. Two such organizations are the Puerto Rican Legal Defense and Education Fund (PRLDEF) and the Mexican American Legal Defense and Education Fund (MALDEF).

Civil rights and equal opportunities for Latinos have been the bulwark for both of these groups. Founded in the early 1970s, their central objectives have been protection under law and civil rights for Puerto Ricans and Mexican-origin populations. Over time, the scope has been expanded to be more inclusive of all Latinos. Their membership base consists primarily attorneys, and funding is derived from foundation grants, legal fees and judgments, and fund-raising (private and corporate gifts). For the most part, their areas of focus include educational equity, equal employment, voting rights, equal housing opportunity, and leadership development. MALDEF includes the policy area of immigrant rights as part of its central mission.

These Latino litigation organizations identify specific practices, locations, and plaintiffs to pursue changes in current policies or seek the full implementation of the law. For example, in *Aspira v. New York Board of Education*, PRLDEF raised the area of language rights and access to bilingual education services and resources. MALDEF in *Tyler v. Phloe* challenged the area of free educational access by undocumented school-age children. The local school district required proof of legal status for school-age children to receive a "free" public education. As a result, the court ruled that access to education is a "basic right" that is accorded to all persons residing in the school district jurisdiction. In the area of voting rights, PRLDEF and MALDEF have challenged the election structure of at-large districts since the 1970s (i.e., seeking district elections rather than **at-large systems**), and later focused on redistricting plans in order to increase Latino representation (promoting the creation of majority minority districts).

Both organizations have a board of directors and a general counsel to lead them. Representation comes primarily from the legal and corporate sectors, and they are less connected to a geographic or mass population base. The nature and policy arenas of PRLDEF and MALDEF are not amenable to being mass-based or grassroots-driven organizations. Even though their organizational base is not directly linked to a mass-based Latino constituency, both organizations have ongoing ties with other Latino organizations and leadership that enable them to be effective and strategic in determining which area, issues, and plaintiffs to work with. These organizations have served as policy protectors and initiators of policy expansion for the Latino communities. Pursuing such issues as challenging existing election systems that are detrimental for Latino representation, contesting funding and program inequities in both K-12 and higher education in terms of educational quality, access, and opportunities, and fighting employment discrimination against Latinos due to phenotype, accent, or negative stereotypes all represent policy expansion initiatives.

Exile Organizations: The Cuban Community?

In many respects, a number of Latino subgroups can be viewed as incorporating an exile orientation and organizational vehicles for influence and action. Latinos from Nicaragua, El Salvador, Guatemala, Argentina, and Uruguay (to name a few) have political factors affecting their decision to come to the

United States. At the same time, political refugee immigration status is not automatically accorded to persons from any Latin American country but Cuba. For the most part, on a case-by-case basis, proof of imminent danger due to political beliefs and activities serve as the primary criteria to achieve political refugee status. As noted in chapter 3, the growing Cuban community in the U.S. has been characterized as an exile group (L. Pérez 1985, 1986). In this manner, much of the community's attention and energy has focused on U.S. foreign policy toward Cuba and Castro's regime. Goals have included trade embargoes, establishment of Radio-TV Martí, continued admission of Cuban émigrés as political refugees, and the demise of Fidel Castro and his socialist state.

Thus the major organizations in the Cuban community have the emphases of an exile community oriented toward Cuba. At the same time, Cuban organizations assist the adaptation and adjustment of Cubans in the economic and political arenas of the United States. An example of an exile-oriented organization is the Cuban American National Foundation (CANF), until recently[3] led by Jorge Mas Canosa. CANF actively promotes the self-determination of the Cuban people and the dismantling of Castro's communist regime. It is against a centralized, government-controlled economy and a one-party state. Founded in 1981, CANF has lobbied in Washington, D.C., for political refugee asylum for Cubans, trade embargoes and isolation of Castro's Cuba, aid for refugees, and media broadcasts (radio and television) as part of Radio Free Marti. CANF has offices in Miami, Washington, D.C., and Union City, New Jersey, as well as chapters in Texas, Georgia, Chicago, Los Angeles, Spain, and Puerto Rico.

This actively anticommunist organization has been quite effective in influencing U.S. foreign policy toward Cuba. Programmatically, CANF supports the Cuban Exodus Relief Fund, informational and policy reports serving clearinghouse functions, Mission Martí, Foundation for Human Rights in Cuba, Endowment for Cuban American Studies, and the Commission for Economic Reconstruction of Cuba. In 1988, CANF was able to get legislation that allowed fifteen hundred Cubans in other countries to come to the United States, with fifteen hundred more Cuban "exiles" admitted annually thereafter. By 1995, ten thousand Cubans had been brought to the United States under this program. Their primary focus on removing Fidel Castro and dismantling the communist system reinforces the image of Cuban organizations as exile oriented.

There is strong evidence of broad base support within the Cuban community for CANF, as seven out of ten Cuban households have contributed to CANF, and a Univision poll found that CANF was identified as trustworthy and effective. Given its Cuba-centered focus, it has strong ties to national Republican leadership, especially during the Reagan administration, and has close ties with Senator Jesse Helms (R-NC). This was evident with the passage of the Helms-Burton Act, the 1992 Cuban Democracy Act, which tightens the trade embargo on Cuba, and the 1996 Cuban Liberation and Democratic Solidarity Act.

The pervasive character of the CANF within the Cuban community to some may suggest both uniformity and singularity of vision in all segments of the Cuban community. Yet there are other Cuban-based organizations that take alternative positions regarding Cuba, and others that work on the domestic front. The Cuban American National Council (CANC) is active in the areas of education, housing, and economic development services. As a nonprofit organization, it receives funding from numerous levels of government, private corporations, and foundations. This twenty-year-old organization has Latinos and other minorities as its primary "service" clientele. The service projects include coordination and supportive services for 30,000 Cubans and Haitians in Guantanamo, Cuba, building new housing units, 30,000 direct job placements, at-risk students' intervention programs, and over sixty policy publications and annual national conferences. CANC has dealt with inter-minority relations (especially Cuban–African American), Cubanization effects in Miami, redistricting and bloc voting, and educational attainment and language. Overall, the CANC directs its energies toward issues impacting Cubans and other Latinos once they reside in the United States.

Other organizations focusing on U.S.-Cuban policies are the Cuban Committee for Democracy and Cambio Cubano. Both are moderate in their orientation toward Castro's Cuba. Perhaps characterized as social democrats ideologically, these organizations see a more involved role for government in providing jobs, housing, and bilingual education. Its board members include several Cuban academics, and its policy directions leans toward reconciliation and dialogue with the Cuban regime and open travel to Cuba. The increasing proportion of Cubans born in the United States (Moreno and Warren 1992) is partially at play with a more diverse set of attitudes and policy preferences within the Cuban community. For example, in 1995, a Florida International University poll of Cubans surveyed public opinion about possible actions toward Cuba: 84 percent supported sanctions against Cuba, 57 percent favored invasion, and 68 percent favored open dialogue with the Castro regime. As the organizational life of Cubans developed into the new millennium, the predominance of exile-related issues (in addition to a wider range of policy responses toward Cuba) and focus might be expanded to include a broader range of domestic issues and similar minority-based concerns with other Latinos and minority groups.

Professional Organizations and Latinos

Any description of Latino organizations would be negligent not to include the hundreds of organizations that focus on specific public policy issues and whose membership largely consists of professionals. The range of policy interests includes bilingual education, mental health, small business development, immigration, job training, foreign trade policies, and access and participation in most of the professional associations and societies. There are Latino groups in the health care/medical, legal, academic, and business-related fields, the religious denominations, social welfare professions, unions, and education.

Most of these Latino-based organizations are organized around a specific policy arena such as education, health, social services, and so on. Their membership is composed of Latinos active in these arenas as professionals, activists, and concerned citizens. For example, attorneys (HNBA), dentists NAHD), engineers (SHPE), journalists (NAHJ), and **bilingual educators** (NABE) have access to Latino-related professional organizations. Within the public office sector, the National Association of Latino Elected and Appointed Officials (NALEO) is an umbrella organization for appointed and elected Latino officials at all levels of government. Latinos also have caucuses or affiliated associations within the elected official groups. Overall, these Latino organizations promote access, participation, opportunities/mobility, and nondiscriminatory treatment of Latinos and other minorities.

On the policy front, these organizations seek changes within their respective professional organizations; they also conduct research and advocate policy at all levels of government. For example, NABE describes itself as both a professional and an advocacy association. Through its research, professional development, public education, and legislative advocacy, it strives to implement educational policies and practices to ensure equal educational opportunity for diverse students. Consistent with its organizational objectives, NABE pursues its activities on behalf of language minority students with an added dimension of multiculturalism. NABE pursues its goals through special interest groups (SIGs),[4] which enable its membership to pursue more salient interests in greater depth, as well as benefit the organization with thoughtful ideas, policy positions, and analysis. The SIGs serve as working policy subgroups that enable members who specialize in subfields of bilingual education to focus their expertise on developing policy analysis and recommendations that will be presented to the general membership.

Another cluster of Latino organizations exists in the business and economic realms of public policy. These Latino organizations emphasize the economic contributions of Latinos to economic growth and development, as well as promoting greater participation by Latinos as entrepreneurs. Organizations such as the U.S. Hispanic Chamber of Commerce (USHCC) assist the economic development of Hispanic firms with the corporate sector and governmental initiatives and programs. Similar Latino organizations include the Hispanic Association for Corporate Responsibility (HACR), National Hispanic Corporate Council (NHCC), and U.S.-Mexican Chamber of Commerce.

The USHCC defines its mission as "advocating, promoting, and facilitating the success of Hispanic businesses."[5] Its activities include strengthening national programs to assist Hispanic economic development; increasing business relationships and partnerships between the corporate sector and Hispanic-owned businesses; providing technical assistance to Hispanic business associations and entrepreneurs; and monitoring legislation, policies, and programs that affect the Hispanic business community.

While there are Latino business-oriented organizations that focus on the employers' side of Latinos in the economy, there are others that focus on the "workers' side" of economic issues. For example, the Labor Council for Latin American Advancement (LCLAA) is a trade union association that represents 1.4 million Latino workers in forty-three international unions. It serves as a Latino constituency group within the AFL-CIO and engages in advocacy and political work. Founded in 1973, LCLAA states its mission as a "consciousness-raising organization to 'instill pride and unity among Latino workers and serve as a vehicle to advance issues that affect Latinos within their respective trade unions and communities.'"[7] It addresses issues such as low wages, employment-related discrimination, union recognition, and socioeconomic mobility. Another workers' organization is the United Farmworkers Union (affiliated with the AFL-CIO), founded by César Chávez, Dolores Huerta, and Larry Itlong in the early 1960s (Griswold del Castillo 1995). Focusing on agricultural workers, initially in the Southwest, it directed its efforts toward union recognition, wages, working conditions, health and safety issues, and employment-related benefits. Early struggles entailed organizing native-born and immigrant agricultural workers to seek collective bargaining status and legislation enabling federal and state coverage for these workers. Over the years, the UFW has had its share of victories and setbacks. With the death of César Chávez in 1993, the union has been led by Arturo Rodríquez (president) and Dolores Huerta (secretary-treasurer).

More recently, the United Service Workers union has been involved in organizing the immigrant segment of the workforce. Strikes in Los Angeles and Chicago illustrated the organizational force of office service workers and the extensive involvement of Latino immigrants (both undocumented and permanent resident aliens). During the 1990s, labor reassessed its position on immigration reform and the undocumented segment of the labor force. In contrast, the AFL-CIO leadership stated it would press Congress to grant amnesty to the nation's 6–8 million undocumented immigrants (Rodríquez 2000). It was also during the 1990s that labor looked around the country to identify unorganized workers and found them in agriculture, meatpacking, hotels, and restaurants. For Latino immigrants and other undocumented workers, an alliance with the labor movement was an opportunity to press for legalization and improve wage levels and working conditions. Internal changes are also evident in the AFL-CIO with the gains of Latinos as labor organizers and officials (e.g., Linda Chavez-Thompson) through unions in the manufacturing, service, farming, and food service sectors.

LATINO ORGANIZATIONS WITHIN THE POLITICAL INSTITUTIONS

The end of the second millennium brought a major shift for Latino organizations from more regional and local in scope to a greater national prescncc and involvement. Bridging the various Latino sub-communities to a pan-ethnic focus has been a challenge and an opportunity for Latinos to expand their resource base and agenda. The Latino organizational leadership has become more "institutionalized" in the sense that organizational skills, networks, and institutional positioning have supplanted charismatic appeal. The creation of the Congressional Hispanic Caucus (CHC) and its institute (CHCI) in 1976 marked the creation of a legislative organization within the U.S. Congress. With only five Hispanic congresspersons at that time, the founders' goals were to work with other groups both inside and outside Congress to intensify federal commitment to Latinos, as well as to increase Latinos' awareness of the execution and purpose of the American political system.[7] By 1978, the CHCI formed a 501(c)(3) nonprofit organization to add an educational component for leadership development and educational stipends/internships. Its board of directors has been expanded to include representatives from other Hispanic organizations and the corporate sector.

One of its primary functions is to coalesce its members around a collective legislative agenda for Latino interests, as well as monitor executive and judicial policies that affect Hispanics. For example, for the past several years, the CHC has been advocating from a pool of several Latino federal judges to fill Supreme Court vacancies. In addition, its task force structure focuses on a wide variety of policy areas in addition to the more readily identifiable ones—education, immigration, civil rights, and economic development. The "less traditional" policy areas include arts and entertainment, health, telecommunications, and social security. While the number of Latino congresspersons has increased to twenty-one, not all are members of CHC. The three Hispanic Republican representatives[8] have been part of CHC, but not currently. To some degree, the partisan dominance in CHC and foreign policy differences regarding Cuba have contributed to the non-affiliation of Hispanic Republicans.

The other "insider" organization is the National Association of Latino Elected and Appointed Officials (NALEO). This nonprofit, nonpartisan organization was founded in 1976 as a vehicle for political empowerment for the growing number of Latinos in public office. As of June 1999, there were 4,966 Latino elected officials, a 59 percent increase since 1984.[9] With its base,

Henry Cisneros (1947–)

Henry Cisneros established a reputation as one of the most outstanding young Hispanic politicians of the 1970s and 1980s. In 1992 President Bill Clinton appointed him secretary of Housing and Urban Development (HUD) in recognition of his expertise on cities.

Texan Henry Gabriel Cisneros was born in San Antonio on June 11, 1947. In that city, ninth largest in the United States, he made a nationwide reputation as a four-term mayor who won a series of landslide elections. It was no disadvantage to Cisneros's career that San Antonio has a large Chicano population, but there had not been a Mexican American mayor there since the 1840s.

After receiving his B.A. degree in city management from Texas Agricultural and Mechanical University in 1968, he earned a master's degree in urban planning two years later from the same university. He added a second master's, in public administration, from Harvard University in 1973 and a Ph.D. from George Washington University two years after that. Later achievements in government earned him numerous honorary doctorates.

President Reagan appointed Cisneros to the National Bipartisan Commission on Central America in 1983. In this capacity, Cisneros published an opinion that differed from the commission's majority report. He called for serious negotiations with the leftist government of Nicaragua, before the United States ran the risk of jumping into another situation similar to Vietnam. Later, he was a member of the Bilateral Commission on the Future of U.S.-Mexican Relations.

The Republican White House called on him again in 1987 to assist in

NALEO provides assistance and training to elected officials at all levels, as well as research reports and discussions of policy relevant matters. Its annual conference serves as a focal point for establishing policy priorities and cementing working networks among fellow public officials.

A major NALEO initiative began in the late 1980s and was a pro-active effort to promote naturalization among Latino immigrants. Its analysis regarding further political empowerment was the significant percentage of the Latino community that was unable to participate electorally because of non-citizenship. In the American tradition, immigrants make the naturalization decision on an individual basis without active encouragement from "the government" or civic organizations. NALEO incorporated a major campaign to inform and encourage Latino immigrants to pursue naturalization. Part of briefing Mikhail Gorbachev, then the leader of the Soviet Union, at a U.S.-Soviet summit meeting.

In 1992 he was campaign adviser to Democratic presidential candidate Bill Clinton. When Clinton won the White House, he appointed Henry Cisneros secretary of HUD. In that office, Cisneros launched a plan to fight the high incidence of crime and drugs in public housing estates by gradually moving the residents to other neighborhoods. Cisneros served until 1997, when he went back to private enterprise as president of the Univision television network in Los Angeles.

In 1999 a case concerning his extramarital relationship, which had been one of the reasons for his return to private life eleven years earlier, came to a culmination. Cisneros pleaded guilty to one misdemeanor charge related to the truth of statements that he had made to the FBI, about money he had paid to the woman in question, and was sentenced to pay a fine.

The following year, Cisneros launched a venture called American City Vista to develop affordable residential communities in the central areas of diverse cities.

In 2001, before leaving office, President Clinton gave Cisneros a pardon.

Bibliography

Cisneros, Henry G. *Interwoven Destinies: Cities and the Nation.* New York: Norton, 1993.

Gillies, John. *Senor Alcalde: A Biography of Henry Cisneros.* Minneapolis: Dillon, 1988.

Roberts, Maurice. *Henry Cisneros, Mexican-American Mayor.* Chicago: Children's Press, 1986.

the overall plan entailed research to understand the dynamics of that decision-making process, the level of information regarding the naturalization process, the myths or misinformation about naturalization, and the bureaucratic structures that deal with naturalization applications and approval. As a result, citizenship information lines and public relations programs were initiated. NALEO conducted a study of the Immigration and Naturalization Service regarding the processing and accessibility of the organizations to Latinos. Their study, conducted by David North, documented extensive backlogs and waiting periods of up to twenty-four months for a mandatory interview in some INS offices.

More recently, NALEO was involved in the Census 2000 planning. It supported the bureau's plan to include sampling as part of the decennial enumeration process.[10] NALEO has also been active in promoting the full count of all Latinos with support for complete confidentiality, targeted advertising to Latinos, Spanish-language forms and information, and hiring of bilingual/bicultural enumerators (citizens and permanent resident aliens). These actions are examples of strategies for Latino political empowerment. By pursuing the expansion of the Latino political base (i.e., converting more Latino immigrants into citizens and making a full count of resident Latinos), NALEO sees the connection to increasing the number of Latino elected and appointed officials. An active constituency and greater political representation serve the general purposes of NALEO.

Another set of organizations focusing on the political process is the Southwest Voter Registration and Education Project (SVREP) and the Midwest Voter Registration and Education Project (MWVREP). Both organizations have conducted voter registration campaigns and have linked voting with policy preferences and outcomes. Over the past twenty-five years, these organizations have honed their planning and timing to produce better voter registration results. For example, SVREP used to plan its voter registration campaigns many months prior to any local election or in years when no elections were scheduled. Subsequent registration efforts in the same community would include re-registering several of the same persons who had been purged for nonvoting. The timing of subsequent registration campaigns was closer to upcoming elections and involved one-on-one conversations about Latinos' views on politics, the government, public officials, and political participation.

This "educational process" connects Latinos' interests, elections, and representatives with higher rates of voting and more Latino candidates running for office. As a result, the voter education dimension of these two organizations has enhanced the effectiveness of their voter registration campaigns. Clearly, part of the political empowerment goal for Latinos is to expand its electoral base to more closely approach its overall growth rate. While this book has focused on Latino organizations that are national in scope and tend to be pan-ethnic in representing Latino interests, there are a multitude of Latino organizations (often Latino subgroup only) throughout most communities in which Latinos live.

Latinos at the Grass Roots: Community-Based Groups

By their very nature, grassroots organizations are locally based and political activities are targeted to local institutions and issues. Many of their activities are non-electoral and involve noncitizens as well.

The history of Latino grassroots organizations in the United States is both long and dynamic. Latino organizations date back to the nineteenth century and are found in many communities where Latinos reside. By their very nature, grassroots groups are local in orientation and their "longevity" oscillates

---

Box 8.2   Latino Politics at the Grass Roots

In July 1998 the *Los Angeles Times* reported on an organization, Grupo Pro-Mejoras (Pro-Improvement Group) in Mayfield, California (a middle-class Latino community southeast of Los Angeles). The news story relays the account of a neighborhood movement to address issues regarding the local water company (Maywood Mutual Water Company No. 2). The issues revolved around water rates and residents were contesting rising water bills. The predominantly Mexican immigrant persons experienced a less than friendly response from company personnel and were often ridiculed for their poor English (Tobar 1998). As a result of trying to deal with the water company, neighbors began to meet weekly in a member's garage to discuss issues, concerns, and actions.

Over a three-year period, their membership base grew and specific actions evolved (opposition to road bond initiative, running persons for the water company board, etc). As a result, Grupo Pro-Mejoras "took over" the board with one of its members as president. Among newly involved persons, successes often reinforce continued involvement and an expanded range of activities and interests (e.g., exploring the school district or the chamber of commerce). This largely immigrant enclave (both long-term residents and more recent ones) has been activated and has become involved in "small town democracy" quite extensively. This brief example reflects how local neighborhood groups focus on local ad hoc issues and develop the skills, knowledge, and strategies to effect changes.

---

around specific issues and situations. Since the post–World War II era, there has been a distinctive "brand" of community organizations that has had a major impact in many cities and sub-regions, especially in the Southwest.

The Industrial Areas Foundation (IAF), founded by Saul Alinsky (Alinsky 1971), developed an approach, structure, and general philosophy of organizing have-nots for purposes of securing political and economic power. Alinsky was active in African American neighborhoods, particularly in the Midwest and the East, which played a pivotal force in the local areas. The components of a professional, full-time organizer, an umbrella organization to incorporate already existing groups in the neighborhood, direct action and confrontation tactics, multipurpose and concrete goals, and an active membership base were integral for any Alinsky-based organization. The Community Services Organization (CSO) in Southern California was the first Alinsky-style organization in which Latinos were involved as organizers and neighborhood activists. Latino leaders such as Edward Roybal, César Chávez, and Dolores

Huerta were organizers trained by Fred Ross (the full-time Alinsky organizer assigned to CSO). Issues such as voter registration, housing and landlord problems, and poor schools were the focus of CSO political actions.

In the late 1960s and 1970s the advent of COPS (Community Organized for Public Services) in San Antonio surfaced around the issues of rising utilities rates and inadequate drainage infrastructure on the heavily Mexican American west side of the city. COPS successfully involved previously less active "westsiders" with positive, tangible outcomes (Márquez 1993). Subsequently, COPS continued its local involvement and became a significant political force in San Antonio. Other COPS community organizations were formed in Houston, Corpus Christi, Fort Worth, and Austin, as well as in the Rio Grande valley (Valley Interfaith), El Paso (El Paso Inter-Faith Service Organization), and Los Angeles (United Neighborhood Organizations).

The philosophy of the IAF and Saul Alinsky incorporates the key concepts of empowerment, self-interest, direct action, targeting political and/or economic institutions, and negotiating concrete services and resources. Over time, the IAF expanded effectively into the Latino community. Ernesto Cortés Jr. (currently IAF Southwest regional supervisor) was the community organizer for COPS and then for other IAF-based groups throughout the state of Texas (El Paso, Rio Grande Valley, Houston, Fort Worth, etc.). His influence has modified Alinsky's principles regarding institutional change. Cortes sees politics as engaging in public discourse and initiating collective action that is guided by that dialogue. The dialogue includes disagreements, arguments, confrontations, negotiations, and open conversations as part of the political process that makes it possible for people to act. As a result, most of the professional organizer's early organizing efforts were conducting numerous individual meetings for the purpose of identifying potential leaders. Then successive one-on-one meetings serve to direct networks for agenda building and identifying specific areas and arenas for action.

The other significant component of the contemporary IAF approach is to work through religious congregations in a federation structure. Congregations of faith generally affirm meaningful goals in life and serve as institutions built on personal networks of family and neighborhood (Cortés 1996). This context reinforces congregations' struggles to understand and to act. It is the action component that is central to the IAF philosophy. Delivering concrete "goods" to build and sustain communities has been a benchmark for Alinsky community organizations' longevity. More recently, the IAF strategy has been to use the federal government's CBDG program (Community Block Development Grant) as a process for eligible neighborhoods to meet and discuss potential projects with costs attached. As the result of more projects and total costs that exceed CBDG allocation, the IAF members must bargain, trim some projects and delay others to acquire mutual support (Cortés 1996). This process of negotiating and facilitating the bargaining among neighborhoods is intended to produce a more collective culture.

Finally, the IAF orientation emphasizes leadership development by training its organizers to act as teachers, mentors, and agitators who cultivate leadership for the community organization. This process enables persons to develop a broadened vision of their own self-interest (a key concept that serves as motivation and agenda setting) and makes possible the ability to recognize individuals' connections and responsibilities to others and communities. The IAF has adapted over the past forty years in both their strategies and community bases (broader, more diverse, and less geographically defined to specific neighborhoods). Since the 1960s, they have initiated community-based organizations, initially in the African American community and then in the Latino community.

This brief discussion of Alinsky and the IAF is meant to provide some insight into its significance, at the grassroots level, for a number of Latino communities, especially in the Southwest. While the membership of the organizations is overwhelmingly Latino, **ethnicity** and culture serve as the "means" of connecting with others and their experiences; nevertheless, the IAF approach does not want to define issues racially or ethnically. While the Alinsky philosophy focuses more on the self-interest of the community involved and does not see itself as a minority-oriented organization, it seeks to empower the have-nots. There is a considerable overlap between the have-nots and communities of color. The character of IAF community organizations is also influenced by the background and experiences of its professional organizers. With many Latino-trained IAF organizers, their character and Latino-ness are reflected in many Alinsky organizations. At the same time, the existence of Latino grassroots groups extends beyond the long-standing presence of Alinsky-based organizations.

In any community with a Latino population there are some local organizations that focus on their concerns and lives. As mentioned at the beginning of this chapter, the organizational goals encompass important facets of daily living (work, religion, social networks, family, education, immigration, etc.). For example, LUPA (Latinos United for Political Rights) advocates for immigrant rights. ASPIRA is a long-standing, primarily Puerto Rican organization that focuses on educational issues, usually in the Northeast. Many local areas have social and mutual self-help groups that are largely organized around immigrants' hometown origins in the Caribbean, Mexico, Central and South America. Historically, groups like the Alianza Hispano Americano and Orden de los Hijos de America served as mutual aid societies to assist immigrants economically (rotating credit loans, burial insurance, etc.) and social and cultural support systems. In a contemporary sense, many local Latino organizations assist their life in the United States. There is clearly a rise in grassroots organizations within the more recent Latino subgroups (Salvadorans, Dominicans, Colombians, etc.) as their communities grow in size and establish both presence and concerns.

Box 8.3   Newer Latino Organizations Come Forward

The Dominican American National Roundtable (DANR) is a civic organization trying to bring together the voices of Dominicans residing in the United States. It focuses on issues pertinent to the Dominican community that cut across the existing organized sectors, such as grassroots groups, nonprofits, religious, social, and business entities. Since a significant segment of the Dominican community includes immigrants or first generation in the United States, there is an emphasis on recognizing and maintaining the "rich culture" of the Dominican Republic. The theme of the fall 2001 annual conference (held in Washington, D.C.) was "Empowerment through Education: The Way for Dominican Americans." The DANR provides a national forum for analysis, planning, and actions to advance the educational, economic, legal, social, cultural, and political interests of Dominicans. Over sixty organizations and supporters are affiliated with the DANR, and their locations extend beyond New York City to Rhode Island, Florida, New Jersey, and Washington, D.C. Latino umbrella organizations will become more prevalent and inclusive of existing, locally based Latino subgroups.

CONCLUSION

Students of Latinos and their organizational life in the United States need to keep in mind the various dimensions of organizations and follow-up by looking at specific cities and metropolitan areas for Latino activities. The scope of key aspects related to organizations include their goals, breadth and/or range of goals; their constituents and their characteristics; resources and sources of assets; strategies and methods; leadership styles, selection, and accountability; and arenas for action. In this chapter I have focused on the key aspects of Latino organizations and some of their activities without going into great detail on specific organizational and other types of leadership. Since leadership is primarily organizationally based, identifying and profiling specific Latino activists and leaders would require a much longer narrative.

Organizational life for Latinos is active and has become more evident at the national level. Many of these groups use a broader pan-ethnic configuration to increase their constituent and resource base, as well as greater legitimacy as "national players" in policy arenas. While I have not extensively profiled specific Latino leaders, the role of organizational leadership is central for effective Latino political involvement. This cadre of leaders, at both the national and local levels, contributes to the definition and clarification of group goals and issues, identification and planning of strategies, provision of motivating incentives and rationale for individual involvement, and negotiating institutional responses on issues, demands, requests, and so on. The use of personal networks and a thorough understanding of cultural and personal experiences of Latinos in the United States enable Latino leaders to enlist Latinos to get involved, especially politically. In the following chapter we will explore some of the key substantive policy areas and issues that are part of the Latino policy agenda. This will illustrate the role of organizations and leadership and explain why particular areas are salient for Latinos.

NOTES

1. I am referring to the expansion of Latino-oriented social science research since the mid-1960s that has examined prevailing notions about Latinos. Much of the earlier research focused on the Mexican-origin experience. One of the dominant notions was the absence of organizational history and experience among Chicanos. As a result, earlier research on Chicano organizations was directed toward demythologizing an absence of organizational experiences. Subsequently, additional research identified a wider range of Latino organizations, their strategies, accomplishments and impact, organizational structure, leadership base and styles, and adaptability.

2. The Alianza Hispano Americano existed until the mid-1960s. Then issues of impropriety by its president and misuse of federal funds on employment-related programs resulted in its demise. The Chicano collection at the Arizona State University library holds many of the papers, newsletters, ledgers, and correspondence of the Alianza.

3. José Mas Canosa founded the Cuban American National Foundation and served as president beginning in 1981. When he died in late 1997, his son assumed leadership of the organization.

4. There are eighteen SIGs that focus on such topics as special education, early childhood education, higher education, research and evaluation, and so on. All members can select any of the SIGs with another NABE member serving as the chair.

5. www.ushcc.com/mission.htm.

6. www.lclaa.org/introduction.htm.

7. www.chci.org/about/about.html.

8. The three Hispanic Republican congressional representatives are Henry Bonilla (TX), Ileana Ros-Lehtinen (FL), and Lincoln Diaz-Balart (FL).

9. "Who Is NALEO Inc.?" at www.Naleo.org/Naleoinc/membership.html.

10. The congressional oversight committee and the Republican congressional leadership felt that including a sampling component as part of Census 2000 would provide partisan advantage to the Democrats, as the previously undercounted minorities and lower-income groups would be larger with the adjusted totals. Eventually, the sampling component was challenged in two federal district courts and then reviewed by the U.S. Supreme Court. The Court held that for purposes of reapportionment results from a "full enumeration" would be the sole basis for this decennial census. At that time, the Court did not address directly the use of adjusted population totals (via integration of sampling results) for purposes of federal allocation of funds or redistricting.

9

Immigration and Latino Immigrants

Ah, los pobres inmigrantes, los forasteros, los refugiados, los nativo americanos, con su larga historia en este país—formamos el mosaico de la comunidad hispana. Llevamos dentro muchas vivencias que han sido nuestro desafío para sobrevivir esta jornada a los Estados Unidos. Y a cado uno nos debe interesar oir todas las historias de cada persona en nuestras comunidades.

Ah, the poor immigrants, the foreigners, the refugees, the native-born sons and daughters with their long history in this country—we form a mosaic of the Latino community. We come with many different stories and challenges of survival from our journey to America; and we should listen to all of the stories of all our community members.

What government chooses to do can be seen as the basis for public policy (Dye 1992). The range of actions that government takes can include regulating conflict, organizing society, distributing resources, or extracting money from individuals and corporations. We usually think in terms of building roads, establishing social services, providing educational funds for buildings and/or programs, maintaining national defense and security, collecting taxes, and expanding bureaucracies to manage and oversee governmental operations. The pervasiveness of public policy in people's lives is a daily occurrence.

The purpose of this examination of public policy and Latinos is to identify and analyze the causes and consequences of governmental activities. What impacts do Latinos make on the content of public policies? What are the consequences of public policies on Latinos and/or Latino subgroups? Are there institutional arrangements and political processes that limit access and effectiveness for Latino concerns and actions? Do Latinos pursue particular public policies and exhibit specific preferences?

Throughout this book, I have discussed the concept of community among the various national-origin groups that are identified as Latino. In addition, I have explored the nature of community among Latinos in which cultural practices and values can bridge the experiences of being Mexican or Salvadoran or Puerto Rican. Clearly, Spanish language use and loyalty can contribute to public policies that both impact and concern Latinos. Policy areas of education, especially bilingual education and English-only initiatives reflect the extension of culture and public policy.

I have also discussed community as being established by Latinos experiencing common circumstances, conditions, and issues. For example, the poverty rate among Latinos has increased substantially during the 1990s, so social welfare reforms place that policy area in the Latino arena. These bases for community are important in our examination of Latino politics as they represent the content and direction for Latino **political participation** and influence. Previous discussions of organizations, issues, leadership, and participatory patterns and resources will now be directed to three specific policy arenas—immigration, education, and voting rights as issues that are central to most Latino sub-communities.

The area of policy studies includes the causes and consequences of governmental activities, as well as the development of a policy agenda from which governments move in certain directions and with explicit purposes. Latinos are not only responding to existing public policies but are trying to formulate new policies or reformulate current ones. García (1996) attempted to connect the Chicano movement with politics and public policy by looking at the elements or goals of the Chicano movement and how they translated into the policy arenas. In doing so, García uses the work of Milton Esman (1985), which sets out five conditions that are necessary and sufficient for the politicization of ethnic groups: (1) group identities based on objective social distinctions and feelings of solidarity that they generate; (2) grievances based on perceived social, economic, or cultural deprivation, or discrimination; (3) rising expectations for improvement; (4) declining authority and effectiveness of the political center; and (5) effective political organization. These conditions formulate preconditions for Latinos and public policy. Combining the elements of shared community, common issues, and inter-connected organizations working to influence political institutions, the policy-making process deals with setting the agenda and accessing decision makers.

What makes an issue, a concern, or a situation a Latino policy issue? Some general guidelines can place certain issues on a Latino agenda and designate particular public policy arenas. The first guideline is governmental actions having a different and often negative impact on Latinos. Are there situations or policies that affect Latinos in concrete and tangible ways? Given the cultural patterns of Spanish-language persistence and use, the educational attainment levels of many Latinos have lagged for decades. Thus questions of language use, bilingualism, culture, and curriculum serve to influence Latino involvement in the educational arena. Concerns held by policy makers and

Edward R. Roybal (1916–)

Prior to entering the House of Representatives as a Democrat in 1962, Edward Roybal served on the Los Angeles City Council from 1949 to 1962; he served two years in the U.S. Army from 1944 to 1945. Roybal's district is 64 percent Spanish heritage; it includes Pasadena, Pomona, Ventura, Glendale, Santa Ana, and Boyle Heights. He took the spotlight in the early 1980s, when a new immigration bill was brought to the floor. The bill required employers to pay fines if they employed illegal aliens. Roybal believed that this law would disproportionately affect Hispanic citizens. As chairman of the Congressional Hispanic Caucus, he led the unsuccessful fight to defeat the bill. Roybal did not stand for reelection in 1992.

Bibliography

Díaz, Katherine A. "Congressman Edward Roybal: Los Angeles before the 1960s." *Caminos,* July–August 1983.
Duncan, Philip D., and Christine C. Lawrence. *Politics in America: 1996. The 104th Congress.* Washington, D.C.: Congressional Quarterly Press, 1995.

the general public about too many immigrants coming to the United States and their perceived negative impact can target Latinos as the perpetuators of this situation.

The second key factor is an awareness and understanding among Latinos that the issue and current policies differentially affect many Latinos. It is not sufficient that some policies have an impact on Latinos, but that Latinos identify and portray the issue and/or policy as targeting them specifically. When Congress considers immigration reforms and other related legislation, do Latinos see themselves as the catalyst for such changes, as well as "targets" of such proposals? Clearly the first two factors are interrelated. Both the objective and subjective dimensions of policy impacts the Latino communities so that experiencing and perceiving public policies serve to magnify Latinos' interest and motivation in becoming involved in the political process.

The third key factor is the involvement of Latino organizations and leaders in policy arenas. We are examining Latino politics as a collective or group action directed toward policy formation and implementation. It is through Latino organizations and activists that Latino issues and concerns get framed and directed toward specific policy arenas and policy makers. In some cases, Latino initiatives act to prevent the passage of proposed legislation or referenda/initiatives. The long, involved immigration debate that resulted in passage of the **Immigration Reform and Control Act** (IRCA) of 1986 included extensive lobbying by Latino organizations to minimize or eliminate the employee verification system (or national identification card) from the bill. At the same time, lobbying by Latino organizations and efforts by members of the Hispanic Congressional Caucus pushed to include a wide-reaching amnesty provision within IRCA, as well as civil rights protections.

Finally, since public policy involves what governments choose to do, the focus of Latinos on policy-making centers on governmental institutions and all levels of government. The latter point reflects the federal system and decentralization of authority and decision making in American politics. There are many governments that affect Latinos and the arenas for contesting the policy-making process. It has been suggested that Latino politics mostly takes place at the local level with grassroots organizations and localized issues. Nevertheless, the policy-making process everywhere is similar, and regardless of policy-making arenas, the political processes that Latinos learn and strategically use are applicable in many arenas and over time. Latinos getting involved in the policy-making process find opportunities to translate concerns and issues into concrete proposals, influencing, and bargaining.

In this chapter, we will explore the policy area that has generated significant political activity, organizational involvement, and Latino protest. Immigration and the status of immigrants (legal, undocumented, and refugee), as well as the public policies that have come from the federal government, serve as the main focus of our discussion. Although immigration policy is the policy domain of the national government, state governments and municipalities have tried to enter this arena through referendum and other actions to define and limit immigrants' participation in governmental programs.

IMMIGRATION POLICIES AND THE LATINO COMMUNITIES

In 1998, a billboard in Blythe, California, had the following message: "Welcome to California: The Illegal Immigrant State: Don't Let This Happen to Your State." Just two years earlier, Californians voted on **Proposition 187,** which would have restricted undocumented persons' access to social services, public education, and health services. Persons who enter the United States and reside here without legal authorization are referred to variously as illegal aliens, wetbacks, undocumented workers, *sin papeles* (without papers), and so on. Since not all persons living in the United States "illegally" are workers, I will use the term "undocumented persons." These two policy examples serve as an introduction to the area of immigration and Latinos. Interestingly, the examples I cite refer to undocumented immigration, while receiving much national attention, are not the sole basis from which to relate immigration and Latinos. American immigration policies affect prospective entrants, family members, refugees and individuals seeking asylum, possible investors, border surveillance and enforcement, citizenship rights and protections, and access to federal and state entitlement programs.

U.S. Immigration Policies: A Historical Overview

This discussion of immigration policies and Latinos can only be grounded in the range and depth of issues and policies impacting U.S. immigration over time. Overall, U.S. immigration policy has undergone a number of changes since the founding of this nation. From 1790 to 1875, immigration policy could be characterized as a period of unrestricted open immigration. Very few restrictions were placed on those who wished to enter the United States. Toward the latter part of this period, an organized anti-immigrant group, the Native American party (a forerunner to the No-Nothing party), sought to extend the waiting period for citizenship from five years to twenty-one years. Another noteworthy change was the inclusion of the Fourteenth Amendment of the Constitution with the "law of the soil" as the basis for citizenship.

The years 1876–1924 saw U.S. immigration policy impose a series of qualitative controls on entrance into the United States; for example, prostitutes and convicts were banned from entering. Geographically and culturally, the exclusion of Chinese and Japanese immigrants resulted from formal treaty agreements. The American Protective Association was formed in 1887, as an anti-immigrant group advocating that persons should never vote for a Catholic candidate, never hire a Catholic worker over a Protestant worker, and never join in a strike with Catholics. The anti-immigrant, anti-foreigner, and non-Protestant policies were reoccurring elements in U.S. immigrant history. Finally, Congress enacted a law, which declared that any American woman marrying a foreign man would take on the citizenship of her husband and lose her U.S. citizenship.[1] Literacy tests were finally added in 1917, after several previous presidential vetoes. Fears of anarchists and seditionists also inspired restrictions.

The period from 1924 to the present can be characterized as one of both qualitative and quantitative restrictions for immigrants. The landmark **National Origins Act of 1924** set a ceiling on the number of immigrants admitted annually. A formula was based on 2 percent of the national-origin group registered in the 1890 census, which heavily favored natives of northern and western Europe. In this case, Japanese and citizens of the Asiatic zone were excluded. By 1938, the National Origins Act was fully operative, and 82 percent of those eligible to be admitted were from countries from northern and western Europe, 16 percent from southern and eastern Europe, and 2 percent from the remainder of the world. Given these changes in immigration laws, countries from the Western Hemisphere (Mexico, Central and South America) were excluded from quotas. As a result, the U.S.-Mexican border was an "open border" with freer migration flows.

The key governmental agency involved with federal immigration policies is the Immigration and Naturalization Service (INS). An agency in the Department of Justice, the INS is responsible for enforcing laws regulating the admission of foreign-born persons to the United States as well as administering immigration benefits, including the naturalization of qualified applicants for U.S. citizenship. In addition, the INS works with other federal agencies in the admission and resettlement of refugees. In 1864 the INS was housed in the State Department with a commissioner of immigration. There was a problem of divided authority between the federal statutes being enforced at the state level and authorization at the federal level. As a result the Immigration Act of 1891 solidified federal control over immigration through a superintendent of immigration under the Treasury Department. INS was given authority over naturalization through the Naturalization Act of 1906.

The 1906 legislation shifted naturalization from the courts to the Bureau of Immigration and Naturalization to administer and enforce U.S. immigration laws and supervise the naturalization of aliens. These combined functions lasted for seven years as naturalization became a separate bureau in 1913, with the Departments of Commerce and Labor splitting the two functions. By executive order in 1933 the functions were consolidated again in the Labor Department. In 1940 the INS was transferred to the Department of Justice.

The **Border Patrol** was not established until 1924, and in 1933 the Bureau of Immigration and Bureau of Naturalization were merged with the Department of Labor. The primary mission of this agency has been to detect and prevent the smuggling and unlawful entry of undocumented aliens into the United States and apprehend individuals in violation of U.S. immigration laws. Subsequently, the Border Patrol added drug interdiction along the land borders of the United States.

One of the more important activities of the Border Patrol is referred to as line watch. It involves the detection, prevention, and apprehension of undocumented migrants and smugglers of migrants at or near the border by maintaining surveillance from covert positions. It follows up leads, responds to electronic sensor alarms, and uses infrared scopes during night operations, low light level television systems, aircraft sightings, and interpreting and following tracks, marks, and other physical evidence. Examples of such activities include farm and ranch checks, traffic checks, traffic observation, city patrols, transportation check, administrative, intelligence, and anti-smuggling activities.

There have been times of heightened patrols and surveillance. For example, stricter enforcement of Mexican immigrants was more evident during the Great Depression of the 1930s. Mexican nationals and native-born felt the backlash in 1930–1932 as 330,000 were repatriated (Hoffman 1979) to Mexico, with an estimated 500,000 Mexican people leaving under the "voluntary" program. The throes of the Depression, a negative view of foreigners, and a fear of too many immigrants on the welfare rolls were major factors contributing to this Mexican repatriation.

Another development during the 1930s was the American response to political upheavals and war. Refugees from the Spanish Civil War and Hitler's invasion of France, as well as Jews fleeing persecution in Germany and Eastern Europe, were allowed to emigrate. This pattern held during World War II and subsequent military conflicts. During the 1960s and 1970s, immigrants from communist regimes were generally designated as political refugees. The next major immigration overhaul was the passage of the McCarran–Walter Act (INA) of 1952. The quota system was made even more rigid with annual per country caps. In 1965, amendments to the INA established an annual ceiling for Eastern and Western Hemisphere immigrants of 170,000 and 120,000 respectively.

In addition, a system of preference categories for close relatives and other family members was instituted for citizens and permanent resident aliens. Two categories of occupational preferences with specified skills, especially the health professions, were also established. Finally, a seventh preference category was created for 10,200 refugees a year with particular attention to individuals fleeing communist regimes or the Middle East fearing prosecution on account of race, religion, or political opinion, or people uprooted by catastrophic natural calamity. The per country caps were applied to Western Hemisphere countries in 1976 (20,000 annually). Mexico was originally expanded to 40,000 but eventually subjected to the same cap for all countries in the 1976 amendments to the act.

Overall, U.S. immigration policy can be characterized as trying to determine who is admitted, under what circumstances, how many, and from what parts of the world. Historically the borders of the United States have changed. The Southwest was once part of Mexico, both Cuba and Puerto Rico were U.S. possessions, and the United States has been involved in Central and South America from the early 1800s (Monroe Doctrine and beyond); these circumstances have linked Latinos and U.S. immigration. Historically, immigration policies have impacted Latinos directly, especially Mexicans. At the same time, immigration policies have received more attention since the 1970s. As a matter of fact, much of the national discussion of immigration and policy initiatives has been directed toward Latinos. One significant contributor to this situation has been the dramatic global shift of source countries and the number of immigrants entering the United States.

During the 1990s, immigration reform legislation allocated additional funding to the Border Patrol for added personnel and sophisticated equipment. The September 11, 2001, terrorist attacks in New York City and Washington, D.C., added even greater concern for future terrorist attacks and other national security issues. As a result, already heightened border control scrutiny has increased even more. One effect is to impact traditional flows of Latino immigrants along the border as well as the flow of undocumented immigration. President Vicente Fox initiated major policy initiatives to establish a bilateral agreement for Mexican guest workers in U.S. labor markets in 2000. Yet the terrorist attacks and the U.S. military response have put that negotiation on the agenda backburner.

CONTEMPORARY IMMIGRATION PATTERNS

Table 9.1 provides contemporary immigration information regarding the flow of legal immigrants and their areas of origin. Reviewing the years 1961 to the present demonstrates shifts in regional sources for immigrants to the United States. The past thirty years have seen significantly rising numbers of immigrants from Latin America and Asia. The immigration flows from Mexico and Central and South America are quite noteworthy. Almost half of the immigrants come from the Americas, and the addition of Asian immigrants combines for four-fifths of all immigrants for the 1990s. This represents a marked departure from the predominant European migration in the first half of the twentieth century.

The fixed caps per country, especially for Mexico, have created a backlog of applications for permanent residency, as well as the corresponding economic hardships of unemployment and low earnings. The economic interrelationship between the United States and Latin America, both its formal and informal economies, plays a direct role in the ebb and flow of international migration. The repatriation of Mexicans during the Depression illustrates the fluidity of immigrants as a reserve labor pool subject to economic push-and-pull factors in

Table 9.1 Immigration to the United States by Region/Country for Fiscal Years 1961–1998

Region	1961–1970	1971–1980	1981–1990	1991–1998
All countries	3,321,677	4,493,314	7,338,062	7,605,068
Europe	1,123,492	800,368	761,550	1,132,002
Asia	427,642	1,588,178	2,728,157	2,346,751
North America	1,721,634	1,982,735	3,615,225	3,777,281
Mexico	453,937	650,294	1,655,843	1,831,237
Canada	413,937	169,939	156,938	157,564
Caribbean	470,213	741,126	872,051	822,526
Central America	101,330	134,640	468,847	422,766
South America	257,940	295,741	461,847	443,152
Africa	28,954	80,779	176,893	280,230
Oceania	25,122	41,242	45,205	45,584

Source: Immigration and Naturalization Service, *1998 Statistical Yearbook of the INS* (Immigrants Admitted by Region and Country of Birth Fiscal Years 1820–1998) (Washington, D.C.: U.S. Government Printing Office, 2000), tab. 2, pp. 8–10.

both their country of origin and the United States. The anti-foreigner element of U.S. immigrant policy is reflected in Operation Wetback (J. R. García 1980) during the 1950s, with strong anticommunist reaction and McCarthyism.

The categories for admission fall into either family reunification or occupational/special skills. Persons having close family relationships with a U.S. citizen or legal permanent resident, persons with needed job skills, and those who qualify as refugees account for most of the admissions. The other policy impact on the legal status of many Latino immigrants came from 2.6 million former illegal aliens of 1982–1992 who gained permanent resident status through the legalization provisions of the Immigration and Reform and Control Act (IRCA). For example, over 70 percent of the legalized IRCA immigrants were Mexican. Another 10–14 percent were from other Latin American countries (González-Baker 1996). This adds significantly to the growing immigrant segments within the Latino community. Whereas the pipeline metaphor has been used for educational progression, growing numbers of legal permanent resident aliens enables more Latinos to pursue naturalization in the years to come.

Greater attention is being paid to employment-based preference categories. There are five categories for which persons can be admitted based upon skills critical for the American labor market: (1) priority workers, (2) professionals with advanced degrees, (3) skilled workers, professionals without advanced degrees, and needed unskilled workers, (4) special immigrants, and (5) creation immigrants or investors. Policy discussions have reassessed the greater emphasis on family reunification as opposed to labor market skills. For example, the Jordan Commission for Immigration Reform has suggested giving greater priority to the immigration category of employment needs of the U.S. workforce rather than family reunification.

George Borjas (2001) has argued for a more labor skills and economically driven immigration policy. It is an immigration policy in formula format; it awards points to prospective immigrants based on various characteristics and establishes a passing grade to help the American government select among the applicants. Among other characteristics, the point system would take into account education, English language proficiency, and age at time of entry (Borjas 2001, 194–99). Country of origin would be considered to ensure that no nation, culture, or language dominates the immigrant flow. Finally, point consideration would be given to persons seeking employment in immigrant-dependent industries.

While a full discussion of the merits and policy impact of such proposals is not the subject of this chapter, I have tried to illustrate some policy shifts within the immigration arena. The greater emphasis on an economic model for immigrant admission was reflected in the current U.S. Commission on Immigration Reform, chaired by Shirley Hufstedler, who addressed the House of Representatives about the policy directions of the commission. She noted concerns about immigrants with poor English skills being confined to the lowest "rungs" of the American job market. "The national interest could be served by moderating entry of unskilled immigrants, except when other values prevail, notably nuclear family reunification, and by increasing the skills of those who have arrived" (Hufstedler 1999, 8–9). Continued reexamination of the quota limits based on family reunification and employment-based preferences will affect immigration reform in the future.

How these possible changes might impact Latino immigrants and the Latino community has not been analyzed systematically, but the immigrant flow is likely to be reduced, since Latinos do "dominate the immigrant flow" and family reunification contributes substantially to the admission of many Latino immigrants. Greater proportions of immigrant Latinos are admitted as family-sponsored immigrants than employment-based preferences in relation to immigrants from Asia and Europe. As already noted, immigration will remain a national priority and Latinos will continue to be impacted and to engage in policy making to shape the direction and content of American immigration policies.

Immigration and Naturalization

One clear consequence of increasing numbers of immigrants is the growing pool of eligibles for citizenship. For Latinos, the overall pattern has been a relatively low level of naturalization, especially for Mexican immigrants (J. A. García 1981c). The general naturalization requirements include being at least eighteen years of age; living as a legal permanent resident alien for five years in the United States; having good moral character; being able to read, write, speak, and understand commonly used words in the English language; and demonstrating a knowledge of U.S. history and government. In the 1990s there was a marked rise in the number of immigrants becoming U.S. citizens. Overall, slightly less than one-half of all permanent resident aliens have naturalized (INS 1997).

The proportion of immigrants naturalized varies substantially by country. For example, most of the immigrants admitted in 1977 became eligible to naturalize in 1982, and by 1995 about 46 percent had become citizens. Generally, the leading countries of origin are China, the former Soviet Union, and the Philippines, while those from Mexico and Canada are the least likely. The research literature on the naturalization of Latinos has focused on Mexicans. For the most part, the key factors motivating Mexicanos to naturalize have been English language proficiency, length of residence in the United States, higher levels of educational attainment, age of migration, and income (J. A. García 1981c; Pachón and Desipio 1994; Smith and Edmondston 1998). While patriotism, allegiance, and cultural similarity with America have been seen as key determinants for naturalization, becoming a citizen tends to be a more pragmatic decision. Persons become citizens to ensure access to governmental program participation (Supplemental Security Income, food stamps, Medicaid, etc.), employment, educational financial aid and scholarships, and also to improve their positioning for family reunification preferences in immigration.

While the naturalization rates for Latino immigrants have been lower than for immigrants from other regions of the world, their naturalization rose during the 1990s. With proximity to their mother country, especially Mexico, the Caribbean, and parts of Central America, a strong expectation to return served as a disincentive to become a citizen. Mexicans would lose the right to own and inherit property in Mexico if they became U.S. citizens. The surge in naturalization in the 1990s was rooted in both individual motivation and general circumstances and sociopolitical developments. The INS Green Replacement Program launched in 1993, the approval of Proposition 187, rising levels of immigration in the 1980s, the enactment of the Personal Responsibility and Work Responsibility Act, and Mexico's approval of dual citizenship have contributed to increased naturalization.[2] Table 9.2 demonstrates the dramatic rise of immigrants in the 1990s, with greater proportions from Latin America and Asia. The Green Card Replacement Program of 1992 allowed permanent resident aliens to choose naturalization for a slightly higher fee over replacing their green cards.

Four other pieces of immigration legislation passed in the 1990s contributed to rising naturalization rates. First, the **Immigration Reform and Control Act of 1986** (IRCA) included an amnesty provision in which 2.7 million undocumented residents were granted legal resident status. As a result, the first of these now legalized residents could apply for naturalization in 1994. This significantly increased the pool of potential citizens as Latinos constituted over two-thirds of the eligibles.

Table 9.2   Naturalization in the 1990s

Country of Origin	Naturalized Citizens in 1990	Persons Naturalized in 1996	Percentage Naturalized from 1977 Cohort
All countries	7,996,998	1,044,689	NA
Mexico	969,704	217,418	22.0
Germany	512,018	NA	16.8
Philippines	492,214	45,210	63.0
Cuba	375,952	62,168	46.8
China	233,399	30,656	65.5
Dominican Republic	NA	27,293	29.0
El Salvador	NA	33,240	49.6
Vietnam	231,799	47,625	70.2

Sources: Immigration and Naturalization Service (Department of Justice), *1996 Statistical Yearbook of the Immigration and Naturalization Service* (Washington, D.C.: U.S. Government Printing Office, 1996); Philip Martin and E. Midgley, *Immigration to the United States* (Washington, D.C.: Population Reference Bureau Publications, 1996).

Second, the **Illegal Immigration Reform and Immigrant Responsibility Act** (1996) (IIRIRA) had stipulations to bolster the monitoring of the U.S. border and set up measures to remove criminal and other deportable aliens. This law also provided increased protection for legal workers through worksite enforcement. As a result, the "negative" elements of the IIRIRA created incentives for immigrants to gain greater protections and rights through naturalization.

Third, the **Personal Responsibility and Work Opportunity Reconciliation Act** (PRWORA 1996) severely limited immigrants' access to public benefits, especially social service programs. The Welfare Act restricted the eligibility of legal immigrants for means-tested public assistance, widened prohibitions for public benefits for undocumented immigrants, and mandated the INS to verify immigration status in order to determine which immigrants would receive public benefits. Part of the requirement for immigrant sponsorship included that the sponsor would assume financial responsibility for the immigrant if she/he were unable to sustain him/herself. The PRWORA made the legal affidavit of support legally binding.

Fourth, the **Antiterrorism and Effective Death Penalty Act** (ATEDPA, 1996) greatly facilitated procedures for the removal of "alien terrorists" and authorized state and local enforcement officials to arrest and detain certain undocumented persons and provide access to confidential INS files through court order. The overall effect of the 1996 legislation was to produce a more negative environment for immigrants, and naturalization became a protective and defensive response. The September 11 terrorist attacks (2001) produced broader discretion regarding detainment and civil/legal rights for immigrants.

Rising naturalization rates have seen processing concerns among immigrants and advocacy organizations. For example, the National Association of Latino Elected and Appointed Officials (NALEO) pursued an educational and promotional program to encourage more Latino immigrants to pursue naturalization. Materials and informational hotlines were established to facilitate interested Latino immigrants' pursuit of citizenship. In addition, NALEO began working with the INS to streamline processing as long wait periods were developing in many offices. Finally, NALEO made use of public service announcements featuring well-known Latino personalities. The increased number of applicants has produced bottlenecks within the INS organization. By 1998, the average processing time for applications was twenty-seven months (Singer and Gilbertson 2000). The backlog of unprocessed applications rose to an all-time high of 2 million by March 1999. Even as more Latino resident "aliens" are applying for citizenship, long delays slow down the increased pool of prospective voters and may discourage other Latino immigrants from entering the naturalization process.

The Latino electorate is being boosted by the conversion of a growing Latino immigrant segment into citizens. A study by Bass and Casper (1999)

examined the differences in registration and voting behavior between naturalized and native-born Americans. They found that naturalized citizens who
are more likely to be registered and to vote had the following characteristics:
having more education and higher income levels, being employed, owning a
home, having lived for longer a period of time at their current residence, being
women, being older persons and professionals, being married. Relative to
other naturalized citizens from Europe and Asia, Latinos are more likely to be
registered and voting.

When researchers controlled for length of time in the United States and
region of origin (i.e., Latin America), then Latino naturalized citizens' voting
and registration rates did not differ significantly from Latino native-born. A
similarly focused study by Singer and Gilbertson (2000) using qualitative
approaches found similar key influences among Dominicans in New York
City. That is, education, age at entry in the United States, time in the United
States, and language skills were key determinants of naturalizing.

Rising numbers of naturalization applications and eventual citizenship
among Latinos should continue well into the twenty-first century. The
Latino immigrant segment is not insulated from governmental policies,
national movements, and Latino organizational activities. Local governments, media, community organizations, political leaders, and hostile policy
initiatives have contributed to naturalization increases among Latinos. For
example, Jones-Correa's study of New York City Latino immigrants (1998)
reinforces the important role that encouragement plays in their political
involvement or lack of it. He found that immigrant participation was stymied
by both the lack of support to participate and the requirement to renounce
former citizenship, which raised the fear of never being able to return to the
country of origin. Latino immigrants were learning about citizenship under
siege, which leads to the next area in this discussion of immigration policies
and Latinos.

Proposition 187 and Undocumented Immigration

The 1994 elections, including congressional elections and state legislative
and gubernatorial races, were particularly noteworthy in California. The California electorate passed the Save Our State proposition, or Proposition 187.
This new law banned undocumented immigrants from public education and
other social services provided by the state. Proposition 187 was directed
largely toward Latinos, specifically the influx of Latino immigrants (primarily from Mexico) (Armbruster et al. 1995). The initiative and subsequent
campaign drive to pass Proposition 1987 galvanized inter-group tensions and
activated many native and foreign-born Latinos.

Clearly the impetus for Proposition 187 was anti-immigrant fear and concern about a "negative impact" on the economy, job, social services, schools,

crime, and social-moral fabric of the state. California is the leading port of entry for immigrants, especially from Latin America and Asia. While "illegal" or undocumented immigration has been on the American policy agenda for some time, initiatives at the state level were now becoming more common. Whether it was Official English, billing the federal government for additional social service funds, limiting undocumented immigrants' access to social services and education, and generally "scapegoating" the "illegals" for state economic woes, crime, overcrowded schools, and crowded housing, the undocumented population was identified as the source of many of these problems.

The significance of Proposition 187 lies in the recurring theme of xenophobia and nativism that has existed throughout American history. In the 1970s, estimates of the undocumented population ranged from 1 to 12 million. The images of hordes of humanity and thousands of persons daily lining up on the Mexican side and waiting for the cover of night to enter the United States were prevalent. The debate regarding the undocumented resident population has included emotionalism as well as a cool assessment of the costs and benefits. Many economic sectors were vitalized by the influx of undocumented workers, and business income was being generated in local and regional economies as well as adding to tax revenues.

These patterns figured into the benefits of migration. On the other hand, job competition, depressed wage rates, overcrowded housing, language and other demands on the school system and lost revenues through transfers and unreported tax returns were seen as the downside of undocumented migration.[3] In addition, there were negative perceptions of a group of people whose morals and values are not seen as compatible with the "American way of life." For example, Feagin and Feagin (1996) examined stereotypes of Mexican immigrants and found that many Americans saw them as lazy, unambitious, morally suspect, dirty, and a burden to society. These kinds of negative perceptions led to the Save Our State initiative.

By 1996, the INS reported an estimated 5 million undocumented immigrants residing in the United States with a range of about 4.6–5.4 million (INS 1997). In addition, the INS estimated that the population was growing by approximately 275,000 each year.[4] California was the leading state of residence, with 2 million, or 40 percent, of the total undocumented population. Therefore the advent of Proposition 187 in California was not a major surprise. The seven states with the largest estimated numbers of undocumented immigrants were California (2 million), Texas (700,000), New York (540,000), Florida (350,000), Illinois (290,000), New Jersey (135,000), and Arizona (115,000) (INS 1997). Mexico is the leading country of origin; while over 80 percent of all undocumented immigrants come from countries in the Western Hemisphere, with Mexicans representing approximately two-fifths.

The scope of Proposition 187 denied health care, social services, and education to the undocumented. Some other provisions required school district personnel to verify the legal status of students and notify the Immigration and Naturalization Service of those here illegally. Proposition 187 passed with almost 60 percent of California voters supporting the initiative. Examination of voter support among different racial and ethnic voters revealed the following: whites or Anglos, 81 percent; Asian and African Americans, 54 percent; and Latinos, 23 percent. During the early part of the Proposition 187 campaign, polls indicated Latino support at 52 percent, but that changed dramatically during the campaign.

Some political observers focused on the strategies and responses used by opponents of Proposition 187 that altered the outcome. Latino and civil rights organizations and labor tried to mobilize their constituencies to turn out and vote against the proposition. The message sent out included appeals on infringement of basic human and civil rights, the need for the Latino community to come to its own defense, and the contribution made by immigrants. Yet the Save Our State initiative appealed so strongly to the racial anxieties of California voters that it seems unlikely that any different outcome could have resulted (Adams 1996). Nevertheless, Latinos and both established organizations and ad hoc ones actively mobilized against Proposition 187. Latino voter registration increased at a higher rate than other segments of California voters (Los Angeles Times 1994), and growing antagonism was directed toward the Republican Party and Governor Pete Wilson.

As a result, Latinos (both among voting/eligibles and non-citizens) demonstrated heightened political involvement and awareness. One of the legacies of the Proposition 187 experience was a backlash and diminished support for Republicans among Latinos. Since the Reagan years, the Republican Party had focused more attention on promoting the party's ideology and policy positions as compatible with Latino values and traditions. Yet the anti-immigrant Propositions 227 (elimination of bilingual education) and 209 (anti–affirmation action), along with an initiative to require labor unions to obtain membership approval before using union funds for political contributions, found most Latinos on the opposite side of the Republican party's policy stands and with its leadership.

After the passage of Proposition 187, several lawsuits were filed challenging its constitutionality. The day after the measure passed, a federal court in Los Angeles and a state court in San Francisco barred the enforcement of many of the provisions of Proposition 187 denying public education, social services, and non-emergency health care to undocumented immigrants. Two days later, a federal judge in Los Angeles dismissed significant aspects of the proposition, indicating that they conflicted with federal laws that supercede state laws. Judge Mariana Pfaelzer ruled that the state could not deny health care and social services to undocumented immigrants because they are entitled to those services under federal law. She also ruled that a 1981 Supreme Court decision gave undocumented children the right to attend public schools (K-12), although the judge did not overturn the provision that keeps undocumented people from attending public colleges and universities. Agents of social, health, and educational services were supposed to investigate, notify, and report alleged undocumented immigrants. Judge Pfaelzer ruled that that task belonged to the federal government, not state employees.

Basically, the court rulings found that Proposition 187 violated two provisions of the Constitution—the supremacy clause, by stepping on ground preempted by federal immigration law, and the Fourteenth Amendment. The court ruled that, by effectively ordering the deportation of California residents without hearings or other due process of laws and by denial of public education to undocumented children upheld by *Phyler v. Doe* (457 U.S. 202, 225 [1982]), this proposition was in violation of federal policy and principles. The opinion was a 5–4 decision. Another consequence of Proposition 187 was the subsequent passage of federal legislation barring permanent resident aliens from participating in social welfare programs. Previously, in many social service programs, they have had access. As mentioned earlier, tighter provisions were put on sponsors of immigrants to provide financial support for admitted immigrants who were unable to support themselves. Thus the policy debates and Latinos' involvement with immigration (both legal and undocumented) make this area a critical one for them.

There is some variation within the Latino community as to the "ideal" U.S. immigration policy. For non-Latinos, negative attitudes toward the undocumented stems from perceptions of threat (economic, residential, and job competition), racist attitudes, negative attitudes toward "legal" Mexican Americans, and conservative and authoritarian ideologies (Cowan et al. 1997). A study of Latino attitudes toward greater liberalization of U.S. immigration policies found that levels of acculturation, perception of the undocumented as an economic threat, and residence with a significant undocumented population were associated with less support for liberalization (Hood and Morris 1997). The Latino community may have divided opinions about a more liberal immigration policy, yet it has concerns about fair and humane treatment, civil and human rights, social service benefits for permanent resident aliens, and the elimination of negative stereotypes about Latinos. An important factor for Latino attitudes and involvement in this policy area lies in the fact that immigrants and immigration impact (directly and/or indirectly) the overwhelming percentage of all Latinos.

The demise of Proposition 187 did not cancel out public concern about undocumented immigration. Even with a healthy economy and low unemployment rates, a *Los Angeles Times* poll indicated that two-thirds of the respondents saw immigration as a major problem (Kelly 1997). In addition, one-half of the respondents would deny undocumented people access to health care, welfare benefits, schools, and housing. Additional policy suggestions included denying citizenship status to children born in the United States of undocumented parents (54 percent), and one-half support the abolition of bilingual education.[5] On the other hand, Latino respondents supported health, educational, welfare, and housing services for undocumented resident by margins of 3:2 to 7:3. Clearly, there is a significant policy divide on immigration between Latinos and non-Latinos.

Immigration policy represents a major area of interest for and impact on the Latino community. Latino involvement with national policy arenas in the 1980s primarily focused on obstructing restrictive policy initiatives and protecting the civil rights of all Latinos. For example, during the IRCA debates, Latino congresspersons opposed national identity "cards" proving legal residence and introduced amendments to tighten civil rights protections related to the employer sanction provisions.

More recently, members of the Congressional Hispanic Caucus and other members of Congress with significant numbers of Latino constituents were able to reinstate benefits for disabled Latino permanent resident aliens in Supplemental Security Income and Medicaid. A year earlier Congress had passed the Personal Responsibility and Work Opportunity Reconciliation Act, which barred permanent resident aliens from program participation. Currently there are efforts in Congress to initiate a national version of Proposition 187, deny citizenship birthrights to children born in the United States of undocumented parents, and declare English as the Official Language.

THE POLITICAL NATURE AND INVOLVEMENT OF LATINO IMMIGRANTS

Immigration continues to affect many segments of the Latino communities as well as various facets of their lives (the workplace, schools, social and welfare services, civil rights, and negative stereotypes, etc.). It is an active policy arena with debates and policy initiatives about border enforcement, caps on legal immigration, refugee policies, and immigrant benefits. This brief discussion barely touched the breadth of immigration and the underlying issues associated with it. One other dimension that I want to introduce briefly is the political life of Latino immigrants.

While research has been limited on political behavior and attitudes about Latino immigrants, the general characterization is one of limited involvement and interest in the American political system. Jones-Correa's book (1998) on Latino immigrants in the New York metropolitan region portrays the Dominicans, Colombians, and other Latino immigrants in political limbo. They do not actively engage in the political process such as pursuing citizenship, nor are they involved in political parties or other political organizations. Part of the explanation lies with the "myth" of eventual return to their homeland, and a lack of encouragement from political organizations and leaders to participate politically. Research conducted a decade or so earlier by García and de la Garza (1985) found a similar pattern of limited organizational involvement by Mexican-origin immigrants in their respective communities. If they belonged to any organization, it was likely to be a religious-based one. Nevertheless, these Mexican immigrants are less likely to be politically involved.

At the same time, Latino immigrants exhibit a very positive attachment to the United States in terms of loyalty, extolling the opportunities of living in America, and support for political institutions (Pachón and Desipio 1994; J. A. García 1997; de la Garza et al. 1993). They tend to exhibit participatory attitudes of political support and belief in core American values (de la Garza et al. 1996) but do not follow through with concomitant political activities. Given the national origin of some Latino immigrants (from repressive and non-democratic regimes), it has been posited that these political cultures do not reinforce or provide experiences that lead to democratic participation. More recently, Espenshade and Ramakrishnan (2001) found that coming from a repressive Latin American regime does not affect voting and registration, while anti-immigrant sentiment serves as a catalyst for participation.

Again we see immigration policies and public response to immigration being directly linked to the political world of Latino immigrants. During the latter part of the 1990s, naturalization rose significantly. In 1998 alone, over 1.2 million persons naturalized, which was more than twice that of the previous year. The Clinton administration initiated efforts in 1999 to reduce the backlog of naturalization applications (Pan 1999). Overall, wait periods were cut almost in half; in offices in San Francisco and Houston the wait period was shortened from thirty-two months to nineteen months. Similarly, the thirty-three-month wait period for a green card was reduced to twenty-four months. Ironically, there was a drop in naturalization applications the following year by almost one-half (McDonnell 2001). One partial explanation is a less imminent threat of anti-immigrant sentiment and the significant increase in fees for all INS applications. In addition, Congress had restored access for permanent resident aliens to many federal social service programs.

A limited survey of Latino immigrants was conducted by the Tomas Rivera Policy Center in 1996. One result was a salient interest in educational politics and policy, particularly among Salvadorans and other Central Americans (O'Connor 1998). Schools were seen as inadequate and serious issues were raised about the quality and effectiveness of schooling their children received. This finding was supported by the Latino National Political Survey regarding Latino involvement in school-related matters, for both native and foreign-born Latinos (de la Garza et al. 1993). The second most frequently mentioned issue area related to language difficulties and poverty. This interest in education was also reflected in Latino support for Proposition BB in California, which increased bond funding for schools. Latinos supported the proposition by 82 percent compared to 67 percent for Anglos and 76 percent for African Americans. Other concerns center around immigrant human and civil rights and access to social services.

The 1990s witnessed concrete signs of Latino immigrant political involvement, especially at the local level, through their jobs and unionization. Labor has shown greater interest and recognition of immigrant workers in traditional sectors—agriculture, manufacturing, construction—and more importantly in the service sectors. Immigrant workers in the restaurant and hotel industry, janitorial services, and child and elder care have been subject to unionizing activities and strikes. Janitorial worker strikes in Chicago and Los Angeles marked significant involvement of immigrant workers (both documented and undocumented) in leadership roles as well as on the picket lines (Guarnizo 1994; Figueroa 1996; Milkman 2000). The labor issues, besides wages and benefits, focus on entrance opportunities for legal entry into the United States, access to public services, increased regulation of labor, health, and safety standards, and **limited voting** rights for non-citizens in school board elections (Milkman 2000).

David Broder (2001) discusses the awakening of the Latino immigrant communities, which include the dishwashers, chamber maids, painters, and bellhops who help form the **Organization of Los Angeles Workers** (OLAW). This organization, which advocates for workers rights, worked diligently for the mayoral campaign of Antonio Villaraigosa. The Service Employees International Union and the Hotel and Restaurant Employees Unions were an integral part of OLAW and political **mobilization** activities in the city. OLAW was able to recruit over 600 canvassers and distribute over 80,00 registration cards and forms. Similar organizational efforts were evident in Miami with the Hispanic Coalition. With over 130,000 immigrants naturalizing in Florida, the coalition helped register new citizens and the partisan effect was a 5–1 Democratic advantage (Booth 1996). This was due to anxiety among immigrants and anti-immigrant sentiments associated with many Republican leaders and policy initiatives. The election of George W. Bush reoriented the Republican Party's stance on immigration and Latino immigrants.

CONCLUSION

The awakening and greater political involvement of Latino immigrants should continue into the twenty-first century. The saliency and impact of public policies on this sub-community and the broader Latino community serve to maintain and build on the political "capital" of efforts in the late 1990s. Another example is Salvador Espino, who is seeking political office as a city council member in Fort Worth, Texas. This thirty-three-year-old Mexican-born, naturalized citizen sees his candidacy as an opportunity to show that the Latino community has a stake in what occurs in city hall (Tórrez and Jackson 2001). Other Latinos in this city are also seeking political opportunities at the city and county levels and transferring their work and business experiences into political organizing and mobilization. We have touched only lightly on the political world of Latino immigrants and the dynamics of activating this segment of the Latino community. Much research is being directed toward a better understanding of the political integration of Latino immigrants. Clearly this is an important demographic and political segment of the Latino community. NALEO recognized this potential over fifteen years ago, as it was the first Latino organization to target permanent resident aliens for naturalization drives and education. Now more Latino organizations and leaders are directing their attention to them, as well as the American labor movement and the religious institutions. A recurring theme in this book, the dynamics of Latino politics is its continual development and processes of change.

NOTES

1. The U.S. Supreme Court reasoned that the principle of the identity of the husband and wife was a reasonable requirement in making foreign policy. The Cable Act of 1922 repealed automatic loss of female citizenship but did not include females who married alien men ineligible for citizenship. They continued to lose their citizenship upon marriage until 1931, when Congress repealed the 1907 law.

2. A green card is a form of identification administered by the Immigration and Naturalization Service that certifies an individual as a legal permanent resident alien (PRA) in the United States. Originally, a green card was the vehicle for identification and bearers had to register annually to maintain their legal residence. PRA's can be required to produce their green cards at any time. Even though the identification is no longer a green card, it is still referred to as such.

3. "Transfer of payments" refers to immigrants sending part of their earnings back to family and relatives in their country of origin. It has been argued that such remittances represent an imbalance of money flow, as earnings derived in the United States are not "fed" back into the economy but are sent to fuel a foreign economy.

4. INS estimates are constructed by combining detailed statistics by year of entry for each component of change that contributes to the undocumented population residing in the United States. The undocumented usually enter the country through temporary stay visas and then stay beyond the specified period of admission. Approximately 40 percent of the undocumented are nonimmigrant overstays. The remainder of the undocumented cross the border between ports of entry. Thus there are five primary sets of data: (1) entered before 1982; (2) net overstays from 1982 to present; (3) net entered without inspection (EWIs); (4) mortality estimates of annual deaths to the resident undocumented population; and (5) emigration: number of undocumented immigrants who emigrated to the United States in the following four-year period.

5. In 1998, the Unz initiative, or Proposition 227, would eliminate bilingual education in California schools (K-12) within a year after its passage. Then limited proficiency or non–English speaking students would be placed in a language immersion program for a year. I discussed this proposition and its politics in the previous section of this chapter.

10

Education
and Voting Rights

~~~~~~

Adquirir conocimiento, profundizar la sabiduría y proteger nuestros derechos humanos comienzan con la formación académica que sostiene nuestro afán por aprender. Lo usamos para afirmar nuestro auto concepto y vivir con dignidad.

Acquiring knowledge, deepening our wisdom, and protecting our human and civil rights begins with an education that sustains our desire to learn. We use that knowledge to affirm our own self-esteem and to live with dignity.

The Department of Commerce (U.S. Census Bureau 2000) announced that the Hispanic population showed gains in educational attainment. More specifically, the proportion of Latinos aged twenty-five and older with a high school degree or higher increased from 51 percent in 1987 to 56 percent in 1999. During the same time period, the proportion of Latinos who have some college training increased about seven percentage points (from 22 percent to 29 percent), and those with a bachelor's degree increased about two points (from 8 percent to 10 percent). These indicators of educational progress for Latinos demonstrate gains in educational attainment; yet relative to other populations, the educational gap is still widening (i.e., the percentage of non-Hispanic white adults over twenty-five years who are high school graduates is 87.8 percent). Although Latinos are improving their educational achievement, other groups in the nation are improving as well. African Americans and Asian Americans have made similar or even greater gains in educational attainment. For example, while the percentage of Latinos who have completed high school is now 56 percent, the percentage of Asian Americans exceeds 85 percent.

EDUCATION: A LATINO CONTINUAL PRIORITY

In chapter 9, I laid out the nature of the American public policy process and the resources and strategies Latinos need to pursue to secure policy outcomes and implementation that can make a difference. For over thirty-five years, the Mexican American community and subsequently other Latino groups have focused their attention and activities on the educational system. Issues of insufficient resources, segregation, exclusion from decision making, lack of representation in the teaching and administrative ranks, poor facilities, curricular needs, and bilingual programs represent a major portion of the educational issues facing the Latino communities. In 1970, the U.S. Commission on Civil Rights published the six-volume *Mexican American Education Project.* This report outlined the major problems confronting Mexican American children and their parents. The thrust of the report (looking at the five southwestern states) documented the extensive problems Mexican Americans encountered in the educational system, which resulted in low educational achievement, high dropout rates, and thwarted aspirations.

Nearly thirty years later, a recent report, *Our Nation on the Fault Line,* by the **President's Advisory Commission on Educational Excellence for Hispanic Americans** (1999), reported that the educational achievement gap between Latinos and non-Latinos persists and recurring problems have not changed. The magnitude of the crisis is unparalleled, according to the commission. Examining conventional educational indicators, Hispanic Americans are making progress at alarmingly slow rates from preschool through grade school, middle school, high school, and on to higher education. The cumulative effect of such neglect is obviously detrimental not only to Hispanics but also to the nation (1999, 1).

The particulars of Latino "educational well-being" indicators identified by the commission include the following:

1. Less than 15 percent of all Latinos participate in pre-school programs.
2. More than twice as many Latinos as non-Latinos are enrolled below grade level (are older than the age associated with the grade level).
3. Latinos drop out earlier and at unacceptably high rates.
4. The total proportion of bachelor's degrees for Latinos has risen only 1.4 percent from 1985 to 1993, even though Latino college enrollment has increased by 3.2 percent.
5. Illiteracy for Latino adults has remained high compared to other groups.
6. Latino students are segregated in schools that are resource poor (1999, 3–4).

To compound poor Latino educational achievement, inadequate school funding, bilingualism treated as a liability, and a lack of representation on educational policy-making boards are additional obstacles that need to be overcome in order to improve Latinos' educational experiences and outcomes. While this latest national commission on the status of Latinos and the educational system portrays a "crisis situation," this pattern is a long-standing one. In 1972 the U.S. Commission on Civil Rights characterized the Mexican American educational experience as one of neglect, isolation, discrimination, inadequate resources, and linguistic ostracization. So while the documentation of the substance and scope of Latinos and the educational system has produced repetitive and consistent findings, the range of recommendations has also carried prescriptions similar to the ones recommended by previous federal commissions. The President's Advisory Commission generated an extensive set of recommendations to try to alleviate the educational neglect of Latinos.

The recommendations include the following:

1. Model effective programs and intervention strategies in preschool education, dropout prevention, bilingual education, and student motivation.
2. End segregation of Latinos.
3. Oppose the prevention and termination of educational opportunities for immigrant children.
4. Train teachers to deal effectively with multicultural children.
5. Ensure adequate funding and proper funding for bilingual education programs, Title VII of the Improving American Schools Act and Goals 2000.
6. Increase four-year access for Latino high school graduates and community college transfer students, especially financial support initiatives (1999, 4–6).

These recommendations represent only a partial list of "solutions" designed to improve Latinos' educational progress and equity. Yet our focus on public policy needs to extend beyond a listing of the problems and possible solutions. The educational system must extend beyond professional educators. Administrators and policy makers, like parents, communities, and Latino organizations, play a viable role in defining the policy agenda and impacting legislation. The Latino community has been trying to impact the educational system for decades and continues its struggle. One of the difficulties of this policy area lies in the multi-layered nature of education.

Historically and politically, the crux of educational decision-making is located at the local level. Local school boards and superintendents make policy decisions, and educational professionals are major participants in the decision-making process. At the same time, state governments play a major role in financing with their ability to raise tax revenues for local school districts. More recently, state government has also gotten involved in standardizing testing of student performance and exit exams for graduation. Finally

the federal government, with its significant revenues, provides intergovernmental aid, especially for desegregation programs, compensatory education
programs, and bilingual education funding. Thus the educational decision-
making process involves several policy arenas, political jurisdictions, and key
actors. The multiple points of access allow Latinos to develop many different
strategies and pressure points to effect change.

A persistent theme resulting from social surveys during the past thirty
years is the importance of education among Latinos. Originally, surveys were
conducted with Mexican Americans in the Southwest and nationally (Arce
1982) and later with Mexicans, Cubans, and Puerto Ricans (de la Garza et al.
1993). In every case, when Latinos were asked to identify key issues and concerns, education was consistently ranked among the top three. At the same
time, there are popular notions about the reasons for the poor educational
"track record" among Latinos: a lack of commitment and value placed on
education by Latinos themselves. Again the cultural dimension of being
Latino comes into play as a possible explanation for poor educational attainment. The Latino response has centered on examining the structural dimensions and policy biases instead of "blaming the deficiencies" within the
Latino community.

Consistent with our theme of policy emanating from cultural and situational conditions, the policy area of education embroils both. The persistence
of Spanish-language use has meant that many Latino children begin their
school experience with limited or no English-language facility. With learning
and understanding based on an English curriculum, the role of language
impacts progress through the grades (K-12) and beyond. For many Latinos,
grade repetition, placement in remedial classes, poor standardized test performance, lower participation in "college preparatory classes," and more inci-
dences of disciplinary actions (Duran 1983; Carter and Segura 1979; Meier
and Stewart 1991) are common patterns.

Mexican Americans still attend many **de facto segregated schools** (schools
that due to residential segregation and school attendance zones produce
schools that are highly segregated by race, **ethnicity,** and class). Until the
mid-twentieth century, de jure segregation (legally mandated segregation of
students based on race and ethnic background) was evident in California and
Texas. Two court cases, *Westminster v. Mendez* and *Bastrop I.S.D. v. Gonzalez,* challenged the segregation of Mexican American students. Part of the
rationale for the segregation was based on educational or pedagogical needs.
School administrators used Latinos' cultural "distinctiveness" as the basis
for separating them from the rest of the other students in order to educate
them properly, while taking nothing away from the educational progress of
other students. In this case, culture served to define the best way to deal with
the educational needs of Latino children, viewing their culture as a hurdle for
educational success.

A subsequent policy question of who Latinos are, arose in the 1970s and

Lauro F. Cavazos Jr. (1927–)

After winning many awards in various fields, Lauro F. Cavazos served as secretary of education from 1988 to 1990. This appointment made him the first Hispanic American to be a cabinet member.

Cavazos, a sixth-generation Texan, was born on January 4, 1927, on the huge King Ranch, where his father worked. He received a B.A. and an M.A. in zoology in 1949 and 1952, respectively, at Texas Technological University. In 1980 he became president of the university and of its Health Sciences Center. He was the first Hispanic and the first Texas Tech graduate to hold those posts.

In August 1988, President Ronald Reagan appointed Cavazos to head the United States Department of Education. Reagan called his new cabinet member a leader in helping minorities gain educational opportunities.

Cavazos had explained, in a speech to Texas school administrators two years earlier, his commitment: "We will never really succeed in having the kind of world we want unless our children are educated. . . . While it is important to be prepared to defend the nation militarily, it is important also to be prepared intellectually to provide quality education for every child."

Cavazos pointed out that Hispanics, who at that time had a 45 percent dropout rate, were becoming an increasingly larger percentage of students in United States public school systems, "and getting them to stay in school is going to be difficult."

Thanks in great measure to Cavazos's influence, the President's Council on Educational Excellence for Hispanic Americans was created to stimulate scholarship among Latino youth. Cavazos's performance as secretary of education was criticized by some, but Cavazos was reappointed by the next president, George H. W. Bush.

Both Reagan and Bush picked Cavazos for the job despite the fact that he was a Democrat. Bush's Republican White House chief of staff, John Sununu, however, forced Cavazos to tender his resignation in 1990.

The League of United Latin American Citizens (LULAC) honored Cavazos with the title Hispanic Educator of the Year (1983) and with a Hispanic Hall of Fame Award four years later. Among his honors are a Medal of Honor from the University of California, the President's Medal for Distinguished Achievement from the City College of New York, the Medal of Merit from the Pan American University, and the Distinguished Service Medal from the Uniformed Service University for the Health Sciences.

Hispanic Business magazine named him one of the one hundred influential Hispanics in 1987.

Bibliography

Meier, Matt S. *Mexican American Biographies.* Westport, Conn.: Greenwood, 1988.

Box 10.1   Latinas and the Educational System

A recent report by the American Association of University Women on Latinas and schools (Ginorio and Huston 2000) joins the debate over whether educational failings result from deficiencies within Latino culture and practices or from institutional or systemic factors. According to the report, Latinas lag behind other racial and ethnic groups in graduation rates; they are less likely to take the SAT, and scores are lower for those who do; they are under-enrolled in gifted and talented education and Advanced Placement classes; and they are less likely to complete a bachelor's degree. Ironically, Latinas often perform better than their male peers, with higher scores in reading, history, mathematics, and science over their high school years. The gender gap for Latinas is greater than that for other racial/ethnic groups. Finally, the report provides strong evidence that both Latinos and Latinas experience stereotyping and other obstacles that discourage achievement in school. Latinas were three times more likely than other girls to fear for their personal safety in school. In addition, teachers and counselors often assume that Latinos(as) are gang members because they speak Spanish.

The AAUW report introduces the positive role of Latino cultural values and educational policies. Ginorio and Huston state that "schools need to work with and not against their families and communities and the strengths that Latinas bring to the classroom . . . to recognize cultural values and help Latinas harmonize these values with girls' aspirations to education and learning." Essentially their recommendations focus on greater cooperation between education professionals and parents to produce a more conducive climate for academic success. This report serves as a good example how "situations" can be defined, problems framed, responsibility placed, and culture viewed.

1980s regarding desegregation plans for many southern and southwestern communities. It was brought to a head in the cases of *Nichols v. Houston I.S.D.* and *Keyes v. Denver I.S.D.* In both situations, the school districts' original desegregation plans involved pairing and/or reassigning Latino children with African American students. In this manner, the school district would satisfy the racial mix targets without impacting many Anglo students. The courts ruled that for purposes of desegregation plans, Mexican Americans and other Latinos constituted a separate "ethnic group" and introduced a tri-ethnic formula to determine how desegregation plans would be designed. Establishing Latinos as an official part of the desegregation mix opened the legal door to questions of educational quality and equity. Latinos were concerned about the educational curriculum, bilingual educational programs (or their absence), and overall quality of education, in addition to racial/ethnic isolation.

Even though these cases and others prohibited de jure segregation, the 1990s saw increasing numbers of Latinos being concentrated in ethnically segregated schools and school districts. As mentioned in previous chapters, the youthfulness of Latino populations is reflected in their growing numbers in school districts throughout the country. In many major school districts (e.g., Los Angeles, Houston, Tucson, New York, Denver), Latinos now are the majority group and their percentages will continue to increase in the future. Thus a condition associated with rising numbers of Latino students is their location in resource-poor districts in terms of tax base, expenditure levels, facilities, teacher salaries, and so on.

In the 1970s and 1980s these resource disparities were raised in *Serrano v. Priest* and *Rodriquez v. San Antonio I.S.D.* Basically relying on property taxes to underwrite most school funding disadvantaged poorer communities. Much higher tax rates had to be instituted in order to generate revenues comparable to more affluent communities. Underlying the legal arguments for the plaintiffs was the matter of educational equity and access to a quality education as a fundamental right. Subsequently, state governments were brought into the policy area of school financing with court orders to equalize school financing statewide.

Over time, more significance is given to the importance of educational achievement for all students in order to lead productive and economically rewarding lives. The association of successful completion and achievement in schooling with employability, earnings, overall quality of life, economic mobility, and improved social status emphasized the centrality of educational success in a modern American society. While the courts did not completely embrace the fundamental rights arguments, the significant resource disparities across school districts and heavy reliance on property taxes were matters that states needed to address. This resulted in state legislatures dealing with school equalization at the statewide level. As a result, the role of the state increased in providing school financing throughout their respective states. Yet some twenty years later, successful implementation of school equalization remains a problem.

Sandy Astin (1982, 1985) advanced the idea of an educational pipeline in which identifiable "leaks" illuminate the problem areas for students. Normally, the example begins with a cohort of one hundred students entering kindergarten and counts the number who progress to high school graduation. In the case of Latinos, more than half (approximately 55) of the original students do not make it to high school graduation. The list of explanations can range from lack of pre-schooling, English language "deficiency," lack of

Joseph Manuel Montoya (1915–1978)

In 1936, at age twenty-two, Joseph M. Montoya, who was still at George-town University, became the youngest person in the history of the state to be elected to the New Mexico House of Representatives. In 1938 Montoya graduated from law school and was reelected. The following year he was elected Democratic majority floor leader. In 1940, Montoya was elected to the state senate, once again becoming the youngest person ever elected. By the time he left the senate in 1946, Montoya had been reelected twice and held the position of majority whip as well as chairman of the Judiciary Committee. From 1947 to 1957 he was elected lieutenant governor three times and also served two additional terms in the state senate.

In 1957 Montoya was elected to the U.S. House of Representatives in a special election after the sudden death of the recently reelected New Mexican Congressman Antonio Manuel Fernandez. In Congress Montoya gained recognition as a political moderate, a dedicated Democrat, and a diligent legislator. In 1963 he became a member of the House Appropriations Committee. A strong advocate of education measures, he authored the Vocational Education Act. In 1964 Montoya won the 1964 U.S. Senate election to complete the term of Dennis Chavez, beginning an eleven-year career in the Senate, where he served on the Appropriations Committee, the Public Works Committee, the Joint Committee on Atomic Energy, and, most memorably, the Senate Select Committee on Presidential Campaign Activities, popularly known as the Watergate Committee. Montoya also worked on behalf of civil rights, education, health care, and alien workers, and he maintained a strong interest in the economic well-being of his constituents. In 1976 Montoya was defeated by Harrison Schmitt, a former astronaut.

Bibliography

Hispanic Americans in Congress. Washington, D.C.: U.S. Government Printing Office, 1995.

Vigil, Maurilio, and Roy Luján. "Parallels in the Career of Two Hispanic U.S. Senators." *New Mexico Historical Review,* October 1972, 362–81.

bilingual and/or English as a second language programs, grade repetition, poor facilities and resources, segregation in poorer school districts, discriminatory disciplinary actions, tracking into vocational programs or into the general curriculum, inadequate support systems, under-representation on school boards, among administrators and teachers, and insensitive and culturally inappropriate standardized testing and assessment (Meier and Stewart 1991; Orfield 1991a,b) The net result in the educational pipeline is the loss of many Latinos, particularly in the middle school years. For example, 40 percent of the sixteen-to-twenty-four-year-old Latino dropouts left school with less than a ninth-grade education, compared to 13 percent of non-Latino white dropouts and 11 percent of African Americans.

So far I have catalogued a long list of poor educational outcomes and the need for Latinos to interject themselves into the education policy process. With the primary assumption of successful educational progress being connected to better jobs and earnings potential and a better quality of life, why are there differential outcomes based on race, ethnicity, gender, and class? One way to examine education public policy is to raise questions about why the educational experiences and outcomes are the way they are. Are Latinos, as a group, less able, less motivated, less supportive of educational attainment, or culturally limited to succeed in education? Does the "educational establishment" operate in a way that creates obstacles and is it designed so that Latinos will consistently do poorly? These questions, while polar in nature, can serve to sort through the policy perspectives and policy alternatives that come from Latinos and other interested parties.

The first perspective points to the primary source of the problem as emanating from Latinos themselves. Poor educational progress and performance results from a lack of supportive educational values and efforts by families and the community. The cultural dimension for Latinos also comes into play, negatively affecting their educational progress. Persistent Spanish-language use and linguistic isolation reinforce many Latinos' lack of receptivity to an English-language curriculum. In addition, purported cultural values of traditionalism, superstition, machismo, and fatalism are attributed to Latinos (Carter and Segura 1979). Latinos' cultural values and beliefs are viewed as inappropriate to the American educational system. For example, someone with more traditional values and outlook assumes that the student will have less interest in and ability to deal with science and mathematics. The segregation of Mexican Americans in their own schools or separate classrooms is justified on pedagogical reasons. It was better to isolate Mexican American children to teach them separately in light of their cultural "drawbacks," as well as not inhibiting the learning of non-Latino children.

Language has been central in the analysis of the poor educational performance of Latino children. In the 1960s, advocates for bilingual education began to pursue federal legislation to support a bilingual education curriculum. It was felt that learning both content and subject matter as well as honing English skills (not just verbal, but syntax, writing, etc.) would be enhanced with the use of the student's home language. Given this broader view of English-language mastery, the bilingual curriculum would cover a number of grades and/or periods of time. In 1968, the Bilingual Education Act was passed with the congressional leadership of Senator Ralph Yarborough (TX) (Crawford 1992b).

At the same time, Latino educational activists and organizations like the National Association of Bilingual Educators lobbied diligently to get federal status and funding. By 1973, the federal government was spending $45 million a year to support bilingual education in twenty-six languages. The early expert witnesses, mostly Latinos, were linguists, psychologists, state legislators, curriculum specialists, school administrators and teachers, and labor and business leaders (Crawford 1992b). Part of the rationale for bilingual education has centered around the psychological effects of a monolingual English curriculum on non-English or limited-English-speaking children.

A. Bruce Gaarder, head of the modern language programs for the U.S. Office of Education, stated in subcommittee testimony:

> Language is the most important exteriorization or manifestation of the self, of the human personality. If the school, the all-powerful school, rejects the mother tongue of an entire group of children, it can be expected to affect seriously and adversely those children's concept of their parents, their homes, and . . . themselves. (Crawford 1992a, 78)

Thus the policy debates about bilingual education fold in many issues, concerns, values, and controversies. The multitude of issues and interpretations including the following:

- the continuance of non-English languages and the extent of assimilation and integration into American life;
- persistence of "foreign" cultural practices and norms;
- cultural and linguistic balkanization;
- how learning and intelligence is associated with language use;
- the appropriateness of bi-or multilingualism in America;
- the state's involvement in promoting other cultures and languages; and
- what constitutes educational opportunities for all.

In the final analysis, bilingual education is about the growing political empowerment of Latinos in the United States. While bilingual education focuses on curricular methodologies and approaches for children with limited English proficiency, the long-standing problems those Latino children have encountered in school reflect a disempowered position in policy-making bodies. For Mexican Americans, school walkouts in the 1960s and 1970s raised bilingual education needs, as well as teacher and administrator recruitment, cultural studies courses, ethnic foods in the cafeteria, review of disciplinary policies, access to extra-curricular activities, and segregated schools. The underlying theme was recognition and direct involvement in the educational decision-making process. Similarly, school decentralization efforts in New York City (Gittell and Fantini 1970), especially in the Ocean Hill-Brownsville areas, reflected major initiatives by Latinos and other minorities to have a greater impact on education.

This discussion of bilingual education is inter-meshed with an overall move by Latinos for greater empowerment in all relevant realms of Latino educational needs and concerns. The more recent "lightning rod" for bilingual education and the entire corollary of Latino concerns lies with **Proposition 227** in California, officially entitled the English Language Initiative for Immigrant Children, or the Unz initiative. Californians voted on it in June 1998. The goal of Proposition 227 was to teach English to children in public schools as rapidly as possible. Most instruction would be in English, and limited English proficiency students would be placed in English immersion classes for a year and then "mainstreamed" into regular classes. Finally, the legislature would appropriate $50 million annually for ten years to subsidize English classes for adults who agree to tutor English learners. Early polls indicated strong support for Proposition 227 across all racial and ethnic groups and partisans. The *Los Angeles Times* reported that almost two-thirds of Latino voters indicated support for Proposition 227.

During the course of the campaign, political **mobilization** by both established Latino organizations (**National Association of Bilingual Educators,** Mexican American Political Association, LULAC, etc.) and ad hoc groups pushed for Latinos to oppose Proposition 227. The bases for the opposition ranged from the misrepresentation of what bilingual education entails, the limited benefits of English immersion for non–English speaking students, the proposition as a general attack on the Latino community in California, and the overall educational status of Latinos in the state. While the early pre-election pools indicated strong support across all groups, on Election Day, Latinos voted 63 percent to 37 percent against Proposition 227. Overall, the proposition passed 60.9 percent (for) to 39.1 percent (against). Only two counties voted against the proposition (San Francisco and Alameda) and a majority of Anglos (67 percent), African Americans (57 percent), and Asian Americans (52 percent) voted for the Unz initiative.

Interestingly, some of the exploratory items in the *Los Angeles Times* exit poll revealed real differences between Latinos and non-Latinos. Twelve percent of Latinos were first-time voters compared to 4 percent for all voters. Also, 39 percent of Latino voters indicated that they were motivated to vote because of Proposition 227 compared to 27 percent of all voters. Fully 49 percent pro-Unz voters indicated that all persons should speak English (as a reason to vote for Prop. 227) in contrast to 24 percent of Latino voters (*Los Angeles Times* 1994a). On the other hand, 36 percent of Latinos versus 16 percent of non-Latinos indicated they were motivated to vote on Proposition 227 because they felt that the proposition discriminated against non–English speaking persons. As the campaign progressed, Latinos became more invested and opposed to the proposition.

It has been posited (Crawford 2000) that as individuals became more informed about the issues and many of the particulars about bilingual education curriculum, they were less likely to support it. Part of the underlying issue was a continued activation within the Latino community in California in response to "negatively" targeted initiatives. Opponents of Proposition 227 connected the Unz initiative to several statewide referendums (discontinuing state affirmative action programs, denying immigrant social and educational services, and limiting union contributions to political campaigns) that placed undue burdens on Latinos. Activating the Latinos of California, due in part to the rise of "hostile" propositions, stimulated greater participation not only in ballot propositions but also in elections of more Latino legislators and local officials.

Most surveys done during the 1990s indicated that the vast majority of Latinos acknowledged the need to acquire proficiency in English. On the other hand, there is a strong tendency among Latinos to maintain their culture, which includes the Spanish language, and to be bilingual. Thus while Proposition 227 eliminated bilingual programs, the issue area was not just a pedagogical one. Bilingualism and the perpetuation of a bi- or multilingual American society were also at stake for Latinos.

A recent survey of Hispanics asked their respondents to indicate the more pressing issues facing the Latino community. The policy area with the greatest concern and attention was education (*Washington Post* 1999). Surveys conducted in the 1960s and 1970s reflect the same prioritization in which the education policy area was the most salient. Although education continues to be a high priority among Latinos, some issues persist while others take on new forms. For example, the issues of bilingual education in the 1960s and 1970s addressed its implementation and funding. Once federal legislation was adopted, the focus turned to expanding the number of programs in place and broader inclusion of limited English speaking students. It was only in the 1990s that an organized "backlash" was directed toward bilingual education curriculum. At the same time, matters of overcrowded schools, more racially and ethnically segregated schools and school districts, disciplinary actions, social promotions, continued poor standardized test performances, and lack of political and administrative representation on school boards fill the Latino educational agenda.

The commitment to educational attainment and progress and its importance for social and economic mobility form a strong core for Latinos to invest in the educational policy arenas. Our continuing theme of forming and operating as a community of culture and/or interest is quite applicable in this policy area. While there is no absolute consensus on every policy dimension associated with education, Latinos exhibit more of an active, working community in this area.

VOTING RIGHTS, THE VOTING RIGHTS ACTS, AND LATINOS

While education and the challenges that Latinos continue to face in achieving educational excellence and equity, another policy area of long-standing priority is representation and access to office holding. We have already seen the concerns for power and influence among Latinos, and the linkages between electoral participation, political influence, and policy outputs. Active electoral activities (voting, campaigning, contributing money, etc.) by Latinos can increase their political capital. During Campaign 2000 both major political parties devoted increasing attention to Latinos. In addition, more Latinos(as) pursued elective offices at all levels throughout the country. The electoral gains that occurred in the 2000 elections for Latinos can be attributed to such factors as a maturing or aging population, greater numbers of naturalizations, heightened political awareness, more effective mobilizing by Latino organizations and leaders. This section explores another contributing dimension to the positive developments of electoral participation and representation by reviewing and analyzing the voting rights acts.

The **Voting Rights Act** (VRA) of 1965 marked a major policy initiative to deal with long-standing practices that had excluded African Americans and other minorities from the electoral process. Such persistent problems had included annual registration systems, literacy tests, hostile election poll locations, economic and physical intimidation of minority group members, and limited registration locations and hours. These practices had a direct bearing on the relative absence of minority elected officials and the resulting policy responsiveness by all levels of government. While the major impetus of the VRA was targeted toward African Americans in the South, subsequent amendments focused on Latinos and other linguistic minorities in other parts of the United States. Basically, the Voting Rights Act extended federal authority over matters related to all aspects of elections. For the most part, elections were administered by the states. A major factor was the rise of the civil rights movement, which pressured Congress and the White House to deal with civil rights, voting rights, housing, public accommodations, and employment discrimination.

Even though the Fourteenth and Fifteenth Amendments to the U.S. Constitution were designed specifically to guarantee African Americans the right to vote, implementation was far less than effective. For example, the Fifteenth Amendment forbids both states and the federal government to deny American citizens the right to vote on "account of race, color, creed, or previous condition of servitude." In addition the **Enforcement Act of 1870** specifically prohibited denial of the right to vote in state and local elections. The **Force Act of 1871** gave federal court appointed supervisors the power to oversee registration and election processes when two citizens make that request. Later in the 1800s, Congress repealed the Enforcement and Force Acts, and protective voting rights legislation was virtually nonexistent until the 1950s. Then a series of legislative enactments (Civil Rights Acts of 1957, 1960, and 1964) attempted to provide protection, but the remedy was enabling individuals to sue in federal court for voting rights violations. However, this case-by-case character did not lend itself to any systematic or complete design (Cottrell 1986).

In the summer of 1965 all the inadequacies of previous federal attempts to address basic voting rights and protections were brought to a "policy head." The VRA passed the House by a vote of 328–74, and the Senate by 79–18. The involvement of many civil rights organizations and the civil rights movement played a major role in pressuring Congress to act. The major provisions of this historic piece of legislation included both nationwide applications and special provisions that applied only to certain states and political subdivisions or covered jurisdictions (the Voting Rights Act applied to political jurisdictions in which registration and turnout is less than 50 percent of the potential electorate). For the most part, states in the South, including Texas and Arizona, were part of the covered jurisdictions. In addition, specific counties in states throughout the country[1] were also part of the VRA coverage. The previous use of discriminatory tests, devices, and practices in the electoral process were key determinants for which states, counties, and towns were brought under the VRA.

Essentially, the role of the federal government was to take a more active role in monitoring state and local jurisdictional practices to ensure the availability of open and fair access to all residents. Section 2 of the VRA set out the bases in which voting requirements would be evaluated in terms of their effects on minority populations.[2] Section 5 of the VRA required covered jurisdictions to submit any election-related changes before the Department of Justice for **preclearance.** Preclearance involved the Voting Rights section of the Justice Department, which reviewed proposed election changes (different election dates, changed poll locations, election materials, annexations, etc.) in order to assess their impact on minority group representation and possible voter dilution. The change could not result in minority voter dilution or negatively impact the equal protection provisions for all citizens.

Additional examples of possible changes include changes in electoral boundaries resulting from reapportionment, changes in the method of election, changes in the composition of the electorate resulting from annexations, consolidations, or incorporations, provisions establishing voter registration requirements and candidate qualifications, changes in the form of government, and provisions that set bilingual election procedures and assistance (Cottrell 1986). Amendments to the Voting Rights Act in 1972 and 1977 expanded coverage to include more jurisdictions in the Southwest and were applicable to Native American and Latino populations.

For the most part, if groups could show that election changes or existing election provisions "harmed" the minority community electorally, then the Justice Department or the courts would deny the proposals or require placement of more neutral election procedures and practices. With the 1982 amendments to the VRA, the results test was included for litigation that challenged the discriminatory effects of election systems and other voting practices. An earlier Supreme Court decision in *Mobile v. Bolden*[3] had placed the burden of proof on the plaintiffs to prove a purpose or intent to discriminate on the part of state or local officials, besides showing the effects of such election practices. The 1982 VRA amendment revised the requirements of proof to center on the results of discrimination instead of having to show intent. With that change, the plaintiffs did not have the highly difficult task of proving racial intent or purpose. The VRA also made use of federal observers to oversee elections and make sure minority voters have access to the electoral process. Local organizations could request federal examiners to observe local elections.

The greater significance of the VRA for Latinos came with the 1975 amendments (sec. 203) with extended coverage to linguistic minorities and broadened coverage to 14 states). The minority language groups included Asian Americans, Alaskan Natives, various linguistic groups among the American Indians, and persons of Spanish heritage. As a result, these political jurisdictions had to provide all election materials in the language of the covered language minority group. This included registration materials, election notices, and the ballot. Until 1992, there had to be the equivalent of 5 percent of a linguistic minority in the covered jurisdiction to produce bi-or multilingual materials. This was determined through the decennial census and the questions related to language use and abilities. For persons who spoke a language other than English, their responses as to their inability to understand English determine the threshold for VRA coverage. With the 1992 amendments, the minimum language threshold was set at 10,000 for each political jurisdiction.

THE VRA AND LATINO POLITICS

Federal involvement in electoral systems at the state and local levels was designed to remove a legacy of exclusionary practices that impeded the par-

William ("Willie") Cárdenas Velásquez (1944–1988)

Willie Velásquez created and ran an unparalleled drive to give Hispanics in the United States greater political power through voting. He spearheaded a process that convinced millions to vote and thousands to run for office. He also filed scores of successful lawsuits to reshape election districts more fairly. He changed the face of U.S. politics for Hispanics, though he never held political office.

Velásquez was born on May 9, 1944, in San Antonio, Texas, the son of a butcher. While San Antonio remained his home base for life, his work made him well known in U.S. political circles and in the Mexican American community simply as "Willie."

He graduated from college in 1966 and plunged into Hispanic civil rights activism. He began graduate studies in 1968 but dropped out in order to work full-time as an activist.

After leaving graduate school, Velásquez participated in an effort, led by civil rights pioneer César Chávez, to unionize farmworkers in Texas. He also helped found, or participated in the early operation of, a number of Hispanic civil rights organizations, including the Mexican American Legal Defense and Education Fund (MALDEF) and the Southwest Council of La Raza (The Race), which later became the National Council of La Raza.

However, in time, Velásquez began to believe that many existing organizations, particularly La Raza, were too quixotic. He felt that they were more concerned with dramatically establishing a position than with

ticipation of minority citizens. Our knowledge about levels of minority voter participation is also the result of the VRA. The law stipulated that the Bureau of the Census biannually collect data on voter registration and turnout. In the Bureau's 1972 survey, only 46.0 percent and 52.7 percent of Mexican Americans and Puerto Ricans respectively were registered to vote. Since then, there have been modest gains in the percentage of Latinos that are registered. Yet as noted in the discussion of Latino electoral participation in an earlier chapter, these electoral levels have not changed dramatically.

In addition to opening the electoral process for Latino voters, a main benefit of the VRA was the opportunity to elect more Latino officials. There is a connection between more Latino voters, a pattern of opening the political process, and continued non-responsiveness with greater efforts to have more Latino elected officials. As Latinos got more involved electorally, the obtaining practical results, and Velásquez was interested in the outcome. He thought that the key to results for Hispanics was voting power.

If many Hispanic Americans did not vote, he decided, it was not because of apathy or ignorance but because of a feeling that they could not win. This could change if the numbers of voters grew large enough. To help achieve this, he founded the Southwest Voter Registration Education Project in 1974. Known as SVREP, or simply Southwest Voter, the new group employed a variety of tactics in its drive to empower Hispanics. One was to keep activities at the grassroots level, maintaining close contact with individuals and with small community organizations. Another was to encourage people not only to vote but also to enter the political process as candidates. A third tactic was to conduct and then publish serious research into the voting patterns and the voting potential of Hispanics and the potential of Hispanic candidates.

Velásquez cooperated with groups such as MALDEF to bring lawsuits to redraw many election districts. These districts were often found to have been shaped in a way that diluted Hispanic voting power. An example was the joining of a heavily Hispanic downtown city area with largely Anglo suburbs to create a single voting district.

In the fourteen years that Velásquez led SVREP, it was credited with spectacular results: Hispanic voter registration in the United States rose from 3 million to 5 million; half of that increase—a jump of 1 million—was directly attributed to Southwest Voter. Hispanics went from having the lowest voter-registration rate among U.S. minorities to the highest, and the number of Hispanics in political office doubled to 3,200.

issue of **descriptive representation**[4] became more realistic. Descriptive representation refers to the population makeup racially and ethnically and the characteristics of the political representatives. The population percentages of racial and ethnic groups would mirror the background characteristics of their elected officials. Early records of Latino elected officials were kept in the late 1960s and early 1970s (J. A. García 1986a). Less than six hundred elected officials were holding office at any level of government. Over the period of the Voting Rights Act, there has been a marked increase of Latino elected officials. In 1998 the number of Latino elected officials exceeded 10,000. At the same time, the distribution of Latino elected officials is heavily concentrated at the local governmental area. More Latinos now serve on school boards, city councils, and county boards of supervisors than at state or federal levels.

Studies by the U.S. Commission on Civil Rights and the Joint Center for

Political Studies have documented significant gains among African American elected officials since the passage of the 1965 Voting Rights Act. The rate of change for Latinos since 1970 has been much slower than the African American experience. A number of explanations have been explored for the pace of Latino representation. One factor is the existence and effectiveness of Latino organizations to capitalize on the VRA and convert Latino non-registrants into registered voters. Organizations like the Southwest Voter Registration and Education Project (SVREP) and MALDEF/PRLDEF have focused much of their energy on voter registration drives and educating more Latinos about the electoral process. At times, these organizations encounter reluctance among Latinos to register, and the hesitancy includes distrust of the political system, lack of familiarity with American government and elections, fear of being called for jury duty, and disinterest.

Limited resources (education, income, and life cycle status) also come into play regarding Latinos electoral participation. These types of factors suggest that Latinos have limited social capital and less strong participatory orientations to be as active electorally. The concept of social capital focuses on the connections that exist among members of civic and political society that serve as a glue connecting citizens to form a community. It is characterized as a set of horizontal associations between people such as social networks and common norms that affect productivity and collective endeavors for a recognized community. According to Putnam (2000), the accumulation of social capital is the "lubricant" for the working of a democratic society. Therefore, the short-term opportunities afforded through the VRA have had limited returns for registration and turnout levels. At the same time, it has been argued that the absence of any voting rights legislation would have made the situation worse.

There is a legacy of exclusion and informal practices that have discouraged participation. Despite significant gains in the South for African Americans, economic intimidation and physical threats continued after the VRA. Similarly, in areas of the Southwest such as the Rio Grande valley, powerlessness, economic intimidation, and very limited social capital made it difficult to improve the representative position in the 1970s. Yet mobilization efforts, active political and social organizations, and leadership have resulted in significant gains in the 1980s and beyond. One area of VRA coverage deals with the reapportionment process. Any plans for states under the VRA jurisdiction have to undergo preclearance. As a result, redistricting, since the 1980s, has helped produce legislative districts (congressional, state, and local) that are more conducive to attracting and electing Latinos to public office.

The structural and historical conditions of many communities with a Latino presence help provide a contextual basis to understand how Latinos have participated or not (Montejano 1987). Latino participation does not solely depend on the individual and collective actions of Latinos, but political and social institutions and legal provisions that can impede, prohibit, or facilitate political involvement. These legacies and continuing practices can mitigate individual initiatives and motivation to get involved politically. Also, hostile environments and biased "rules of the game" can make it quite difficult for Latino organizations to be effective politically. The VRA provisions recognized the role of social and political structures and historical legacies, and attempted to remove these particular obstacles. It was hoped that underrepresented group members would be able to enter the electoral arenas more easily.

Political maturation and development have taken place within the Latino community. Since Latinos as a group have had lower levels of electoral involvement, it has been suggested that they have not understood the American political system well enough to be more competitive. With the passage of the VRA and its subsequent extensions and amendments, the Latino organizations and their leadership had to more effectively design their strategies and actions regarding voter registration, educational campaigns, and developing a cadre of Latinos to run for elected office. For example, earlier efforts at voter registration were timed many months prior to a election, and newly registered voters did not follow through using their vote. Door-to-door campaigns, more than just trying to convince Latinos to register and vote, also discussed concerns and issues. The timing of voter registration campaigns was changed to be closer to the election dates. Talking to potential Latino registrants about issues and concerns during the registration campaigns helped identify important issues and recognized community leaders who could be encouraged to seek elected office.

Gains in the number of Latino elected officials have increased over the past twenty years. At the local level, the gains have been more noticeable on school boards, especially in terms of Latina elected officials. At the same time, there have been some Latino successes at the state and federal levels. Since the 1980s, there have been two Latino governors (Tony Anaya in New Mexico and Bob Martínez in Florida). It was not until the 2000 elections that another Latino served in a statewide office. Cruz Bustamante, currently the highest-ranking Latino elected state official is lieutenant governor of California. Modest gains have been made in state legislatures, with California experiencing the most dramatic increases from the early 1990s. At the turn of the twentieth century, Latino candidates were seeking office in Kansas, Michigan, Missouri, Oregon, and Washington. There were five Latinos in Congress in 1970 but twenty-four in 2002. The 1970 congressional cohort consisted entirely of Mexican Americans, while the current Latino congresspersons include four Cubans and three Puerto Ricans. The last elected Latino senator was Joseph Montoya of New Mexico, who left the Senate in 1978. The more visible and broader base the elected office holds, the greater the resources and organization necessary for Latino candidates and the greater the difficulty of mounting a successful campaign.

There have been two major contributors to Latino increases in the number of elected representatives that have been associated with the VRA (J. A. García 1986a): (1) the changeover of **at-large election systems** to **single-member districts** and (2) reapportionment and redistricting. In the case of the former, litigation initiated by the Mexican American Legal Defense and Education Fund (MALDEF) and the Southwest Voter Registration and Education Project (SVREP) has challenged the discriminatory effects of at-large election system. Under this system, candidates would not run or be elected from any specific part of the community. The plaintiffs showed the exclusionary effects for Latinos in these communities by demonstrating the following patterns: a history of exclusion in many facets of local life schools, housing, representation, public access, etc.); unsuccessful attempts by Latino candidates to win elected office; evidence of voter polarization such that non-minority voters seldom vote for any Latino candidates; evidence of racially biased campaigns; and identifiable preference among Latino voters for Latino candidates. Once the litigants could demonstrate these patterns, the defendants (municipalities, counties, school districts, etc.) would have to show that these patterns were not the result of discriminatory actions.

These successful litigation attempts resulted in the ordering of single-member districts, which would improve the opportunity for Latino candidates. Single-member districts are elective positions in which voters in a specific area of the city or county nominate and elect their representative. Thus persons in other sections of the community elect representatives who live in their area. When these districts were drawn up, specific attention was given to the racial and ethnic makeup of the proposed districts. The preclearance process tied to the VRA approved districts with substantial and/or majority Latino constituencies in the districts. By doing so, it opened up access for Latino representation.

During the Reagan administration, the Department of Justice shifted the burden of proof to the plaintiffs, who must not only demonstrate patterns of exclusion but must prove discriminatory intent on behalf of the political jurisdiction. When the VRA was extended in 1982, Congress "reinstated" the "results" so that plaintiffs needed to prove that the results of election systems, practices, and so on, diluted Latino voter participation and impact, but not intent. Again the political jurisdiction would then have to show that the results were not due to their discriminatory practices. Over the next fifteen years, the federal courts, particularly, established the guiding principles used to determine if the voting rights of Latinos or other covered groups were violated or not.

A critical court case that set the standard for creating **majority–minority districts** was ***Thornburg v. Gingles*** (106 S. Ct. 2752 [1986]). Majority–minority districts are political jurisdictions with primarily minority residents (over 50 percent of the population). Election measures and actions that resulted in minority voter dilution have been a central protection from the VRA. In *Gingles*, the courts upheld the constitutionality of creating majority–minority districts when their voting strength has been submerged in multimember districts with white majorities. The courts recognized a state compelling interest to rectify a pattern of exclusion. The remedy of majority–minority districts is appropriate when there has been racially polarized voting that has minimized or cancelled out the potential for minority voters to elect candidates of their choice from their own community (Grofman 1995). In addition, if it can be shown that the minority community is sufficiently large and geographically concentrated, then a district can be drawn.

The *Gingles* ruling applied when there was substantiating racial bloc voting and when minority voter dilution existed. Then the court laid out three conditions to design a remedy: minority community is sufficiently large and geographically concentrated; it is a politically cohesive community; and the majority, when voting as a bloc, customarily defeats the minority community's preferred candidate (Pinderhughes 1995). Thus majority–minority districts became viable alternatives for Latinos and other minority communities to improve chances that their political representatives would come from that minority community.

In the early 1990s, a number of lawsuits were filed that challenged the creation and existence of majority–minority districts. These suits originated in Texas *(Vera v. Richards)*, Louisiana *(Hays v. Louisiana)*, North Carolina *(Shaw v. Reno)*, Georgia *(Miller v. Johnson)*, New York, Illinois, and Florida. Congresspersons Gutierrez (D-IL) and Velázquez (D-NY) were affected by litigation challenging their district boundaries. In each case, the plaintiffs challenged the predominance of race as the guiding force in the design of legislative or congressional districts, resulting in peculiarly shaped districts. The term "racial gerrymandering" was used to describe majority–minority districts. While the courts have supported such guidelines as compactness, contiguousness, and maintenance of **community of interests,** it is not the district shape per se that generated concerns among critics of voting rights redistricting (Grofman 1995). The plaintiffs objected to what was seen as racially motivated districting that takes the appearance of a system of proportional representation.

Shaw v. Reno brought majority–minority districts into question. The state of North Carolina submitted its redistricting plan to the Department of Justice preclearance division for review. One of its congressional districts was a majority–minority district (out of twelve districts), but the Justice Department rejected the plan, stating that it had demonstrated neither the purpose nor the effect of diluting minority-voting strength (Grofman 1995). At the

Box 10.2   Two Redistricting Stories

The following two redistricting stories (one from Odessa, Texas, and the other from northern Virginia) illustrate the promise, realities, and challenges confronting Latinos and the political parties. The Republican-controlled Virginia state legislature has designed a mostly Latino district in northern Virginia (Timberg and Melton 2001). Virginia Republicans have proposed creating the first legislative district without a white or African American majority. Instead, the district boundaries would link fast-growing Latino and Asian communities in Arlington, Alexandria, and the Baileys Crossroads section of Fairfax. The demographic breakdown would be 42 percent Latino, 20 percent African American, and 10 percent Asian American. The partisan elements involve a Republican effort to improve their inroads among Latinos by creating a minority district. At the same time, the plan also puts two Democratic delegates from Arlington into the same district.

Partisan efforts by politicians to position themselves in good stead with the Latinos in the Washington, D.C., area reflects their substantial population growth and potential voting support. In northern Virginia, the Latino population increased by 107 percent in the 1990s and by 90 percent in the D.C. area. Latino Republicans (the Virginia chapter of the National Republican National Assembly) have endorsed the plan. While party registration in the proposed district would favor the Democratic Party, Republicans are expected to recruit competitive minority candidates. It seems likely that if the proposed plan gets adopted, one of the two incumbent Democrats in the area will relocate to compete for that seat.

Both Latino and Asian American activists call the proposed district a step forward for minority representation, but they still question whether a minority (i.e., Latino) would be elected, since it is primarily an immigrant community. Most of the Latinos are Salvadorans and Bolivians, with non-citizenship being a significant factor. This example points out the mix of factors affecting Latinos and redistricting plans: growth to make up a sub-

same time, the Justice Department suggested a potential second African American majority district could be drawn in the southeastern part of the state. The state legislature responded with a new plan, although the second majority–minority district was drawn elsewhere in the state.

As a result, an elongated and snake-shaped twelfth district was challenged, as its shape was deemed bizarre in the extreme. Eventually the case stantial portion of any district, the mix of different minority groups within a district, the diminishing effects of a sizable non-citizen component, and assessment of the partisan effects and payoffs.

Texas has been redistricting, and the percentage of Latino growth in the state is quite momentous. In Ector County (Odessa), Latinos make up 42.4 percent of the county's population, compared to 31.4 percent ten years ago (Stevens 2001). At the same time, Latino representation in Ector County on various governing boards is 12.5 percent. For example, one of the seven Odessa College board is Latino, and the same is true for the school and hospital boards. The Odessa city council has one Latino among six representatives, and none of the five county commissioners is Latino.

The proposed county redistricting plan has three districts with Latino majorities ranging from 56.5 percent to 63.1 percent, and another district that is 42.6 percent. Local Latino leaders see this as an opportunity for more representation and potentially different policy agendas and decisions. At the same time, there are concerns about a drop-off in Latino voting strength, taking into account the voting-age population and the non-citizen segment. A Midland Latino city council member sees the new redistricting plans as an opportunity for the Republican Party to recruit Latinos. On the other hand, The Democrat Latina on the Odessa City council cites a challenge for Latinos to step up to leadership positions and "more importantly, exercise their power at the polls" (Stevens 2001).

This situation characterizes the opportunities and challenges that redistricting offers to Latinos now. The need to convert the population growth into a registered and active voting community is one challenge. Second, identifying and recruiting Latinos to contest for elected offices and assembling the necessary organizational and financial resources to be effective is another challenge. Finally, registration, education, and linkages with Latino adults and candidate support make up the third piece of the redistricting window of opportunity. Demonstrating a stronger Latino voting bloc, electing more Latinos or not, also has the effect of increasing their value to the major political parties.

went to the Supreme Court. The majority did not rule that the redistricting scheme violated white voter rights because it led to unfairly diluting or canceling out the votes of white voters because white voters were not being underrepresented. Ten of twelve districts had white majorities (Grofman 1995). The majority of the court asserted that equal protection could be betrayed if redistricting legislation "is so extremely irregular on its face that it rationally can be viewed only as an effort to segregate the races for purposes of voting, without regard for traditional districting principles and without sufficiently compelling state justification" (*Shaw v. Reno* 1993). Clearly this ruling brought the issue of the shape of legislative districts into question. Justice O'Connor pointed out those placing African American voters into a district "who are otherwise widely separated by geographic and political boundaries, and who have little in common with one another, but the color of their skin" (*Shaw v. Reno* 1993).

Thus the courts placed some real limitations on race-conscious decision making while, at the same time, not ruling that it was unconstitutional. There is still debate on this ruling regarding the vagueness of the new equal protection test laid down in *Shaw v. Reno* (for future challenges).[5] At the same time, court decisions in 2000 and 2001 upheld majority–minority districts with "irregular shapes" due to the state's compelling interest to remedy past exclusionary practices. In addition, the courts have not indicated any violation of group rights as a basis for ruling against the North Carolina redistricting and subsequent cases. How can the equal protection clause be violated when there is no group whose rights are violated? While this case does not hold race-conscious districting as prima facie unconstitutional, it does indicate the court has placed some parameters on a "race-conscious remedy." In both cases where a Latino congressperson was involved in a redistricting challenge, the redrawn district and subsequent election resulted in their retaining the seat.

While the VRA provides monitoring and opportunities for legal challenges to election systems and procedures, the increased difficulty of race-conscious redistricting plans is particularly important for Latinos and increased representation. While the U.S. Constitution requires Congress to be reapportioned after each decennial census, Supreme Court cases such as *Baker v. Carr* and *Westberry v. Sanders* have similar effects for state legislatures and local governments. As a partial result, the more noticeable gains for Latino representation have come after reapportionment (J. A. García 1986a, 1991). Growth gains of Latinos in the district or redrawn districts that concentrate more Latinos is closely associated with more Latino candidates and elected officials. For example, after the 1970 congressional reapportionment, Latinos in Congress went from five to nine. During the 1980s and 1990s the number of Latinos in Congress increased to twenty-one. The reapportionment process is also potentially beneficial to Latinos in the future because of their geographical location in states such as California, Arizona, Texas, Florida, and Colorado, which will receive additional congressional seats due to population growth.

For example, Arizona's population grew by 40 percent over the past decade and Latinos now constitute over 25 percent of the state's population. An independent redistricting commission (IRC) was established through referendum in the 2000 elections to reduce the partisan nature of redistricting politics. To the extent possible, Arizona's growth added two more congressional districts to draw. Under the IRC working plan, only the Latino incumbent remains favorable for his reelection, and a second proposed district in the southern region of the state has a majority Latino population base. In the 2002 election Raul Grijalva was elected from the new 8th Congressional district in southern Arizona. As suggested in other places in this book, population growth alone does not guarantee immediate representational gains for Latinos, but it does create many opportunities. Concentration in key states, regions, and urban areas is an asset, in combination with effective leadership and organization and an expanded voting base.

SAFE DISTRICTS AND VOTER PARTICIPATION

While the VRA, with its preclearance and coverage provisions, has contributed to gains in Latino registration and voting, there is concern about unintended consequences for Latino districts. Researchers such as de la Garza and Desipio (1993) have raised some concerns about declining voter participation in Latino districts stemming from the creation of majority Latino districts, which has contributed to the increase of elected officials. The issue in these districts is that with a Latino representative less in question, the voters in the district, especially Latino voters, decline in their turnout levels. De la Garza and Desipio have argued that Latino voters should take more interest and participate in elections with Latino elected officials. These **safe districts** establish a Latino in that elected office almost indefinitely (absent term limits). The idea of a safe district generally suggests that the incumbent and her party are firmly entrenched in the elected office. A safe district can be secure for a particular political party, member of racial/ethnic group, and/or current incumbent. Thus the debate centers on the responsiveness of the Latino elected official to her constituency and the voting turnout level. If Latino turnout declines, that means Latino voters are less involved and officials do not need to pay much attention to their constituencies (Wolfinger 1993; Cain and Kiewiet 1992).

The interplay of representation, participation, responsiveness, and accountability bring together a wide range of considerations and indicators. The criticism of Latino majority districts and declining voter turnout is characteristic of most safe districts, regardless of the racial/ethnic background of the representative and the district. Linking voter turnout and policy responsiveness is but one of several ways for constituents to influence their representatives and the policy agenda. Political scientists have examined the meaning of low turnout in terms of apathy, satisfaction, cynicism, disinterest, and representative-constituent issue congruence. To a significant degree, all of these dimensions operate in this constituent-representative relationship. Participation and representation is more inclusive than vote turnout. The networks between the Latino representative and local groups and leadership, issue and policy congruence, constituent evaluation of the representative, and the representative's voting record provide a more comprehensive picture of the relationship between Latinos and Latino elected officials.

It is estimated that in most congressional house elections, less than 10 percent of the seats are competitive, and over 90 percent of incumbents are reelected (Tate 1993; Browning, Marshall, and Tabb 1984). While the numbers of Latino elected officials have been increasing steadily, it may be premature to conclude that the side effect of a declining voter turnout is negative. The larger social context of voter participation decline and how participation manifests itself in a more technological world and other political developments are affecting turnout levels more than having a Latino representative.

Nevertheless, the future for increased Latino political representation under the influence of the VRA lies in three more recent developments and opportunities. The first deals with the continued redistricting process of 2001–2002. All states and other jurisdictions (cities, counties, school, etc.) are developing plans from which all elected officials will operate in the 2002 elections and beyond. The composition of these district boundaries impacts party influence, current incumbents, potential challengers, and level of minority representation in this country.

While the creation of new majority–minority districts is likely, the creation of influence or impact districts and/or multiracial/ethnic districts is even more likely. **Impact or influence districts** represent areas in which the Latino community (the principle can be applied to other minority groups or defined interests) constitutes a significant portion of the population and electorate. In this manner, the creation of districts with a sizable proportion of Latinos (30–40 percent) establishes a "critical mass." Presumably representatives would be more responsive and Latinos could exert pressure more effectively. The second development is the closer proximity of Latino neighborhoods with other communities of color (i.e., African Americans and Asian Americans). In addition, there is a greater mix of Latino subgroups (Salvadorans, Dominicans, Puerto Ricans, Mexican Americans, etc.) in urban areas such as Los Angeles, Miami, New York City. This greater racial/ethnic mix of communities of color in political jurisdictions (i.e., congressional and legislative districts) affords an opportunity for inter-minority group coalitions, such as efforts in Boston and Los Angeles (Jennings 1992; Sonenshein 1990) to create cohesive and coordinated electoral redistricting strategies. The number of racially and ethnically diverse districts will be substantial after this current round of redistricting. How and in what ways Latinos pursue coalitional partners in the redistricting process can produce increased Latino representation, in both short and long term.

The third development in which the VRA has had a more direct effect is the installation of **alternative voting systems** as a remedy for minority voting dilution. Alternative voting systems are options from the conventional plurality (i.e., winner takes all) or majority system, which is the common mode in American elections. They range from cumulative voting, **limited voting,** and single transferable vote to proportional voting schemes. In several small communities in Texas (and North Carolina, as well) (García and Branton 2000), the result of voting rights litigation (initiated by the Southwest Voter Registration and Education Project) has changed at-large election systems to a **cumulative voting system.** A cumulative voting system enables voters to distribute their votes (the amount is equivalent to the number of positions available). If five city council seats are available, voters can give one candidate all five of their votes or split the votes among two candidates or any other combination. This election system and limited voting allows cohesive interests (racial/ethnic groups, issue organizations, minority political parties, etc.) to direct their votes to their preferred candidate(s). Limited voting is a voting system in which each voter has fewer votes than the total number of seats or positions to elect. For a five-seat election, the voter may have only one vote or up to four votes to cast. This method allows voters to target their support for a particular candidate or smaller subset of candidates. Studies by Engstrom et al. (1998) in the South and Southwest have demonstrated noticeable gains among minority groups, especially for African Americans.

Engstrom, Taebel, and Cole (1997) and Brischetto and Engstrom (1997) indicate that more minority candidates run for office with cumulative or limited voting systems than under the previous system, and they enjoy greater success in winning office. There are some differences also. African Americans have been more active in fielding candidates and winning than Latinos. Recently Texas and North Carolina (García and Branton 2000) passed legislation that allows local governments the option to change to either cumulative (Texas) or limited (North Carolina) voting systems. In May 2000 the Amarillo, Texas, school district held its first cumulative election in which a Latina and an African American were elected to the school board. As voting rights litigation continues to be filed on behalf of Latinos, especially during the next round of redistricting, the attention to alternative voting systems will be more carefully evaluated and promoted.

While the VRA was enacted in 1965, it has undergone numerous extensions and amendments. The inclusion of linguistic minorities and bilingual materials provisions served as major opportunities for Latinos to enhance their electoral participation. Over the subsequent extensions and congressional hearings associated with the VRA, efforts have been made to eliminate the bilingual materials provisions, allow covered jurisdictions to be removed from preclearance review, and provide stricter tests for minority plaintiffs to prove minority vote dilution and exclusionary practices. Currently the VRA extends until 2002, when Congress will decide whether to extend it or not. Debate about the need for the VRA and bilingual materials for elections in the twenty-first century will surely be substantial. The role of Latino organizations, Latino leaders, and Latino members of Congress, as well as the civil rights communities, will be pivotal in both extending the VRA and determining whether its provisions take into account recent court rulings on redistricting.

CONCLUSION

In this chapter and the previous chapter, we have focused on three key research areas that are salient for Latinos: education, immigration, and voting rights. Policy areas within the education area include the quality of education, bilingual education and curriculum to meet the needs of Latino children, equitable funding for education, quality of school facilities, representation in decision-making bodies and school personnel, disciplinary policies and enforcement, greater local control and involvement. To a significant extent, the educational issues that are confronting the Latino communities are much the same issues outlined and discussed by the U.S. Civil Rights Commission (1973) over a generation ago.

The ebb and flow of immigration to the United States and the state of the American economy are closely connected to public policy debates and legislation regarding more restrictive immigration. For the most part, issues surrounding immigration, especially undocumented immigration, have been directed largely toward Latino immigrants and Latino communities. As a result, Latino core concerns include matters of immigration admission policies and processing times, militarization of the U.S.-Mexican border, protection of civil and economic rights, participation in social service programs, more efficient naturalization processing, and political refugee status for Central Americans. A brief history of the voting rights acts and its impact on Latino representation and electoral participation shows that it assisted the political development of Latinos. The provisions of the VRA, especially preclearance and coverage status, enable Latino organizations, especially litigation-oriented ones, to challenge voting systems and practices. The introduction of bilingual materials was part of the amendment process that focused on linguistic minorities. Court decisions in the 1990s placed much tighter restrictions on the use of majority–minority districts as remedies for minority voter dilution. The number of local Latino representatives has increased dramatically, with less dramatic gains at the statewide and federal levels.

What constitutes important policy areas for Latinos can extend beyond the ones discussed in this chapter. In many regards, issues and/or conditions that impact Latinos directly can fall under the Latino policy agenda. For example, if Latinos are concentrated residentially in certain parts of the city and lack basic urban amenities (paved streets, drainage, lighting, etc.) then basic services are a Latino policy issue. In a similar manner, crime, housing, the environment (Pardo 1998), and the like impact Latinos and motivate the community for political engagement. The effectiveness of such involvement can rest on Latinos working by themselves or in concert with other groups who share similar concerns and/or are impacted significantly. The latter approach, cooperative ventures with other segments of the American political scene, serves as the focus of the next chapter.

NOTES

1. Particular counties and towns are covered by special provisions in Connecticut, California, Colorado, Florida, Hawaii, Idaho, Massachusetts, Michigan, New Hampshire, New York, North Carolina, South Dakota, and Wyoming.

2. The language in section 2 included: "(a) no voting qualification or prerequisite for voting or standard, practice or procedure shall be imposed or applied by any State in a manner which results in a denial or abridgement of the right of any citizen . . . to vote on account of race or color, or in contravention of the guarantees set forth in section (1973b(f)(2) of this title, as provided in subsection (b) of this section; and b) a violation of subsection (a) . . . if, based on the totality of circumstances, it is shown that the political processes are not equally open to participation by members of a class of citizens protected by subsection (a) . . . in that its members have less opportunity than other members of the electorate to participate in the political process and to elect representatives of their choice".

3. The plaintiffs challenge the at-large election system in the city and county of Mobile, Alabama, with serving as a major obstacle for African American candidates and, subsequently, the local African American community from having opportunities to win elected office. Racial voter polarization, high campaign costs, and racialized campaigning were associated with this election system.

4. For example, the U.S. House of Representatives includes 435 congresspersons. If Latinos were about 11 percent of the population, then descriptive representation would be approximately forty-five representatives.

5. The lack of grounding of the test lay in the absence of established criteria. For example, if two districts are drawn on similarly race-based principles, how does the court determine the injurious effect of either plan by virtue of its snake-like design? How does the court conclude any differential racial impact?

11

Building
Political Alliances

Nos damos cuenta que no dejamos de preguntarnos ¿cuál es el verdadero significado de "comunidad" y a quien consideramos nuestro pueblo? Reconocemos la relación que tenemos con nuestro propio pueblo o con otras personas cuya cultura y tradiciones son como las nuestras. O quizás hasta buscamos otras comunidades para explorar y con quien unirnos.

We realize we have not finished answering, "What is the real meaning of 'community' and whom do we consider to be our people?" We recognize the relationship that we have with our own people and with other people whose culture and traditions are similar to our own. Or perhaps more answers will come when I we seek out other communities to understand, and with whom to unite.

One of the themes in this book is the concept of community and how it is present, to varying degrees, in the Latino community. I have portrayed Latinos in terms of key and salient issues that are significant to most segments of the Latino communities. In addition, I have identified and discussed the rise and adjustment of specific Latino organizations and leaders as extending beyond any one national-origin group and its interests. Finally, we have explored the development of group identity and the rise of a pan-ethnic awareness and consciousness. While there may be some debate as to the cohesiveness and viability of a Latino political community, we take the position that linkages and interactions already occur regularly among Latinos.

Moreover, the recognition and cultivation of Latino-ness by the mass media, political parties, and leadership serve to establish even more community links. In this chapter, we will explore further the theme of community building and linkages and how it is evident among Latinos. It is a mistake to assume that persons of Mexican origin (or any other Latino subgroup) automatically come together with other Latinos. Community is forged with interactions, commonalties, and mutual interests. This discussion of expanding community will include Latinos' working coalitions or

Lucille Roybal-Allard (1941–)

Lucille Roybal-Allard's trajectory to political office has been through her involvement in Comisión Femeníl Mexicana and her relationship with Gloria Molina. Perhaps because she comes from a prominent Democratic political family—her father is the distinguished retired California Congressman Edward Roybal—and had experienced a lack of privacy and personal identity, Roybal-Allard had concluded that she did not want to enter the electoral political arena. Instead, after completing her college education, she chose community and advocacy work. But she quickly learned about barriers to resolution of community problems, barriers often imposed by elected officials themselves. Thus, when Molina's state assembly seat in the fifty-sixth Los Angeles district became available in 1986, Roybal-Allard was ready. Once elected, she set about a number of formidable tasks, for example, stopping the construction of a new prison in East Los Angeles. Other similar battles earned Roybal-Allard a solid reputation as an advocate for her constituency. Since her election to the U.S. Congress from the Thirty-third Congressional District in Los Angeles in 1992, she is emerging as a very effective legislator. As the first California Latina elected to Congress, Roybal-Allard's successes have opened the door for more Latinas to run for statewide national elected office.

Bibliography

Bornemeier, James. "Marshaling California's Democratic Forces." *Los Angeles Times*, February 7, 1997, 3.

Renwick, Lucille. "They're Out in the Cold: The New Conservative Agenda in Washington Could Spell Trouble for Many Inner City Services and Funding." *Los Angeles Times*, January 1, 1995, 12.

alliances with other minority communities, especially the African American community.

I began this book by introducing a community based on commonalties of culture and interests. The common cultural base extends itself when individuals are connected closely together by their participation in a common system of meaning with accompanying patterns of customary interactions and behaviors that are grounded in a common tradition (Cornell 1985). Common language, religion and religious practices, familial networks, celebrations and holidays, folklore and customs, and the arts can be inclusive of Latinos' common culture. On the other hand, a **community of interests** exists when Latinos are united by a common set of economic and political concerns due, in part, to their concentration in certain industries and/or occupational domains, being residentially segregated (Denton and Massey 1988; Bean and Tienda 1987), or politically disenfranchised (Smith 1990; Acuña 1996). Common conditions and interests should lead to the development of a shared sense of group identity, perceived common conditions and contributing **structural factors** (discrimination, institutional racism, exclusionary practices, etc.), and a common policy agenda.

LATINO COMMUNITY FORMATION: BASIS FOR PARTNERSHIPS

I will try to augment the notion of shared Latino culture and interests by identifying concrete indicators forging a Latino community. The data vehicle for this exploration is the Latino National Political Survey (de la Garza et al. 1993). One benefit of the survey's results is the range of questions that can provide good indicators of commonalties. On the other hand, the LNPS is limited to Cubans, Puerto Ricans, and Mexican-origin respondents. Although these three groups represent almost four-fifths of the Latino population, the notable increase of Central and South Americans prevents it from furnishing a complete picture of the dynamic Latino community. So we can create snapshots and actual indicators of the basis for community. The indicators that we will use are (1) Latino group identity, (2) interactions among Latinos, (3) perceptions of Latino group discrimination, (4) Latinos' affinity across groups and their home countries, and (5) perceived common cultural practices and political/economic interests.

Latino Group Identity

The LNPS asked each respondent if he or she identified with national-origin or pan-ethnic terms (Latino, Hispanic). Examples ranged from Mexicano, Boricua, and Cuban to Latino, Hispano, and Hispanic. Overwhelmingly, most of the respondents selected their corresponding national-origin terms (Puerto Ricans selected Puerto Rican or Boricua, etc.) (García et al. 1993). The pan-ethnic options were Hispanic and Latino. Over one-fourth of the Mexican-origin and Puerto Rican respondents chose Hispanic as their identification and another one-fourth to one-seventh selected Latino. The respondents could select more than one Latino descriptor. Interestingly, only 12.9 percent of the Cuban respondents selected Hispanic, while 18.5 percent selected Latino. There was some variation among those choosing Latino: Mexican-origin, 14.8 percent; Puerto Rican, 24.6 percent; and Cuban, 18.5 percent. While each respondent selected a national-origin label, the presence of Latino or Hispanic choices provided some evidence of a broader sense of inter-group identification.

Research by Jones-Correa and Leal (1996) uses the same data source to explain the extensiveness of Latino/Hispanic identity and its role in these communities. The use of a primary and/or secondary identification places **pan-ethnicity** within a constellation of multiple identities. Latinos born in the United States, as well as Latinos with several generations here, were more likely to select a pan-ethnic identification, particularly the Mexican-origin respondents. Jones-Correa and Leal (1996) suggest that pan-ethnicity has been socially constructed over time, which has contributed to increases in pan-ethnic identification among Latinos. At the same time, Jones-Correa and Leal (1996) do not find a significant relationship between persons using a Latino identifier and acknowledging political similarities across the Latino subgroups. What does seem clear is that members of Latino national-origin groups are recognized by the larger society as Latinos (more so than a specific Latino subgroup). There is a growing awareness that Latinos consciously describe themselves as a pan-ethnic group, in addition to their own nationality group. What is less clear is how much a broader identity as Latino influences their inclination to work more closely on common concerns and issues.

Interactions among Latinos

How many interactions take place among Latinos, within their own subgroups and across the various Latino subgroups? The extent and nature of interactions can be analogous to a family setting, in which persons are linked to one another's lives, situations, and circumstances. Again drawing on the LNPS, there are series of questions that explore the extent of interactions with each of the Latino subgroups (the LNPS is limited to Cubans, Puerto Ricans, and Mexican-origin). The range of responses went from a lot of contact to none. The results are shown in table 11.1, which indicates that Latinos have a lot of contact within their own group, but very limited (if any) contact with any other Latino subgroup. Almost three-fifths of the Mexican-origin respondents have a lot of contact with other "Mexicanos," while only one-eighth of the Puerto Ricans and one-sixteenth of the Cubans had a lot of contact with Mexican Americans.

Similarly, over 67 percent of the Puerto Rican respondents had a lot of contact with fellow Puerto Ricans, while only 1.8 percent had contacts with Mexicans and 1.5 percent had extensive contact with Cubans. Obviously, a major factor is the presence of Latinos in the same communities. I commented earlier on the distribution of Latinos in the United States and the relative concentration of each group in certain parts of the country. The LNPS was conducted in 1990, and the mix of Latino subgroups is greater now. The results of Census 2000 strongly support the greater mix of Latino groups in areas where Mexican Americans, Puerto Ricans, or Cubans were the predominant group (Miami, Houston, New York City, Philadelphia, etc.).

Table 11.1   Contact or Interaction among Latinos with Other Latinos

Variables	Mexican-origin	Puerto Rican	Cuban
Contact with Mexican-origin persons			
A lot	923 (59.7%)	80 (13.8%)	37 (6.0%)
Some	378 (24.5%)	110 (19.0%)	71 (11.4%)
Little or none	244 (15.8%)	388 (67.1%)	513 (82.6%)
Contact with Cubans			
A lot	24 (1.6%)	59 (10.2%)	552 (81.4%)
Some	71 (4.6%)	101 (17.5%)	74 (10.9%)
Little or none	1,445 (93.9%)	417 (72.3%)	52 (7.7%)
Contact with Puerto Ricans			
A lot	27 (1.8%)	395 (67.1%)	96 (15.5%)
Some	132 (8.6%)	105 (17.8%)	191 (30.8%)
Little or none	1,381 (89.7%)	89 (15.1%)	334 (53.7%)

Source: De la Garza et al., *Latino Voices: Mexican, Puerto Rican, and Cuban Perspectives on American Politics* (Boulder: Westview, 1993).

Of the Cuban respondents, over four-fifths have a lot of contact with other Cubans in contrast to very limited contact with either Mexican-origin or Puerto Ricans. This pattern is quite similar for each of these Latino subgroups with a slightly greater intra-group contact among Cubans. The fact that each group is regionally concentrated reduces the opportunity for inter-group interactions. In addition, the longer-term residency of Mexican-origin in the Southwest, and to a lesser extent in the Midwest, has allowed more Mexican Americans (particularly second and third generation) greater metropolitan residential dispersions throughout the metropolitan areas. Works by Massey and Denton (1993) and Farley (1996) indicate that Latino residential segregation is lower than African American and slightly higher than Asian American. On the other hand, Census 2000 findings indicate that a growing number of urban areas, such as San Francisco, Chicago, Los Angeles, and New York City, now have a greater mix of Latino subgroups, which increases the opportunities for greater contact. The significant influx of Central and South Americans since the late 1980s has broadened the notion of Latino interactions beyond that of Cubans, Puerto Ricans, and Mexican-origin. These Latino subgroups could well serve as a nexus of interactions for all Latinos and broaden a sense of a Latino community.

Perceptions of Latino Group Discrimination

One of the key criteria that characterize minority group status, besides a sense of group identity, is differential treatment. Discriminatory practices directed toward Latinos can serve to enhance group solidarity. While the direct experience of discrimination has an important effect on individuals (de

Table 11.2   Perception of Discrimination of Latino Subgroups by Latino Subgroups

Discrimination Variables	Mexican-origin	Puerto Rican	Cuban
Degree of discrimination toward Mexican-origin			
A lot	487 (31.6%)	209 (35.8%)	147 (22.1%)
Some	657 (42.6%)	229 (39.3%)	212 (31.9%)
Little or none	397 (25.9%)	145 (24.9%)	306 (46.0%)
Degree of discrimination toward Puerto Ricans			
A lot	203 (13.6%)	203 (34.7%)	57 (8.5%)
Some	608 (40.9%)	230 (39.3%)	231 (34.4%)
Little or none	676 (45.5%)	152 (26.0%)	384 (57.2%)
Degree of discrimination toward Cubans			
A lot	254 (17.2%)	127 (21.7%)	45 (6.6%)
Some	620 (42.1%)	215 (36.7%)	226 (33.4%)
Little or none	599 (40.7%)	244 (41.6%)	406 (60.0%)

Source: De la Garza et al., *Latino Voices: Mexican, Puerto Rican, and Cuban Perspectives on American Politics* (Boulder: Westview, 1993).

la Garza et al. 1993), individual perceptions of discrimination are equally important in developing a sense of minority group status. Similar conditions, perceptions, and experiences can serve to establish a sense of a "siege" community. Our earlier discussion of **Proposition 187** provided insight into the external actions of a state initiative that clearly targeted Latinos as having negative impacts on California.

As a result, heightened group awareness and consciousness developed to combat the initiative and other political issues. In the United States, practices of discrimination based on race and **ethnicity** have been a prime motivation for group solidarity (Dawson 1994). In the LNPS, each respondent was asked about her or his perceptions on the extent of discrimination faced by each of the Latino subgroups, in addition to other groups in American society. The results in Table 11.2 represent the perceived extent of discrimination directed against the Latino subgroups.

Mexican-origin respondents perceived themselves as experiencing the greatest degree of discrimination. More than 30 percent of the Mexican-origin respondents, and 35.8 percent of the Puerto Ricans, felt that Mexican-origin persons encountered a lot of discrimination. In contrast, Cubans responded at 22.1 percent for the upper level of discrimination. Overall, 54–75 percent of the Latino respondents from these three subgroups felt that Mexican-origin persons experienced a lot or some degree of discrimination.

While the majority of these Latinos rated Mexicans as most discriminated against, Puerto Ricans followed with Cubans at a distant third. Of the Puerto Rican respondents, 34.7 percent perceived themselves as experiencing a lot of

Box 11.1   The *Washington Post* Latino Survey

In 1999 the *Washington Post,* in conjunction with the Henry J. Kaiser Family Foundation and Harvard JFK School of Government, conducted a national survey of Latinos. A similar question was asked about the Latino respondents' perception of discrimination directed toward Latinos. In addition to Mexican-origin, Puerto Ricans, and Cubans, ample numbers of Central and South American respondents were queried. Overall, 82 percent of all the Latinos indicated that discrimination was a problem for Latinos in the United States, with a range of Latino subgroup responses from 77 percent (Puerto Ricans) to 90 percent for Central/South Americans. A follow-up question asked the respondents if discrimination was a big problem for Latinos. This question assessed the saliency of this perception in light of other concerns the Latinos respondents might have. For this item, among all Latinos, some 67 percent indicated that discrimination was a big problem. By Latino subgroup, the range was from 67 percent (Mexican-origin) to 72 percent (Central/South Americans). These results illustrate the relatively high degree of agreement among Latinos regarding perception of discriminatory treatment directed toward group members. In addition, these perceptions are highest among the Central/South American respondents, who are the fastest-growing segment of the Latino community.

discrimination, in comparison to 13.6 percent for Mexican-origin respondents and 8.5 percent for Cubans. When the "a lot" and "some" categories are combined, then 42.9 percent to 74.0 percent perceived some level of discrimination directed against Puerto Ricans.

Cubans perceived lower levels of discrimination, responding that 6.65 percent of Cubans are discriminated against; 17.2 percent and 21.7 percent respectively for the Mexican-origin and Puerto Rican respondents felt that Cubans are discriminated against a lot. Clearly, Mexican Americans and Puerto Ricans perceived higher levels of discrimination directed toward Cubans than the Cuban respondents themselves. There is evidence that discrimination aimed at Latinos cuts across the various Latino subgroups. At the same time, the extensiveness of this experience is uneven. Another question from the LNPS asks each respondent if he or she had ever experienced a discriminatory encounter. One-third (Mexican-origin) to one-seventh (Cubans) indicated actually experiencing discrimination. Some degree of "out-group" status is not uncommon for many Latinos. What is less clear is how these experiences are interpreted and internalized within and across the different Latino sub-communities.

Table 11.3   Feeling Thermometer among Latinos toward Each Group and Country of Origin

	Mexican-origin	Puerto Ricans	Cubans
Country of origin			
United States	mean = 92.1	mean = 93.1	mean = 95.6
	SD = 14.8	SD = 15.0	SD = 12.9
Puerto Rico	mean = 57.4	mean = 89.5	mean = 76.2
	SD = 21.8	SD = 18.1	SD = 22.5
Cuba	mean = 38.3	mean = 35.7	mean = 53.7
	SD = 24.5	SD = 28.4	SD = 42.7
Mexico	mean = 75.2	mean = 57.1	mean = 45.9
	SD = 24.7	SD = 23.5	SD = 25.1
Latino subgroups			
Mexican Americans	mean = 84.8	mean = 61.2	mean = 58.0
	SD = 19.5	SD = 23.3	SD = 24.2
Mexican immigrants	mean = 75.1	mean = 53.6	mean = 55.9
	SD = 24.1	SD = 25.5	SD = 25.0
Cubans	mean = 53.1	mean = 56.1	mean = 84.9
	SD = 23.7	SD = 26.1	SD = 19.6
Puerto Ricans from the island	mean = 59.1	mean = 89.2	mean = 68.2
	SD = 24.2	SD = 18.0	SD = 23.1
Puerto Ricans from the mainland U.S.	mean = 57.2	mean = 88.1	mean = 66.5
	SD = 23.6	SD = 17.8	SD = 22.8

Source: De la Garza et al., *Latino Voices: Mexican, Puerto Rican, and Cuban Perspectives on American Politics* (Boulder: Westview, 1993).
Note: SD = standard deviation.

Latinos' Affinities across Groups and Their Home Countries

While contact across the different Latino sub-communities is limited, the existence of positive sentiments about one another can enhance a sense of broader community. We will pursue this aspect of community building by examining several other items in the LNPS. A feeling thermometer[1] was used to gauge the respondents' feelings toward the specific Latino countries of origin and specific Latino subgroups. A fifty-degree response would represent a neutral postion. The specific countries identified were the United States, Mexico, Cuba, and Puerto Rico. In addition, each respondent was asked to rate his or her feelings toward Mexican Americans, Mexican immigrants, Puerto Ricans from the mainland (i.e., United States), Puerto Ricans from the island, and Cubans. The ratings across each of the Latino subgroups as well as ratings for their own group members would be indicative of affinity for a Latino community. A critical set of responses comes from the Latino subgroup ratings of members other than their own group members.

While loyalty among Latinos to their cultural heritage and home countries has been discussed, one consistent affinity for all of the Latino respon-

dents is a very high rating for the United States. The range of the thermometer scores for the three groups is 92.1 to 95.6. Such a positive attachment to
the United States suggests a strong loyalty to their country of residence (there
are Latinos in the LNPS who are multi-generational in the United States),
while also maintaining positive feelings about one's country of origin. Each
Latino subgroup rates his or her country of origin higher than any other
Latino country. For example, Puerto Rican respondents gave an average thermometer rating of 89.5 for the Commonwealth of Puerto Rico compared to
76.2 for Cubans and 57.4 for Mexican-origin respondents.

A similar pattern existed for the country ratings of Cuba and Mexico.
Mexican-origin respondents rated Mexico higher (75.2) than Puerto Ricans
(57.1) or Cubans (45.9). In the latter case, the Cuban rating of Mexico was the
only one that fell below 50. Cubans rated their country of origin 53.7, versus
35.7 for Puerto Ricans and 38.3 for the Mexican-origin. The ratings for Cuba
represent a mixture of sentiments regarding the ruling regime and the people
of Cuba. During the interview, several of the respondents asked whether the
question referred to Cuba the country versus Cuba the people (see table 11.3).

The series of items that asked the Latino respondents to rate their feelings
of affinity toward specific Latino subgroup members provides a more personal
connection. Again, a similar pattern occurred as each respondent graded his
or her "compatriot" higher than the other Latino subgroups. For Mexican
Americans and Mexican immigrants, the Mexican-origin respondents gave
average scores of 84.8 and 75.1 respectively, while the ratings for Puerto
Ricans (mainland and the island) and Cubans were 61.2, 53.6, and 58.0 respectively. Mexican-origin respondents expressed less affinity for Mexican immigrants. Nativity (U.S.-born versus foreign-born) played a role in the lower rating, although the average score was in the upper quartile. Even though the
Mexican-origin native respondents share a common ancestry, family relationships, and cultural ties, they may compete with Mexican immigrants for
jobs, housing, and different levels of acculturation. Puerto Rican respondents
rated Puerto Ricans from the mainland and the island highly, with average
scores of 89.2 and 88.1.

Similarly, Cuban respondents rated Cubans highly, 84.9, versus 56.1 for
Puerto Ricans and 53.1 for Mexican-origin. The drop-off in ratings for each
Latino subgroup ranges consistently from twenty-one to twenty-four points.
Puerto Ricans and Cubans gave higher ratings to each other than to Mexican-
origin persons. At the same time, virtually all of the ratings were above the
fifty-point mark, indicating positive affinities. Considering the timing of the
LNPS, 1989–1990, the demographic and geographic shifts among these Latino
subgroups and the significant influx of Central and South Americans, especially in the 1990s, have increased residential contact among all Latinos. Still
regionally concentrated, the mix of Latinos in each region of the country is
affecting familiarity, interactions, and possibly affinities.

Perceived Common Cultural Practices and Political/Economic Interests

Throughout this discussion of Latino politics, I have identified the concepts of community of interests and culture as building blocks for a broad-based Latino community. If Latinos, across the various national-origin subgroups, perceive and interact in a manner in which they see common cultural and structural conditions, then there will be greater motivation to engage in collective efforts. We have tried to identify salient issues and bridging organizations and leaders that promote an integrated Latino community. In this chapter, we are exploring the responses of individual Latinos as to whether they perceive common cultural and/or political-economic ties that cut across their own Latino subgroup's situation. In the LNPS, specific questions asked the respondents about their view of the broader Latino community.

The first question asked if the respondent perceived a similarity of culture among all of the Latino subgroups. The range of responses was from very similar to not similar at all. There was a conscious effort to not define culture in any particular way so that each person would interject his or her own notions of what culture includes and whether it is shared with other Latinos. Somewhat surprisingly, the extent of perceived similar cultures across the LNPS (the very similar response) represented only one-fifth of all of the Latino respondents. The biggest response category was the "somewhat similar," over one-half of all of respondents answering affirmatively (from 54.3 percent to 56.9 percent). Only one-quarter of the Latino respondents did not see any cultural similarities across three Latino subgroups (see table 11.4). One conclusion that can be drawn is that the existence of strands or threads across the various Latino sub-communities and public celebrations (National Hispanic Heritage Month, Cinco de Mayo, Puerto Rican Independence Day, etc.) will add supplementary links toward creating a more overlapping cultural map.

Whereas some degree of cultural similarity is present, the responses for commonly shared political and economic concerns were less evident than the cultural dimension. The series of questions paired all combinations for the three groups (Mexican-origin and Cubans, Cubans and Puerto Ricans, etc.). With almost every combination, the very similar response did not exceed 10 percent. The somewhat similar category ranged from 24.2 percent (Mexican–Cuban) to 42.0 percent (Puerto Rican–Cuban and Puerto Rican–Mexican). In fact, the "not very similar" category was the larger response for virtually every combination. Interestingly, the Cuban respondents felt that they shared fewer common political and economic concerns with the other two Latino subgroups. The persistence of approximately two-fifths of the Latino respondents responding that Latinos have somewhat similar political and economic situations may serve as an indicator that organizations and Latino leadership need to foster awareness of more concrete connections. If these Latino subgroups see few commonalties politically and/or economically, then a community of mutual interests has major limitations. Another impli-

Table 11.4   Perceptions of Commonalties of Culture and Political and Economic Conditions among Latinos

	Mexican-origin	Puerto Ricans	Cubans
Extent of cultural similarities			
Very similar	304 (19.7%)	118 (20.1%)	122 (18.0%)
Somewhat similar	842 (54.6%)	318 (54.3%)	366 (56.9%)
Not very similar	395 (25.6%)	150 (25.6%)	187 (27.5%)
Extent of political similarities between Mexicans and Cubans			
Very similar	116 (7.8%)	46 (8.3%)	32 (4.8%)
Somewhat similar	556 (37.3%)	209 (37.7%)	160 (24.2%)
Not very similar	820 (55.0%)	300 (54.1%)	469 (71.0%)
Extent of political similarities between Mexicans and Puerto Ricans			
Very similar	191 (12.7%)	46 (8.2 %)	47 (7.2%)
Somewhat similar	607 (40.5%)	235 (42.0%)	196 (30.2%)
Not very similar	700 (46.7%)	279 (49.8%)	406 (62.6%)
Extent of similarities between Puerto Ricans and Cubans			
Very similar	191 (12.7%)	46 (8.2%)	47 (7.2%)
Somewhat similar	607 (40.5%)	235 (42.0%)	196 (30.2%)
Not very similar	700 (46.7%)	279 (49.8%)	406 (62.6%)

Source: De la Garza et al., *Latino Voices: Mexican, Puerto Rican, and Cuban Perspectives on American Politics* (Boulder: Westview, 1993).

cation is that some inter-Latino group pairing (i.e. Puerto Rican–Mexican or Puerto Rican–Cuban) forms part of the community building blocks.

The timing of the LNPS at the beginning of the 1990s cannot take into account the development of Latino activities and networks that have continued into the new millennium. As noted in chapter 9, issues like immigration and redistricting serve to create alliances and communications across the Latino sub-communities. Many Latino organizations and activists make contact, consult, and work to strengthen relations across the various Latino sub-communities. The other element is the growing presence of Central, South American, and Dominicans in the Latino mosaic. The building blocks are slowly evolving and further results come from both elite and local grassroots activities and dialogues.

One way we can extend these insights to community building is to look at particular "traits" among Latinos that are currently "demonstrating indicators of community of interests." By doing so, we might be able to derive greater insight into the building blocks of a Latino political community. Are

Box 11.2   Another Look at the *Washington Post* Survey

Three questions on the *Washington Post* survey tap a sense of the attraction and utility of Latino subgroups politically. The first asked the respondents to agree or disagree with the statement that Latinos share "few" political interests and goals. Overall, 44 percent of the Latino respondents disagreed. The range of Latino subgroup responses that disagreed with this statement ran between 37 percent (Central/South Americans) to 51 percent (Puerto Ricans). The following question asked if the respondent felt that "Latinos today are working together to achieve common goals or not." Overall, a majority (56 percent) of the Latino respondents felt that Latinos are working together. The range of working together responses ranged from 59 percent (Mexican-origin) to 52 percent (Puerto Ricans). Finally, the third item asked the respondents if Latinos would be better off if Latino groups worked together politically, worse off, or no difference. Overwhelmingly, the Latino respondents answered affirmatively (84 percent) with virtually no difference for any of the subgroups (either 85 percent or 86 percent).

How do these additional pieces of information add to the previous results in the LNPS? While it appears that Latino subgroups are "quicker" to recognize their cultural similarities, it is not as evident when assessing their political/economic commonalities. At the same time, a significant segment in each subgroup makes those connections; this reinforces that organizations and individuals are actively engaged on behalf of Latino political matters. These responses indicate strongly that greater Latino awareness and involvement would be aided by more visible and disseminated information and activities before broader segments of the Latino community.

foreign-born Latinos more likely to exhibit a sense of cultural and/or political community than native-born or younger Latinos? To explore this, we will examine intra-group differences based on nativity and age groupings. The results in table 11.5 examine the same items of common cultural and political/economic similarities or not, but the responses are broken down by age groupings.

The four age groups were 18–25, 26–39, 40–54, and over 55. The results of the common culture item do not indicate any real differences except for the Mexican-origin respondents. The 40–54 group is more likely to see greater cultural similarity than any other age-group. Yet variations by age groupings does not denote any significant deviation regarding the distribution of this item from that found in table 11.4. Similarly, an examination of age with the political/economic item between Mexican and Cuban respondents suggests that age does have some effect. Perceptions of less common political and economic concerns are more evident among the older respondents (40 years and older), particularly with Cubans. In the case of Puerto Ricans, it is the 26–39 age grouping in which greater dissimilarity is present.

The results of the age comparisons for political similarities or not between Mexicans and Puerto Ricans produce some noteworthy results. For the 26–39 age-group, as well as the 40–54 group of Mexican origin, political dissimilarity is the standard view. In the examination of political similarity between Puerto Ricans and Cubans, it is the Mexican-origin respondents, particularly the younger ones, who see more common political concerns than any other grouping. Older Cubans and the middle-age Puerto Ricans see fewer common political concerns between these two groups. To the extent that some sense of common political concerns and conditions exist, it is found among younger Latinos, and they fall in the somewhat similar response.

Looking at possible intra-group differences based on nativity may reflect both different experiences and perspectives about being Latino or how one sees one's own group in comparison with other Latino subgroups. For example, a third-generation Mexican-origin person residing in Wyoming may be more Americanized and have very limited contact with other Mexican-origin persons or other Latinos. At the same time, absence of direct contact is not the only means by which a person maintains his or her Latino-ness. The mass media, especially the Spanish-language media, as well as other high-tech forms of communication serve as vehicles for maintaining, redefining, and bridging communities among Latinos. The mass media and its influence on Latinos attitudes, cultural practices and awareness, and political communication represents a vital area for more in-depth analysis. We will now turn our attention to table 11.6 for the responses of both foreign-born and native-born Latinos regarding cultural and political/economic similarities across the Latino subgroups.

The responses on the commonalty of culture indicate that foreign-born respondents see more similarities than their native-born counterparts. If you combine the responses of "very similar" and "somewhat similar," from 70 percent to 73 percent of foreign-born respondents registered affirmatively. The native-born Mexican-origin respondents provided the only exception, as 78.6 percent indicated "very or somewhat similar culture" across the Latino subgroups. These responses make it difficult to assess the impact of nativity. Overall, approximately one-fourth of all Latino respondents expressed little cultural similarity across the Latino subgroups. It was higher among foreign-born Mexicanos (30.1 percent), as well as native-born Cubans (33.4 percent). Potentially, the experiences in each subgroup, whether native or foreign-born, may be more self-defined than similar.

In terms of political and economic similarities between Mexican-origin and Cubans, the difference between native and foreign-born is significant.

Table 11.5 Explorations of Commonalities among Latinos by National Origin and Age Group (percentage)

Latino Subgroups and Age Groups	Extent of Common Culture			Political Similarities between Mexicans and Cubans			Political Similarities between Mexicans and Puerto Ricans			Political Similarities between Puerto Ricans and Cubans		
	Very Similar	Somewhat Similar	Not Very Similar	Very Similar	Somewhat Similar	Not Very Similar	Very Similar	Somewhat Similar	Not Very Similar	Very Similar	Somewhat Similar	Not Very Similar
Mexican												
18–25	3.1	16.1	6.0	1.1	11.1	13.0	2.9	10.7	11.8	2.7	13.9	8.9
26–39	7.7	21.9	10.7	3.1	13.9	23.5	3.4	17.1	19.9	4.4	19.4	16.7
40–54	5.4	8.8	4.7	2.2	6.3	10.4	3.9	6.2	8.8	4.7	7.2	6.7
55+	3.6	7.9	4.2	1.3	5.9	8.1	2.4	6.5	6.3	2.3	7.6	5.4
Puerto Rican												
18–25	4.4	11.5	5.3	3.2	9.4	7.9	2.1	10.5	8.2	1.1	8.4	11.4
26–39	7.5	22.1	10.3	2.3	14.4	24.0	3.6	15.2	21.2	2.3	13.2	24.8
40–54	5.5	12.7	6.2	1.8	8.1	13.9	1.4	9.8	12.6	2.1	7.7	14.8
55+	2.7	8.0	3.9	.7	5.6	8.5	1.2	6.4	7.4	1.8	5.0	8.0
Cuban												
18–25	2.4	8.1	3.9	.6	4.2	9.8	0.3	5.7	8.2	1.4	4.8	8.4
26–39	5.2	13.6	6.7	1.2	7.8	16.7	2.9	8.3	14.6	2.0	9.8	13.7
40–54	4.0	14.1	6.8	.8	4.1	20.0	1.1	7.1	16.8	1.4	7.7	15.8
55+	6.7	18.4	10.2	2.3	7.9	24.7	2.9	9.1	23.0	3.6	11.3	20.2

Source: De la Garza et al., *Latino Voices: Mexican, Puerto Rican, and Cuban Perspectives on American Politics* (Boulder: Westview, 1993).

Table 11.6   Perceptions of Cultural and Political Similarities among Latinos: Native- and Foreign-Born Respondents (percentage)

	Mexican-origin		Puerto Rican		Cuban	
	Native	Foreign	Native	Foreign	Native	Foreign
Cultural similarities among Latinos						
Very similar	18.2	21.1	16.6	21.9	11.4	19.0
Somewhat similar	60.4	48.7	57.1	52.5	54.9	53.8
Not very similar	20.9	30.1	25.5	25.4	33.4	26.6
Political similarities between Mexicans and Cubans						
Very similar	8.6	6.7	10.4	7.1	3.5	8.1
Somewhat similar	42.9	31.7	44.8	33.9	35.4	28.3
Not very similar	48.3	61.6	44.8	55.6	64.6	63.5
Political similarities between Mexicans and Puerto Ricans						
Very similar	13.4	12.1	7.9	8.5	1.2	7.5
Somewhat similar	44.6	36.4	52.6	36.5	43.5	33.0
Not very similar	42.0	51.4	39.5	55.0	55.3	59.4
Political similarities between Cubans and Puerto Ricans						
Very similar	14.4	13.8	11.4	6.7	12.9	18.2
Somewhat similar	52.0	44.0	54.9	43.4	36.7	60.4
Not very similar	33.5	41.9	33.4	49.8	50.4	20.9

Source: De la Garza et al., *Latino Voices: Mexican, Puerto Rican, and Cuban Perspectives on American Politics* (Boulder: Westview, 1993).

That is, native-born Latinos were more likely to acknowledge a higher percentage of similarity than their foreign-born counterparts. Again the Cuban respondents were at a slightly lower percentage, especially in the "very similar" category. Similar response patterns were evident for the pairing of Puerto Rican–Mexican origin. In this case, all three subgroups of native-born Latinos indicated a greater percentage of similarity than the foreign-born Latinos. The response category most affected was the "somewhat similar" category. Finally, the results of the political and economic similarity item between Puerto Ricans and Cubans displayed a similar pattern for the Mexican and Puerto Rican respondents such that native-born saw greater similarity of political concerns. At the same time, the Cuban foreign-born saw greater dissimilarity.

A note of caution about these results, particularly regarding the Cuban respondents, is the very high percentage of foreign-born in the sample (90 percent for the Cuban community and over 60 percent for all of the respondents). Such a distribution on nativity will influence any statistical results. Nevertheless, there is some indication that differences do occur between native and foreign-born Latinos. Apparently experiences in the United States, particularly growing up in America, cause the native-born to see themselves as a minority group rather than as immigrants (Wilson 1977). Immigrant populations are more likely to compare their situation in the United States with that of counterparts who remained in their home country.

This includes comparisons of status, progress, and opportunity. Native-born Latinos assess their status relative to other groups in American society. In this case, the idea of a minority group in the United States can have greater potential to mobilize persons for common action. In addition, perceptions of similarity (cultural and/or political) are influenced by the composition of their networks—culturally, linguistically, and residentially. Finally, the foreign-born segment responded more favorably to culturally similarities, in part due to their closer proximity of Latino cultural practices than their native-born counterparts. Perceived similarity based on the idea of being Latino or Hispanic is less familiar to the foreign-born Latino.

The concepts of Latino and Hispanic are U.S.-based and have meaning in terms of a collection of communities from Latin America and the Iberian Peninsula. Thus awareness of and orientation toward other Latinos may be more evident among the native-born. The additional factor of others (non-Latinos) seeing Latinos as a monolith (culturally, physically, socioeconomically, etc.) can affect how Latinos respond to one another. The work of Hayes-Bautista et al. (1988) explores the idea of dis-assimilation in which Latino medical students (who had been largely assimilated into the American culture) were admitted to the medical school program as "affirmative action" efforts. Being served by special programs that assist their progress in medical school and being tagged as minorities and Hispanics has the effect of motivating these students to reexamine who they are. If other people or institutions see and treat you as different (whether or not particular Latinos saw themselves as such), then there is a tendency to explore why and perhaps reexamine why being of Latino background, one does not exhibit the expected behaviors and attitudes. The Hayes-Bautista study chronicled the transformation or "dis-assimilation" of many of these Latino students in becoming more Latino and identifying as such (in this case a closer affinity with seeing oneself as Mexican origin or Chicano). Thus the development of a broader-based Latino community results from not only how Latinos see each other but the effects of being defined by non-Latinos, public policies, mass media, and political leaders.

Our examination of a broader-based Latino community centers upon a network of interactions, common understanding of concerns and issues, and a sense of mutual respect. At the same time, the dynamic nature of any community does not require complete unanimity, consensus, or common activities at all times. We have only begun to examine and explore the community-building process across the various Latino communities in a systematic manner. At the same time, it can be useful to think of building community across Latino subgroups as a coalition-formation process. Latino subgroups come together for very specific purposes and at different times. Research on coalitions (Jackson and Preston 1991; Ture and Hamilton 1992) suggests that there are key elements that need to be in place in order for groups to agree to combine resources on specific situation and issues. I will extend this discussion of coalition formation by briefly looking at potential common political strands between Latinos and African Americans.

COALITIONAL AFFINITIES: DISCRIMINATION AND SOCIAL DISTANCE

While there has been much emphasis on the growth of the Latino community, especially in the past decade, there has also been much discussion about the political influence achieved by the African American community (Walton 1997; Dawson 1994). Works by McClain and Karnig (1990) and McClain and Stewart (1999) have established the prospects and limitations of an inter-racial/ethnic coalition between Latinos and African Americans. Competitive forces have been the primary area of emphasis between these two groups. As a result, coalitions are made tenuous (competing for municipal employment positions, business contracts, elected positions, etc.), although they have served as the focal point of Latino–African American relations. At the same time, some recent research (J. A. García 2000; Jennings 1994; Jaynes 2000) has outlined possible inducements and/or situations to work together.

While entire books and major research projects are trying to examine the nature of working coalitions between Latinos and African Americans, my purpose here is to suggest (with some evidence) a basis for coalition formation and the character of coalition formation. First, why would Latinos and African Americans come together to work cooperatively? Second, the nature of coalitions is purposeful, situation specific, and temporary. A discrimination model of coalition formation (Uhlaner 1991; J. A. García 2000), along with collective group orientations (sense of empowerment, efficacy, and consciousness) and socioeconomic status, can work concurrently to determine areas of cooperation and obtain resources to be effective. This type of model suggests that both Latinos and African Americans experience discriminatory practices in the United States, and that creates a common link or bond.

Connected with discriminatory experiences is the sense of a group identity as Latinos, African Americans, and/or minority group members, which motivates persons to get involved politically on behalf of common concerns. Finally, socioeconomic status helps provide the political resources to be effective in political arenas. Works like Browning et al. (1990) looked at local politics in the

San Francisco Bay area to illustrate that minority coalitions could include Anglo liberals for effective policy outcomes. In California, Jackson and Preston (1991) and Sonenshein (1994) examined electoral efforts that connected the Latino and African American communities, especially in Los Angeles.

The basis of the **discrimination-plus model** (J. A. García 2000) depends on common experiences, issue priorities, and values among minority group members in order for them to be receptive to joint political activities and collective efforts. Even if individuals make those kinds of connections, of course, minority organizations and leadership play a critical role in implementing strategies and plans to act on these common goals and issue concerns. Organizations and their leaders function to outline specific political strategies, activities, communication links to the community, and motivational cues to stimulate action. Carmichael and Hamilton (1967) identified necessary requisites for any coalition to form, which include (1) recognition of each party's self-interests, (2) recognition that each party's self-interest is benefited by alliances, (3) each party having an independent base of support, and (4) the coalition effort focusing on specific and identifiable goals. In essence the continual political empowerment of Latinos strengthens their partnership contribution to any coalition effort. The link is the discrimination experienced and perceived by Latinos and African Americans.

Uhlaner (1991) suggests that recognition of differential treatment could lead minority groups to feel sympathetic across groups, more disadvantaged than others, or inclined to protect their own group more. The discrimination connection also suggests that individuals who have experienced or perceived discrimination directed at their group are likely to possess a strong sense of racial and/or **ethnic identity** and support for specific issues or problems (Uhlaner 1991). The key for Latino–African American coalitions lies with each assessing its disadvantaged status and seeing the inter-connectedness. Each group confronts similar problems and conditions and, perhaps, a common target. McClain and Karnig (1990) demonstrated that in American cities with a critical mass of both Latinos and African Americans, political coalitions are viable if both minority groups see themselves combating the "white power structure." When they share a common target in vying for elective office, Latino and African American officials make gains at the expense of current non-minority officeholders. At the same time, a minimal level of trust between the two groups is essential for any degree of success. Oliver and Johnson (1984) showed that a low level of trust between Latinos and African Americans existed in Los Angeles.

The range of experiences that can link Latinos and African Americans in cooperative ventures lies outside the scope of this discussion. Yet their attitudes toward each other and commonalties regarding discrimination are of interest. At approximately the same time as the Latino National Political Survey was being conducted, the third wave (1990) of the **National Survey of**

Box 11.3   Racial/Ethnic Coalitions in Los Angeles?

Recent works on Los Angeles (Waldinger and Bozorgmehr 1996; Yu and Chang 1995; Ong et al. 1994) have introduced the added factor of the growing Asian American community and some corresponding political developments. The unsuccessful mayoral campaign of Michael Wu to succeed Tom Bradley included the strategy of forging a multiethnic/racial coalition. Inter-minority electoral coalitions elected Bradley in Los Angeles, Dinkins in New York, Peña and Wellington in Denver, and Washington in Chicago. In essence, being a global city afforded Los Angeles, with its diverse ethnic/racial mix, greater opportunities and accumulated experience to build on working relationships. After Tom Bradley decided not to run for mayor again, there were numerous discussions among African Americans, Latinos, Asian Americans, and white liberals (Sonenshein 1994) to reach accord on a common candidate to support for mayor. Michael Wu, a longtime member of the city council and a close ally of the Bradley coalition, emerged as the bearer of the Bradley coalition. The level of support and voting strength that Tom Bradley developed was not transferred to the Wu mayoral candidacy. While the strength of the rainbow-like Los Angeles coalition was not the sole factor in his defeat, it did play an important role.

Black Americans (Jackson 1992) was also in the field. Latinos' responses concerning their sense of social distance from other Latinos and perception of discrimination have already been described. Similar questions were asked of African American respondents for use in exploring possible common experiences and perspectives. Table 11.7 presents the "feeling thermometer" from respondents in the Latino and black surveys. The newer information is the feeling of "closeness" these groups had toward each other. The wording of the items is such that respondents were asked to rate on a 0 to 100-thermometer scale their feeling of closeness, with a 50 representing a middle or neutral point.

Table 11.7 suggests some positive links between these communities. As expected, respondents felt closer to their own group than to the other groups (88.7 percent of African Americans responded that they felt somewhat or very close to other African Americans), while overall positive ratings existed among Latinos. Latinos responding as somewhat or very close to African Americans ranged from 41.8 percent to 51.2 percent. The largest aggregation was at the mid-point, where about 33 percent of the Latinos were found. In

Another dimension of interethnic relations in Los Angeles is the recent gains in political representation, especially among Asian Americans and Latinos. This development has altered political alignments and networks in Los Angeles local politics, in some ways challenging political positions and networks in the African American community, as well as between them and white liberal networks. In addition, gains among Latinos in the California assembly, particularly in the leadership positions, were achieved by creating working coalitions. The combination of changing demographics, continued growth and political development (representation, organizational resources and skills, raised political capital, etc.) among minority groups, especially Latinos and Asian Americans, and broader networks across activists and organized groups make both cooperative and competitive activities take place more frequently.

Multi-centers of power and influence across several minority communities have created opportunities and challenges to interact with one another as potentially significant partners or adversaries in the Los Angeles political arena. As a result, members of different groups weigh overlapping interests and calculate the "cost-benefit" ratios of cooperation versus competition for enhancing their individual group's benefits (Henry and Muñoz 1991). By its very nature these interracial coalitions tend to be short-lived and sustained by specific, identifiable goals and interpersonal connections and respect.

reality, about 80 percent of Latinos fell at the midpoint or above. For the African American respondents, a similar result was found. That is, 47.7 percent indicted that they felt somewhat or very close to Hispanics/Latinos. These results can be interpreted as foundational in the sense of possibilities for cooperative efforts. At the same time, activists, leaders, and minority organizations serve as the mobilizing catalysts to convert positive feelings into political actions.

A second component of this preliminary exploration of cooperative coalitional efforts is a common sense of experiencing discrimination. Common experiences, especially negative ones, can bring communities together. Part of the basis of minority status in the United States has been differential treatment or discrimination. Earlier in this chapter, I presented data on the perception of discrimination among Latinos. In this section, I present data on Latinos' perception of discrimination toward African Americans, as well as African Americans' own perceptions of discrimination. Previously Latinos indicated that a majority of Latinos encounter some and/or a lot of discrimination (see table 11.8).

Table 11.7   Extent of Closeness to Latinos and African Americans among Respondents in the Latino and Black National Surveys

Group Social Distance Variables	African Americans[a]	Mexican-origin[b]	Puerto Ricans	Cubans
African Americans				
Not very close	11 (1.7%)	107 (7.4%)	49 (9.0%)	58 (9.4%)
Somewhat not close	41 (7.2%)	137 (9.5%)	55 (10.1%)	58 (9.4%)
Midpoint or neutral[c]		484 (33.6%)	162 (29.7%)	243 (39.4%)
Somewhat close	258 (39.6%)	173 (12.0%)	65 (11.9(%)	86 (13.9%)
Very close	320 (49.1%)	539 (37.4%)	214 (39.3%)	172 (27.9%)
Hispanics				
Not very close	133 (20.4%)			
Somewhat not close	189 (29.0%)			
Somewhat close	217 (33.3%)			
Very close	94 (14.4%)			

Source: National Survey of Black Americans (Institute for Social Research, University of Michigan, 1992). James Jackson, principal investigator.

[a]The responses for the NSBA were not very close; somewhat not close; somewhat close; and very close. The question in the LNPS were based on a 0 to 100 so that the corresponding categories are not very close (0–24); somewhat not close (25–49); neutral or midpoint = 50; somewhat close (51–74); and very close (75–100).

[b]For the LNPS, items related to social distance were broken down by each specific Latino subgroup: Mexicans, Puerto Ricans, and Cubans. There was not any item that grouped all persons as Latinos.

[c]The NSBA did not have a midpoint or neutral position.

Table 11.8   Experience with Discrimination among Latinos and African Americans in the Latino and Black National Surveys

Experience with Discrimination	African Americans	Mexican-origin	Puerto Ricans	Cubans
Yes	216 (34.8%)	516 (33.4%)	176 (30%)	95 (14%)
No	405 (65.2%)	1024 (66.6%)	413 (70%)	584 (86%)
Total respondents	621	1540	589	679

Sources: National Survey of Black Americans [James Jackson, principal investigator] (Institute for Social Research, University of Michigan, 1992); de la Garza et al., *Latino Voices: Mexican, Puerto Rican, and Cuban Perspectives on American Politics* (Boulder: Westview, 1993).

Similar percentages of experiences with discrimination among Latinos and African Americans indicate very comparable levels. Again, Cuban respondents reported the fewest encounters with discrimination, but the percentages for African Americans, Puerto Ricans, and Mexican-origin were almost identical (about 33 percent). Respondents encountering discrimination had knowledge of family, friends, and coworkers who also experienced it.

We know that persons' perceptions and attitudes influence their assessment of societal treatment and how their group is regarded. Another table examines African American and Latino responses toward their perceptions

Table 11.9   Perception of Discrimination toward African Americans and Latinos by Respondents in the Latino and Black National Surveys

Discrimination Variables[a]	African Americans	Mexican-origin	Puerto Ricans	Cubans
A lot	237 (40.2%)	596 (38.8%)	336 (57.3%)	169 (24.9%)
Some	182 (30.8%)	599 (38.9%)	168 (28.7%)	218 (32.2%)
A little/none	171 (29.0%)	231 (15.0%)	52 (8.9%)	100 (14.7%)
None	—	111 (7.2%)	30 (5.1%)	191 (28.2%)

[a]The construction of this variable (i.e., perception of opportunities for African Americans in overall life chances, education, and jobs) resulted in three categories of perceptions.

about the extent of discrimination directed toward African Americans. A previous table presenting Latinos' perceptions of discrimination indicated that one-half to three-fourths of the Latino respondents perceived a lot or some degree of discrimination. Again, the Cuban respondents (see table 11.2) recorded lower levels of discrimination than other Latino respondents did. Perceptions of discrimination were about 40 percent for Cubans and slightly higher for Puerto Ricans (42.9 percent) and Mexican-origin persons (53 percent).

Table 11.9 shows that Latinos perceived higher levels of discrimination toward African Americans than the African American respondents did. About 75 percent of the Puerto Rican and Mexican-origin respondents perceived a lot or some discrimination, as did 66.1 percent of Cubans. For the African American respondents, summated across the three category options (i.e., a lot, some, and a little or none), a total of 71 percent indicated a perception that fellow African Americans experience a lot or some discrimination. To the extent that a common occurrence of experiencing as well as perceiving discriminatory practices toward minority groups can bridge racial and ethnic communities, there is good evidence that a bridge does exist. As mentioned earlier, there is no guarantee that with a common evaluation of the treatment and cost of being a Latino or an African American in American society, working alliances between these two communities or other communities of color will automatically result.

Given this preliminary examination and the works of Uhlaner (1991) and J. A. García (2000), the preconditions for successful alliances or coalitions would include each group having independent bases of leadership, resources, and well-defined goals. Agreeing on a common "target" and well-defined objectives increases the possibilities for cooperative efforts. Finally, the commonalty of negative differential treatment (discrimination) serves as a bridge to coalesce in cooperative ventures. In essence, I am outlining a common minority status model for cooperative efforts.

Box 11.4   Vieques and Coalitional Partners

A good example of this swinging pendulum between cooperation and competition is illustrated in a recent news story by *Orlando Sentinel* reporters Jeff Kunerth and Sherri Owens (2001). The recent involvement of Jesse Jackson and Al Sharpton in protests over the navy's continued use of Vieques, Puerto Rico, for bombing tests can be interpreted as African American leaders extending protest concerns into the Latino policy arena. And in Osceola County, the NAACP chapter has selected a Hispanic as its vice president. These moves are welcomed by such Latino leaders as Raul Yzaguirre (NCLR) because he feels that broadening the scope of civil rights beyond a black-white paradigm enables the issue and the participants to be more diverse and inclusive. The reporters also commented that both the NAACP and the National Urban League have increased their efforts to recruit Hispanic members by addressing important issues to that community. Hugh Price, national president of the Urban League is quoted as saying, "There are major issues that confront our communities—education, discrimination, employment. . . . We will move forward faster if we coalesce." A local chapter president of Orange County also states that "reaching out to Hispanics [makes sense] because we have some of the same issues. If we do not form some kind of unity, neither one of us will get anywhere." Further evidence of joint efforts in Osceola County, where Latinos grew 292 percent in the 1990s, is that whites and Latinos now compose one-third of NAACP membership.

At the same time, there are concerns among segments of the African American community regarding Latinos. One of their worries is that significant Latino growth could weaken the political influence that blacks have

In light of research literature on **political participation** and **mobilization,** the additional dimensions of political interest, group identity, gains in socioeconomic status (educational attainment, income levels, higher-status occupations), and assertive organizational direction and involvement provide the needed political capital and motivation to work collectively. Clearly more opportunities and challenges will present themselves or will be initiated by Latino and African American leadership and organizations. Physical proximity, at times sharing common residential and commercial areas, can also increase interactions. At the same time, undercurrents of greater competition for limited political and economic gains highlight the zero-sum calculations that working together may incur unequal costs and benefits to one's own group.

worked to build. Decreasing numbers or smaller percentages become a numbers game in which blacks could lose access to opportunities earned from past struggles of the civil rights movement. In addition, there are sentiments that the level of discrimination faced by Latinos is not as great as it is for African Americans. Since the number of Latinos is based on the Spanish-origin question in the census and other government agencies, race is a different question asked. As mentioned before, a Latino can be of any race. As a result some African Americans (e.g., Orlando Patterson, *New York Times* op-ed) suggest that many Latinos consider themselves racially white and some may not consider themselves a minority. Thus the NAACP and Urban League and other primarily African American organizations should keep their civil rights efforts focused on the needs of their own community. The banter works on both sides as some Latino activists interpret Jackson and Sharpton at Vieques as motivated by a desire for high-profile visibility. They criticize Jackson and Sharpton for absence and silence on the violence and death along the Mexican border. Finally, distinctions are drawn between different policy emphases. Immigration and bilingual education are major issues for Latinos, whereas the African American community does not assign them high priority and may see immigration as a threat to jobs held by African American workers. Another contested arena for these groups is redistricting, as mentioned in the previous chapter. Thus both factors and forces exist (i.e., movement toward cooperative and conflicting or competitive directions), and this will likely remain the case for the near future. Our discussion of current or possible future partnerships is meant to identify and analyze some bases for either of these directions. In reality, both options and directions are viable and necessary as each community continues to build on its resource and organizational bases.

CONCLUSION: A PAN-ETHNIC COMMUNITY AND BROADER PARTNERSHIPS

In light of the examination of community building based on the LNPS and the *Washington Post* Latino survey, what is the extent of a working community among Latinos? Community building and working together, as presented in this chapter, are based on common status (cultural, political, and minority) and positive affinities toward one another. The data suggests promise and limited optimism. There is clear evidence that the Latino communities are both aware of one another and connected in a variety of ways (geographic proximity, common issues, organizational activities and leadership, and pan-ethnic identification). At the same time, affinity is highest within Latino sub-groups more so than among all Latino groups or the broader definition of Latinos/Hispanics. External events, social movements and treatment by interest groups, politicians, and parties serve to coalesce Latinos as an identifiable and working community. The density of Latino–African American networks has increased, and lines of communication and mutual awareness are more evident.

The activities directed toward Latinos in the 2000 elections increased the value of building a more active Latino community and attracted the attention of the major political parties, the media, and leadership in the economic sectors of America. In the concluding chapter I will present four scenarios about the future of Latino communities and the political system. What is clear is that the Latino community is a dynamic force both within its own sub-communities and in the larger aggregation of a national Latino community. Dynamism within the Latino community involves the process of defining itself further (its cultural and group boundaries, interests and breadth of its organizational landscape) and establishing itself as a political participant whose goals, interests, and impact become more identifiable in the greater realm of political and economic life in the United States. This can manifest itself at times as a unified pan-ethnic effort and at other times as independent efforts within each Latino subgroup. The process of coalition formation remains more one of strategic maneuvering and pragmatic considerations. Yet identifying someone you are willing to work with is enhanced by familiarity, trust, and commonalties.

NOTE

1. The feeling thermometer is constructed so that the respondent is asked to indicate his or her feelings about a group or country based on a 0 to 100-degree thermometer. Thus the 100-degree marking represents the most positive feeling and a zero degree is the lowest rating.

1 2

The Latino Community: Beyond Recognition Politics

Hicimos nuestra peregrinación y nos preguntamos—¿Dónde esta nuestra comunidad y cuales son los elementos más importantes que sostienen nuestra comunidad? La verdad es que somos muchas diferentes comunidades que a la vez nos desarrollamos hasta alcanzar otro nivel como comunidad. Tenemos que insistir en preguntarnos ¿Dónde está nuestra comunidad?

We have made our pilgrimage and we have asked ourselves, "Where is our community and which are the most important elements that sustain our community?" The truth is that we are many different communities simultaneously evolving toward a higher level of community. We have to persist in asking ourselves "Where is our community?"

I began this book by asking about the nature and extent of the community that exists within the various Latino sub-communities in the United States. Using the concepts of community of culture and interests, I constructed guidelines and analytical narratives to explore what kind of "political shape" the Latino community was in. I focused on political resource development among Latinos, their organizations, leadership, and the responses of the U.S. political system. In addition to their stunning population growth, particularly over the past twenty-five years, are Latinos increasing their political capital? Are they making significant gains in education, income, and occupational status, increased numbers of naturalized citizens, elected officials at all levels, and in operating more cohesive and effective organizations?

I have suggested that community building among the twenty-plus Latino national-origin groups can provide greater resources, visibility, and political-economic leverage in the American political system. At the same time, the costs and energy required to establish the degree of community necessary for the inclusion of all Latino subgroups remains a significant challenge. This concluding chapter will develop some possible and quite probable scenarios to characterize the politics of the Latino community as we move through the early part of the new millennium.

BASIC COMMUNITY FACTS

Continued Latino Growth and Diversity

Before developing these scenarios, I will establish key advancements and developments that have already occurred within Latino communities and in the American political system. The first "fact" lies with the projected population growth of Latinos. While much has been made of the rapid and continuous growth of the "largest minority," this pattern will be reinforced in the future. Census Bureau population decennial counts and future projections (U.S. Bureau of the Census 2002) into mid-century continue to show the Latino growth rate exceeding that of all other populations. It is estimated that by 2050, Latinos will make up one-fourth of the U.S. population (currently they constitute one-eighth). The other major development in this continued population growth is their geographic dispersion throughout all regions of the United States. In 1990 approximately 90 percent of all Latinos lived in ten states.

The influx of Latinos into less "traditional" areas is becoming more evident. For example, during a Christmas season Protestant service in suburban Portland, Oregon, a call went out to congregational members to give clothing, books, and other practical gifts to needy individuals. The organizer said that the first twenty-eight of the seventy-five households on the list were Spanish speakers. There was another call for persons who could speak Spanish to help deliver the gifts. Similar indicators are present in Portland, Oregon, as signs in Spanish are posted throughout the Oregon Museum of Science and Industry, as well as signs and voice recordings on the MAX (the light rail system).

A Latino transformation is occurring in Dalton, Georgia (northwestern part of the state), where Latinos have been migrating, mostly from Mexico, to the "carpet capital of the world." In fall 2000, Latinos constituted a majority (51.4 percent) of the students in the public schools in this town of 23,000 (Roedemeier 2000). Across northern Georgia, an influx of mostly Latino immigrants is arriving to work in the poultry processing plants and carpet mills. This scenario can be recounted in many other communities throughout the South, the Rocky Mountain States, America's heartland, New England, and the suburban Northeast.

Finally, there is the burgeoning growth of Central and South Americans within the Latino community. While persons of Mexican origin continue to maintain high growth rates (both birth rates and immigration), it is Latinos from the Dominican Republic, Colombia, El Salvador, Guatemala, and the like, who are growing faster and becoming more geographically important. Latinos from Central and South America have settled for the most part in areas where Mexican-origin, Cubans, and Puerto Ricans are located. While contributing to the overall Latino growth, this pattern also represents a broader mix of Latino interests and potential resource building.

For example, Dominicans in New York in 1980 numbered 125,380, which grew to 332,713 by 1990, and was projected to reach 700,000 by 2000. Such growth represents policy interests and demands on the New York educational system, housing, employment, and basic city services. The growing Dominican community has created its own organizations and seeks to enhance its political and economic influence in the "City" overall and in relation to Puerto Ricans and other Latino communities.

Similarly, at a recent redistricting conference in Los Angeles (sponsored by the Southwest Voter Registration and Education Project), activists from the Los Angeles Salvadoran community attended and involved themselves in providing their perspectives and interests in the strategy sessions and proposing boundaries for legislative and congressional districts. For the future, the continual significant growth of Central and South American-origin Latinos will help shape the nature of Latino politics in terms of issues, leadership, and challenges for collective efforts and cooperation.

The expansion of Latinos into metropolitan areas and regions of the country where they have been less evident serves a couple of political and social purposes. First, the continuing growth (but more geographically varied settlement patterns) provides Latinos with an even greater national presence. Even though the public and political-economic institutions are aware of the Latino communities, there are regions, especially the South, Northwest, and upper Midwest, in which public awareness of and experience with Latinos had been virtually nonexistent. At the same time, the expansion of Latinos into more locales can produce positive and negative consequences. The above-mentioned Latino movement to Dalton, Georgia, has helped meet the demand for jobs and workers. The other side of this rapid transformation is inter-group tensions and anti-immigrant sentiments among "native" Georgians.

For example, in 1989 there were 3,131 non-Latino white students enrolled in Dalton schools, or almost 80 percent of the student enrollment. In the fall of 2000, there were only 1,893 white students, many having transferred to private schools (Roedemeier 2000). Some parents complained that their English-speaking children were ignored as teachers paid more attention to children learning the English language. One store's plywood sign condemns "uncontrollable immigration" and declares, "Congress sold us for cheap labor" (Roedemeier 2000). On the other hand, Dalton's carpet industry clearly supports the Latino immigrants. Dalton produces 40 percent of the world's carpet, and in a community where the unemployment rate is less than 3 percent, carpet mills are worried about maintaining reliable workers.

Obviously, part of the future of Latino politics is the process of community building within the Latino community, as well as bridging within existing community interests and institutions in more recently settled areas. Continued growth exceeding the national average and movement into lower and/or fewer Latino populated areas are some of the basic facts about the future profile of Latinos in the United States. They represent both challenges and opportunities for Latinos to establish their roots in the community and develop the resource base and interest to influence local policy makers and employers.

Latino Pan-Ethnicity and Its Viability

The second basic "fact" that bears relevance to the future of Latino politics is the existence of a pan-ethnic community. I have questioned the existence and form of community that may exist among the various Latino subgroups in the United States. Our examination of this question demonstrates that some level of pan-ethnic community exists among Latinos. Organizations continue to represent and advocate on behalf of Latinos, and numerous newer organizations have been formed. They have organized around issues of civil and political rights and salient policy areas (immigration, language policies, etc.), as well as work-related groups and culture- and neighborhood-based interests. Political and economic elites have established networks and, at times, cooperative activities that cut across specific Latino subgroups (Cubans, Dominicans, Salvadorans, etc.).

The dispersion of Latinos across different regions of the country has brought more Latinos into contact where only one group previously predominated. For example, the Latino mix in the Miami metropolitan area has changed, and a majority of Latinos are now non-Cubans. While inter-Latino group interactions may vary by group and they may be more competitive than cooperative in nature (competition for scarce public and private resources, political resources, etc.), the changed Latino landscape has created pressures and incentives to come together as a broader community. These developments in conjunction with the media's attention have continued to reinforce the expansion and activities of Latinos throughout the country. These developments serve to influence Latino community building. I have suggested that community can come together as a result of internal efforts by Latinos themselves, as well as how the "larger" society, its institutions and key elites, perceive and act in recognition of their presence.

A central question for Latinos in the area of **pan-ethnicity** is, who is defining Latinos and the Latino community, and for what purpose does it exist? The development and advancement of organizations and leadership address Latino interests, obtaining public recognition and definition(s) of the social construct of Hispanic/Latino, and enhancing more extensive interactions and contact among different Latino subgroups that help construct a Latino community. Thus the question about the existence of a Latino community is answered in the affirmative. The follow-up question centers around the development of a functioning, effective Latino community that has impact on political, economic, and social matters at the various levels of government and the economy.

The Latino Vessel Has Arrived

The mid-1990s firmly established the real "political capital" of Latinos in American politics. Metaphors of "invisibility," "a sleeping giant," and "soon to have your place in the sun" have been used for decades, especially in references to the Mexican-origin population. More recently, similar themes of potentiality and conversion of a significant, growing population into a major political, economic, and cultural force were evident in the mass media, espoused by political and economic leaders, and by activists and organizational leaders from the different Latino communities. Since the mid-1990s, there is greater evidence that Latinos have moved to more concrete indicators that the "Latino vessel has arrived" on the American political and social shores.

An example of the more visible political front is the rise of Latino elected officials at the state and federal levels. California serves as one of the better cases, with Cruz Bustamante as lieutenant governor and Richard Polanco as California senate majority leader. Significant gains in the California state legislature have marked a major breakthrough for Latinos in that state. California had the greater number and percentage of Latinos, primarily Mexican-origin, for a number of decades; yet electoral representation was not manifested in similar proportions. California Latinos now hold 762 elective offices statewide, from city council to Congress (Verdin 2000). Latinos account for 20 percent of the 120 state senators and assemblypersons. In twenty-nine of the fifty-two congressional districts, the Latino population is 100,000 or more. In spring 2002, two Latinos (Sanchez and Cardoza) secured the Democratic Party nomination in the primaries. In both cases their districts are majority Democratic registrants. The political developments in California augment the advances made by Latinos in Texas and Florida.

The combination of factors—such as more widespread and effective voter registration campaigns, the California initiatives (Propositions 187, 227, 229, etc.),[1] anti-immigrant and Latino responses, increased numbers of Latino candidates, the opportunity to compete for elective offices due to term limits, greater Latino organizational effectiveness and cooperation, more visible and active local community efforts (labor movements, service delivery issues, police matters, etc.), and higher rates of naturalization—all contributed to the "real" results of Latino politics.

Over one-half million more Latinos voted in the 1998 congressional election than in 1994, increasing their presence at the polls from 3.5 million to 4.1 million (Day and Gaither 2000b). The number of Latinos of voting age increased from 10.4 million to 12.4 million in 1998. These changes occurred at a time when other groups (whites, especially) were evidencing a decline in voter registration. Projections for 2000 and beyond indicate that states with the largest number of voting-age Latinos will reside in California (7 million), Texas (4 million), New York (1.8 million), and Florida (1.8 million) (Day and Gaither 2000a). Finally, the voting-age population of Latinos and of Asian and Pacific Islanders was expected to be 16 percent higher in November 2000 than in November 1996. Rather than any one catalyst or event, the culmination of sustained efforts by Latinos over the years, in addition to key external developments, created a more hostile and targeted environment causing Latinos to mobilize more effectively.

Socioeconomic developments among Latinos have contributed to a more concrete reality for Latinos and their impacts. That is, part of the growing population represents a greater percentage of younger Latinos reaching eighteen years of age. The continuing growing percentage of Latinos who are voting age and/or becoming naturalized citizens is now a critical mass of the Latino voting-age population. This development is also reflected in the increasing numbers of Latinos who are registered and their proportion of the electorate (Jamieson et al. 2002). Similarly, there are continuing incremental gains in education attainment and income growth among Latinos. The year 1992 marked the first time that over 50 percent of the Latino adults over the age of twenty-five years had achieved a high school diploma. By 1998, that group increased to 57.5 percent. At the same time the gap between Latinos and others still remains around 20–25 percent. The proportion of Latino households earning above $30,000 has grown by 70 percent over the past two decades.

Economically, the growth of Latino-owned firms and their gross revenues have quadrupled over the past decade. These serve as indicators of economic and educational progress. The Latino population in Chicago increased by 18 percent from 1980 to 1990, and it was expected to grow to almost 1 million by 2000. Statistics from Chicago city planners Russell and Russell (1989) show that Latinos make up a majority of five of Chicago's seventy-seven communities, and marketing research revealed that Latinos constitute a $9 billion consumer market. Similarly, there are 2.6 million Latinos living in the twenty-eight counties in and around New York City with an estimated $18.9 billion in buying power for 1989 (Schlossberg 1989). Nevertheless, a relative gap persists between Latinos and other groups, especially nonminority America.

Socioeconomic improvement among Latinos reinforces the social capital that is accumulating among Latinos individually and collectively as a viable community. The results of the 2000 census also show the growing middle class among Latinos. There are over 2.5 million Latino households earning between $40,000 and $140,000. From 1979 to 1999, the Latino middle class grew by 71.2 percent (Pimentel 2002). These households have a total purchasing power of $278 billion annually. If Latino households earning over $140,000 are added, then the figure rises to $333 billion. With an expanding middle class, as well as a larger percentage of the population over eighteen years, the political resource base for the Latino community will continue to provide opportunities for empowerment.

Similar developments are evident in other parts of the country. The Cuban community continues to expand its political presence in Florida, especially southern Florida. Mayors and city council members of most southern Florida cities (Miami, Hialeah, Coral Gables, etc.), as well as administrators and public employees, are well represented by members of the Cuban community. Likewise, Cubans serve in the state legislature, both from southern Florida and other parts of the state (Tampa-St. Petersburg, etc.). With the political redistricting in 2001, Cubans continued to expand their political representation at the local, state, and federal levels.

In 2000, Latino candidates appeared on the ballot in states not commonly associated with Latino candidates (Kansas, Massachusetts, Michigan, Wisconsin, etc.), and some were elected. The past trend of Latinos selected to cabinet-level positions under previous presidential administrations is already apparent in appointments by George W. Bush (i.e., Antonio González, formerly Texas Supreme Court Justice as chief White House counsel, and Mel Martínez, formerly housing administrator of Orange county, Florida, to head the Department of Housing and Urban Development). The more sustained attention that Latinos received during the 2000 and 2002 elections, both at the presidential and other levels, reinforces the rising Latino political capital and raises expectations among Latinos about the impact they can have in terms of public policy and partisan politics.

Other developments that are occurring in communities throughout the United States include Latino subgroups such as El Salvadorans, Colombians, Dominicans, Nicaraguans, and other Central and South American Latinos. These communities have active organizations and leaders who are exerting influence and shaping local policy agendas. A more politically and economically visible Latino community at several levels of the American system is a fact of Latino life and American politics.

LATINO POLITICS AND THE NEW MILLENNIUM: SOME POSSIBLE SCENARIOS

Community constitutes ongoing links and interaction between leaders and general Latino publics in a variety of venues (residential, work, organizational life, public policy concerns, and regular contact and interactions). At the same time, community does not require complete consensus and uniformity of thought. In this discussion of Latinos and politics community is characterized as an interconnected and interacting set of members who share basic goals and visions and regularly work collectively to advance these objectives. This type of community is pragmatic and goal-oriented rather than ideologically "pure."

Do significant gains in **political participation** and representation represent a short-term pattern for Latinos or does it indicate a more active political and economic future? We will expound on three possible scenarios for the future of Latino politics.

Scenario 1: Continual Latino Political Development

Some major contributing factors in the contemporary political development of Latinos include (1) activation of a greater part of the Latino community into various forms of political involvement (local community involvement, organizational affiliation, political awareness, campaigning, voting, etc.); (2) external actions and developments that serve as catalysts for political involvement (anti-immigrant initiatives, **English only,** concerns about cultural balkanization, attention by national political parties and leaders, etc.); (3) increase of individual social capital among Latinos (gains in educational attainment, income, expanding adult population and citizens, occupational mobility, etc.); (4) expanding organizational networks across Latino subgroup lines and collaborative efforts; and (5) heightened local political activities in communities throughout the United States.

This scenario portrays the future of Latino politics as one of continued political progress in political capital and effectiveness. In order for this progress to occur, the intersection of leadership, organizations, and Latinos needs to be expanded and made more integrative and cooperative. This necessary ingredient is building on the momentum established in the late 1990s. Maintaining political involvement and communication in both directions—leaders and general Latino publics—serves to delineate more clearly the Latino policy agenda and its priorities. In addition, enhanced political development occurs when pursued on a continual basis. Earlier accounts of Latinos' limited impact on the political system were tied to their low political capital, their limited experiences with political processes, and lack of broad-based, active support. Latinos are now located in the formal political institutions and operate in established organizational vehicles of advocacy and influence, and constitute an expanding electorate.

This scenario includes specific areas Latino political development could build on. One is the accelerated conversion of Latinos as political actors (becoming more politically engaged). Organizational and local community efforts continue to encourage eligible Latino permanent resident aliens to naturalize. Such activities not only educate and activate Latino immigrants to file for citizenship, but also ensure the efficient and receptive workings of the Immigration and Naturalization Service. There are now policy initiatives to separate the border enforcement and monitoring functions from the naturalization function of the INS. Coupled with the rising fees of filing for citizenship and green cards, Latino organizations and leaders are faced with designing immigration-related reform policies that not only serve the Latino "immigrant" community but enhance further Latino political development. Latino organizations must work with and/or "pressure" the INS to shorten the time lapse between filing for naturalization and final swearing in, and civil rights protections (due process concerns for deportation hearings, access to higher education for undocumented students, workplace protection for workplace conditions, etc.).

While there is a tendency to portray politics in national terms, attention to local issues and politics is a critical element for greater Latino political development. Local issues such as housing, jobs, crime and law enforcement, social services, gentrification, schools and educational services, and access to decision makers are primary concerns and conditions that many Latinos face on a daily basis. By focusing on issues that are most pertinent and "visible," Latinos continue to expand political skills and accumulate experiences from which to evaluate and learn for future political involvement. I have presented evidence indicating that "politics is local" so that getting persons involved in matters affecting them "daily" affords the opportunity for interaction, using one's skills, gaining greater political awareness and knowledge, and accumulating valuable civic experiences.

A second area of attention is the "greater density" of interactions across the multitude of Latino subgroups. How do Latinos of many different national origins interact and come together in a variety of social and economic situations? The regional concentration of Latino subgroups has become less defined; greater residential and labor market overlap (living and working in the same areas) affords Latinos greater opportunities to establish a broader sense of community. Yet increased interactions do not guarantee harmonious and cooperative ventures. In this sense, the role of leadership and framing of common issues and visions become important elements in this equation.

Earlier discussions of Latinos and politics in this book revolved largely around the Mexican-origin community, as well as Cubans and Puerto Ricans. As a contemporary portrayal of the changing Latino community indicates, the inclusion and involvement of Central and South Americans, as well as Dominicans, are an integral part of the Latino political development scenario. These other Latino subgroups are becoming more actively engaged in issues particular to their respective communities. In many respects, issues about immigration status and adjustment, basic services, employment training and opportunities, educational quality and language assistance are quite similar with issues of Mexican-origin, Puerto Ricans, and Cubans.

Each Latino subgroup must develop its own political capital (political resources, organizations, leadership base, political knowledge, and experience with its own political and economic institutions). As it does so, issues, interests, and the utility of collaborative efforts with other Latino subgroups become clearer. An emphasis on lines of communication and mutual discussions across Latino subgroups can further collective political empowerment and political/economic agendas. There is evidence that such linkages in the 1990s and continuation of these developments enhance Latino political development.

Another concrete example of lines of communication is the Congressional Hispanic Caucus. The CHC has been in operation for almost thirty years, and its membership has grown from five to over twenty members. While the majority of the congresspersons are of Mexican-origin, as well as Democratic, the number of Puerto Rican and Cuban members has grown. Unanimity has not always been the case for the CHC, especially on matters of U.S. policy regarding Cuba and the Castro regime. Currently the two Republican Cuban members of the House do not officially belong to the CHC.

There is a history of shared common concerns about social welfare policies, immigration and refugee adjustments, language-focused legislation, expanding Latino political influence, and numerous other issues and concerns. It would be less than realistic to assume complete consensus across all members of any caucus all of the time. Even if the CHC does not include all Latino members of Congress, continuing dialogues and interactions among this core set of political representatives can serve the continued political development of this working community. The Congressional Hispanic Caucus is expected to grow even larger in 2002, with the latest round of redistricting configurations and more Latino elected officials.

The third area of further Latino political development is an extension of the first area. I have already discussed converting more Latinos to become politically involved in their communities, more politically informed, and more experienced in civic affairs. Converting the significant population base into a more powerful political force was the earlier point. The third area focuses on expanding economic resources from which Latino political endeavors would benefit. Studies like the Latino National Political Survey (de la Garza et al. 1993) indicate that the percentage of Latinos contributing to political campaigns and/or organizations is small. Increasing Latino political capital also includes receiving a greater economic commitment from community members for Latino efforts and organizations.

The economic resources come from individuals and the business sector. Recent gains in Latino political and economic advancement, the persistence of salient issues, and economic mobility and growth among Latino professionals and entrepreneurs serve as identifiable sources of economic resources for the Latino community. Obviously the linkage of more Latinos assessing their needs, interests, and affinities to the activities of Latino organizations and groups is a necessary condition. While many may see this type of focus directed toward more nationally visibly Latino-based organizations, the act of directing money toward a variety of efforts (charitable, neighborhood activities, specific projects, local organizations, etc.) both benefits particular recipients and establishes further the need and impact of greater economic resources derived from Latinos to address common concerns and issues.

Scenario 2: A Symbolic Community and Independent Actions

Our second scenario reaffirms the existence of some level of community among the various Latino subgroups. Community connotes identifying and associating with perceived similar persons, as well as maintaining a level of awareness and public recognition of Latinos as a social category. This level of community is now quite evident. A dynamic community would include regular and positive interactions and collaborative activities. Thus our second scenario suggests that the Latino "umbrella" takes on a symbolic, ceremonial connection for public display. The advent of Latinos is the result, in part, of governmental policies that combined or "merged" the various "Latino" subgroups into a new larger grouping. The mass media, choosing to characterize persons and nationalities of Spanish origin under the general category of Latinos or Hispanics, also reinforces general awareness of a symbolic community. This scenario posits a limited basis for the idea of a Latino community, which confines its practicality as a political/social movement. Therefore, the similarities and/or cultural connections that may exist among the various Latino subgroups are not sufficient to form a working community setting.

In more specific terms, issues regarding Cuba, Fidel Castro and his communist regime, trade embargoes, expanding refugee admissions, and the like are much more salient for the Cuban community than the rest of the Latino subgroups. In addition, political perspectives and policy preferences toward Cuba may be quite different for other Latino communities and their leadership. Legalizing the immigration status of Central Americans or recognizing political refugee status may be more salient among Salvadorans, Guatemalans, and Nicaraguans than among Puerto Rican or Mexican-origin communities. The political status of Puerto Rico (statehood, independence, commonwealth) or immediate closing of the Vieques site for bomb testing are concerns for the Puerto Rican community primarily. Similarly, the focus and perspective of each Latino subgroup are either limited to their respective communities and/or occupy a lower priority for other Latinos. This scenario would reinforce the decision of each Latino subgroup to pursue its own interests, consistent with its own salient issues, through its own organizations and activities.

As Latino subgroups pursue their respective agendas, they may use "Latino" as the context for their politics, but the reference is limited to their own group. For example, Dominicans in New York City may be seeking redress for poor educational quality (poor facilities, lack of curricular offerings, need for bilingual programs, etc.) in their neighborhood schools. In their public actions and public discourse, especially with the media, Dominican leaders may refer to these specific problems or concerns as Latino ones. It can afford the opportunity for other Latino subgroups to support their efforts as well as "piggy-back" their specific issues to the same political institutions.

The other factor that may influence the preference and reality of each Latino subgroup going its own way is the assessment that each Latino subgroup is in competition with the others. Again referring to the Dominican community in the New York City area, Dominican political and economic issues and concerns are viewed as vying for recognition and policy responsiveness in competition with Puerto Ricans, Colombians, or other Latino subgroups. Advancement becomes a potential zero-sum game in which the political system pits one group against the other for limited resources. Thus Latino politics become a competition among various Latino subgroups for political recognition, policies, and rewards. Specific Latino groups that have accumulated political resources and positions will try to maintain their power situation, while the other Latino subgroups see them as part of their obstacles for progress.

Another example is inter-Latino tension in southern Florida between the Cuban community, several Central American groups (Panamanians, Nicaraguans, etc.), and Puerto Ricans. This competition centers, in part, around access, influence, and power in southern Florida. Competition over economic policies that affect non-Cuban Latinos and concerns over political representation and access may be directed toward the Cuban political leadership and organizations.

The competitive nature of relations among Latino subgroups tends to accentuate inter-group differences rather than commonalties. As a result, maintaining any competitive advantage restricts cooperative and collaborative ventures. Within this scenario, a broader representation of Latino politics can be advanced, despite the competitive tensions, by each Latino subgroup portraying a more public depiction of cooperativeness and some unity, while dealing directly with differences in private forums. The analogy of keeping family matters and disparities *en la casa* and having a different public face outside the home describes this scenario of Latino politics. Thus this scenario requires an adjustment by looking at Latino communities as a confederation of overlapping interests; under certain conditions, the communities may come together.

Scenario 3: A Latino Community with an Outlier

This third scenario represents a limited community membership in which some Latino subgroups engage in collaborative and cooperative activities and/or regular joint dealings. The latter form of Latino political community would mean broad-based organizations that are inclusive (in terms of constituencies, staffing, and agenda) of the various Latino subgroups. Thus our theme of common interests and culture brings together most of the Latino subgroups to function as a political community, and it implies that Latino subgroups or coalitions may join forces outside the Latino communities.

The outlier component of this scenario suggests that one or more Latino subgroups will pursue its own agenda rather than negotiate or compromise with other Latino subgroups on public policy (those in force or proposed) and identify its own issue priorities. In addition, each Latino subgroup sees its political resources, base, and previous effectiveness as sufficient to continue on its "own path." Intra-group solidarity, established lines of political and economic communication and influence, clarity of political objectives, and relative unanimity among its leaders are factors that may encourage an outlier to operate in the American political system without "active membership" in the broader Latino community.

Based on earlier remarks about the different Latino subgroups and their organizations and political objectives, I am suggesting that the Cuban community fits the description of an outlier. For example, its long-standing, defined, and active involvement in shaping U.S. foreign policy regarding Castro's Cuba remains a central core of the Cubans' policy agenda. Both the primacy of this issue and, more recently, different policy orientations (normalizing relations, removing the trade embargo, adjusting refugee admission of Cubans) by other Latino activists/politicians have served as contributing factors for Cubans to distance themselves (policy-wise) from the "larger" Latino community. The extended political "battle" over Elian González[2] and the fervency and sustained effort within the Cuban community were not mirrored to the same degree among other Latino communities and leaders. The amount of expended political capital and mass media portrayal of the Cuban community served, in part, to accentuate policy divergence and tensions between Cubans and other Latinos.

Another item on the "list" of other situations and patterns that may work for an outlier model for Cubans is their close ties to the Republican Party, not shared by most other Latino subgroups. This relatively long-standing pattern heightens inter-group competitiveness as the Republican Party seeks to make greater inroads with other Latinos and highlight differences of policy preferences. The regional concentration of Cubans (almost 90 percent live in Florida, especially southern Florida) functions as a political base coupled with greater socioeconomic status and resources than other Latinos. Their strong

Nydia Margarita Velázquez (1953–)

Nydia Velázquez in 1992 became the first Puerto Rican woman to win a seat in the U.S. Congress representing a New York City district.

A veteran of voter registration drives among Hispanics, like the Atrevete (Dare to Do It) crusade launched in 1987, Velázquez is also a tireless campaigner for the rights and welfare of all minorities. She is proud to point out that New York's Chinese community named her the biggest defender of immigrant groups in general.

Velázquez began her career as an educator. First, she taught school in Puerto Rico; then, after earning her master's degree in New York, she was a lecturer in political science at the University of Puerto Rico in Humacao; finally, she was a professor in the Department of Black and Puerto Rican studies at the City University of New York's Hunter College. (This back-and-forth movement between Puerto Rico and New York established a pattern that she continued when she entered politics.)

Velázquez began to put her political science education into practice in 1983. She had a commitment to improve the lives of the poor and others on the margins of society—a sense of obligation that she attributes to her father's example. As assistant to a former congressman who sought her advice on immigration matters, she testified about immigration before Congress. After that, she served on the New York City Council. In 1986 she headed Puerto Rico's Migration Division Office, within the island's Department of Labor and Human Resources. Three years later, she was back in New York, this time as head of the Department of Puerto Rican Community Affairs in the United States.

In 1991 Velázquez created an AIDS research and education campaign in the Hispanic community, Hispanos Unidos Contra el SIDA (Hispanics United Against AIDS).

The 1990 census led to the redrawing of many election districts to reflect the increased presence of minorities among the population. This helped Velázquez in a hard-fought but successful campaign to be elected to the U.S. House of Representatives in 1992. In Congress she continues battling for progressive causes. In 1998 Velázquez received 84 percent of the vote for return to Congress. Velázquez was reelected again in 2000 and 2002.

Bibliography

"Congresswoman Nydia M. Velázquez's Home Page." www.house.gov/velázquez. Downloaded October 11, 2000.

Telgen, Diane, and Jim Kamp, eds. *Notable Hispanic American Women.* Detroit: Gale Research, 1993.

group politicization operates as an independent basis of action and encourages them to follow their own path. Contributing strongly to the outlier strategy or position are the following: the political development of Cubans in the United States, the strength of their organizations, their relative success in penetrating political institutions, economic resources, and entrepreneurial activities, and their commitment to a clear agenda. Whether other Latino subgroups can pursue this scenario with similar results is not clear at this time.

A question that can arise from this scenario is, does a Latino subgroup operate as an outlier for an indefinite period of time? Even if the outlier scenario continues, there are symbolic and public perceptions of linkages between Cubans and other Latino communities. In addition, this scenario does not preclude interactions, dialogues, and joint support between the outlier and the rest of the Latino community. For example, on matters of economic development initiatives, sampling adjustments for Census 2000, affirmative action, benefits and services to immigrants, language policies, and voting rights (National Council of La Raza 1999), Cuban members of the U.S. House of Representatives voted in accord with the other Latino representatives. Therefore, this scenario lays out an independent direction and control of the agenda, strategies, and priorities within a specific Latino subgroup.

The Latino subgroup does not function in isolation. Other Latino subgroups may move in that direction if good working relations do not exist within the broader Latino community, or if the Latino subgroup's agenda and priorities do not receive adequate attention and support. An assessment of the group's resources and strengths may indicate that pursuing an independent path may be an effective approach. This last scenario shows how the concept of community can organize itself so that some semblance of community exists while functioning more meaningfully within the various sub-communities.

CONCLUSION: LATINOS, COMMUNITY, AND POLITICS—
A DYNAMIC PROCESS

In this book the concept of community is developed as a series of interacting links among persons of Spanish origin and their experiences in the United States as a basis for the formation of a political community. The concept of communities of culture and interests served as the organizing theme for the discussion of Latinos and their involvement in American politics. Given the diversity of national origins captured by the general description of Latinos or Hispanics, an immediate challenge lies in portraying and integrating important characteristics and experiences among twenty-plus national-origin groups. Demographic profiles, historical developments and experiences, and issue concerns provide some evidence of Latino community dynamics. Clearly the political development of Latino subgroups and Latinos as a broader community has evolved and will continue to so do.

Political actors, political institutions, political parties, the mass media, and the larger public recognize that Latinos are not only altering the demographic landscape but also affecting the political processes, agendas, and decision-making institutions. The theme of potentiality and promise, which has characterized discussions of Latinos for decades, has moved dramatically beyond speculation since the mid-1990s. I have tried to discuss those developments, as well as the issues and challenges that still confront greater Latino political effectiveness and more widespread political involvement.

Future analysis, interpretation, and discussion of Latinos and their politics and impact need to be placed within a dynamic context. The internal forces of Latino activists, their ideas and perspectives, and strategy assessments will affect the development and continued shaping of Latino politics and inter-group dialogues, along with the external climate and actions taken by political institutions, actors, and interest groups. Continued attention to improving inter-group communication and cooperation is part of future Latino political development. Further expansion of political resources (active participants, financial resources, positive participatory orientations, organizational infrastructures and resources) serves to enhance the growing political capital of Latinos and define its direction and purpose. Our examination of Latino politics has (1) a historical context and (2) a dynamic nature. The second point deals with an evolving sense of community and how it can work in the American political system. In a very real sense, the ongoing discussion of these developments and important contributors precludes any formal ending to this book.

NOTES

1. Propositions 187, 227, 229 were referendums in California in the mid-1990s that proposed restricting immigrants' access to educational, medical, and social services, rescinding state affirmative action programs in education and employment, and replacing bilingual educational programs with one-year English-language immersion programs.

2. Elian González was a six-year-old Cuban émigré whose mother and her significant other ventured the Caribbean Sea in the spring of 2000. They took Elian with them. Both adults died at sea, and young Elian was rescued by the Coast Guard and taken to a hospital in Miami. Subsequently an uncle in Miami sought to secure asylum for Elian González, which began a major national debate and political incident, involving the Cuban government, Fidel Castro, the INS, Department of Justice, the

Cuban community and leadership, and eventually the Office of the President. Through a protracted legal battle, and despite rulings by the INS and the federal courts for the return of Elian González to his father in Cuba, the Cuban family, supported by the Cuban community, refused to surrender him to the authorities. Eventually an early morning INS "raid" secured Elian from the Miami relatives, and ultimately he was reunited with his father.

Glossary

~~~~~~

Alternative voting systems are options that differ from the conventional plurality (winner takes all) or majority system used in American elections. They range from cumulative voting, limited voting, and single transferable vote to proportional voting schemes.

Antiterrorism and Effective Death Penalty Act (ATEDPA) (1996) greatly facilitated procedures for the removal of "alien terrorists" and authorized state and local enforcement officials to arrest and detain certain undocumented persons and provide access to confidential INS files through court order.

At-large election system is a process whereby candidates would not run or be elected from a specific part of the community but would compete city or countywide.

Border Patrol was not established until 1924, and in 1933 the Bureau of Immigration and Bureau of Naturalization were merged in the Department of Labor. The primary mission of this agency is to detect and prevent the smuggling and unlawful entry of undocumented aliens into the United States and apprehend individuals in violation of U.S. immigration laws.

Community of interest represents the conditions, statuses, and experiences that Latinos share with members of other Latino subgroups.

Community of common/similar cultures exist when individuals are linked closely by their participation in a common system of meaning with concomitant patterns of customary interactions of culture (language, customs, art, etc.).

Cumulative voting system enables voters to distribute their votes (the amount is equivalent to the number of positions available) in whatever manner they desire. For example, if there are three offices to be decided, voters can cast their votes in any combination (all three votes to one candidate; two for one and one for another, etc.).

De facto segregated schools are those schools that due to residential segregation and school attendance zones produce schools that are highly segregated by race, ethnicity, and class.

Descriptive representation refers to the population makeup racially and ethnically and the characteristics of the political representatives. The population percentages of racial and ethnic groups mirror the background characteristics of their elected officials.

Discrimination–plus model characterizes coalition formation as being influenced by common experiences, issue priorities, and values of minority group members, making them receptive to joint political activities and collective efforts.

Enforcement Act of 1870 specifically prohibited denial of the right to vote in state and local elections.

English only initiatives are statewide initiatives that establish as English the official language of the state and require that all official business and activities be conducted only in English. Similar efforts have been focused in the U.S. Congress for national legislation.

Ethnic group identification is a cognitive process of seeing one's social identity defined in ethnic terms. The person undergoes a process by which she feels a sense of commonality of association with other members of her ethnic group.

Ethnic identity is a set of self-ideas about one's own ethnic group membership, which includes knowledge, feelings, and preferences about one's ethnicity. It includes a sense of self as a member of an ethnic group.

Ethnicity can be defined as a collectivity within the larger society having a real or putative common ancestry, memories of a shared historical past, and a cultural focus on one or more symbolic elements defined as the epitome of peoplehood. Also, ethnicity is seen as a web of sentiments, beliefs, worldviews, and practices that individuals hold in common.

Force Act of 1871 gave federal court–appointed supervisors the power to oversee registration and election processes when two citizens make that request. Later in 1800s, Congress repealed the Enforcement and Force Acts, and protective voting rights legislation was virtually nonexistent until the 1950s.

Human capital concept is found in the economics literature. As individuals invest in their human resource "portfolio," motivated to obtain more education, greater degrees of training, and more experience, they are advantaged for greater returns in the job market via earnings. The idea is that acquiring greater human resources produces economic returns. The idea of human capital can also be thought of as political capital: individuals with greater skills, knowledge, and interest in the political process can be more effective in their actions.

Illegal Immigration Reform and Immigrant Responsibility Act (IIRIRA) (1996) had stipulations to bolster the monitoring of the U.S. border and set up measures to remove criminal and other deportable aliens. In addition, this law provided increased protection for legal workers through worksite enforcement.

Immigration and Reform and Control Act (IRCA) (1986) was a major reform bill that sought multiple policy goals. It attempted to restrict legal immigration by establishing more fixed annual admission ceilings; increasing border enforcement and staffing to interrupt the flow of undocumented migration; establishing criteria for an amnesty program for residing undocumented persons (agricultural workers and other workers/families); sanctioning employers and monitoring the of hiring undocumented workers; and requiring proof of legal status for employment.

Impact or influence districts represent areas in which the Latino community (the principle can be applied to other minority groups or defined interests) constitutes a significant portion of the population and electorate. Usually a population threshold of 30 percent is viewed as a sizable demographic presence to which officials are responsive.

Latino National Survey Project is the first national probability survey of adults who are Mexican, Cuban, and Puerto Rican origin that was conducted in 1989-1990. The survey focused on political attitudes and behavior, group identity, policy preferences, and other aspects of political life.

Limited voting is a system in which the voter has fewer votes than the total number of seats or positions to be elected. For example, if three seats are up for selection, the voter has only one or two votes to cast. There is no uniform practice ruling the number of votes allowed, other than there must be at least one less than the number of elected positions being contested.

Majority–minority districts are political jurisdictions in which residents are primarily minority (over 50 percent of the population).

Mobilization is the process by which political candidates, political parties, activists, and groups try to induce other people to participate and get involved. Participation involves three key ingredients: resources, psychological orientations, and recruitment.

National Association of Bilingual Educators is a professional organization at the national level wholly devoted to representing both the interests of language-minority students and the bilingual education professionals who serve them.

National Origins Act of 1924 set a ceiling on the number of immigrants admitted annually. A formula was based on 2 percent of the national-origin group registered in the 1890 census. The implementation of the act heavily favored natives of northern and western Europe. Japanese persons and citizens of the Asiatic zone were excluded.

National Survey of Black Americans (NSBA) was a national probability study of 2,107 self-identified black Americans eighteen years of age and older interviewed in 1979–1980. These respondents were recontacted in eight-, nine- and twelve-year intervals, forming four waves of interviews. NPSBA provided the basis on which social scientists could address social, political, and economic factors in African American life.

Organization of Los Angeles Workers (OLAW) is an organization that promotes workers rights. It worked diligently for the mayoral campaign of Antonio Villaraigosa. The Service Employees International Union and the Hotel and Restaurant Employees Union were an integral part of OLAW and political mobilization activities in the city. OLAW was able to recruit over six hundred canvassers and distribute over 80,000 registration cards and forms.

Pan-ethnicity refers to a sense of group affinity and identification that transcends one's own national origin group. Thus a pan-ethnic identity does not necessarily replace one's national origin affinity, but includes a broader configuration to define the group: Latinos or Hispanics, including several national origins. Pan-ethnicity can also be seen as a sociopolitical collectivity made up of people of several different national origins.

Political participation involves the process of influencing the distribution of social goods and values. The critical factors for involvement are resources, time, opportunities, beliefs, values, ideology, and participatory political attitudes. In addition, participation is affected by organizations, leaders, and political parties who strategically choose to activate specific individuals and/or groups.

Personal Responsibility and Work Opportunity Reconciliation Act restricted the eligibility of legal immigrants for means-tested public assistance, widened prohibitions on public benefits for undocumented immigrants, and mandated the INS to verify immigration status before immigrants would receive public benefits. Immigrant sponsorship required the sponsor to assume financial responsibility for an immigrant who was unable to sustain himself. The PRWORA made the affidavit of support legally binding.

Political incorporation focuses on how persons learn and involve themselves with the American political system. It generally focuses on newcomers to the political system (young persons assuming adult status or immigrants) and "marginalized" populations such as minority group members. For our purposes, political incorporation is the process by which group interests are represented in the policy-making process

Power relations focus on political resources, agenda setting, organizational development, leadership and mobilization, authority, influence, and legitimacy. Power is distributed among individuals and groups in society, and power relationships deal with the use of power and interactions between groups and individuals.

Preclearance involves the Voting Rights section of the Justice Department, which reviews proposed election changes (affecting election dates, poll locations, election materials, annexations, etc.) of covered jurisdictions, in order to assess their impact on minority group representation and possible voter dilution. A change may not result in minority voter dilution or negatively impact the equal protection provisions for all citizens. The Voting Rights division clears or rejects any proposed changes.

President's Advisory Commission on Educational Excellence for Hispanic Americans produced a report entitled *Our Nation on the Fault Line.* This presidential commission was created by President Bill Clinton to examine the state of Hispanics and the educational system.

Proposition 187, or Save Our State Proposition, was passed by the California electorate in 1994. This new law barred undocumented immigrants from public education as well as other social services provided by the state (welfare and health).

Proposition 227, officially entitled the English Language Initiative for Immigrant Children (Unz initiative), was designed to eliminate bilingual education programs. Limited-English-proficiency children would take a one-year English immersion program and would then be mainstreamed into the regular English-based curriculum.

Redistricting is a decennial process by which political jurisdictions reconfigure their electoral districts to meet standards of equal size, compactness, contiguity, and maintain communities of interest. The body that implements the redistricting plan can be the state legislature, local governmental body, the courts, or an independent redistricting commission.

Safe district generally suggests that the incumbent and her party are firmly entrenched in the elected office. Thus a safe district can be secure for a particular political party, member of a racial/ethnic group, and/or current incumbent.

Single-member districts are elective positions for which voters in a specific area of a city or county nominate and elect their representative.

Social construct of race usually refers to a group of persons that defines itself as distinct due to perceived common physical characteristics. The sense or categorization of race is the result of self-identification, institutional definitions of racial categories, and organized segments that develop or construct notions, ideas, and elements of racial membership.

Structural factors have to do with the rules of the game and how political institutions function, especially focusing on access, individual or group legal standing, rights and protections, and the formal requirements for participation.

Targeted mobilization involves the identification of persons who, when contacted, are more likely to respond to calls for involvement.

Thornburg v. Gingles (106 S. Ct. 2752 [1986]) is a Supreme Court ruling that upheld the constitutionality of creating majority-minority districts when minority voting strength has been submerged in multimember districts with white majorities. The courts recognized a state compelling interest to rectify a pattern of exclusion. The remedy of majority-minority districts is appropriate when there has been racially polarized voting that has minimized or cancelled out the potential for minority voters to elect candidates of their choice of their own community.

The Voting Rights Act (VRA) (1965) was a major policy initiative addressing long-standing practices that had served to exclude African Americans and other minorities from the electoral process, including annual registration systems, literacy tests, hostile election poll locations, economic and physical intimidation of minority group members, and limited registration locations and hours. Consequently, suspension of literacy tests, use of federal monitors, review of election-related changes, legal challenges by local persons or groups, and standards for voter dilution were key elements of the legislation.

References

~~~~~~

Acuña, Rodolfo. 1976. *Occupied America: A History of Chicanos.* 2d ed. New York: Harper & Row.

———. 1981. *Occupied America: A History of Chicanos.* 3d ed. New York: Harper & Row.

———. 1988. *Occupied America: A History of Chicanos.* 4th ed. New York: Harper & Row.

———. 1996. *Anything but Mexican: Chicanos in Contemporary Los Angeles.* New York: Verso.

Adams, Greg D. 1996. "Legislative Effects of Single-Member vs. Multi-Member Districts." *American Journal of Political Science* 40 (February): 129–44.

Alinsky, Saul. 1971. *Rules for Radicals: A Practical Primer for Realistic Radicals.* New York: Vintage.

Allsup, Carl. 1982. *The American GI Forum: Origins and Evolution.* Austin: University of Texas Press.

Almond, Gabriel, and Sidney Verba. 1963. *The Civic Culture.* Princeton: Princeton University Press.

Alvarez-López, Luis, S. Baver, J. Weisman, R. Hernandez, and N. Lopez. 1997. *Dominican Studies: Resources and Research Questions.* New York: Dominican Research Monographs, CUNY Dominican Studies Institute.

Arce, Carlos. 1982. "A Reconsideration of Chicano Culture and Identification." *Daedulus,* 177–91.

Armbruster, Ralph, K. Geron, and Edna Bonacich. 1995. "The Assault on California Immigrants: The Politics of Proposition 187." *International Journal of Urban and Regional Research* 19 (December): 655-64.

Astin, Alexander. 1982. *Minorities in Higher Education.* San Francisco: Jossey-Bass.

———. 1985. *Achieving Academic Excellence.* San Francisco: Jossey-Bass.

Barrera, Mario, Charles Ornelas, and Carlos Munoz. 1972. "The Barrio as an Internal Colony." In H. Hahn, ed., *People and Politics in Urban Society,* 465–98. Los Angeles: Sage.

———. 1979. *Race and Class in the Southwest: A Theory of Race and Class Inequality.* Notre Dame, Ind.: University of Notre Dame Press.

———. 1988. *Beyond Aztlan: Ethnic Autonomy in Comparative Perspectives.* New York: Praeger.

Barvosa-Carter, Edwina. 1999. "Multiple Identities and Coalition Building: How Identity Differences within Us Enable Radical Alliances among Us." *Contemporary Justice Review* 2, no. 2: 111–26.

Bass, Loretta, and Lynne Casper. 1999. *Are There Differences in Registration and Voting Behavior between Naturalized and Native-born Americans?* Population Division Working Paper, no. 28. Washington, D.C.: U.S. Bureau of the Census.

Bean, Frank, and Marta Tienda. 1987. *The Hispanic Population of the United States.* New York: Russell Sage Foundation.

Bernal, Martha, and Phylis Martinelli, eds. 1993. *Mexican American Identity.* Encino, Calif.: Floricanto.

Bonilla, Frank, and Rebecca Morales. 1998. *Borderless Borders: Latinos, Latin Americans, and Paradox of Interdependence.* Philadelphia: Temple University Press.

Booth, William. 1996. "In a Rush: New Citizens Register Their Political Interest as Mexican Immigrants Become Naturalized." *Washington Post,* September 26, 1996.

Borjas, George. 2001. *Heaven's Door: Immigration Policy and the American Economy.* Princeton: Princeton University Press.

Boswell, Thomas, and J. R. Curtis. 1984. *The Cuban American Experience: Culture, Images, and Perspectives.* Totowa, N.J.: Rowman & Allanheld.

Boswell, Thomas. 1994. *A Demographic Profile of Cuban Americans.* Miami: Cuban American National Planning Council.

Brady, Henry, Sidney Verba, and Kay Scholzman. 1995. "Beyond SES: A Resource Model of Political Participation." *American Political Science Review* 89 (June): 271–94.

Briegal, Kaye. 1970. "The Development of Mexican American Organizations." In Manuel Servin, ed., *Mexican Americans: An Awakening Minority,* 160–78. Beverly Hills: Glencoe.

———. 1974 " Alianza Hispano Americano and Some Civil Rights Cases in the 1950s." In Manuel Servin, ed., *Mexican Americans: An Awakening Minority,* 174–87. 2d ed. Beverly Hills: Glencoe.

Brischetto, Robert, and R. Engstrom. 1997. "Cumulative Voting and Latino Representation: Exit Surveys in Fifteen Texas Communities." *Social Science Quarterly* 78, no. 4: 973–1000.

Brischetto, Robert, and R. de la Garza. 1983. *The Mexican American Electorate: Political Participation and Ideology.* Austin: Center for Mexican American Studies, University of Texas.

———. 1985. *The Mexican American Electorate: Political Opinions and Behavior across Cultures in San Antonio.* Austin: Center for Mexican American Studies, University of Texas.

Broder, David. 2001. "Awakening of the Latino Community Will Change the Political Map." *Washington Post* Writers Group, May 23, 2001.

Browning, Rufus, D. Marshall, and D. Tabb. 1984. *Protest Is Not Enough: The Struggle of Blacks and Hispanics for Equality in Urban Politics.* Berkeley: University of California Press.

———. 1990. *Racial Politics in American Cities.* New York: Longman.

Cain, Bruce, and R. Kiewiet. 1992. *Minorities in California.* A report to the Seaver Foundation.

Carmichael, Stokely, and Charles Hamilton. 1967. *Black Power: Politics of Liberation in America.* New York: Vintage.

Casper, Lynne, and Loretta Bass. 1998. *Voting and Registration in the Election of 1996.* Current Population Reports. Washington, D.C.: Bureau of the Census.

Carter, Thomas, and Roberto Segura. 1979. *Mexican Americans in School: A Decade of Change.* New York: College Entrance Examination Board.

Chapa, Jorge. 1995. "Mexican American Class Structure and Political Participation." *New England Journal of Public Policy,* Fall.

Cornell, Stephen. 1985. "The Variable Ties That Bind: Context and Governance in Ethnic Processes." *Ethnic and Racial Studies* 13: 368–88.

———. 1988. *The Return of the Native.* New York: Oxford University Press.

Cornell, Stephen, and Douglas Hartman. 1998. *Ethnicity and Race: Making Identities in a Changing World.* Thousand Oaks, Calif.: Pine Forge.

Cottrell, Charles. 1986. "Introduction: Assessing the Effects of the U.S. Voting Rights Act." *Publius* 16, no. 4: 5–17.

Cortés, Ernesto. 1996. "What about Organizing?" *Boston Review* 21 (6).

Cowan, Gloria, Livier Martinez, and Stephanie Mendiola. 1997. "Predictors of Attitudes toward Illegal Immigrants." *Hispanic Journal of Behavioral Sciences* 19, no. 4: 403–17.

Crawford, James. 1992a. *Hold Your Tongue: Bilingualism and Politics of English Only*. Menlo Park, Calif.: Addison-Wesley.

———. 1992b. *Language Loyalties: A Sourcebook on the Official English Controversy*. Chicago: University of Chicago Press.

———. 2000. *At War with Diversity: U.S. Language Policy in an Age of Anxiety*. Buffalo, N.Y.: Multilingual Matters.

Croucher, Sheila. 1997. *Imagining Miami: Ethnic Politics in a Postmodern World*. Charlottesville, Va.: University of Virginia Press.

Cruz, Jose. 1998. *Identity and Power: Puerto Rican Politics and Challenges of Ethnicity*. Philadelphia: Temple University Press.

Cuello, José. 1996. *Latinos and Hispanics: A Primer on Terminology*. Detroit: Wayne State University Press.

Dawson, Michael. 1994. *Behind the Mule: Race and Class in African American Politics*. Princeton: Princeton University Press.

Day, Jennifer. 1998. *Hispanics Population Shows Gains in Educational Attainment*. Census Bureau Reports CB98-107. Washington, D.C.: U.S. Bureau of the Census.

Day, Jennifer, and Avalaura Gaither. 2000a. "California, Texas, and Florida Will Show Biggest Increases in Voting Age Populations in November, 2000." *Census Bureau Projects*, CB00-125. Washington, D.C.: U.S. Bureau of the Census.

———. 2000b. "Voting and Registration in the Election of November 1998." *Current Population Reports*, P20-523RV. Washington, D.C.: Department of Commerce.

De la Garza, Rodolfo Z., Anthony Kruszewski, and Tomas Arciniega, eds. 1973. *Chicanos and Native Americans: The Territorial Minorities*. Englewood Cliffs, N.J.: Prentice-Hall.

De la Garza, Rodolfo Z., and David Vaughn. 1984. "The Political Socialization of Chicano Elites: A Generational Approach." *Social Science Quarterly* 65: 290–307.

De la Garza, Rodolfo, and L. Desipio. 1992. *From Rhetoric to Reality: Latino Politics in the 1988 Elections*. Boulder: Westview.

———. 1993. "Save the Baby: Change the Bath Water, Get a New Tub: Latino Electoral Participation after Seventeen Years of Voting Rights Coverage." *University of Texas Law Review* 71: 1029–42.

———. 1996. *Ethnic Ironies: Latino Politics in the 1992 Elections*. Boulder: Westview.

De la Garza, Rodolfo, L. Desipio, F. C. García, J. A. García, and A. Falcón. 1993. *Latino Voices: Mexican, Puerto Rican, and Cuban Perspectives on American Politics*. Boulder: Westview.

De la Garza, Rodolfo, A. Falcón, F. C. García, and J. A. García. 1994. "Mexican Immigrants, Mexican Americans, and American Political Culture." In B. Edmondston and J. Passel, eds., *Immigration and Ethnicity: The Integration of America's Newest Arrivals*. Washington, D.C.: Urban institute Press.

De la Garza, Rodolfo, M. Menchaca, and L. Desipio. 1994. *Barrio Ballots: Latino Politics in the 1992 Elections*. Boulder: Westview.

De la Garza, Rodolfo, A. Falcón, and F. Chris García. 1996. "Will the Real Americans Please Stand Up: A Comparison of Anglo and Mexican American Support for Core American Values." *American Journal of Political Science* 40, no. 2: 335–51.

Del Olmo, Frank. 1998. "Giant Is Awake and Is a Force in California: Latino Voters Pivotal Role in the Elections Puts All Politicians on Notice." *Los Angeles Times,* June 7, 1998.

———. 2001. "Bush Is Reaching Out to Latinos beyond the Beltway." *Los Angeles Times,* April 22, 2001.

Denton, Nancy, and Douglas Massey. 1988. "Residential Segregation of Blacks, Hispanics, and Asian Americans by Socioeconomic Status and Generation." *Social Science Quarterly* 69: 797–817.

———. 1989. "Racial Identity among Caribbean Hispanics: The Effects of Double Minority Status on Residential Segregation." *American Sociological Review* 54, no. 5: 790–809.

Desipio, Louis. 1996. *Counting the Latino Vote: Latinos as a New Electorate.* Charlottesville, Va.: University of Virginia Press.

Desipio, Louis, and Rodolfo de la Garza. 1998. *Making Americans and Remaking Americans: Immigration and Immigrant Policy.* Boulder: Westview.

Díaz-Briquets, Sergio. 1989. "The Central American Demographic Situation: Trends and Implications." In Frank Bean, J. Schmandt, and S. Weintraub, eds., *Mexicans and Central Americans Population in U.S. Immigration Policy.* Austin: University of Texas Press.

Duran, Richard. 1983. *Hispanics' Education and Background: Predictors of College Achievement.* New York: College Entrance Examination Board.

Dye, Thomas R. 1992. *Understanding Public Policy.* 7th ed. Englewood Cliffs, N.J.: Prentice-Hall.

Elliston, Jon. 1995. "The Myth of the Miami Monolith." *NACLA Report on the Americas* 29, no. 2: 40–42.

Engstrom, Richard. 1992. "Modified Multi-Seat Election Systems as Remedies for Minority Vote Dilution." *Stetson Law Review* 21: 743–70.

———. 1994. "The Voting Rights Act: Disenfranchisement, Dilution, and Alternative Election Systems." *PS: Political Science and Politics* 27, no. 4: 685–88.

Engstrom, Richard, D. Taebel, and R. Cole. 1997. "Cumulative as a Remedy for Minority Vote Dilution: The Case of Alamogordo, New Mexico." *Journal of Law and Politics* 5: 469–97.

Esman, Milton. 1985. "Two Dimensions of Ethnic Politics: A Defense of Homeland and Immigrant Rights." *Ethnic and Racial Studies* 8: 438–50.

———. 1995. *Ethnic Politics.* Ithaca, N.Y.: Cornell University Press.

Espenshade, Thomas, and S. Ramakrishnan. 2001. "Immigrant Incorporation and Political Participation." *International Migration Review* 35, no. 3.

Espiritu, Yen Lee. 1992. *Asian American Pan Ethnicity: Bonding Institutions and Identities.* Philadelphia: Temple University Press.

———. 1996. "Colonial Expression, Labour Importation, and Group Formation: Filipinos in the United States." *Ethnic and Racial Studies* 19: 28–48.

———. 1997. *Asian American Women and Men: Labor, Laws, and Love.* Thousand Oaks, Calif.: Sage.

Falcón, Angelo. 1988. "Black and Latino Politics in New York City." In F. C. García, ed., *Latinos and the Political System.* Notre Dame, Ind.: University of Notre Dame Press.

———. 1992. "Time to Rethink the Voting Rights Act." *Social Policy,* Fall-Winter, 17-23.

———. 1995. "Puerto Ricans and the Politics of Racial Identity." In Ezra Griffith, Howard Blue, and Herbert Harris, eds., *Racial and Ethic Identity: Psychological Development and Creative Expression,* 193-207. New York: Routledge & Kegan Paul.

Falcón, Angelo, and J. Santiago, eds. 1993. *Race, Ethnicity, and Redistricting in New York City: The Garner Report and Its Critics.* IPR Policy Forums Proceedings. New York: Institute for Puerto Rican Policy.

Farley, Reynolds. 1996. *The New American Reality: Who We Are, How We Got There, Where We Are Going.* New York: Sage.

Feagin, Joseph, and Clarice Feagin. 1996. *Race and Ethnic Relations.* 5th ed. Englewood Cliffs, N.J.: Prentice-Hall.

Fernández, Edward. 1985. "Persons of Spanish Origin in the United States." March 1982, Series P-20, no. 396. Washington D.C.: U.S. Government Printing Office.

Fernández, Maria Elena. 1999. "Prop. 187 Backers Pushing New Initiatives." *Los Angeles Times,* December 3, 1999.

Figueroa, Hector. 1996. "The Growing Force of Latino Labor." *NACLA Report on the Americas* 30 (November-December): 19–24.

Fitzgerald, Joseph. 1971. *The Meaning and Migration to the Mainland.* Englewood Cliffs, N.J.: Prentice-Hall.

Fitzpatrick, P., and L. T. Parker. 1981. "Hispanic Americans in the Eastern U.S." *Annals of the American Academy of Political and Social Sciences* 454: 98–110.

Fix, Janet. 2001. "The Changing Face of Unions." *Detroit Free Press,* April 30, 2001.

Foley, Douglas. 1988. *From Peones to Politicos: Class, Ethnicity in a South Texas Town.* Austin: University of Texas Press.

Fox, Geoffrey. 1997. *Hispanic Nation: Culture, Politics, and Construction of Identity.* Tucson: University of Arizona Press.

Fuchs, Lawrence. 1990. *The American Kaleidoscope: Race, Ethnicity, and the Civic Culture.* Middleton, Conn.: Wesleyan University Press.

García, F. Chris, ed. 1974. *La Causa Politica: A Chicano Politics Reader.* Notre Dame, Ind.: University of Notre Dame Press.

———. 1988. *Latinos and the Political System.* Notre Dame, Ind.: University of Notre Dame Press.

———. 1997. *Pursuing Power: Latino Politics.* Notre Dame, Ind.: University of Notre Dame Press.

García, John A. 1977. "Chicano Voting Patterns in School Board Elections: Bloc Voting and Internal Lines of Support for Chicano Candidates." *Atisbos,* Winter, 1–14.

———. 1981a. "The Political Integration of Mexican Immigrants: Explorations into the Naturalization Process." *International Migration Review* 15: 608–25.

———. 1981b. "Yo Soy Chicano: Self-Identification and Sociodemographic Correlates." *Social Science Quarterly* 62: 88–98.

———. 1981c. "Political Integration and Mexican Immigrants: A Preliminary Report." In U.S. Commission on Immigration Reform, *U.S. Immigration Policy and the National Interest.* Washington, D.C.: U.S. Government Printing Office.

———. 1982. "Ethnic Identification, Consciousness, Identity: Explanations of Measurement and Inter-Relationships." *Hispanic Journal of Behavioral Sciences* (September): 295–313.

———. 1986a. "The Voting Rights Act and Hispanic Political Representation." *Publius* 16: 49-66.

———. 1986b. "Caribbean Migration to the Mainland: A Review of Adaptive Experiences." *Annals of the American Academy of Political and Social Science* 487 (September): 114–26.

———. 1987. "Political Orientations of Mexican Immigrants: Examining Some Political Orientations." *International Migration Review* 21: 377–89.

———. 1989. "Chicano Electoral Behavior and Orientations." In Gary Keller, ed., *Curriculum Resources in Chicano Studies.* New York: Bilingual Review Press.

———. 1992. "Hispanic Americans in the Mainstream of American Politics." *Public Perspective* 3, no. 5: 19–23.

———. 1995. "A Multi-Cultural America: Living in a Sea of Diversity." In D. Harris, ed., *Multiculturalism at the Margins: Non-Dominant Voices on Differences and Diversity.* Westport, Conn.: Bergen & Garvey.

———. 1996. "The Chicano Movement: Its Legacy for Politics and Policy." In David Maciel and Isidro Ortiz, eds., *Chicana/os at the Crossroads: Social, Economic, and Political.* Tucson: University of Arizona Press.

———. 1997. "Hispanic Political Participation and Demographic Correlates." In F. Chris García, ed., *Pursuing Political Power: Latinos and the Political System.* Notre Dame, Ind.: University of Notre Dame Press.

———. 2000. "The Latino and African American Communities: Bases for Coalition Formation and Political Action." In Gerald Jaynes, ed., *Immigration and Race: New Challenges for American Democracy.* New Haven: Yale University Press.

García , John A., and Carlos Arce. 1988. "Political Orientations and Behavior of Chicanos." In F. Chris García, ed., *Latinos and the Political System.* Notre Dame, Ind.: University of Notre Dame Press.

García, John A., and Regina Branton. 2000. "Alternative Voting Systems: Explorations into Cumulative and Limited Voting and Minority Representation and Participation." Paper presented at the annual meeting of the American Political Science Association, Washington, D.C.

García, John A., and R. de la Garza. 1985. "Mobilizing the Mexican Immigrant: The Role of Mexican American Organizations." *Western Political Quarterly* 38: 551–64.

García, John A., R. de la Garza, F. C. García, and A. Falcón. 1994. "Ethnicity and National Origin Status: Patterns of Identities among Latinos in the U.S." Paper presented at the meeting of the American Political Science Association, Washington, D.C.

García, John A., and Sylvia Pedraza-Bailey. 1990. "Hispanicity and the Phenomenon of Communities of Interest and Culture among Latinos." Paper presented at the American Political Science Association meeting, Washington, D.C.

García, Juan R. 1980. *Operation Wetback: The Mass Deportation of Mexican Undocumented Workers in 1954.* Westport, Conn.: Greenwood.

———. 1995. *Mexican American Changing Images.* Tucson: Mexican American Studies and Research Center.

García, Mario. 1989. *Mexicans and Americans: Leadership, Ideology, and Identity.* New Haven: Yale University Press.

Gittell, Marilyn, and Mario Fantini. 1970. *Community Control and the Urban School.* New York: Praeger.

Ginorio, Angela, and Michelle Huston. 2000. *Si, Se Puede! Yes We Can: Latinas in School.* Washington, D.C.: American Association of University of Women Educational Foundation

Gómez, David. 1982. *Somos Chicanos: Strangers in Our Own Land.* 2d ed. New York: Macmillan.

Gómez, Laura. 1992. "The Birth of the Hispanic Generation: Attitudes of Mexican American Political Elites toward the Hispanic Label." *Latin American Perspectives* (February): 45–59.

Gómez-Quiñones, Juan. 1990. *Chicano Politics: Realities and Promise.* Albuquerque: University of New Mexico Press.

———. 1994. *The Roots of Chicano Politics, 1640-1940.* Albuquerque: University of New Mexico Press.

González-Baker, Susan. 1996. "Su Voto es Su Voz: Latino Political Empowerment and the Immigration Challenge." *PS: Political Science and Politics* 29, no. 3: 465–69.

Grassmuck, Sheri, and Patricia Pesser. 1996. "Dominicans in the United States: First and Second Generation Settlement." In Sylvia Pedraza and Ruben Rumbault, eds., *Origins and Destinies: Immigration, Race, and Ethnicity.* Belmont, Calif.: Wadsworth.

Griswold del Castillo, Richard. 1995. *Cesar Chavez: A Triumph of Spirit.* Norman: University of Oklahoma Press.

Grofman, Bernard. 1995. *"Shaw v. Reno* and the Future of Voting Rights." *PS: Political Science and Politics* 28 (March): 25–26.

Grofman, Bernard, and Chandler Davidson, eds. 1992. *Controversies in Minority Voting: A 25-Year Perspective on the Voting Rights Act of 1965.* Washington, D.C.: Brookings Institution.

Grofman, Bernard, L. Handley, and R. Niemi. 1992. *Minority Representation and the Quest for Voting Equality.* New York: Cambridge University Press.

Grossman, Milton M. 1964. *Assimilation in American Life: The Role of Race, Religion, and National Origins.* New York: Oxford University Press.

Guarnizo, Luis. 1994. "Los Dominicanyorks: The Making of a Bi-National Society." *Annals of the American Academy of Political and Social Science* 533: 70–86.

Guzman, Betsy. 2001. *The Hispanic Population: Census 2000 Brief.* May. C2KBR/01-3. Washington, D.C.: U.S. Bureau of the Census.

Hansen, Kristen, and Carol Faber. 1997. "The Foreign-Born Population, 1996." *Current Population Reports.* P-20-497. Washington, D.C.: U.S. Bureau of the Census.

Hardy-Fanta, Carol. 1993. *Latina Politics and Latino Politics: Gender, Culture, and Political Participation.* Philadelphia: Temple University Press.

———. 2000. "A Latino Gender Gap: Evidence from the 1996 Election." *Milenia* 2 (February). Notre Dame Inter-University Program for Latino Research.

Hardy-Fanta, Carol, and Carol Cardoza. 1997. "Beyond the Gender Gap: Women of Color in the 1996 Election." Paper presented at the annual meeting of the American Political Science Association, Washington, D.C.

Hayes-Bautista, David. 1980. "Identifying Hispanic Populations: The Influence of Research Methodology on Public Policy." *American Journal of Public Health* 70: 353–56.

Hayes-Bautista, David, and Jorge Chapa. 1987. "Latino Terminology: Conceptual Basis for Standardized Terminology." *American Journal of Public Health* 77: 61–68.

Hayes-Bautista, David, Werner Schenk, and Jorge Chapa. 1988. *The Burden of Support: Young Latinos in an Aging Society.* Stanford, Calif.: Stanford University Press.

———. 1992. *No Longer a Minority: Latinos and Social Policy in California.* Los Angeles: UCLA Chicano Research Center.

Henry, Charles, and Carlos Munoz. 1991. "Ideology and Interest Linkage to California's Rainbow Coalition." In B. Jackson and M. Preston, eds., *Race and Ethnic Politics in California.* Berkeley, Calif.: Institute for Governmental Research, University of California.

Hernández, Jose, L. Estrada, and D. Alvirez. 1973. "Census Data and the Problem of Conceptually Defining the Mexican American Population." *Social Science Quarterly* 53, no. 4: 671–87.

Hernández, Ramona, and Francisco Rivera-Batiz. 1997. *Dominican New Yorkers: A Socioeconomic Profile, 1997.* New York: Dominican Research Monographs. CUNY Dominican Studies Institute.

Hernández, Ramona, and S. Torres-Saillant. 1996. "Dominicans in New York: Men, Women, and Prospects." In G. Haslip-Viera and S. Baver, eds., *Latinos in New York: Latinos in Transition,* 30-56. Notre Dame, Ind.: University of Notre Dame Press.

Hero, Rodney. 1988. "The Election of Frederico Peña as Mayor of Denver." *Western Political Quarterly* 40: 93–105.

———. 1992. *Latinos and the Political System.* Philadelphia: Temple University Press.

———. 1996. "Ethnic Ironies: Latino Politics in the 1992 Elections." In R. de la Garza and L. Desipio, eds., *Latinos and the 1992 Elections,* 75-94. Boulder: Westview.

Hill, Kevin, and Dario Moreno. 1996. "Second-Generation Cubans." *Hispanic Journal of Behavioral Sciences* 18, no. 2: 175–93.

Hirsch, Herbert, and Armando Gutierrez. 1973. "The Militant Challenge to the American Ethos: Chicanos and Mexican Americans." *Social Science Quarterly* 53: 830–45.

———. 1974. "Political Maturation and Political Awareness: The Case of Crystal City Chicanos." *Aztlán* 5: 295–312.

Hoffman, Abraham. 1979. *Unwanted Mexican Americans in the Great Depression: Repatriation Pressures, 1929–1939.* Tucson: University of Arizona Press.

Hood, M. V., and Irwin Morris. 1997. "Amigo or Enemigo? Context, Attitudes, and Anglo Public Opinion toward Immigration." *Social Science Quarterly* 78, no. 32: 309–24.

Hood, M. V., Irwin Morris, and Kurt Shirkey. 1997. "Quedete or Vete: Unraveling the Determinants of Hispanic Public Opinion toward Immigration." *Political Research Quarterly* 50: 627–47.

Hufstedler, Shirley. 1999. "The Final Report on the Commission on Immigration Reform." Statement before the U.S. House of Representatives Subcommittee on Immigration and Claims, Washington, D.C.

Immigration and Naturalization Service. 1997. *Annual Report on Legal Immigration: Fiscal Year 1997.* Washington, D.C.: U.S. Government Printing Office.

Jackson, Bryon, E. Gerber, and B. Cain. 1994. "Coalitional Perspectives in a Multi-Racial Society African American Attitudes toward Others." *Political Research Quarterly* 47, no. 2: 277–94.

Jackson, Bryon, and Michael Preston, eds. 1991. *Racial and Ethnic Politics in California.* Berkeley: University of California Press.

Jamieson, Amie, Hyon Shinn, and Jennifer Day. 2002. "Voting and Registration in the Election of November 2000." *Current Population Reports.* P20-542. Washington, D.C.: Department of Commerce.

Jaynes, Gerald, ed. 2000. *Immigration and Race: New Challenge for American Democracy.* New Haven: Yale University Press.

Jennings, James. 1977. *Puerto Rican Politics in New York City.* Washington, D.C.: University Press of America.

———. 1992. *The Politics of Black Empowerment: Transformation of Black Activism in Urban America.* Detroit: Wayne State University Press.

———. 1994. *Blacks, Latinos, and Asians in Urban America.* Westport, Conn.: Greenwood.

Jennings, James, and M. Rivera. 1984. *Puerto Rican Politics in Urban America.* Westport, Conn.: Greenwood.

Johnson, Hans, Belinda Reyes, Laura Mameesh, and Elisa Barber. 1999. *Taking the Oath: An Analysis of Naturalization in California and the United States.* San Francisco: Public Policy Institute of California.

Jones-Correa, Michael. 1998. *Between Two Nations: The Political Predicament of Latinos in New York City.* Ithaca, N.Y.: Cornell University Press.

Jones-Correa, Michael, and David Leal. 1996. "Becoming Hispanic: Secondary Pan-Ethnic Identity among Latin American Origin Population in the U.S." *Hispanic Journal of Behavioral Sciences* (May): 214–54.

Jordan, Barbara. 1994. *U.S. Immigration Policy: Restoring Credibility.* Washington, D.C.: U.S. Government Printing Office.

Jordan, Howard. 1995. "Immigrant Rights: A Puerto Rican Issue." *NACLA Report on the Americas* 29, no. 3: 35–39.

Kasarda, John D. 1985. "Urban Change and Minority Opportunities." In Paul Peterson, ed., *The New Urban Reality,* 33–68. Washington, D.C.: Brookings Institute.

———. 1989. "Urban Industrial Transformation and the Underclass." *Annals of the Academy of Political Science and Sociology.*

Keefe, Susan, and Amado Padilla. 1989. *Chicano Ethnicity.* Albuquerque: University of New Mexico Press.

Kelly, Daryl. 1997. "Illegal Immigrants Remain a Concern Despite Economy." *Los Angeles Times,* November 2, 1997.

Krantz, Colleen. 2001. "Responses Are Mixed to Latino Immigrants." *Des Moines Register,* March 18, 2001.

Kunerth, Kenneth, and Sherri Owens. 2001. "Hispanics Reshape Civil Rights Agenda." *Orlando Sentinel,* July 1, 2001.

Lindholm, Kathryn, and Amado Padilla. 1981. "Socialization Communication: Language Interaction Patterns Used by Hispanic Mothers and Children in Mastery Skill Communication." In Richard Duran, ed., *Latino Language and Communicative Behavior.* New Jersey: ABLEX.

López, David, and Yen Espiritu. 1990. "Panethnicity in the United States: A Theoretical Framework." *Ethnic and Racial Studies* 13, no. 32: 198-223.

Los Angeles Times. 1994a. "Study no. 413 Exit Poll: California Primary Election." *Los Angeles Times,* June 2, 1994.

———. 1994b. "The Post Election Study." *Los Angeles Times,* June 7, 1994.

Márquez, Benjamin. 1985. *Power and Politics in a Chicano Barrio: A Study of Mobilization Efforts and Community Power in El Paso.* Lanham, Md.: University Press of America.

———. 1988. "The Politics of Racial Assimilation: League of United Latin American Citizens." *Western Political Quarterly* 42: 355–77.

———. 1993. "The Industrial Areas Foundation and the Mexican American in Texas: The Politics of Mobilization." In Paula McClain, ed., *Minority Group Influence: Agenda Setting, Formation, and Public Policy,* 127–46. Westport, Conn.: Greenwood.

Massey, Douglas. 1979. "Effects of Socioeconomic Status Factors on Residential Segregation of Blacks and Spanish Americans in United States Urbanized Areas." *American Sociological Review* 44: 1015–22.

————. 1981. "Hispanic Residential Segregation: A Comparison of Mexicans, Cubans, and Puerto Ricans." *Sociology and Social Research* 65: 311–22.

Massey, Douglas, and Nancy Denton. 1993. *American Apartheid: Segregation and Making of an Underclass.* Cambridge: Harvard University Press.

McClain, Paula, and Albert Karnig. 1990. "Black and Hispanic Socioeconomic Status and Political Competition." *American Political Science Review* 84: 535–45.

McClain, Paula, and Joseph Stewart. 1999. *Can We All Get Along: Racial and Ethnic Minorities in American Politics.* Boulder: Westview.

McDonnell, Patrick. 2001. "Citizenship Process Is Streamlined, but Applications Decline." *Los Angeles Times,* July 4, 2001.

Meier, Ken, and J. Stewart. 1991. *The Politics of Hispanic Education.* Albany: SUNY Press.

Meyer, David, and Sidney Tarrow, eds. 1997. *The Social Movement Society: Politics for a New Century.* Boulder: Rowman & Littlefield.

Milbank, Dana. 2000. "The Year of the Latino Voter? Only in Campaign Rhetoric." *Washington Post,* May 21, 2000.

Milbrath, Lester, and M. L. Hoel. 1977. *Political Participation.* 2d ed. Skokie, Ill.: Rand McNally.

Milkman, Ruth. 2000. *Organizing Immigrants: The Challenge for Unions in California.* Ithaca, N.Y.: Cornell University Press.

Miller, Arthur, P. Gurin, Gerry Gurin, and Oksana Malanchuk. 1981. "Group Consciousness and Political Participation." *American Journal of Political Science* 25: 494–511.

Montejano, David. 1987. *Anglos and Mexicans in the Making of Texas, 1836–1986.* Austin: University of Texas Press.

Montoya, Lisa, Carol Hardy-Fanta, and Sonia Garcia. 2000. "Latina Politics: Gender, Participation, and Leadership." *PS: Political Science and Politics* 33: 555–61.

Moore, Joan, and Raquel Pinderhughes, eds. 1993. *In the Barrios: Latinos and the Underclass Debate.* New York: Russell Sage Foundation.

Morales, Rebecca, and Frank Bonilla, eds. 1993. *Latinos in a Changing U.S. Economy: Perspectives in Growing Inequality.* Newbury, Calif.: Russell Sage Foundation.

Moreno, Dario, and C. Warren. 1992. "The Conservative Enclave: Citizens in Florida." In R. de la Garza and L. Desipio, eds., *From Rhetoric to Reality: Latinos and the 1988 Elections.* Boulder: Westview.

Muñoz, Carlos. 1989. *Youth, Identity, and Power: The Chicano Movement.* London: Verso.

National Council of La Raza. 1999. *Legislative Update.* Washington, D.C.: National Council of La Raza.

National Hispanic Leadership Agenda. 1998. *Congressional Scorecard, 105th Congress.* Washington, D.C.: NHLA.

————. 2000. *Congressional Scorecard, 106th Congress.* Washington, D.C.: NHLA.

Nagel, Joanne. 1996. *American Indian Renewal: Red Power and Resurgence of Identity and Culture.* New York: Oxford University Press.

Nelson, Candice, and Marta Tienda. 1985. "The Structuring of Hispanic Ethnicity: Historical and Contemporary Perspectives." *Ethnic and Racial Studies* 8: 49–74.

Nelson, Dale C. 1979. "Ethnicity and Socioeconomic Status as Sources of Participation: The Case for Ethnic Political Culture" *American Political Science Review* 73, no. 4: 1024–38.

Nie, Norma, Jane Junn, and Kenneth Stehlik-Barry. 1996. *Education and Democratic Citizenship in America.* Chicago: University of Chicago Press.

O'Connor, Ann Marie. 1998. "School Is Top Issue for Two Immigrant Groups." *Los Angeles Times,* March 19, 1998.

Oliver, Melvin, and Charles Johnson. 1984. "Inter-Ethnic Conflict in an Urban Ghetto: The Case of Blacks and Latinos in Los Angeles." *Social Movement, Conflict, and Change* 6: 57–94.

Omni, Michael, and Howard Winant. 1994. *Racial Transformation in the U.S.: From the 1960s to 1980s.* New York: Routledge & Keegan Paul.

Ong, Paul, Edna Bonacich, and L. Cheng. 1994. *The New Asian Immigration in Los Angeles and Global Restructuring.* Philadelphia: Temple University Press.

Orfield, Gary. 1991. *Status of School Desegregation, 1968–1986: Segregation, Integration, and Public Policy—National, State and Metro Trends.* Alexandria, Va.: National School Board Association.

Orfield, Gary, and Carole Ashkinaze. 1991. *The Closing Door: Conservative Policy and Black Opportunity.* Chicago: University of Chicago Press.

Pachón, Harry. 1987. "An Overview of Citizenship: Naturalization in the Hispanic Community." *International Migration Review* 21: 199–210.

Pachón, Harry, and Louis Desipio. 1990. "Future Research on Latino Immigrants and the Political Process." Paper presented at the Inter-University Program for Latino Research, Pomona, Calif.

———. 1994. *New Americans by Choice: Political Perspectives of Latino Immigrants.* Boulder: Westview.

Padilla, Amado. 1974. "The Study of Bilingual Language Acquisition." Report to the National Science Foundation GY 411534. Spanish-speaking Mental Health Center no. 1191. Los Angeles, Calif.: UCLA.

Padilla, Felix. 1986. *Latino Ethnic Consciousness: Case of Mexican Americans and Puerto Ricans.* Notre Dame, Ind.: University of Notre Dame Press.

Pan, Phillip. 1999. "INS Says Citizenship Backlog Cut." *Washington Post,* October 29, 1999.

Pardo, Mary. 1998. *Mexican American Women Activists: Identity and Resistance in Two Los Angeles Communities.* Philadelphia: Temple University Press.

Patterson, Ernest. 1975. "Context and Choice in Ethnic Allegiance." In Nathan Glazer and Daniel Moynihan, eds., *Ethnicity, Theory, and Experience.* Cambridge: Harvard University Press.

Patterson, Orlando. 2001. "Race by the Numbers." *New York Times,* May 8, 2001, p. A27.

Payne, Richard J. 1998. *Getting Beyond Race.* Boulder: Westview.

Pedraza-Bailey, Sylvia. 1985. *Political and Economic Migrants in America: Cubans and Mexicans.* Austin: University of Texas Press.

Pedraza-Bailey, Sylvia, and Ruben Rumbault, eds. 1995. *Origin and Destinies: Immigration, Race, and Ethnicity.* Belmont, Calif.: Wadsworth.

Peña, Devon. 1998. *Chicano Culture, Ecology, and Politics: Subversive Kin.* Tucson: University of Arizona Press.

Pérez, Lisandro. 1985. "The Cuban Population of the United States: Results from the 1980 Census of Population." *Cuban Studies* 15, no. 2: 1–18.

———. 1986. "Immigrant Economic Adjustment and Family Organization: The Cuban Success Story Reexamined." *International Migration Review* 20: 4–20.

Petersen, Mark. 1995. "Leading Cuban American Entrepreneurs: The Process of Developing Motives, Abilities, and Resources." *Human Relations* (October): 1193–1216.

Phillips, Dan. 1999. "INS Said Citizen Backlog Cut." *Washington Post,* October 29, 1999.

Pimentel, O. Ricardo. 2002. "Hispanic Middle Class Growing Fast." *Tucson Citizen,* January 10, 2002.

Pinderhughes, Dianne. 1995. "The Voting Rights Act: Whither History." *PS: Political Science and Politics* 28, no. 2: 55–56.

Pitt, Leonard. 1966. *The Decline of the Californios: A Social and Political History of Spanish-Speaking California.* Berkeley: University of California Press.

Piven, Frances, and Richard Cloward. 1979. *Poor People's Movements: Why They Succeed, How They Fail.* New York: Random House.

———. 1988. *Why Americans Do Not Vote.* New York: Pantheon.

———. 2000. *Why Americans Still Don't Vote and Why Politicians Want It That Way.* Boston: Beacon.

Portes, Alejandro, and R. Mozo. 1984. "The Rise of Ethnicity and Determinants of Ethnic Perspectives of U.S. Society among Cuban Exiles." *American Sociological Review* 49: 383–497.

———. 1985. "The Political Adaptation Process of Cubans and other Ethnic Minorities in the United States: A Preliminary Analysis." *International Migration Review* 19: 35–63.

Portes, Alejandro, and Rubén Rumbaut. 1990. *Immigrant America.* Berkeley: University of California Press.

Portes, Alejandro, and A. Stepnick. 1993. *City on the Edge: The Transformation of Miami.* Berkeley: University of California Press.

———. 1998. "Morning in Miami: A New Era for Cuban-American Politics." *American Prospect,* May-June, 28-33.

President's Advisory Commission on Educational Excellence for Hispanic Americans. 1999. *One Nation on the Fault Line.* Washington, D.C.: U.S. Government Printing Office.

Pulído, Laura. 1996. *Environmental Racism and Economic Justice.* Tucson: University of Arizona Press.

Putnam, Robert. 2000. *Bowling Alone: The Collapse and Revival of American Democracy.* New York: Simon & Schuster.

Ramírez, Roberto. *The Hispanic Population in the United States: Population Characteristics.* P20-527. Washington, D.C.: Bureau of the Census.

Reed, John. 1997. *The Hispanic Population in the United States: March 1995.* Current Population Reports. Washington, D.C.: Bureau of the Census.

———. 1998. *Hispanic Population Nears 30 Million.* Census Bureau Reports. Washington, D.C.: Bureau of the Census.

Reed, John, and Roberto Ramirez. 1998. *The Hispanic Population in the United States, March 1997.* Washington, D.C.: Bureau of the Census.

Reza, H. G. 1998. "Group Stirs Outrage with Billboard Deploring Illegal Immigration." *Los Angeles Times,* May 6.

Rodríquez, Clara. 1998. *Puerto Ricans: Born in the USA.* Boston: Unwin Hyman.

———. 2000 *Changing Race: Latinos, the Census, and the History of Ethnicity in the U.S.* New York: New York University Press.

Rodríquez, Gregory. 1996. "The Browning of California: Proposition 187 Backfires." *New Republic,* September, 18–28.

———. 1998. "Latino Voters Are Finally Awakening to Their Political Power: But Will Cultural Attitudes Reduce Their Effect?" *Los Angeles Times,* January 11, 1998.

Rodríquez, Lori. 2000. "Top Candidates Court Latino Vote in Key Primaries." *Houston Chronicle,* February 26, 2000.

Roedemeier, Chad. 2000. "Hispanic Transformation: Immigrants Stream into North Georgia for Jobs, Changing the Social Fabric of Town and Schools." Associated Press.

Rosenstone, Steve, and Mark Hansen. 1993. *Mobilization, Participation, and Democracy in the U.S.* New York: Macmillan.

Russell, Mark, and Martha Russell. 1989. "Chicago's Hispanics." *American Demographics* (September): 58–60.

Saito, Leonard. 1998. *Race and Politics: Asian Americans, Latinos, and Whites in a Los Angeles Suburb.* Urbana: University of Illinois Press.

San Jose Mercury News. 1998. "Vote Turnout Was a Record for Latinos." June 7.

San Miguel, Guadalupe. 1987. *Let Them All Take Heed: Mexican Americans and the Campaign for Educational Equality.* Albuquerque: University of New Mexico Press.

Santillán, Richard. 1985. "The Latino Community and State and Congressional Redistricting, 1961–1985." *Journal of Hispanic Policy* 1: 52–66.

Sassen-Koob, Saskia. 1979. "Formal and Informal Associations: Dominicans and Colombians in New York." *International Migration Review* 13, no. 2: 314–29.

———. 1985. "The Changing Composition and Labor Market Location of Hispanic immigrants in New York City." In Marta Tienda and George Borjas, eds., *Hispanics and the Economy.* Orlando, Fla.: Academic.

———. 1988. *The Mobility of Labor and Capital: A Study in International Investment Flow.* New York: Cambridge University Press.

Schlossberg, Jeremy. 1989. "Hispanic Hot Seat: Hispanics Who Live in New York City." *American Demographics* 10 (August): 49–52.

Schermerhorn, R. A. 1970. *Comparative Ethnic Relations: A Framework for Theory and Research.* New York: Random House.

Shaw v. Reno. 1993. 509 U.S. 630; 113 S. Ct. 2816.

Shockley, John S. 1974. *Chicano Revolt in a Texas Town.* Notre Dame, Ind.: University of Notre Dame Press.

Sierra, Christine. 1987. *Latinos and the New Immigration: Response for the Mexican American Community.* Renato Rosaldo Lecture Series Monograph, no. 3. Tucson: Mexican American Studies and Research Center.

———. 1991. "Latino Organizational Strategies on Immigration Reform: Success and Limits of Public Policy-Making." In R. Villareal and N. Hernandez, eds., *Latinos and Political Empowerment for the 90s.* New York: Greenwood.

Singer, Audrey, and Greta Gilbertson. 1996. "Naturalization among Latin American Immigrants." Paper presented at the annual meeting of the American Sociological Association, New York.

———. 2000. *Naturalization in the Wake of Anti-Immigrant Legislation: Dominicans in New York City.* Working Papers, no. 10. Washington, D.C.: Carnegie Endowment for International Peace.

Skerry, Peter. 1993. *Mexican Americans: the Ambivalent Minority.* Boston: Free Press.

Smith, Anthony. 1981. *The Ethnic Renewal in the Modern World.* Cambridge: Cambridge University Press.

Smith, Tom. 1990. *Ethnic Survey: The General Social Survey.* Technical Report no. 19. Chicago: National Opinion Research Center, University of Chicago.

Smith, James P., and Barry Edmondston. 1998. *The Immigration Debate: Studies in the Economic, Demographic, and Fiscal Impacts of Immigration.* Washington, D.C.: National Academy Press.

Sonenshein, Raphael. 1990. "Bi-racial Coalitions Politics in Los Angeles." In R. Browning, D. Marshall, and D. Tabb, eds., *Racial Politics in American Cities.* New York: Longman.

———. 1994. *Politics in Black and White.* Princeton: Princeton University Press.

Stavans, Ilan. 1996. *The Hispanic Condition: Reflections on Culture and Identity in America.* New York: Harper.

Stevens, Jeff. 2001. "Hispanics Next in Line for Power." *Odessa American,* May 17, 2001.

Tarrow, Sidney. 1998. *Power in Movement: Social Movements and Contentious Politics.* New York: Cambridge University Politics.

Tate, Kathleen. 1993. *From Protest to Politics: The New Black Voters in American Elections.* Princeton: Princeton University Press.

Tilly, Charles. 1978. *From Mobilization to Revolution.* Reading, Mass.: Addison-Wesley.

Timberg, Craig, and R. H. Melton. 2001. "GOP Designs Mostly Latino N. VA. District." *Washington Post,* April 11, 2001.

Tirado, Miguel. 1970. "The Mexican American Minority's Participation in Voluntary Political Associations." Ph.D. diss., Claremont Graduate School (the Claremont Colleges).

Tobar, Hector. 1998. "Water Bill Triggers Off a Revolt from a Tiny Garage in Maywood, California." *Los Angeles Times,* July 24.

Torres-Saillant, Silvio. 1998. "The Tribulations in Blackness: States in Dominican Racial Identity." *Latin American Perspectives,* May: 126–46.

Torres-Saillant, Silvio, and Ramona Hernández. 1998. *The Dominican Americans.* Westport, Conn.: Greenwood.

Tórrez, Adrianna, and Bechetta Jackson. 2001. "Hispanics Planning to Run for Council: Leaders Emerging, Latinos Say." *Ft. Worth Star Telegram,* April 22, 2001.

Ture, Kwame, and Charles Hamilton. 1992. *Black Power: The Politics of Liberation.* Vintage ed. New York: Vintage.

Uhlaner, Carole. 1991. "Perceived Prejudiced and Coalitional Prospects among Black, Latinos, and Asian Americans." In Byron Jackson and Michael Preston, eds., *Ethnic and Racial Politics in California,* 339–71. Berkeley, Calif.: Institute for Governmental Studies.

Uhlaner, Carole, B. Cain, and R. Kiewiet. 1989. "Ethnic Minorities in the 1990s." *Political Behavior* 11: 195–231.

United States Bureau of the Census. 1993. *We the Americans . . . Hispanics.* Washington, D.C.: Department of Commerce.

———. 2002. *The Hispanic Population of the United States: Population Characteristics.* Current Population Reports P20-527. Washington, D.C.: Department of Commerce.

United States Civil Rights Commission. 1972. *The Unfinished Education: Outcomes of Minorities in Five Southwestern States.* Vol. 2 of *The Mexican American Education Project.* Washington, D.C.: U.S. Government Printing Office.

———. 1974. *Toward Quality Education for Mexican Americans.* Vol. 6 of *The Mexican American Education Project.* Washington, D.C.: U.S. Government Printing Office.

———. 2001. *Voting Irregularities in Florida during the 2000 Presidential Elections.* Washington, D.C.: U.S. Government Printing Office.

Verba, Sidney, and Jae-on Kim. 1978. *Participation and Political Equality.* New York: Cambridge University Press.

Verba, Sidney, and Norman Nie. 1972. *Participation in America: Political Democracy and Social Equality.* New York: Harper & Row.

Verba, Sidney, Kay Scholzman, and Henry Brady. 1995. *Voice and Equality: Civic Voluntarism in American Politics.* Cambridge: Harvard University Press.

Verba, Sidney, Kay Scholzman, Henry Brady, and Norman Nie. 1992. "Race, Ethnicity, and the Resources for Political Participation: The Role of Religion." Paper presented at the annual meeting of the American Political Science Association, Chicago, September 3-6.

Verdin, Tom. 2000. "Hispanic Influence Grows in California." Associated Press.

Waldinger, Roger. 1989. "Immigration and Urban Change." *Annual Review of Sociology* 15: 359–85.

Waldinger, Roger, and M. Bozorgmehr. 1996. *Ethnic Los Angeles.* New York: Sage.

Walton, Hanes. 1997. *African American Power and Politics: The Political Context Variable.* New York: Columbia University Press.

Warren, Mark. 1996. "Creating a Multi-Racial Democratic Community: A Case Study of Texas Industrial Areas Foundation." Paper presented at the Conference on Social Welfare and Urban Poverty. New York: Russell Sage Foundation.

Washington Post. 1999. "Survey Portrays Hispanic Poverty: In Alexandria, a Stark Picture of Growing Group." December 9, 1999, p. V1.

Welch, Susan, and John Hibbing. 1985. "Hispanic Representation in the U.S. Congress." *Social Science Quarterly* 65: 328–35.

West, Cornell. 1994. *Race Matters.* New York: Vintage.

Wilson, Paul. 1977. *Immigration and Politics.* Amistral: Australian National University Press.

Wolfinger, Raymond. 1993. "Improving Voter Participation." In P. Frank and W. Mayer, eds., *What to Do: Improving the Electoral Process.* Boston: Northeastern University Press.

Wolfinger, Raymond, and Steven Rosenstone. 1980. *Who Votes.* New Haven: Yale University Press.

Yu, Eu, and Edward Chang. 1995. "Minorities Talking Coalition Building in Los Angeles" A two-day symposium.

Index

〰〰〰〰〰〰〰〰〰〰〰〰〰〰〰〰〰〰〰〰〰〰〰〰〰〰

Page references followed by a *b*, *n*, or *t* refer to boxed text, endnotes and tables respectively.

reapportionment and, 132, 210–11; redistricting and, 132, 204, 206–11, 212–13

About the Author

~~~~~~

John A. García is professor of political science at the University of Arizona and has been at the University since 1972. His primary areas of research have been American politics—minority-group politics, especially Latinos, and urban governments; survey research; and public policy. His research has focused on policy issues of political mobilization, political participation, and policy implementation and formation. He has published articles and book chapters in these fields for the past thirty years. He was coauthor of *Latino Voices: Mexican, Puerto Rican, and Cuban Perspectives on American Politics* (Westview Press, 1993) and a chapter, "Expanding Disciplinary Boundaries: Black, Latino, and Racial Minority Group Politics in Political Science" in *The State of the Discipline II* (1993). Professor García was one of the coprincipal investigators on the original National Chicano Survey in 1979, and also one of the four principal investigators on the Latino National Political Survey in 1989–1990. He has extensive expertise on Latino demographic change and its political effects, and the methodological issues of both sample-design and census-taking among Latinos. His works bridge basic and applied research as evident by his participation on the decennial Census Race and Ethnic advisory (Hispanics) committee, ICPSR executive council, and the NSF Social and Behavioral and Economic Science Directorate Advisory committee. He has served in various capacities in the American Political Science Association including coprogram chair (1999) and secretary.